UNIVERSITY OF WINNIPEG
LIBRARY
515 PORTAGE AVENUE
WINNIPEG, MAN. R3B 2E9
DISCARDED

BOLLINGEN SERIES XXXVII

ERWIN R. GOODENOUGH

JEWISH SYMBOLS

in the

Greco-Roman Period

VOLUME FIVE

FISH, BREAD, AND WINE

(*The first of two volumes*)

BOLLINGEN SERIES XXXVII

PANTHEON BOOKS

Published for Bollingen Foundation Inc.
by Pantheon Books Inc., New York, N. Y.

Published in Canada by McClelland and Stewart, Ltd., Toronto

THIS BOOK IS VOLUME FIVE OF THE THIRTY-SEVENTH PUBLICATION
IN A SERIES SPONSORED BY AND PUBLISHED FOR
BOLLINGEN FOUNDATION

Library of Congress Catalog Card No. 52–10031

Manufactured in the United States of America
by Kingsport Press, Inc., Kingsport, Tenn.

TO
KARL LEHMANN
AND
WILLIAM EDGERTON
VOLUMES V AND VI OF THIS STUDY
ARE DEDICATED IN
FRIENDSHIP, GRATITUDE, AND RESPECT

PREFACE TO VOLUMES V AND VI

IN THE FIRST THREE volumes of this series we reviewed the data of Jewish art (except for the Old Testament paintings of Dura) and saw that they presented a new problem. Jews had borrowed a vocabulary of pagan symbols which they mingled with their own symbols of menorah, shofar, and the rest in such a way as to make it seem inevitable that the pagan symbols were as meaningful for the Jews who used them as were the Jewish ones. The phenomenon was not local, for it appeared with amazing uniformity in almost every place from Rome to Mesopotamia where Jewish remains were found at all. It was not a phenomenon of a few paganized Jews or a small sect, for these symbols appear not only in wide geographical distribution, but on almost all official Jewish structures, such as synagogues and catacombs. Since many of the symbols appear also on amulets with Jewish divine or human names, amulets which seem for the most part made for Jewish use, there is strong suggestion that the forms had operative power and were not mere decoration. The conclusion is thus beyond debate that this vocabulary of forms was an integral part of the Judaism of the Roman world, though at the end of Volume III I left open the question of whether it was more than a decorative vocabulary.

The phenomenon, in itself indisputable, raised the question which the first three volumes only defined as a problem: what this art, and especially the pagan borrowings, implied for the Jews who used it. As a thesis I suggested in those volumes that the borrowed symbols showed the Jews to have been deeply affected by the sort of mystic and eschatological hope which the same symbols indicated for paganism and Christianity. I hoped to give evidence in the later volumes to support this thesis. My more intelligent reviewers took the attitude that we should have to see in these later volumes whether I made my case. Others, of course, at once said with finality that I had or had not done so.

The first task in appraising the art forms was obviously to see what light the literary sources of the period could give us. There are a variety of ancient Jewish writings, but virtually only one body of them come from the period when most of the designs were made. The writings of Philo, as well as the bulk of the so-called apocryphal and pseudepigraphical books, were apparently composed during the first century before or the first century after Christ, while the archeological material suggests that the public use of pagan symbols began really in the second century and that most of the material is from the third to the fifth centuries. From these centuries we have a few Jewish mystic documents, or references to such documents, but none of them is at all satisfactory for showing the general trends of Judaism in the period. The great documents—and a great literature they truly constitute—were written by the rabbis. So true is this that modern Jewish historians of the period have largely described the Judaism of those years on the basis of rabbinic writings.

In setting out to answer the question put by the art remains, accordingly, I had to begin Volume IV by examining what the rabbis had had to say on the subject of art. Here we at once met with disappointment. A few rabbis had given grudging permission to make some sorts of art objects, "had not stopped them," but the whole weight of rabbinic judgment had been much against artistic representations, and we accordingly had to conclude that the initiative in such borrowing would never have come from them and that most of them would have thought it blasphemy.

Our problem is: What sort of Jews could have borrowed these art forms—art forms, indeed, especially associated with pagan gods and their cults—and why did Jews want them? When we try to explain a movement in history, we are looking for the source of initiative, not for passive observers. And this, at most, is what the negative statements of the rabbis, or their silences, would make them.

Furthermore the inscriptions show that throughout the Roman world, even for the most part in Palestine, the language of Jews was Greek (later, in the West, Latin): they had lost Hebrew and Aramaic so early that the Septuagint had been begun at least in the middle of the third century B.C. The rabbis had recognized the necessity of providing a second Greek translation when the Christians appropriated the Septuagint, but they had never made any attempt to translate their own writings. The talmudic life of the Jews of medieval and modern times was possible only through knowledge of Hebrew and Aramaic. These languages the Jews of the Roman world did not have.

There seemed no reason to suppose, therefore, that the Jews who made the monuments must all have been guided by the rabbis and their writings. Yet it is quite as unjustified to jump at once to Philo, the apocrypha, and the pseudepigrapha and to treat their ideas as authoritative for these hidden Jews. To be sure, the writings of Philo are at least in Greek, and I am sure that they are not so isolated from the thinking of other Jews as many scholars insist who do not like to face their implications for either Judaism or Christianity. But one of my most sympathetic reviewers said that I "consider Philo the principal teacher of the hellenized Jews throughout the Greco-Roman era. His books, written in Greek, were in a sense the scriptures of the literate hellenized Jews who derived their knowledge of the Bible and the Law from his works."

If I am giving that impression I want earnestly to correct it. As my publication continues, it will be explained why I believe that Paul and the authors of the Letter to the Hebrews and of the Fourth Gospel cannot be understood apart from Philonic conceptions, but I see no reason to suppose that any one of the three had ever read a line of Philo's writings. Similarly the biblical allegory of Justin Martyr is clearly Philonic, but I could never believe Justin had worked with texts of Philo. I feel the same to be probably true of hellenized Jews throughout the Roman world. I turn to Philo because he is a palpably existent product of hellenistic Judaism and by and large except for the archeological monuments palpably the only one. But Philo is the product of the hellenization of Jews, not the creator. There is not the slightest reason to suppose that his writings were ever official for hellenized Jews, and it is a great question even how representative of them as a whole Philo was. Clearly his writings cannot be supposed to give us all the facets of the Jewish thought and life in the Greco-Roman diaspora from 300 B.C. to A.D. 600. The life of business, family relations, synagogue organization and worship, ethical standards, the forms of observing the Sabbath and the Festivals—these are a very small number of aspects of Jewish life about which Philo tells us almost nothing, certainly nothing which we can at once transfer to Jews in Rome and Tunisia. Actually the monuments do not tell us about these things either, and any picture of the Judaism which lay behind the monuments must remain largely incomplete. If I tried to answer all the questions people would like me to answer about these Jews, and that I should like to answer, I would leave my data, the archeological data, far behind indeed.

One of my most acute reviewers complained that, as he could see it in the first three volumes, my picture of hellenized Judaism was "oversimplified." This is like pointing out that we need iron for our civilization and complaining that in a copper mine we find only copper. The picture of Judaism in the Greco-Roman world that finally will emerge from this study is still fluid in my own mind, and I shall attempt to formulate it only when I have completed a study of the material and its implications. But I warn the reader at once that from a group of symbols primarily funerary and mystical in their origin the whole of the life of these Jews can never be inferred. If I can get only copper from this mine, however, I propose to get all the copper possible. We shall do this by using all the Jewish literary evidence of any kind that I can control. I warn the reader again that the symbols, themselves largely borrowed from mystic and funerary hellenism in its later forms, will over and again find their most congenial association with ideas in hellenistic Jewish sources. This does not seem strange to me; but I hope it will not appear to the careful reader that I am forcing the material into Philonic pigeonholes. It is only that repeatedly he and later Jewish mystics will be found saying things which fit the mystic and funerary symbols.

The process is like that of fitting a formula to a curve. From many experiments in ballistics, for example, one can get a series of dots representing what happens in a gun as one increases the charge exploded within it. These dots can be joined in a curve, and then the mathematician sets to work to find out what kind of mathematical formula will, when plotted, produce a similar curve. In that way the rough beginning of a science of ballistics, the physical laws of the phenomena, can be first envisaged.

In this study we are similarly at the crude beginnings, with a body of data we want to explain. We must fit literary material to it as we can. It will be a great advance step if another scholar can show that I have ignored a body of rabbinical material which in spirit fits these mystic-funerary borrowings from Greco-Roman art better than the material which often seems to me to be closest to it. But I have examined the field extensively enough to doubt that such a body of material exists within strictly rabbinic tradition.

Some of my Jewish reviewers have protested against my distinguishing between Cabbalists and the rabbinic tradition, and have pointed out very properly that the Cabbalists were all very observant halachic—that is, legalistic—Jews. With this I agree fully, but my sense of the contrast between Cabbalism and rabbinic tradition proper is one I was taught by Jews themselves. For although the Jewish mystics have been legally observant, most of the legalistic rabbis have not been mystics and have not liked mysticism. Within Judaism the mystic tradition is as anomalous and as persistent as it is within Catholicism, where the Church has canonized many of its mystics but the parish priest and local bishop have rarely encouraged mysticism, or practised it. Mysticism and the cabbalistic writings have just as rarely been standard training in the Yeshivahs. Indeed, the very scholar who in a review protested that I had contrasted rabbinic and mystic Judaism too strongly, himself said exactly what I had in mind: "What the Rabbis opposed were the extremes of mysticism. They did not bestow sainthood on men who assumed that they saw visions or heard heavenly voices, or communed with the Infinite, or sought escape from life. They preferred to call those men saints who sanctified the routine details of life, who retained respect for the human mind in striving for the Infinite." This list of mystic activities and aspirations contains precisely what I meant in saying that the rabbis as a whole did not like mysticism.

A scholar has to talk about types of religious experience, and the legalistic and mystical types are, as types, quite different. That they are many times combined in individuals is perfectly true. In the great majority of cases, however, these two are not combined; indeed most legalists regard mystics with disfavor. It is therefore interesting that in Jewish literature it is for the most part the Cabbalists along with the hellenists whose "curve" approximates the curve of the data. Occasionally we found that rabbinic tradition fitted the curve beautifully, as in the rabbinic interpretation of the sacrifice of Isaac. But usually it is the mystic literature which fits it best.

From all this we return to the fact that although we must expect many things which we find in rabbinic and mystic literature to "fit" the data, the "curve" itself is a simplification set by the archeological data themselves. Generalizations for the Judaism of the time as a whole can be made from any Jewish documents only as they harmonize with the archeological remains, since except for the Bible we have not a single written work that we know Jews were then universally reading. We know that the Jews of the Empire were loyal Jews, living as observantly as they could by the Bible in Greek translation and by local legal traditions, since otherwise they would not so painstakingly have preserved their identity, built their synagogues, and buried one another in graves marked with Jewish symbols. But were they loyal Jews as Philo was a loyal Jew, or as Akiba—or as the apocalyptists, or in still some other sense?

To try to get an answer to such a question from the monuments we had obviously to go on in Volume IV to construct a methodology of studying symbols in transition from one religion to another. It was suggested that borrowed symbols keep a basic value, what we should often call an emotional value. If a new religion that takes in foreign symbols is to keep its identity and not simply merge with the other religion from which it borrows, it must reject the mythical background in terms of which the old religion had explained those values. The new religion must give the old symbols a new explanation—that is, a new mythological background and nomenclature from its own store. A reader beginning with these volumes should by all means go back to read the second chapter of Volume IV, where this matter is more fully expounded.

For the general task of the present series of volumes is to see how far this hypothesis will help in understanding the Judaism expressed in the borrowed symbols. We had to begin, in the rest of Volume IV, by studying the symbols on graves, synagogues, and the like which were not borrowed at all but had recognizably been taken from Jewish cult: the candlestick (menorah), the Torah shrine and scroll, the ethrog and lulab from Tabernacles, the shofar or ram's horn from the New Year and the Day of Atonement, and a peculiar shovel, apparently one for ashes or incense.

In the present volumes we are now at last ready to consider the borrowed symbols themselves, and we begin with symbols of food: fish, bread, and wine. These constitute a transition from the symbols of the fourth volume to those in the volumes which follow, for while the symbols examined in Volume IV are distinctively Jewish in nature and origin, the symbols we shall study later are obvious invasions from the outside, usually from Greco-Roman civilization, especially in its eastern forms. Between these stand the three symbols we consider here, food symbols which in form of representation are borrowed but which refer to common materials of eating and drinking certainly not used by the Jews for the first time at this period. The question of this volume then is: Why did Jews suddenly want to put symbols of fish, bread, and especially wine on their graves and synagogues, and what did they tell themselves and one another when they did so?

As I have tried to answer this question I have received help from many friends. My research assistants contributed much to the preparation of these two volumes, chiefly Miss Beatrice Goffe and Mrs. Claude Lopez. Mrs. Katherine Sohler and my wife also took turns in the work. As to help I had from other scholars, it is useless to rehearse all the names listed in previous volumes, but I must again mention my colleagues in the Departments of Classics and of the Near East, and Leon Nemoy, of the Yale University Library. When we were in Egypt in 1951, everyone was most helpful. I must name especially Alexandre Piankoff as well as the staffs of the Egyptian Museum in Cairo and the Chicago House in Luxor. Charles Nims, of the latter group, spent days with us in the Theban tombs and the temples of Luxor and Karnak. Pahor Labib, of the Coptic Museum in Old Cairo, similarly devoted himself to our interests. For this volume and those which will follow, Miss Edith Porada and the officers of the Pierpont Morgan Library have provided many valuable photographs. I should like again to thank the Soncino Press, London, for permission to quote from their translations of Hebrew texts; I have done so freely in these volumes. I am also indebted to the following publishers for quotation from the works indicated: Cambridge University Press, for J. H. Bernard, *The Odes of Solomon;* Bloch Publishing Co., New York, for S. Singer, *The Standard Prayer Book;* Longmans, Green, New York, for S. A. B. Mercer, *Pyramid Texts;* Pontificium Institutum Biblicum, Rome, for Cyrus H. Gordon, *Ugaritic Literature;* Princeton University Press, for James Pritchard, *Ancient Near Eastern Texts;* and Routledge and Kegan Paul, London, for E. A. W. Budge, *The Book of the Dead.* The two scholars to whom I have dedicated this book have done me immeasurable service, though they will disapprove of many things I say and leave unsaid. The Bollingen Foundation has continued to be extremely helpful. Those who think the scholar a lone wolf, or a dweller in a private tower, little know how deeply social a product he and his work must always be.

As before, acknowledgments for illustrations reproduced in these volumes will be found in the footnotes, at the pages indicated in the Lists of Illustrations; and likewise in the footnotes, acknowledgments for textual quotations.

ERWIN R. GOODENOUGH

Jonathan Edwards College
Yale University
October, 1954

Contents

VOLUME V

VOLUME VI

PART VIII. WINE (*conclusion*)

ABBREVIATIONS

AA, AZ. *Archäologischer Anzeiger zur Archäologischen Zeitung.*

AA, JDAI. *Archäologischer Anzeiger: Beiblatt zum Jahrbuch des Archäologischen Instituts.*

AAL, M. *Atti della R. Accademia dei Lincei, Memorie della Classe di Scienze Morali, Storiche e Filologiche.*

AAL, N. *Atti della R. Accademia dei Lincei, Notizie degli scavi di antichità della Classe di Scienze Morali, Storiche e Filologiche.*

AASOR. *Annual of the American School of Oriental Research in Jerusalem.*

Abrahams, *Jewish Life.* Israel Abrahams, *Jewish Life in the Middle Ages*, London, 1932.

AJA. *American Journal of Archaeology.*

AJP. *American Journal of Philology.*

AJSL. *American Journal of Semitic Languages and Literature.*

Amelung, *Sculp. Vatican.* Walter Amelung, *Die Sculpturen des Vaticanischen Museums*, Berlin, 1903–1936.

ARW. *Archiv für Religionswissenschaft.*

ASAE. *Annales du Service des Antiquites de l'Egypte.*

ASE. Archaeological Survey of Egypt.

AZ. *Archäologische Zeitung.*

BA. *Bollettino d'arte del Ministero della Pubblica Istruzione.*

BAC. *Bullettino di archeologia cristiana.*

BASOR. *Bulletin of the American Schools of Oriental Research.*

BCH. *Bulletin de correspondance hellénique.*

BD. *Book of the Dead.* Unless otherwise stated, as transl. by E. A. W. Budge, *The Book of the Dead: An English Translation*, 2d ed., London, 1923.

BD, ed. Davis. C. H. S. Davis, *The Egyptian Book of the Dead*, London, 1895.

BD, ed. Renouf and Naville. P. L. Renouf and E. Naville, *The Egyptian Book of the Dead*, London, 1904.

Berliner, *Juden in Rom.* A. Berliner, *Geschichte der Juden in Rom*, Frankfort, 1893.

Beyer and Lietzmann, *Torlonia.* H. W. Beyer and Hans Lietzmann, *Jüdische Denkmäler*, I: *Die Jüdische Katakombe der Villa Torlonia in Rom*, Berlin-Leipzig, 1930 (Studien zur spätantiken Kunstgeschichte, IV).

BICA. *Bullettino dell'Istituto di Corrispondenza Archeologica*, Rome, 1829–1885. Continued by publications of Archäologisches Institut des Deutschen Reichs, in Rome.

Billiard, *La Vigne.* Raymond Billiard, *La Vigne dans l'antiquité*, Lyons, 1913.

BJPES. *Bulletin of the Jewish Palestine Exploration Society.*

Bodenschatz, *ADRH.* J. C. G. Bodenschatz, *Aufrichtig deutsch redender Hebräer*, 1756.

Bonner, *Amulets.* Campbell Bonner, *Studies in Magical Amulets, Chiefly Graeco-Egyptian*, Ann Arbor, 1950.

Bonner, "BM." Campbell Bonner, "Amulets Chiefly in the British Museum," *Hesperia*, XX (1951), 301–345.

Bousset, *Religion.* Wilhelm Bousset, *Die Religion des Judentums im späthellenistischen Zeitalter*, 3d ed., Tübingen, 1926 (Handbuch zum Neuen Testament, XXI).

Breasted, *Records.* J. H. Breasted, *Ancient Records of Egypt; Historical Documents*, Chicago, 1906–1907.

BSAE. British School of Archeology in Egypt.

BT. Babylonian Talmud, with references to the various treatises. ET refers to the Engl. transls. made by various scholars under the general editorship of I. Epstein, London, Soncino Press, 1935 et seq. Similarly, GT refers to the German transl. of Lazarus Goldschmidt, pub. with the Hebrew text, Berlin, 1897; rev. ed. (German transl. only), Berlin, 1929.

Bullet. Commiss. archeol. *Bullettino della Commissione Archeologica comunale di Roma.*

Butler, *Architecture, 1899.* Howard C. Butler, *Architecture and Other Arts*, New York, 1903 (Publications of the American Archaeological Expedition to Syria in 1899–1900, II).

Butler, *Architecture, 1904–1905.* *Syria: Publications of the Princeton University Archaeological Expeditions to Syria in 1904–1905 and 1909.* Div. II, Architecture, by Howard C. Butler: Sec. *A*, "Southern Syria"; Sec. *B*, "Northern Syria." Leyden, 1919–1920.

By Light, Light. See Goodenough.

Caylus, *Rec. d'ant.* A.-C.-P. Caylus, *Recueil d'antiquités égyptiennes, étrusques, grecques et romaines*, VI, Paris, 1764.

Charles, *Apoc. and Pseud.* R. H. Charles, *The Apocrypha and Pseudepigrapha of the Old Testament in English, with Introductions and Critical and Explanatory Notes to the Several Books*, Oxford, 1913.

CIG. *Corpus inscriptionum Graecarum.*

CIJ. See Frey.

CIL. *Corpus inscriptionum Latinarum.*

CL. *Dictionnaire d'archéologie chrétienne et de liturgie*, ed. by Fernand Cabrol and H. Leclercq, Paris, 1907 et seq.

Cohn-Wiener. Ernst Cohn-Wiener, *Die jüdische Kunst, ihre Geschichte von den Anfängen bis zur Gegenwart*, Berlin-Leipzig, 1929.

Contenau, *Glyptique.* G. Contenau, *La Glyptique syro-hittite*, Paris, 1922 (Bibliothèque archéologique et historique, II).

Contenau, *Manuel.* G. Contenau, *Manuel d'archéologie orientale depuis les origines jusqu'à l'époque d'Alexandre*, Paris, 1922–1947.

Cook, *Zeus.* Arthur B. Cook, *Zeus: A Study in Ancient Religion*, Cambridge, 1914 et seq.

CR, AIB. *Comptes rendus des séances de l'année*, Academie des Inscriptions et Belles-Lettres.

Creuzer, *Symbolik.* G. F. Creuzer, *Symbolik und Mythologie der alten Völker, besonders der Griechen*, 3d ed., Leipzig, 1837–1843.

CSEL. *Corpus scriptorum ecclesiasticorum Latinorum, Vienna*, 1866 et seq.

Cumont, *After Life.* Franz Cumont, *After Life in Roman Paganism*, New Haven, 1922.

Cumont, *Symbolisme.* Franz Cumont, *Recherches sur le symbolisme funéraire des Romains*, Paris, 1942 (Bibliothèque archéologique et historique, XXXV).

CVA. *Corpus vasorum antiquorum*, Union Academique International.

Danby, *Mishnah.* Herbert Danby, *The Mishnah*, transl. from the Hebrew with introduction and brief explanatory notes, Oxford, 1933.

Davies and Gardiner, *Paintings.* Nina M. Davies and A. H. Gardiner, *Ancient Egyptian Paintings*, Chicago, 1936.

DE. *Description de l'Egypte*, *Antiquités*, Descriptions, Planches, 1809.

Dölger, *Ichthys.* See *Ichthys.*

DS. *Dictionnaire des antiquités grecques et romaines d'après les textes et les monuments*, ed. by C. Daremberg and E. Saglio, Paris, 1873 et seq.

Du Mesnil, *Peintures.* Comte du Mesnil du Buisson, *Les Peintures de la synagogue de Doura-Europos, 245–256 après J.-C.*, Rome, 1939.

Dussaud, *Monuments.* René Dussaud, *Les Monuments palestiniens et judaïques*, Paris, 1912.

Dussaud, "Mythologie." René Dussaud, "La Mythologie phénicienne d'après les tablettes de Ras Shamra," *RHR*, CIV (1931), 353–408.

Dussaud, *Religions.* René Dussaud, *Les Religions des Hittites et des Hourrites, des Phéniciens et des Syriens*, in the volume with E. Dhorme, *Les Religions de Babylonie et d'Assyrie*, Paris, 1945 (Mana, I, ii).

EA. *Ephemeris archaiologikē.*

EB. *Encyclopaedia Biblica*, ed. by T. K. Cheyne and J. S. Black, New York and London, 1899–1903.

EES. T. Schreiber et al., *Expedition Ernst Sieglin, Ausgrabungen in Alexandria*, Leipzig, 1908.

Eisler, "Fisch." Robert Eisler, "Der Fisch als Sexualsymbol," *Imago*, III (1914), 165–196.

Eisler, *Orph.-dion.* Robert Eisler, *Orphisch-dionysische Mysteriengedanken in der christlichen Antike*, Berlin-Leipzig, 1925 (Vorträge der Bibliothek Warburg, II, 1922–1923, ii).

Eisler, *Orpheus.* Robert Eisler, *Orpheus the Fisher: Comparative Studies in Orphic and Early Christian Cult Symbolism*, London, 1921.

EJ. *Encyclopaedia Judaica: Das Judentum in Geschichte und Gegenwart*, Berlin, 1928 et seq.

Erman, *Relig. Ägypt.* Adolf Erman, *Die Religion der Ägypter*, Berlin-Leipzig, 1934.

EXF. Egyptian Exploration Fund.

Farnell, *Cults.* Lewis R. Farnell, *The Cults of the Greek States*, Oxford, 1896 et seq.

FR. A. Furtwängler and K. Reichhold, *Griechische Vasenmalerei*, Munich, 1904 et seq.

Frey, *CIJ.* Jean-Baptiste Frey, *Corpus inscriptionum Iudaicarum, Recueil des inscriptions juives qui vont du IIIe siècle avant Jésus-Christ au VIIe siècle de notre ère*, Rome, 1936, I: *Europe.*

Furtwängler, *Besch.* A. Furtwängler, *Beschreibung der Vasensammlung im Antiquarium*, Berlin, 1885 (Königliche Museen zu Berlin).

Garrucci, *Arte cristiana.* Raffaele Garrucci, *Storia della arte cristiana nei primi otto secoli della chiesa*, Prato, 1872–1880. References, unless otherwise stated, are to the Jewish material in Vol. VI, 1880.

Gautier, *Fêtes.* Henri Gautier, *Les Fêtes du dieu Min*, Cairo, 1931.

GB. J. G. Frazer, *The Golden Bough*, 3d ed., 1935.

GCS. *Die griechischen christlichen Schriftsteller der ersten drei Jahrhunderte*, pub. by Kirchenväter Commission der Preussischen Akademie der Wissenschaften, Leipzig.

Gerhard, *Auser. Vasen.* Eduard Gerhard, *Auserlesene griechische Vasenbilder*, Berlin, 1840–1858.

Gerhard, *GAA.* Eduard Gerhard, *Gesammelte akademische Abhandlungen und kleine Schriften*, Berlin, 1866–1868.

Ginzberg, *Legends.* Louis Ginzberg, *The Legends of the Jews*, Philadelphia, 1909 et seq.

Goodenough, *By Light, Light.* Erwin R. Goodenough, *By Light, Light: The Mystic Gospel of Hellenistic Judaism*, New Haven, 1935.

Goodenough, *Introduction.* Erwin R. Goodenough, *An Introduction to Philo Judaeus*, New Haven, 1940.

Gordon, *Ug. Lit.* Cyrus H. Gordon, *Ugaritic Literature*, Rome, 1949.

Gressmann, *AOTB.* Hugo Gressmann, *Altorientalische Texte und Bilder zum Alten Testament*, 2d ed., Berlin-Leipzig, 1926–1927.

Gressmann, "Jewish Life." Hugo Gressmann, "Jewish Life in Ancient Rome," *Jewish Studies in Memory of Israel Abrahams*, New York, 1927, 170–191.

Hamburger, *RE.* J. Hamburger, *Real-Encyclopädie für Bibel und Talmud, Wörterbuch zum Handgebrauch für Bibelfreunde, Theologen, Juristen, Gemeinde- und Schulvorsteher, Lehrer*, etc., 2d ed., Strelitz, 1883 et seq.

Harris, *Fragments.* J. Rendel Harris, *Fragments of Philo Judaeus*, Cambridge, 1886.

Harrison, *Prolegomena.* Jane E. Harrison, *Prolegomena to the Study of Greek Religion*, 3d ed., Cambridge, 1922.

HDB. James Hastings, *A Dictionary of the Bible*, New York, 1898–1904.

HERE. James Hastings, *Encyclopaedia of Religion and Ethics*, 1908 et seq.

Hopfner, *Fontes.* Theodor Hopfner, *Fontes historiae religionis Aegyptiacae*, Bonn, 1922 (Fontes historiae religionum ex auctoribus Graecis et Latinis collecti, II, i).

HTR. *Harvard Theological Review.*

HUCA. *Hebrew Union College Annual.*

ICC. *International Critical Commentary.*

Ichthys. Franz Joseph Dölger, *Das Fisch-Symbol in frühchristlicher Zeit, ΙΧΘΥΣ als Kürzung der Namen Jesu,* ΙΗΣΟΥΣ ΧΡΙΣΤΟΣ ΘΕΟΥ ΥΙΟΣ ΣΩΤΗΡ, 2d ed., Münster, 1928 et seq.

IG. *Inscriptiones Graecae.*

Jahn, *Besch.* O. Jahn, *Beschreibung der Vasensammlung K. Ludwigs in der Pinakothek zu München,* Munich, 1854.

JAOS. *Journal of the American Oriental Society.*

JBL. *Journal of Biblical Literature.*

JDAI. *Jahrbuch des Kaiserlich Deutschen Archäologischen Instituts.*

JE. *Jewish Encyclopedia: A Descriptive Record of the History, Religion, Literature, and Customs of the Jewish People from the Earliest Times to the Present Day,* ed. by Isidore Singer, New York, 1901 et seq.

JEA. *Journal of Egyptian Archeology.*

JHS. *Journal of Hellenic Studies.*

JÖAI. *Jahreshefte des Österreichischen Archäologischen Institutes in Wien.*

JPOS. *Journal of the Palestine Oriental Society.*

JQR. *Jewish Quarterly Review.*

JRS. *Journal of Roman Studies.*

JT. Jerusalem Talmud, with references to the various treatises. FT refers to French transl. of Moïse Schwab, Paris, 1871 et seq.

Kircher, *Wein.* Karl Kircher, *Die sakrale Bedeutung des Weines in Altertum,* Giessen, 1910 (RgVV, IX, ii).

Kopp, *Pal. crit.* U. F. Kopp, *Palaeographica critica,* Mannheim, 1817 et seq. (4 vols.).

Krauss, *Synag. Altert.* Samuel Krauss, *Synagogale Altertümer,* Berlin-Vienna, 1922.

KW. Heinrich Kohl and Carl Watzinger, *Antike Synagogen in Galilaea,* Leipzig, 1916 (Wissenschaftliche Veröffentlichung der Deutschen Orient-Gesellschaft, XXIX).

Langlotz, *Würzburg.* Ernst Langlotz, *Griechische Vasen in Würzburg,* Munich, 1932 (Martin von Wagner Museum der Universität Würzburg, Bildkatalogue . . . I).

Lanzone, *Dizionario.* R. V. Lanzone, *Dizionario di mitologia egizia,* Turin, 1881 et seq.

Leclercq, *Manuel.* H. Leclercq, *Manuel d'archéologie chrétienne depuis les origines jusqu'au VIIIe siècle,* Paris, 1907.

Lehmann, *Baltimore.* Karl Lehmann-Hartleben and E. C. Olsen, *Dionysiac Sarcophagi in Baltimore,* Baltimore, 1942.

Leisegang, *Index.* Hans Leisegang, *Indices ad Philonis Alexandrini opera,* Berlin, 1926 (L. Cohn and P. Wendland, *Philonis Alexandrini opera quae supersunt,* VII).

Lepsius, *Denkmäler.* C. R. Lepsius, *Denkmäler aus Aegypten und Aethiopien,* Berlin, 1849–1856.

Levy, *Wörterbuch.* Jacob Levy, *Wörterbuch über die Talmudim und Midraschim,* 2d ed., Berlin-Vienna, 1924.

Licht, *Sitt. Gr.* H. Licht, *Sittengeschichte Griechenlands,* Dresden-Zürich, 1925.

LS. Henry Liddell and Robert Scott, *A Greek-English Lexicon.* New ed. of H. S. Jones, Oxford, 1925 et seq.

Lutz, *Viticulture.* H. F. Lutz, *Viticulture and Brewing in the Ancient Orient,* Leipzig, 1922.

Macalister, *Gezer.* R. A. Stewart Macalister, *The Excavation of Gezer, 1902–1905 and 1907–1909,* London, 1912.

Maisler, *Beth She'arim.* Benjamin Maisler, *Beth She'arim: Report on the Excavations during 1936–1940,* I, Jerusalem, 1944. *English Summary,* Jerusalem, 1950.

Mariette, *Dendérah.* A. Mariette, *Dendérah,* Paris, 1870–1875.

MDAI, Ath. *Mitteilungen des Kaiserlich Deutschen Archäologischen Instituts, Athenische Abteilung.*

MDAI, Röm. *Mitteilungen des Kaiserlich Deutschen Archäologischen Instituts, Römische Abteilung.*

Mém., AIB. *Mémoires présentés pars divers savants,* Académie des Inscriptions et Belles-Lettres.

Mém. Inst. *Mémoires* publiés par les membres de l'Institut Français d'Archéologie Orientale du Caire.

Mém. Miss. *Mémoires* publiés par les membres de la Mission Archéologique Français au Caire.

Mercer, *Pyramid Texts.* Samuel A. B. Mercer, *The Pyramid Texts in Translation and Commentary,* New York, 1952.

MGWJ. *Monatschrift für Geschichte und Wissenschaft des Judentums.*

Mon. Ant. *Monumenti antichi, pubblicati per cura della R. Accademia Nazionale dei Lincei.*

Mon. ined. *Monumenti inediti pubblicati dall'Instituto di Corrispondenza Archaeologica (Deutsches Archäologisches Institut)* Rome, 1829–1895.

Mon. Piot. *Monuments et Mémoires,* Académie des Inscriptions et Belles-Lettres (Fondation Eugène Piot).

Monuments. See Dussaud.

Moore, *Judaism.* George Foot Moore, *Judaism in the First Centuries of the Christian Era, the Age of the Tannaim,* Cambridge, 1927.

MR. *Midrash Rabbah,* with references to the various treatises. ET refers to the Engl. transl. made by various scholars under the general editorship of I. Epstein, London, Soncino Press, 1939 et seq.

Müller, *Monteverde.* Nikolaus Müller, *Die jüdische Katacombe am Monteverde zu Rom, der älteste bisher bekannt gewordene jüdische Friedhof des Abendlandes,* Leipzig, 1912. (Pub. in Italian in *Dissertazione della Pontifica Accademia Romana di Archeologia,* Ser. II, Vol. XII [1915], 205–318.)

NBAC. *Nuovo bullettino di archeologia cristiana.*

NF. A. D. Nock and A.-J. Festugière, *Corpus hermeticum,* 1945 (Association Guillaume Budé).

NJ. *Neue Jahrbücher für das klassische Altertum.*

Nilsson, *Griech. Rel.* Martin P. Nilsson, *Geschichte der griechischen Religion,* Munich, 1941–1950 (Walter Otto, Handbuch der Altertumswissenschaft, V, ii).

OB. W. O. E. Oesterley and G. H. Box, *The Religion and Worship of the Synagogue,* New York, 1907.

Osten, *Brett.* H. H. von der Osten, *Ancient Oriental Seals in the Collection of Mrs. Agnes Baldwin Brett,* Chicago, 1936 (University of Chicago Oriental Institute Publications, XXXVII)

Osten, *Newell.* H. H. von der Osten, *Ancient Oriental Seals in the Collection of Mr. Edward T. Newell*, Chicago, 1934 (University of Chicago Oriental Institute Publications, XXII).

Oxé, *Arret. Relief.* A. Oxé, *Arretinische Reliefgefässe vom Rhein*, Frankfort, 1933 (Materialen zur römisch-germanischen Keramik, V).

Parrot, *Refrigerium.* André Parrot, *Le "Refrigerium" dans l'au-delà*, Paris, 1937.

PC, *Histoire.* G. Perrot and C. Chipiez, *Histoire de l'art dans l'antiquité*, Paris, 1882–1914.

PEF, *An.* Palestine Exploration Fund, *Annual.*

PEF, *QS.* Palestine Exploration Fund, *Quarterly Statement.* After 1938 called *Palestine Exploration Quarterly* (abbr., *PEQ*).

PEQ. See PEF, *QS.*

Pfuhl, *Malerei.* Ernst Pfuhl, *Malerei und Zeichnung der Griechen*, Munich, 1923.

PG. Migne, *Patrologia Graeca.*

Piankoff, *Disque solaire.* Alexandre Piankoff, *La Creation du disque solaire*, Cairo, 1953 (Institut Français d'Archéologie Orientale, Bibliothèque d'Etude, XIX).

Pirke Eliezer. *Pirkê de Rabbi Eliezer* (*The Chapters of Rabbi Eliezer the Great*) *according to the Text of the Manuscript belonging to Abraham Epstein of Vienna*, transl. and annot. by Gerald Friedlander, London, 1916.

PJ. *Palästinajahrbuch des Deutschen Evangelischen Instituts für Altertumswissenschaft des Heiligen Landes zu Jerusalem.*

PL. Migne, *Patrologia Latina.*

PME. Publications of the Metropolitan Museum of Art Egyptian Expedition.

Porada, *Morgan.* *Corpus of Ancient Near Eastern Seals in North American Collections;* Vol. I, *The Collection of the Pierpont Morgan Library*, ed. by Edith Porada [New York], 1948 (Bollingen Series XIV).

Pritchard, *Texts.* James B. Pritchard, ed., *Ancient Near Eastern Texts Relating to the Old Testament*, Princeton, 1950.

PSBA. *Proceedings of the Society of Biblical Archaeology.*

PT. John P. Peters and Hermann Thiersch, *Painted Tombs in the Necropolis of Marissa* (*Marêshah*), London, 1905.

PW. *Paulys Real-Encyclopädie der classischen Altertumswissenschaft*, ed. by G. Wissowa, Stuttgart, 1894 et seq.

QDAP. *Quarterly of the Department of Antiquities in Palestine.*

RA. *Revue archéologique.*

RAC. *Rivista di archeologia cristiana*, Pontificia Commissione di Archeologia Sacra.

RB. *Revue biblique.*

RE. See Hamburger.

REG. *Revue des études grecques.*

Reifenberg, *Coins.* Adolf Reifenberg, *Ancient Jewish Coins*, Jerusalem, 1940. Reprinted from *JPOS*, XIX (1939/40), 59–81, 286–318.

Reinach, *Peintures.* S. Reinach, *Répertoire de peintures grecques et romaines*, Paris, 1922.

Reinach, *Reliefs.* S. Reinach, *Répertoire de reliefs grecs et romains*, Paris, 1909–1912.

Reinach, *Statuaire.* S. Reinach, *Répertoire de la statuaire grecque et romaine*, Paris, 1910.

Reinach, *Vases.* S. Reinach, *Peintures de vases antiques*, Paris, 1891.

REJ. *Revue des études juives.*

RgVV. Religionsgeschichtliche Versuche und Vorarbeiten.

RHR. *Revue de l'histoire des religions.*

Robert, *Sarkophag-Reliefs.* Carl Robert, *Die antiken Sarkophag-Reliefs im Auftrage des Kaiserlich Deutschen Archäologischen Instituts*, Berlin, 1890 et seq.

Roscher, *Lex. Myth.* *Ausführliches Lexikon der griechischen und römischen Mythologie*, ed. by W. H. Roscher, Leipzig, 1884 et seq.

Rostovtzeff, *Dura-Europos.* *The Excavations at Dura-Europos, Conducted by Yale University and the French Academy of Inscriptions and Letters*, ed. by M. I. Rostovtzeff et al. *Preliminary Reports*, New Haven, 1928 et seq.

RQ. *Römische Quartalschrift für christliche Alterthumskunde und für Kirchengeschichte.*

RT. *Recueil de travaux relatifs à la philologie et à l'archéologie égyptiennes et assyriennes.*

Schauss, *Lifetime.* Hayyim Schauss, *The Lifetime of a Jew throughout the Ages of Jewish History*, Cincinnati, 1950.

Scheftelowitz, "Fisch-Symbol." I. Scheftelowitz, "Das Fisch-Symbol im Judentum und Christentum," *ARW*, XIV (1911), 1–53, 321–392.

Scholem, *Jewish Mysticism.* Gershom G. Scholem, *Major Trends in Jewish Mysticism*, Jerusalem, 1941 (Hilda Stroock Lectures, delivered at the Jewish Institute of Religion, New York, 1938).

Schürer, *Jüd. Volk.* Emil Schürer, *Geschichte des jüdischen Volkes im Zeitalter Jesu Christi*, 4th ed., Leipzig, 1901 et seq. ET refers to the Engl. transl. of J. Macpherson, S. Taylor, and P. Christie, *A History of the Jewish People in the Time of Jesus Christ*, New York, 1891.

Sethe, *Pyramidentexte.* Kurt Sethe, *Übersetzung und Kommentar zu den altägyptischen Pyramidentexten*, Hamburg, 1935–1940.

Shulchan Aruch, GT. Heinrich G. F. Löwe, transl. *Schulchan Aruch, oder die vier jüdischen Gesetzbücher*, 2d ed., Vienna, 1896 (written in Hebrew by Joseph Karo in the sixteenth century).

Simon, *Verus Israel.* Marcel Simon, *Verus Israel: Etude sur les relations entre Chrétiens et Juifs dans l'empire romain*, Paris, 1948 (Bibliothèque des Ecoles Françaises d'Athènes et de Rome, CLXVI).

Singer, *Prayer Book.* S. Singer, *The Standard Prayer Book*, New York, 1928. (Reprinted many times in England and in the United States.)

Speleers, *Textes des Pyramides.* Louis Speleers, *Traduction, index et vocabulaire des textes des pyramides égyptiennes*, Brussels, 1936.

Stebbins. E. B. Stebbins, *The Dolphin in the Literature and Art of Greece and Rome*, Menasha, Wisconsin, 1929.

Stephani, *Compte rendu.* *Compte rendu de la Commission Impériale Archéologique*, St. Petersburg, 1860–1880.

Strack, *Intro.* Hermann L. Strack, *Introduction to the Talmud and Midrash*, Philadelphia, 1931.

Strack-Bill. Hermann L. Strack and Paul Billerbeck, *Kommentar zum Neuen Testament aus Talmud und Midrasch*, Munich, 1922–1928.

Tischbein, *Hamilton Vases.* W. Tischbein, *Collection of Engravings from Ancient Vases . . . Now in the Possession of Sir William Hamilton*, Naples, 1791–1795.

Torlonia. See Beyer and Lietzmann.

TSBA. *Transactions of the Society of Biblical Archaeology.*

TTS. The Theban Tombs Series.

TU. Texte und Untersuchungen zur Geschichte der Altchristlichen Literatur, Leipzig, 1882–1952.

UJE. *Universal Jewish Encyclopedia*, ed. by Isaac Landman, New York, 1939–1943.

Walters, *Engraved Gems.* H. B. Walters, *Catalogue of the Engraved Gems and Cameos, Greek, Etruscan and Roman, in the British Museum*, London, 1926.

Ward, *Seal Cylinders.* William Hayes Ward, *The Seal Cylinders of Western Asia*, Washington, 1910.

Watzinger, *Denkmäler.* Carl Watzinger, *Denkmäler Palästinas*, Leipzig, 1933–1935.

Wilamowitz, *Glaube.* Ulrich von Wilamowitz-Moellendorff, *Der Glaube der Hellenen*, Berlin, 1931–1932.

Wilpert, *Mosaiken und Malereien.* Josef Wilpert, *Die römischen Mosaiken und Malereien der kirchlichen Bauten vom IV. bis XIII. Jahrhundert*, 2d ed., Freiburg im Breisgau, 1917.

Wilpert, *Pitture.* Josef Wilpert, *Roma sotteranea: Le Pitture delle catacombe romane*, Rome, 1903.

Wolfson, *Philo.* Harry Austryn Wolfson, *Philo: Foundations of Religious Philosophy in Judaism, Christianity and Islam*, Cambridge, 1947.

ZaeS. *Zeitschrift für ägyptische Sprache und Alterthumskunde.*

ZAW. *Zeitschrift für die alttestamentliche Wissenschaft.*

ZDMG. *Zeitschrift der Deutschen Morgenländischen Gesellschaft.*

ZDPV. *Zeitschrift des Deutschen Palästina-Vereins.*

ZNW. *Zeitschrift für die neutestamentliche Wissenschaft.*

Zohar. *The Zohar.* ET refers to Engl. transl. of Harry Sperling and Maurice Simon, London, Soncino Press, 1931 et seq. FT refers to French transl. of J. de Pauly, rev. by E. Lafuma-Giraud, Paris, 1906 et seq.

ZWT. *Zeitschrift für wissenschaftliche Theologie.*

EXTANT TREATISES ATTRIBUTED TO PHILO

The English titles, except as noted hereafter, are those of F. H. Colson and G. H. Whitaker, with Supplements by Ralph Marcus, in the Loeb edition of the works of Philo. Roman numerals in italics refer to the number of the volume of that series in which the given treatise appears. I have furnished English titles for the Armenian works not in the Loeb edition.

Abr. *De Abrahamo.* On Abraham (*VI*).

Aet. *De aeternitate mundi.* On the Eternity of the World (*IX*).

Agr. *De agricultura.* On Husbandry (*III*).

Animal. *Alexander, sive de eo quod rationem habeant bruta animalia.* Alexander, or That Dumb Animals Have Reason. (Accessible only in Armenian and in Aucher's Latin transl.)

Antiq. *Liber antiquitatum biblicarum.* (Pseudo Philo, ed. by Guido Kisch, 1949, transl. M. R. James, 1917: *The Biblical Antiquities of Philo.*)

Cher. *De cherubim.* On the Cherubim, and the Flaming Sword, and Cain the First Man Created out of Man (*II*).

Conf. *De confusione linguarum.* On the Confusion of Tongues (*IV*).

Cong. *De congressu eruditionis gratia.* On Mating with the Preliminary Studies (*IV*).

Cont. *De vita contemplativa.* On the Contemplative Life (*IX*).

Decal. *De decalogo.* On the Decalogue (*VII*).

Deo. *De deo.* On God. (Accessible only in Armenian and in Aucher's Latin transl.)

Det. *Quod deterius potiori insidiari soleat.* That the Worse Is Wont to Attack the Better (*II*).

Ebr. *De ebrietate.* On Drunkenness (*III*).

Flac. *In Flaccum.* Against Flaccus (*IX*).

Fug. *De fuga et inventione.* On Flight and Finding (*V*).

Gig. *De gigantibus.* On the Giants (*II*).

Heres. *Quis rerum divinarum heres.* Who Is the Heir of Divine Things (*IV*).

Hyp. *Apologia pro Iudaeis.* Hypothetica (*IX*).

Immut. *Quod deus sit immutabilis.* On the Unchangeableness of God (*III*).

Jona. *De Jona.* On Jonah. (Accessible only in Armenian and in Aucher's Latin transl.)

Jos. *De Josepho.* On Joseph (*VI*).

LA. *Legum allegoria.* Allegorical Interpretation of Genesis (*I*).

Legat. *Legatio ad Gaium.* Legation to Gaius (*X*, forthcoming).

Migr. *De migratione Abrahami.* On the Migration of Abraham (*IV*).

Mos. *De vita Mosis.* Moses (*VI*).

Mund. *De mundo.* On the World.

Mut. *De mutatione nominum.* On the Change of Names (*V*).

Opif. *De opificio mundi.* On the Account of the World's Creation Given by Moses (*I*).

Plant. *De plantatione.* Concerning Noah's Work as a Planter (*III*).

Post. *De posteritate Caini.* On the Posterity of Cain and His Exile (*II*).

Praem. *De praemiis et poenis.* On Rewards and Punishments (*VIII*).

Prob. *Quod omnis probus liber sit.* That Every Virtuous Man Is Free (*IX*).

Provid. *De providentia.* On Providence (*IX*).

QE. *Quaestiones et solutiones in Exodum.* Questions and Answers on Exodus. (Supplement II to the Loeb edition, transl. Ralph Marcus.)

QG. *Quaestiones et solutiones in Genesim.* Questions and Answers on Genesis. (Supplement I to the Loeb edition, transl. Ralph Marcus.)

Sacr. *De sacrificiis Abelis et Caini.* On the Birth of Abel and the Sacrifices Offered by Him and His Brother Cain (*II*).

Samp. *Sine preparatione de Sampsone* [*sermo*]. On Samson. (Accessible only in Armenian and in Aucher's Latin transl.)

Sobr. *De sobrietate.* On the Prayers and Curses Uttered by Noah When He Became Sober (*III*).

Som. *De somniis.* On Dreams, That They Are God-sent (*V*).

Spec. *De specialibus legibus.* On the Special Laws (*VII*, *VIII*).

Virt. *De virtutibus.* On Virtues Which, together with Others, Were Described by Moses; or on Courage, Piety, Humanity, and Repentance (*VIII*).

PART VII

FISH AND BREAD

CHAPTER ONE

Creatures of the Sea

IT HAS LONG been the general assumption that the fish was a Christian symbol, to the point that almost any appearance of fish from the Roman world has usually been considered Christian. Although the existence of the fish as a symbol in paganism has been thoroughly understood by experts, only two scholars, to my knowledge, have suggested that the fish might have been a symbol in Judaism also.[1] Yet the fish has appeared on many of the monuments discussed in the previous volumes of this study, and, we shall see, it frequently reappears to the present in Jewish life. As a symbol we cannot consider it what I have called idiomatically Jewish, since nothing in the Jewish Bible suggests such a symbolic use of the fish.

A. JEWISH REPRESENTATIONS

TO COME to any understanding of the possible meaning of the fish in Judaism we must first review its appearance on Jewish monuments of the period. Throughout we must consider not only the various kinds of genuine fish, but the dolphin, which is of course a mammal, and mythical sea monsters, since it will become clear that the symbolic values of all merge so closely that we can consider and discuss them all as fish.

1. The Fish

WHEN REPRESENTED by Jews as a sign of the zodiac, the fish takes its usual place as Pisces. As such it is shown in the customary way as a pair of fishes, usually facing in opposite directions and often connected by a line which runs in an ogival curve from the mouth of one to that of the other.[2] Of the signs of the zodiac, Pisces seems to have been especially important to Jews of the period, for it appears without the other signs in the Catacomb Vigna Randanini at Rome,[3] where the connecting cord is a garland which the fish hold between them; at the synagogue of Er-Rafid,[4] carved as the fragment of a

1. Scheftelowitz, "Fisch-Symbol"; Eisler, "Fisch"; Eisler, *Orpheus*, 221–225.

2. For fish in Jewish zodiacs see above, III, figs. 515 (?), 640, 644.

3. See III, figs. 742 (at left), 748 (at top); cf. II, 19.

4. See III, fig. 541; cf. I, 211.

frieze which may or may not have included the other signs; and on two of the ceiling tiles at the Dura synagogue, fig. 1.[5] Capricorn, represented as a sea goat, is the only zodiacal sign given similar prominence as an independent symbol.[6]

In the synagogue at Beth Alpha in Palestine a border surrounds the three main panels of the mosaic floor. In this border are collected a large number of the symbols we are to discuss, including baskets of bread and fruit. Just above the Torah shrine at the top of the design stand two emblems, a bunch of grapes on a vine at the right, and a fish on the left.[7] In the mosaic, for special emphasis, the fish's tongue is bright red.

The mosaic floor of the synagogue of Hammam Lif in Tunisia reveals the most arresting instances of the fish among the Jewish remains.[8] There, beside a flowery shore, is indicated a sea in which swim a huge fish, a dolphin, and two ducks.[9] From the mouths of both the fish and the dolphin extend objects which seem to me clearly ropes by which they have been caught. Between the fish and the dolphin is a wheel with eight or nine spokes (drawings of the wheel differ). At the top is a peculiar object which Biebel takes to be a conventionalized hand of God.[10] He has made the interesting suggestion that the whole scene represents creation; the sea, the dry land, the birds, the fishes, and the flowers. He has ignored, for this, the wheel, the ropes from the mouths of the fishes, and the fact that the "dry land" with its little flowers is the "mead of asphodel," the form which frequently represented in art the Elysian Fields, the Island of the Blessed—the heaven of antiquity.[11] We shall discuss the wheel with fish below.[12]

We recall that in the panel immediately beneath this scene peacocks confront each other on either side of a cup, from which water or wine spouts up in a fountain, and that a palm tree with pendant fruit and a bird stand on either side beyond the peacocks. The fish and dolphin with ropes from their mouths may be adaptations of some fishing scene, as in those we shall discuss shortly from Antioch, where Eros rides the back of a dolphin while he catches it with rod and line by the mouth.[13] Or an Orpheus the Fisher may have originally been at the other end of the line in the Jewish mosaic and been deliberately cut out by later Jewish iconoclasts. Representations of seascapes with fish in the water are very common in the mosaics of North Africa, but although many of them show fishing scenes, I have found none in a form at all comparable to this.[14]

5. Courtesy of the Yale University Art Gallery; cf. Margaret Crosby in Rostovtzeff, *Dura-Europos*, VI, 386, and plate XLVI, 3.

6. See below, p. 11.

7. See III, fig. 635.

8. See III, figs. 887 f., 897, 900. For discussion of the many problems presented by this synagogue see II, 89–100.

9. The symbolism of ducks will be discussed in Vol. VIII.

10. "The Mosaics of Hammam Lif," *The Art Bulletin*, XVIII (1936), 551.

11. For the identity of the Elysian Fields with the Island of the Blest in antiquity see Waser in PW, V, 2470–2476. This place was considered abundantly fruitful, and always with delightful climate. The flowers seem to conflate this with the "mead of asphodel," where the shades of heroes went: *Odyssey*, XI, 539; XXIV, 13; *Homeric Hymn to Hermes*, 221, 344; Wagler, in PW, II, 1730–1733. We saw a similar flowery field in the future world in III, fig. 842; cf. II, 46.

12. The wheel, with two fish, also appears on an inscription from Ravenna, which is dubiously Jewish; see below, n. 57. On the combination of wheel and fish see below, pp. 56 f.

13. See below, p. 25.

14. See, for example, R. M. du Coudray la Blan-

From the synagogue at Hammam Lif has come another mosaic fragment which shows a fish.[15] Nothing is known of its original setting, but Biebel guesses the fragment may have been in the lost part, which I have called the "Elysian Field." It seems to me more probable that this was not its setting and that it came from another room in the synagogue.

In the little catacomb at Rome on the Via Appia Pignatelli a fish was painted on the wall above a peculiar row of reeds and between two large palm trees, according to a report by N. Müller.[16] No drawing or photograph of the design was ever published, so far as I know. Müller's argument [17] that this little catacomb was Jewish has not been challenged, and I see no reason to do so.

One of the few carved stone fragments from the synagogue at Sheikh Ibreiq in Galilee appears to be a triglyph from a frieze,[18] with little objects carved in the spaces: two trees, an animal (perhaps a rampant lion, perhaps, from its hump, a bull), and a fish. Here again we seem to be presented with symbols.

A fragment of a carved stone found in Acrae, Sicily,[19] has been taken to be Jewish, though Dölger protested.[20] On this stone is another palm tree with pendant fruit, two varieties of birds, a two-handled jar of the type usually considered Jewish,[21] a number of "round objects" generally supposed to be bread or, specifically, mazzoth, and a fish. Amid the diversity of the symbols with the fish we are beginning to feel a uniformity. We have met all but the "round objects" already, and the relevance of these also will become increasingly apparent as we continue. There are no grounds for deciding finally whether this is a Jewish piece or not, but I am impressed with Orsi's argument that here is a strange group of symbols for Christianity. Though fish or dolphins are common on Punic tombstones, Dölger's suggestion that the stone from Acrae is a Punic piece has no foundation.[22] From the point of view of symbolic meaning the group of symbols on this stone is important whatever its origin, but the usual guess seems to me to be the most likely one, that the stone is Jewish.

On two tiles from the ceiling of the synagogue at Dura, we have said, are presented

chère and P. Gauckler, *Catalogue du Musée Alaoui*, 1897 (Description de l'Afrique du Nord): plate III, 7, a fishing scene, with a duck among the fishes; plate VII, 111, Neptune on a sea horse surrounded by fish. P. Gauckler et al., *Catalogue du Musée Alaoui* (Supplément), 1910 (same series), plate II, shows a very complicated marine and fishing scene, with a shrine in the center and Aphrodite on her shell at the bottom, the four Winds in the corners, and in the border a vine with birds in the interstices; ibid., plate V, a fishing scene with a city on the shore; and plate XIV, which shows a single plaque with fish. Another complicated mosaic from the Baths of Thina was published by R. Massigli, *Musée de Sfax*, 1912 (same series), plates I–V (cf. pp. 1–5), where Arion as Orpheus is on a dolphin at the center. For Nereids and Neptune on sea horses see also G. Doublet, *Musée d'Alger*, 1890 (same series), plates XVI f.; S. Gsell, *Musée de Tébessa*, 1902 (same series), plate VIII (cf. pp. 64–67). See also P. Gauckler et al., *Musées de Sousse*, 1902 (same series), plate I and plate IX, 4, fish swimming from a basket; and plate VI, 2, a fishing scene.

15. See III, fig. 914.

16. "La Catacomba degli Ebrei presso la via Appia Pignatelli," *MDAI*, *Röm.*, I (1886), 54. See above, II, 34.

17. Op. cit., 49–56.

18. See III, fig. 545; cf. I, 209.

19. See III, fig. 856; cf. II, 56.

20. *Ichthys*, I, 441 f.

21. See I, 96.

22. He has a typical collection in *Ichthys*, III, plates XXVI f., but the parallelism with the Acrae stone is to me not impressive.

the pair of fishes of the zodiacal sign Pisces, fig. 1.[23] We shall see that much more frequently the dolphin and Capricorn were also on the tiles of the ceiling.[24] Systematic examination of the designs of these tiles will have to await the final volume of this study, but they appear to me to be very important. Miss Crosby said that since so many tiles with similar patterns were found in private houses in the city, the ones in the synagogue seem to her not to have been specially made for Jewish use but to have been stock patterns procurable from the pagan manufacturers.[25] At least it is obvious that the Jews of Dura did not object to the designs on these tiles and they selected designs from the symbolic lingua franca of the day, most of which can be demonstrated to have had value for pagans and Jews alike. It must be recalled that several tiles have inscriptions [26] and that two of them have the "much-suffering eye," one with *Iaō* above it.[27] As for Pisces, the sign also appears, apart from an inscription, carved in the synagogue of Er-Rafid.[28]

The fish appears on several lamps from Palestine. The first is a lamp with seven holes from Tell en-Nasbeh.[29] Such lamps with seven holes are usually taken to be Jewish, though this detail seems in itself not decisive to me, and I should call the lamp in question only probably Jewish. Under the seven holes is an arcade of the type common on Jewish lamps. There are five columns joined by arches with a boss under each arch. Between the columns are placed symbols: in the two outer spaces is a design of two lozenges, with "round objects" between them, arranged vertically; in each of the two inner spaces is a fish. We have found that objects are put thus under arches to indicate their special sanctity. The similarity of this design with that on the stone from Sheikh Ibreiq [30] is striking.

The second lamp, fig. 6,[31] has a palm branch under each of its seven holes. In the lower half a fish with open mouth is beside the filling hole on either side. Its open mouth seems about to seize an elaborately represented "round object" before it; a smaller "round object" fills in the space beside the larger one. This lamp and the one which will next be mentioned are the property of Mrs. Miriam Schaar Schloessinger, who said that she bought them in Jerusalem and was told they came from an unrifled tomb at Walaja, near Betther. Mrs. Schloessinger has written me that she can add nothing to this information.

The third lamp, fig. 5, must be considered with the second, since both are reported to have come from the same tomb. It has five holes, each set in a little arch as though, following the use of the arch, to indicate the sanctity of the flames. From these to the circles round the filling hole are two tiers, each made of seven "round objects" with bosses. On either side of these is a fish. The one at the left is eating two little "round objects." Before each fish is a peculiar object made of three concentric ovals. "Round objects" fill in the spaces by the fish, and a scroll, which may be a variant of what I have

23. See above, p. 4.
24. See below, pp. 11, 13.
25. In Rostovtzeff, 385.
26. Ibid., 387–390.
27. See above, III, figs. 1065 f.; cf. II, 238.
28. See III, fig. 541; cf. I, 211.
29. See III, fig. 261; cf. I, 149.
30. See III, fig. 545.
31. From a photograph kindly sent me by M. Schaar Schloessinger, who published it in her "Five Lamps with Fish Reliefs: from Israel and Other Mediterranean Countries," *Israel Exploration Journal*, I (1950/1), plate 23; see pp. 84–95.

called "cursive round objects," [32] runs round the bowl of the lamp from the fish to the handle. On the handle is a palm branch resembling the palm branches on the preceding lamp. Definite identification of the ovals is impossible, but Mrs. Schloessinger has pointed out the frequency with which the motif (or variants of it) is represented on Neo-Babylonian seals, often with fish.[33] Writers in this field frequently call it the rhomb, and it seems identical to what we have often spoken of as a lozenge. In its early form it was almost certainly the vulva of the fertility goddess, of whatever name,[34] but probably it had many identifications and explanations through the centuries. We shall see a lamp shortly where such a pair of ovals appear to have become the eyes of Horus. Again it seems to me that we must think in symbols, not in words for the symbols. It is the fish themselves with this form, of which the "round objects" of the preceding lamp may well be variants, which are the factor of continuity, not any identification or name for either the fish or the centered object.

Were these two lamps, then, made by or for Jews, and was it a Jewish corpse with which they were buried? Mrs. Schloessinger says they should be dated in the second or third century.[35] She thinks that this is too early for the lamps to be Christian, and that to take the ovals as loaves is to strain the identification. She is quite confident that both lamps refer to the cult of the Syrian Atargatis; certainly there is no question that both symbols had historic roots in Atargatis. The possibility that the lamps are Jewish, however, she merely mentions in passing. Here is the chief justification for the bulk of the present study. Only, for example, if one has in mind all the Jewish fishes in comparison with the fishes of paganism and Christianity can one safely deal with isolated or atypical objects. Before we are done we shall see that there are definite parallels to the symbolism of these lamps in remains from paganism, Judaism, and Christianity alike. I should say that at the outset the possibilities that the lamps in question belonged to any one of the three are about equal. As we proceed, the likelihood that they are Jewish will become steadily greater, but we shall never feel certain about any of the lamps.

The fourth Palestinian lamp, fig. 371 of Volume III, is from Gezer. It has a design of four fishes—two on each side swimming toward the nozzle—and two ovoid objects with round centers, so drawn as to look like eyes. Galling said that the lamp was Christian, and he may be right, but his grounds for such a conclusion are by no means conclusive.[36] That the ovoids have here been identified with eyes would indicate that the ovoids had come to be rather uncertain in explanation. As eyes they are what are usually called "Horus eyes," but from the discussion of amulets we have come to understand them as the "sound eye" in contrast to the "much-suffering eye." [37] They were always used for

32. See above, I, 186.

33. See, for example, Porada, *Morgan*, figs. 636, 689, 707, 709, 711 f., 759, 768, 1002, 1055. See my fig. 16, and below, p. 15.

34. See Schloessinger, 90.

35. Ibid., 88. She follows Iliffe in *QDAP*, III (1934), 84; and Avi-Yonah in *QDAP*, X (1942), 144.

36. See I, 163. Kurt Galling, "Die Beleuchtungsgeräte im israelitisch-jüdischen Kulturgebiet," *ZDPV*, XLVI (1923), 18.

37. See II, 238–241. In I, 163, we noticed the resemblance of these eyes to representations of leaves and lozenges with centers, and felt even there the kinship of the form to the vulva of the ancient goddess.

their talismanic value, and it is to be presumed that the fish with them had such a value also.

The fifth lamp, fig. 8, was also published by Mrs. Schloessinger[38] as of unknown provenance. It would date, she thinks, from the fourth to the eighth century. It shows only four fishes, two on each side, but this time swimming one behind the other round the filling hole. She regards the four little bosses in front of the filling hole as an abbreviation of the cross and so as "conclusive evidence" that the lamp is Christian, but for this there is no warrant whatever.[39] In view of the absence of information about the provenance of the lamp, it would seem that the design, if Christian at all, is an adaptation of a design of fish which Jews used, and there is every possibility that this lamp, too, is Jewish. In fact it seems to me much more likely to be either pagan or Jewish than Christian.[40]

The sixth lamp, this one from Jerusalem, fig. 372 of Volume III,[41] shows that its decoration consisted primarily of fishes. Two whole fishes and the head of another are left on the fragment. They were drawn confronting each other, with some object, perhaps the trunk of a palm tree, between them. It is reasonable to assume that we have again the association of fish with the palm tree.

The seventh lamp has just been published by Mrs. Schloessinger from her collection, fig. 7.[42] Again it shows a pair of fish flanking a tree or a palm branch, presumably the latter. As she points out, these fishes are made with open mouths, and are in detail of manufacture so surprisingly like the fishes of the lamps of fig. 5 that she seems quite right in supposing that the molds for both were made by the same person. It is notable that the open-mouthed fishes this time approach the palm branch. They are probably still the fish eating something. In Christian art we shall see that such fish eat a wafer, presumably that of the Eucharist.[43] It would seem that the fish eating and the fish with the palm branch are interchangeable ways of saying the same thing.

This is confirmed by an eighth lamp, which is in the Whiting Collection of Pales-

38. Op. cit., 93, and plate 24A.

39. In op. cit., n. 43, she refers to M. Meurdrac, "Une Sépulture chrétienne à Sidon," *Berytus*, IV (1937), plate XXX (she mistakenly gives plate XIII), fig. 3. This is a design of the four bosses under a magical cross; but there are bosses in other places, so that the four by no means mark a specific way of making the Christian cross. The bosses in other designs on the same plate of Meurdrac show how such bosses were used in a variety of places, apparently to give the value of the circles with magical crosses we met so often as "characters." See above, II, index, s.v. "Characters." As a matter of fact Meurdrac herself has exaggerated the Christian character of the tomb. There were indisputably Christian lamps in it, but also others which seem to me purely pagan, and one with a menorah. See above, I, 148; III, fig. 1209.

40. Schloessinger, op. cit., publishes a lamp from Carthage as her lamp E. It has the outer border of palm branches common on lamps from Carthage, both Jewish and Christian, and a wreath like a series of rays round the filling hole. Beneath this wreath, by the spout, is a little fish. The illustration suggests that the fish was not part of the original mold but was scratched in before baking. It is so roughly drawn as to be quite indistinguishable in her excellent photograph. Her statement that the combination of fish and palm branch "leave no doubt as to the Christian significance of this lamp" has no foundation, but I do not include the lamp in this collection, if only because the fish is so hard to recognize.

41. See above, I, 163, n. 187.

42. From M. Schaar Schloessinger, *Israel Exploration Journal*, 1956.

43. See below, pp. 56 f.

tinian Pottery at Yale, fig. 4.[43a] It shows on either side of the filling hole a pair of open-mouthed fishes, again of the same design, that appear about to eat a central device consisting of a wreath with a dot in the center. It seems to me that this wreath and dot are a deliberate identification of the wreath with the "round object" or wafer, in which case it represents the spiritual triumph of the fish that eat the wafer. Another wreath with dot is above the filling hole.

The ninth lamp, from Jerash, is one of the most interesting I know. On its upper face, fig. 374 of Volume III, are a variety of magical "characters," including, on each side of the central opening, a solar cross with its circles. Avi-Yonah mistook them for Christian crosses and hence called the lamp Christian, but there is nothing distinctively Christian about the crosses or the lamp.[44] Beside each of these crosses is a peacock and a fish. On the base of the lamp [45] is a jar of the same Jewish type as that we saw on the stone from Acrae, with five fishes on its belly. This may possibly be a design to represent the fact that the wine of the Eucharist is identical with the five fishes of the Christian story of the Multiplication, in which case the lamp would be Christian.[46] But the line of argument of this whole volume will be that Christian usage of both wine and fish was an adaptation of earlier Jewish usages, so that the identification of fish and wine, which the design seems plainly to indicate, cannot be taken a priori to indicate that the lamp is Christian. The lamp with its various "characters" is clearly an object of talismanic power, and this design on the bottom, where it could not be seen, probably had considerable power in its own right. It is at least possible that the lamp is Jewish.

From the less certain evidence of the lamps we return to securely Jewish representations, where a fixed vocabulary of fish has seemed to emerge, with the tree (especially the palm tree), wine symbols, "round objects," baskets of bread or fruit, and ducks. We are not surprised, then, to see the same vocabulary in a fresh arrangement in the Catacomb Vigna Randanini in Rome. Round one of the ceiling designs,[47] itself another of the domes of heaven, is a band divided into eight sections, four of which contain a basket, probably filled with fruit or flowers but perhaps with loaves of bread. These four sections alternate with four others, all of which have at the center a vase or low column or, most likely, an altar. In two of these sections a pair of ducks confront each other on either side of this central altar. In the other two are fishes grouped around the central object, with one fish

43a. Courtesy of the Yale University Art Gallery. Each of the four fish on this lamp is oddly represented with two eyes, apparently so that the fish may be recognizable as such whichever side is turned toward the observer. The Whiting Collection was made at the American Colony's antiquities shop in the Old City, and was itself got together mostly from Arabs who gave no provenance for their offerings. I have no idea where this particular lamp was found except that it was in Palestine.

44. See I, 163. For magical crosses see III, figs. 999–1004, 1008. Such crosses with points go back indefinitely before Christianity. For their appearance in Greek art of the geometric period see A. Roes, *Greek Geometric Art, Its Symbols and Its Origin*, 1933, index, s.v. "cross, solar."

45. See III, fig. 376.

46. We return to this identification below, p. 53. Avi-Yonah's suggestion (see above, I, 163) that the design is a revival of the ancient Egyptian technique of representing fish in a transparent aquarium seems to me to go far afield indeed.

47. See III, figs. 748 f.

on top of it. Harnack could only exclaim about them, "Surely not pure decoration." [48]

That the fish were not pure decoration for Jews seems at once made certain by the little fish amulet found in a Jewish grave in Palestine.[49] A very similar fish amulet has just been found near Jerusalem in a grave with ossuaries.[50] Because of various marks Bagatti takes the cemetery, and with it the fish, to be Christian. He may be right, but there is no evidence that the signs he calls Christian had already become so in first-century Palestine. The total evidence for Jewish use of fish did not, it seems to me, enter into Bagatti's judgment. It has always been assumed that ossuary burial in Palestine was a distinctively Jewish practice, and nothing in these burials would make me alter that judgment. Accordingly, I take it that we have two fish amulets from Jewish graves of the period. Amulets, especially those buried with a corpse, must be regarded seriously as manifestations of the religious orientation of those who use them,[51] and, however vague our reconstructions of their exact reference may have to be, an amulet always implies an active and potent symbol. We shall see that the fish is still used in this way by Jews.[52]

It seems very probable, however, that the Jewish fishes at this time were not mere fetishes, used for a vague and unexplained protection, but were eaten as a special food. This, one finally concludes, is the implication of the designs on two Jewish gold glasses.[53] On both glasses is represented the typical rounded bolster famous especially from early Christian representations of the Eucharist but, as we shall see, originally pagan, with the table in front of it and the fish on a platter upon the table. Even Frey's reluctance to admit religious implications in Jewish pictures had to break down before these. He classed them with the fish on the stone from Acrae as a reference to the fish meal of the *cena pura*, which precedes the Sabbath.[54]

Two inscriptions survive, beside each of which stood two fishes, perhaps as Pisces, which have been thought Jewish but which Frey ruled out of that category. His reasons are curious. One of them [55] he pronounced pagan because, he said, the fish is so common on pagan inscriptions; he thought the other [56] was Christian "because of the two fishes, which, in isolation, have hardly any meaning except in Christianity." Actually there was never any reason for ascribing either of these to Judaism, so far as I can see, so that in spite of Frey's amusingly contradictory reasons for eliminating them, we shall not include them.[57]

48. *Zur Abercius-Inschrift*, 1895, 16 (TU, XII, ivb).

49. See above, III, fig. 380.

50. See B. Bagatti, "Scoperta di una cimitero giudeo-cristiano al 'Dominus Flevit'," *Studii Biblici Franciscani Liber Annuus*, III (1952/3), 168, fig. 23, 8; 169, 184.

51. See above, II, 208–295.

52. See below, p. 22.

53. See above, III, figs. 973 f.; cf. II, 112.

54. *RAC*, VIII (1931), 308 f. See below, p. 43.

55. *CIJ*, no. 58.*

56. *CIJ*, no. 83.*

57. The first is a grave inscription from Ravenna, set up, among others, by one Mariem (Mariam). Above the inscription is a disk with six spokes between the letters *MM* (*Moestae Memoriae*) along with two fish, headed in opposite directions. Scheftelowitz, "Fisch-Symbol," 27, and Hans Achelis, *Das Symbol des Fisches*, 1888, 62 f., both claimed the inscription for Judaism, as Frey pointed out ad loc., just because the name Mariem seemed definitely Semitic. The inscription itself would be equally proper in paganism, Judaism, or Christianity. The second inscription is on a glass vessel, of the *pie zēsais* variety. Heuser in F. Kraus, *Real-*

In summary, these representations of the fish show that Jews were by no means haphazard in using it as a symbol. The zodiacal sign Pisces appears, apart from its setting in a zodiac, at both Dura and Er-Rafid. The fish itself was used, apparently as a sacred or magical symbol, on Palestinian lamps and in the synagogue at Sheikh Ibreiq. It is presented with a red tongue at Beth Alpha and with a rope at Hammam Lif, and in these cases, as in Sicily, it is grouped with bread, wine symbols, palm trees, and ducks. It was painted with palm trees in a Roman catacomb. The fish is definitely an article of food twice on Roman gold glass, and its other appearances with bread and wine, especially at Vigna Randanini, suggest that the fish is a food there also. The fish caught with a rope would also seem to be fish for food. Fish, therefore, were presented by Judaism frequently and with established associations, though not at all in what could be described as an artistic convention. That these appearances of the fish are merely decorative seems from the crudity of their presentation the least warranted conclusion.

2. *Other Creatures of the Sea*

BEFORE GOING ON to discuss the tradition of the fish as a symbol we must note the Jewish representations of the dolphin, and the marine monsters—the goat (Capricorn) or the horse with a long fishy tail (hippocampus).

The dolphin very frequently appears on Jewish remains of the period. It was found, notably, on fifteen of the ceiling tiles at Dura. These are poorly preserved; I reproduce the best of the lot in fig. 2.[58] In one of the tombs at Sheikh Ibreiq were found three little inlays, presumably from a wooden coffin that has disintegrated. One inlay represents a boat, one a gadrooned vase, and one a dolphin.[59]

In the "mausoleum," another tomb at Sheikh Ibreiq, parts of a mosaic floor survive; one part shows four dolphins.[60] Here is a rectangle filled by a design of lozenges, with objects at the center of each lozenge. Within this is a second rectangle chiefly occupied by a circular unit with an outer band, but with the central part of the circle destroyed. A dolphin occupies each of the four corners of the rectangle left by the circle. This design of a central circle within a square, each of whose four corners is filled by a figure, is basically that of the solar circle with the Seasons, who may be represented by such figures of the Seasons as we have seen in synagogues of Palestine,[61] by putti,[62] or in some other way, so

Encyklopädie der christlichen Alterthümer, I, 517 (cf. 523) said that beside the inscription were two fishes, and this is the basis of discussions of the object by Scheftelowitz, Loeschcke, and Frey (q.v. at no. 83* for these references), in spite of the fact that all these refer to the much more careful description by O. M. Dalton, *Catalogue of Early Christian Antiquities in the British Museum*, 1901, no. 653, where Dalton says that these objects are leaves and does not mention the fish. There seems no record of the provenance of the object, so that whether with fish or without, there is no reason for calling it Jewish. Mention may also be made of two fish in a strange tomb in Palestine, where there is nothing to indicate the religion of the persons entombed; see John P. Peters in *Art and Archeology*, VII (1918), 192. Projections from the mouths are here represented which recall the ropes we discussed above. See also the tomb with a fish painted on the wall at Gezer: above, I, 163, n. 187.

58. Courtesy of the Yale University Art Gallery.

59. See III, fig. 981.

60. See III, figs. 84 f.; cf. I, 101.

61. See III, figs. 640, 644, 647, 658.

62. It has been suggested that the putti in the ceiling design of Vigna Randanini, III, figs. 748 f., are Seasons.

that it is possible the dolphins have here the value of Seasons. With the inner part of the circle gone, however, nothing definite can be decided about the design.[63]

The most striking appearance of dolphins is on one of the ceilings of the Catacomb Torlonia at Rome.[64] Here is the same basic design as in the mosaic at Sheikh Ibreiq, in this case easily recognized as what Lehmann has taught us to call the Dome of Heaven,[65] a design which seems to me symbolically a variant of the zodiacal circle. At Torlonia the design becomes elaborately Jewish, since a menorah is in its center, where pagans, Jews, and Christians usually put Helios or some other saving symbol. In small circles at the four corners are Jewish objects, one of them a shofar and the other three what on the whole I judge to be lulabs.[66] In this design, at once soteriological in form and Jewish in designation, there are four other prominent spaces, in each of which is a dolphin carrying a trident in its mouth; its long tail curls about the trident and ends in a trefoil. It is rather hard to accept Frey's categorical assertion that here the dolphins alone have no religious or symbolic value for the Jews who used this catacomb.[67] I doubt also that the similar use of dolphins here and at Sheikh Ibreiq is mere coincidence. The dolphin with the trident would seem to have had the powers of Poseidon.

Two dolphins carry a garland between them on a ceiling in the Catacomb Vigna Randanini,[68] a sign that they are bringing immortality. Dolphins perform the same function at both ends of a Dionysiac sarcophagus in Baltimore, fig. 10.[69] Three dolphins swim along the edge of a sarcophagus cover, which is also from the Catacomb Vigna Randanini.[70] The dolphin is at the center of the strigilations on a sarcophagus from the Catacomb Torlonia.[71] One was reported as having been carved on the synagogue at Ed-Dikkeh.[72] Most impressive of all is its appearance with a fish of the same size, presumably a tunny, in the synagogue at Hammam Lif, as already noted.[73] Like the fish it has apparently been caught and is being pulled in by a heavy rope from its mouth. Gressmann[74] took the dolphins of the Roman catacombs to be simply a variant of the fish of the cena pura, but Beyer and Lietzmann,[75] feeling that dolphins could have no reference to a fish meal because they are not eaten, take refuge in the "purely ornamental," as does Frey.[76] It is difficult to agree altogether with any of these scholars. True, the dolphin was not eaten in Greece and could hardly have been used there to suggest the cena pura. But we were told

63. I strongly suspect that the circle contained a head or figure of Helios which later iconoclasts removed.

64. See above, III, fig. 806; cf. II, 36.

65. "The Dome of Heaven," *The Art Bulletin*, XXVII (1945), 1–27.

66. See above, IV, 146 f.

67. Frey, "Il Delfino col tridente," *RAC*, VIII (1931), 306, 314; cf. *CIJ*, I, p. CXXVIII. Frey goes so far in denying symbolic value to such figures that in the *RAC* article, 309, he asserts that the anchor on Palestinian coins of Alexander Jannaeus attests the maritime power of the Jews in Palestine! Before Frey, Beyer and Lietzmann, *Torlonia*, 19, had denied the dolphins any symbolic value.

68. See above, III, figs. 742, 749.

69. Courtesy of the Walters Art Gallery, Baltimore, where it is no. 23.36. It is the left side of a third-century Roman sarcophagus. See Lehmann, *Baltimore*, fig. 29; cf. fig. 28 and p. 20.

70. See above, III, fig. 800; cf. II, 29.

71. See III, fig. 832; cf. II, 42.

72. See I, 206.

73. See III, figs. 887 f., 897. See above, p. 4.

74. Gressmann, "Jewish Life," 187.

75. *Torlonia*, 19.

76. See above, IV, 6–8.

that the dolphin is now eaten in North Africa, and the dolphin caught by a rope suggests food.

Jewish representations of the sea horse and of Capricorn, the goat fish, are less common than those of the fish and dolphin. Capricorn is represented on seventeen ceiling tiles at Dura, of which I show a single example, fig. 3.[77] On a frieze in the synagogue at Capernaum appears a sea monster beside which a pair of eagles hold between them a garland or open wreath.[78] Kohl and Watzinger [79] thought the monster a sea horse but said that the head has a horn and an ear which hangs down and that beneath its chin is a tuft of hair like a goat, so that we may safely assume it is the goat fish which is represented. On a ceiling of the Catacomb Vigna Randanini [80] a sea horse is painted between two dolphins. We shall see that in Roman times sea monsters were apparently interchangeable, so that this may have been designed to represent Capricorn with Pisces.

We ask only one question more at this point. Were the sea monsters which appear on the base of the menorah of the Arch of Titus [81] the work of Roman artists who wanted to decorate the treasure in their own way, or were such creatures so early taken into Judaism that they were actually put upon the Temple menorah by Jews themselves? The question cannot be answered categorically either way, but though we cannot count them among Jewish symbols, the possibility of their Jewish origin seems to me not at all excluded. In any case the sea goat at Capernaum and the sea horse in the Vigna Randanini, to say nothing of the seventeen Capricorns on the ceiling tiles of the Dura synagogue, cannot be ignored in our search for the symbolic meaning of the Jewish fish. If symbolic values did lie behind them, however, what were those values, and what explanations did the Jews give them?

B. PAGAN REPRESENTATIONS

In accordance with our general methodology, Jewish usage of fish and other sea creatures must be compared with pagan usage of the same symbols before we can evaluate the significance of the Jewish instances. Because we must not prejudge that Jewish usage kept pagan values, an examination of the pagan material is essential before any opinion on the matter is formed.

1. The Fish

The material on no one of the symbols we are studying has been so well collected as that on the fish. There is the imposing work of Dölger, as well as less pretentious studies.[82] The most convenient brief review of the pagan remains was made by Cumont.[83]

77. Courtesy of the Yale University Art Gallery; cf. Rostovtzeff, *Dura-Europos*, VI, plate XLVI, 6.

78. See III, fig. 475; cf. I, 188.

79. KW, 33.

80. See III, figs. 742, 749; cf. II, 19.

81. See IV, fig. 1 and p. 72.

82. See especially C. R. Morey, "The Origin of the Fish Symbol," *Princeton Theological Review*, VIII (1910), 93–106, 231–246, 401–432; IX (1911), 268–289; Leclercq in CL, VII, 1990–2086.

83. In PW, IX, 844–850.

Without attempting to reproduce all the material in these collections, I must call attention to the most important aspects of pagan usage for our purpose.

a. Egypt. Egyptian paintings often show fish in one way or another, especially in the water, where they are usually understood as indicating that what is shown is water. Sometimes they are being caught by fishermen. The fish was not one of the more important symbols of Egyptian religion. We do know, however, that there were a number of fish taboos among the Egyptians and that their priests were not allowed to eat fish at all, though fish eating was required of the laity on certain days of the month.[84] Fishes were often preserved as mummies, and one became the symbol of immortality because it led the pious to the realm of the blessed.[85] Fig. 9 [86] shows a mummy in the form of a fish being accompanied to the other world by Anubis; it is in a private Theban tomb of perhaps 1,000 B.C. A fish ate the phallus of Osiris in many forms of the legend, and probably this story arose because the popular mind associated the fish with the phallus, especially with the phallus of Osiris. Since the phallus, as we shall see, was important as a symbol of immortality among the Egyptians,[87] it is interesting to note fig. 11,[88] where a mummy of the hellenistic period lies on the lion bed on his way to the next world, gazing at an Oxyrhynchos fish above him instead of at the usual soul bird. I should guess that in both representations the fish is Osiris, presented thus because of his most life-giving member, his phallus, and that in the earlier of these two the dead man is as usual identified with Osiris as the fish, while in the second he is the Osiris mummy in the more common form, but looking especially to the virtue of the fish for his hope of immortality.

b. Mesopotamia. The place of the fish in the religious traditions of Mesopotamia has recently been studied by Mrs. Van Buren,[89] who has presented an interesting analysis with an abundance of material. For the earliest prehistoric periods Beatrice Goff is collecting material and has kindly let me see much of it. The fish appears on remains of the earliest clearly defined village culture, the so-called Hassunah period, in the fifth millennium. There it is represented with geometric designs, and water birds are devouring the fish, fig. 15.[90] They do so on another plate in a setting of zigzags (water) and lozenges, fig. 12.[91] From the Ubaid period, somewhat later, traces of offerings have been found in a temple in

84. It may be in connection with this that the Egyptians used the "fish plates"—that is, plates with fishes painted on them; see W. Kronig, "Aegyptische Fayence-Schalen des Neuen Reiches," *Mitteilungen des Deutschen Instituts für Aegyptische Altertumskunde in Kairo*, V (1934), esp. 155–164.

85. For references see PW, loc. cit.

86. From Giulio Farina, *La Pittura egiziana*, 1929, plate CLXXIV.

87. See below, pp. 166–176.

88. From Ahmed bey Kamal in *ASAE*, IX (1908), plate I. See his remarks on pp. 23 f., and those of W. Spiegelberg in *ARW*, XII (1909), 574 f. Cf. also A. Wiedemann, "Der Fisch Ant und seine Bedeutung," *Sphinx*, Leipzig, XIV (1899), 231–244; E. Mahler, "Das Fischsymbol auf ägyptischen Denkmälern," *ZDMG*, LXVII (1913), 37–48.

89. E. Douglas Van Buren, "Fish-Offerings in Ancient Mesopotamia," *Iraq*, X (1948), 101–121, with plates XV–XVIII.

90. From Ernst Herzfeld, *Die vorgeschichtlichen Töpfereien von Samarra*, Berlin, 1930, plate VI, no. 6 (Die Ausgrabungen von Samarra, V).

91. From ibid., fig. 7, no. 7, p. 14. Cf. plate XXXIX, 7.

which are fish bones and bones of birds. From the Jamdat Nasr period the fish commonly appears being devoured by birds; it is also on amulets. Mrs. Van Buren's material suggests that throughout the later periods of Mesopotamian civilization fish were offered to and identified with several gods and goddesses. Here they have had a "chthonic [i.e. eschatological] association; it is possible, however, that in quite early times they betokened 'life,' and that the later conception of re-birth caused them to be used in funerary rites." [92]

Fish are frequently represented as offerings or as the food for ritualistic banquets. An example, probably from an early dynastic period, is the seal in fig. 14.[93] It shows what is commonly called a "banqueting scene": a seated figure at each end is being offered food by an attendant. The attendants are naked, and perhaps the seated figures also. Before each of the latter is a fish, and in the center between these two groups is a tier of what appear to be sacred objects. Beginning from the bottom they are: a drinking cup with something emerging or protruding from it, two circles of bread, a fish, and a libation vase flanked by two ovals. We have here then a double association with the fish, that of fertility and of an object to be eaten, probably in funerary association. Parallel to this seal is a later hymn which records that a table was laid for Ishtar of Uruk, on which were butter, milk, dates, cheese, and seven fishes.[94] Because the "magical" number seven is specified, Mrs. Van Buren sees evidence of the "mystic character of the rite." Fish were an appropriate offering for Adad, she points out, to insure growth of crops. They also figured in wedding scenes.

Mrs. Van Buren seems to me successfully to have isolated the unchanging value of the fish as a symbol from the dubious and varied identifications and explanations given it from one period to another: she sees the fish for millennia in Mesopotamia as at once a fertility symbol and a funerary symbol, and in both a life symbol. Miss Goff is convinced that with this went a sense of conflict when the fish was eaten by the birds from earliest times, and indeed fig. 16 [95] may represent a divine intervention in this struggle. This is a later seal which Miss Porada describes:

> Hero grasping two ostriches. Fish and rhomb in field. Terminal: winged sun disk, star, stylus beside tasseled spade, one above other.[96]

The winged "hero" seems to be a divine figure who, under the power of the divine signs, strangles the birds and so keeps them from attacking the fish and rhomb or lozenge beneath them. Whether or not such is the meaning of this particular seal, the fish and rhomb, as we have already mentioned,[97] appear too frequently together on this material to go without comment. If the rhomb, which is shown also in fig. 14, was often the vulva of the goddess,

92. Van Buren, 102.

93. From L. Legrain, *Ur Excavations*, 1936, III, no. 381. It was found in stratum 4, which Ann Perkins, *Comparative Archaeology of Ancient Mesopotamia*, 1949, 142, says contains material as late as the second dynasty. With reasonable probability we can say that the seal dates from before the middle of the third millennium. The seal was republished by Van Buren, fig. 5.

94. N. Schneider, *Götternamen von Ur*, III, 1939, 36a, Sec. 21 of *Innina* (Analecta Orientalia, XIX); Van Buren, 112.

95. From Porada, *Morgan*, fig. 759.

96. Ibid., Text, 92.

97. See above, p. 7.

as even the most reluctant admit, it is a short step to suggest that fertility symbols and phallic symbols were often identical and that from the beginning the fish may have had phallic significance. When the bird eats the fish, all sorts of symbolic possibilities suggest themselves, including the Freudian castration complex and the aggressive instinct. But I should guess that while the fish may have had literal phallic reference, this reference was not especially to the phallus of the individual or to human sexuality but was to the more universal source of life, and that the conflict was one with the forces which destroy life. This conception of the destruction of life as itself a hope of life is a paradox which was mentioned in the discussion of method [98] and which we shall see constantly recurring with other symbols, to the point that it is the dead Savior on the cross which is the most hopeful symbol of life in our civilization. And our hope of life is symbolized as we, like the ancient birds and the people at the banquets, eat the life symbol in the torn flesh of the murdered savior.

Mrs. Van Buren sees the whole range of symbolism in the late stamp-seal shown in fig. 17,[99] which was found at Nippur and is dated at the period of Artaxerxes or Darius I. It has been recognized that the figures at the top represent the sun, the moon, and perhaps a star. Their presence seemed to Mrs. Van Buren to mark as definitely symbolic the fish flanked by birds, the three rising from water which she associates with the "waters of the Under World from which all life germinated." [100] In this she still sees what she calls chthonic symbolism, what we are calling funerary or eschatological symbolism—that is, indicating hope of life after return to the ground in burial.[101]

In discussing the deity with the flowing bowl we shall note that little fishes often swim up the streams, a phenomenon which suggests the confusion we shall especially encounter in Christian symbolism between the great Fish as the Savior and the little fishes as his followers who have taken on his likeness and nature. That this mystical idea of the fish goes back to Mesopotamia we have no literary evidence to substantiate, but the two references of the fish are clearly implied by the representations, and there is no reason to suppose that mystical identification cannot be thought of as very old. At least, Mesopotamian remains reveal a pisciform god—the Fish who was the god and who was ritualistically eaten.

c. Syria. In Syria, although Dagon is no longer considered by scholars a fish god,[102] the fish was highly important. Fishes had saved Atargatis, according to one myth, and so were transported to heaven. Cumont concludes that it was with reference to this myth that fish became popular emblems of protection, though it seems more likely to me that the myth was itself the product rather than the cause of the talismanic value of the fish.

98. See IV, 60.

99. From Van Buren, plate XVIII, 24; cf. Léon Legrain, *The Culture of the Babylonians*, 1925, plates XXXV, and LIII, fig. 802 (The University of Pennsylvania, The University Museum, Publications of the Babylonian Section, XIV). Alongside this design is a name Shamash-ah-iddin, son of Sin-ittanu: ibid., p. 330.

100. Ibid., 121.

101. See ibid., n. 3, where she makes a comparison with a slightly earlier Cypriote vase painting.

102. F. J. Montalbano, "Canaanite Dagon: Origin, Nature," *Catholic Biblical Quarterly*, XIII (1951), 381–397, states the case, with references to earlier studies.

The sacred fishes of later Syria and Phoenicia, to which reference is often made in classical writers,[103] seem to have been regarded by them as eastern phenomena and to have been survivals of the earlier Atargatis traditions. Lucian [104] describes the figure of a goddess whose lower part is that of a fish and in whose honor, significantly, both fish and doves are taboo as food. A legend had it that the Syrian goddess sprang from a large egg brought up from the Euphrates by a fish and hatched by a dove; as a result, the fish was not eaten as food and the dove was thought to possess the power of the gods.[105]

Priests offered fish daily on the altar to Atargatis. "It is hard to avoid concluding," says Cumont, "that in the Syrian mysteries this divine food was eaten, and that the faithful believed they united themselves by this communion with their goddess." [106] But if this is true for ritualistic eating, it was also thought that if a man ate fish as ordinary food the goddess afflicted him with swellings, ulcers, and decay of the loins. Strict penance with confession had to be done at once.[107]

Dölger is plausible in his suggestion that the amulets worn by the soldiers in the army of Judas Maccabaeus, amulets which caused their death according to the pious story, were actually fishes, and he sees the fish amulet from Gezer [108] as an instance of such influence of Atargatis on Jews.[109]

Xenophon tells of the river Chalus, near Aleppo, whose *tame* fish natives thought to be gods. Similar holy fish were recognized throughout Asia Minor. The taboo against catching fish persists to the present in many parts of Asia Minor, and eating them seems to the natives even more shocking. The importance of fish symbolism for Phoenicians appears from its having been carried to North Africa by the Punic settlers, where, we shall see, fish mosaics and fish on tombstones were very popular.

d. Greece. In contrast, the fish was everywhere eaten in Greece, but it had little religious significance there in classical times. Apart from the dolphin, to which we come shortly,[110]

103. Lucian, *Dea Syria*, 45; in his note to this passage A. M. Harmon (in the Loeb ed., IV) has a large collection of classical references to sacred fish in pools, and to the Syrian fish taboo.

104. *Dea Syria*, 14.

105. This is based upon a statement of Nigidius Figulus, who died 45 B.C. It is quoted with parallels and discussed by Dölger, *Ichthys*, II, 195 f. On p. 201 he quotes Plutarch, *Quaestiones convivales*, VIII, viii, 4, who says that the ancient Greeks sacrificed to Poseidon as the "racial father" since "they, like Syrians, supposed that man was born from the 'damp substance'." Plutarch goes on to quote Anaximander to the effect that "the fish is the common mother and father of man." The Syrians are more sensible, says Plutarch, since they worship the fish directly, and hence refuse to eat it. Apparently, however, this taboo applied only to ordinary eating, not to ritualistic eating.

106. On fish at these Syrian festivals, along with wine, see Cumont in *CR, AIB*, 1917, 281–284; cf. *Ichthys*, II, 263–297. A table for offerings is in the museum at Istanbul, no. 7754, from Arapsun, of the fifth century B.C. A plate of fruit and a dove are carved on the top, and on the front is a row with a sheep and a goat, and a fish whose tail is lost behind a wreath. Ritualistic offering or eating seems indicated.

107. R. Pettazzoni, "La Confession des péchés en Syrie aux époques préchrétiennes," *Mélanges syriens offerts à M. R. Dussaud*, 1939, I, 197–202 (Bibliothèque archéologique et historique, XXX).

108. See above, III, fig. 380; cf. I, 166.

109. *Ichthys*, II, 205.

110. See below, pp. 22–27.

this seems to me quite true in spite of sporadic references in Greek literature.[111] The ancient Pythagoreans, for example, had a taboo against eating fish, but it is clear from Plutarch [112] that the Greeks of his day made so many guesses at what might have provoked such a taboo that actually they had no idea what did so.[113] Aelian [114] records that in a certain remote village in Lycia a divination or augury by fishes was practised, a custom, we gather, which was indeed a singular curiosity to the ancients.[115] An Attic vase in the Kunsthistorische Museum at Vienna suggests that fish may have been among the beasts torn and eaten by Dionysiac orgiasts, since the maenad at the left has a fish in each hand and the maenad on the right what looks like a piece of fish in her right hand. But in spite of the material gathered by Eisler [117] on the subject, I do not think there is much evidence for Dionysiac fish eating as an important practice.

Fish eating at Greek wedding feasts may have been important, and, we shall see, it came to be so among Jews, where the fertility symbolism of the fish would in that case probably have been recognized. But Eisler's evidence for it is inadequate.[118] On the contrary, the seventh book of Athenaeus' *Deipnosophists* is given over to an elaborate discussion of the values of various fishes, in alphabetical order, though while a number of them are called "sacred" to this or that deity, the discussion is concerned almost entirely with the edibility of the various kinds, with ample evidence of taboos but no trace of symbolic importance of the fish as such.[119]

A unique Boeotian amphora of the geometric period, however, suggests that in the more primitive days of the "Nurse of Animals" such fish symbolism as we have seen in the East was active also in Greece. On this vase, fig. 18,[120] the goddess has above each shoulder a

111. For a review of the references to fish as food in ancient literature see *Ichthys*, V, 329–358.

112. *Quaestiones convivales*, VIII, viii.

113. Eisler explains this taboo on the ground that the fish was a phallic symbol: "Fisch," esp. p. 168. His study explains all fish symbolism in these terms. We shall see much of that meaning in the fish, but much more besides. His study, therefore, while valuable and rich in the material collected, seems to me by no means to exhaust the subject.

114. *De natura animalium*, VIII, 5.

115. Fish seem to have been used in magic by the ancients, but only rarely: *Ichthys*, V, 181–188.

116. See Eisler, "Fisch," fig. 13, at p. 176; cf. p. 183. It was originally published in A. de Laborde, *Collection de vases grecs de M. le comte de Lamberg*, 1814, Supplément II, plate 3.

117. "Fisch" and *Orpheus*.

118. Athenaeus frequently quotes lists of fishes from the lost play *The Marriage of Hebe* of Epicharmus, but that these lists specified the fish at the wedding banquet, or that, if they did, they had symbolic importance as Eisler concludes, there is nothing to indicate. See Eisler, "Fisch," 176; *Orpheus*, 258.

119. Athenaeus, *The Deipnosophists*, VII, 50, sacrifice of the first tunny of the season to Poseidon; 114, the scari, a sacred fish; 126, fish sacred to Hecate, Apollo, Hermes, Dionysus, Aphrodite, and Artemis, with some reference to fish used in the rites of these gods; VIII, 11 f., fish superstitions. But all of this seems quite incidental in the extended pages on fish as food.

120. From Paul Wolters in *EA*, III (1892), plate X, 1; cf. p. 221. Fig. 1*a* on the same plate shows the vase as a whole from the other side, with scrolls, small birds, a large bird in flight, and a hare, with two more swastikas. The row of little water birds above the goddess continues round the vase. See also Wolfgang Schultz in *Memnon*, III (1909), 197, and fig. 22. Dölger, *Ichthys*, II, 179–181, denies any phallic significance, though he admits the fish is not an ornament on the dress. He sees the goddess represented as powerful in the air (birds), on land (bull), and in the water. That is, he denies any special symbolic value to the fish as such. Eisler, "Fisch," 172, agrees with Schultz. Stebbins, 55 f., calls the figure the "Persian Artemis" and does not take the fish to be a dolphin.

bird (apparently a peacock) and a swastika. Below her outstretched arms are the foreleg of a bull at the right and the head of a bull at the left—each, again, with a swastika. On the ground at either side of her are a pair of confronted and harnessed lions, with swastikas. The goddess herself, as Schultz recognized, although conforming to the general type of the "Nurse of Animals" is shown by her wavy hair and the zigzag lines which go down from her waist to be a goddess of water in some sense. With this is the large fish which Schultz rightly saw was drawn as though in cross section approaching the lower part of her body. Its phallic reference seems obvious. But the fish with the Cypriote goddess is not unique on this piece. Another Cypriote vase has on one side a goat, a water bird, a lyre, a wine pitcher, and a peculiar design which was taken to be a bier. On the other side of this vase, fig. 19,[121] are, above, a goat, a lozenge, and a water bird, and, below, two panels (the design on the third panel is destroyed), in one of which is a water bird with a fish and in the other the goddess, with a string of three fish in her left hand and the thigh of an animal in her right. This association of the goddess with the fish has clearly come to Cyprus from Syria.

While no other such fish goddess appears in the art of the Greek islands of that period, enough evidence is avilable to make it likely that the fish had indeed come over from the East to be an important symbol in that civilization. Discussion of the name by which this goddess was called, whether it was Atargatis, the Syrian Artemis, the Persian Anahita, or some other,[122] seems to me only to obscure the importance of the fish as a symbol in its own right. The Cypriote seals, which are clearly derived from Syrian and hence Mesopotamian prototypes, use the fish in the same way it had been used in the East; see for example the green serpentine seal shown in fig. 13.[123]

Probably earlier than any of these is the remarkable silver bowl found in a grave at Golgoi in Cyprus, fig. 20.[124] The design on the bowl seems intended to express the hope of immortality in Egyptian and Cypriote terms. Against a background of lotus flowers and trees, four funerary boats with various people and objects aboard are drawn in a circle. Two of the boats are pulled by horses, one by bulls or cows, and one by ducks. This design makes an outer band which is finished on the inside by wavy circles to indicate water. Inside the water is a large central rosette of twenty-eight points separated by lotus flowers, and at the heart of this rosette is a smaller one with a round center. The large rosette seems to me to indicate, like the later "Domes of Heaven," the heavenly solar paradise to which the dead hope to come. Hence it is interesting that on this rosette are etched the bull (cow) and horse, both of them means of salvation, the one in Egyptian and the other in more Cypriote terminology. With these are a human male and female, probably the dead man and wife in the tomb, their hands upraised as they hail the new life, a pose which we shall

121. From Maggie Rutten, "Deux vases chypriotes du Musée du Louvre," *Mélanges syriens offerts à M. R. Dussaud*, I, plate I, facing p. 436 (Bibliothèque archéologique et historique, XXX); see figs. 13 and 14 for Syrian parallels.

122. Dölger, *Ichthys*, II, 181–184.

123. From Louis P. di Cesnola, *Cyprus*, 1878, plate XXXI, 8; cf. fig. 11 and plate XXXIII, 24, 28. John L. Myres, *Handbook of the Cesnola Collection of Antiquities from Cyprus*, 1914, 439, no. 4329 (see the photograph on p. 435) calls this Cypro-Mycenean art of a rapidly degenerating style.

124. From Cesnola, plate XI at p. 114; cf. p. 117. See Myres, 457 f., for comment on the date of such bowls of Egyptian inspiration.

see again.[125] In every possible interstice with these are a number of fishes, presumably in this setting another symbol of immortal hope.

A little clay tripod of the early iron age, what Myres calls the Cypro-Mycenean tradition, shows among other things an ithyphallic man with a fish on either side of him, fig. 22.[126] On a slightly later vase a bird eats a fish in whose mouth is a swastika, fig. 23.[127] Myres describes a design on a roughly contemporary vase where there is only a fish, with a swastika again in front of its mouth. These early fish, which are marked as sacred by the fact of their devouring the swastika, at once suggest the connection of the fish associated with, or devouring, "round objects," eyes, lozenges, or little "loaves," which we have seen in Mesopotamia and Judaism and which we shall see again in Christianity.[128] We seem again to have suggestions of a continuity of symbolic value. There is also a vase from Rhodes, fig. 21,[129] again of the mixed geometric and figured period, where the chief decoration is a pair of fishes (only one appears in the photograph) with swastikas.

e. The Roman Empire. Such symbolic use of the fish seems absent from the representations of classical Greece,[130] but the same symbolism suddenly reappears in hellenistic and Roman paganism. Again Dölger has collected the material.[131] For the hellenistic period the evidence is not conclusive, but he seems right in supposing that an offering of fish for the dead came over into western practice from the East. He has shown clearly, however, that many tombstones and lamps with fish from Roman times which had been judged Christian were actually of pagan origin.[132] Such fish symbolism was most frequently used by Punic and Neo-Punic people of North Africa, along with other devices of magical power.[133] On several of these the fishes are represented on plates, so that a fish meal for the dead seems

125. See below, p. 167.

126. From Cesnola, plate XLIV, 33(*b*). Cf. Myres, 67, no. 513.

127. From Cesnola, plate XLVI, 38; cf. Myres, 96, no. 757; 97, no. 760.

128. Indeed in one of the tombs of Cyprus was found, along with two typical eastern fertility goddesses, a peculiar object in thin gold shaped exactly like the rhombs we have seen from Mesopotamia. The lips are pressed lengthwise in the center as in those rhombs. The gold is pierced at each end, and those who found it call it a "mouth piece." See *The Swedish Cyprus Expedition: Finds and Results of the Excavations in Cyprus*, 1927–1931, I, 1934, plate XCLVII, 2–4; Text, I, 564, no. 77. In accord with the oriental significance of the rhombs, it looks to me much more like the vulva of the goddess, especially when found with the fertility goddess herself. One recalls, on the other side, the gold "eye bandages" of Mochlos: see on the whole subject Arthur Evans, *The Shaft Graves and Bee-Hive Tombs of Mycenae*, 1929, 4–14.

129. From C. W. Lunsingh Scheurleer, *Grieksche Ceramiek*, Rotterdam, 1936, plate V, 16; see p. 31.

130. *Ichthys*, III, plate XXXI, shows two examples of black-figure vases, the vines of which have a Dionysiac orientation. In one, Poseidon rides a bull while carrying the vine, the trident, and a fish; in the other two men crowned in ivy kill a large tunny fish while dogs watch. In the first the fish seem only to identify Poseidon, and one can come to no conclusions of fish symbolism from the second.

131. *Ichthys*, II, 377–387. See also the hellenistic sarcophagus from Lycia, in the museum at Istanbul, on one end of which are a lion's head, a mask, two fishes, and two dolphins: in G. Mendel, *Catalogue des sculptures grecques, romaines et byzantines*, Constantinople, 1912, I, 284–287.

132. *Ichthys*, II, 387–410.

133. See ibid., III, plates XXIV, XXVI, XXVII, XXXVII; R. M. du Coudray la Blanchère and P. Gauckler, *Catalogue du Musée Alaoui*, 1897, figs, 695, 748, 777 (Description de l'Afrique du Nord).

indisputable. See figs. 25 [134] and 24,[135] two "offering tables," where the fish are shown with little loaves of bread. The funerary, hence presumably eschatological, fish was, accordingly, something ready in paganism, both eastern and western, for Jews and Christians to take over.

The most important single type of such monuments is that which gives prototypes for the Jewish and Christian symbolism of the fish banquet. These are represented as a three-legged table with a bolster curved behind it for the banqueters. On the table is a platter holding a fish. The same convention, with or without the banqueters, was especially typical among the symbols on plates of lead or stone supposedly dedicated to the "Thracian Rider," a deity who seems to have migrated into the Balkans from the East. This figure with its table and fish has been often published and discussed: [136] I show only two examples, one, fig. 26,[137] where the fish is simply on the little three-legged table at the bottom, along with other sacred animals; the other, fig. 27,[138] where it is actually the center of a banquet. Dölger was most reluctant to see symbolism in pagan representations, yet he said of the fish meal on such plates: "Here the fish is over and over again all too clearly represented as the holy food of a mystery cult." [139]

Closely connected with this is the same table with fish elaborately presented in the Sabazius paintings at Rome, which we have already discussed.[140] The oriental origin of the rites of these pictures is shown by the Phrygian cap worn in the plaques of the Thracian Rider as well as in the Sabazius paintings. This connection continued in the famous scene of the banquet of Dido, fig. 28,[141] which appears in a manuscript of Virgil, perhaps "from upper Italy of late antiquity." [142] With the fish are three little loaves of bread, while attendants bring the wine. I see no trace of Christian influence in the painting.[143]

f. Modern Survivals. The fish has continued to the present as a talismanic device, often used as an amulet in North Africa and Syria. Dölger shows several, usually with the "hand of Fatima," as the hand of God is called by Moslems. I saw the fish in a most interesting place in the desert behind the Theban Tombs in Egypt. Not far from the Tomb of the Nobles there is on top of a hill a little building, unroofed, which our guide told me is a fertility shrine for Mohammedan women, fig. 30.[144] I went in and found just the four walls, with two niches in them. Smoke blackening showed that the niches are used for lights, fig. 31. Perhaps the place is used only at night; perhaps the lights have some significance in the rituals carried out there. On the walls are scratched various designs,

134. From *Ichthys*, III, plate xxv, fig. 1. The original, he says, is at the Musée Alaoui (Bardo) in Tunis.

135. From ibid., fig. 2. Dölger says that the original is at the Collection of the Minervan Temple at Thébessa, Algeria.

136. *Ichthys*, I, 143–150; II, 420–447. Dölger has an excellent bibliographical discussion in II, 421 f.

137. From ibid., III, plate xxxiii.

138. From ibid., plate xxxii, 2.

139. Ibid., I, 147.

140. See above, II, 45–50; cf. III, figs. 839–843.

141. From *AA, JDAI*, XLIX (1934), 294, fig. 6. It is in cod. vat. lat. 3867, Vergil fol. 100, v. Dölger, *Ichthys*, III, plate lii, calls it "fifth century."

142. *AA, JDAI*, XLIX (1934), 295.

143. The haloes seem to me the pre-Christian royal haloes. See above, II, 227 f.

144. Figs. 30, 31, and 32 are from photographs I took at the shrine.

obviously of talismanic importance for fertility. A plant growing from a pot is to be seen between the two niches, and in fig. 32 two fishes (the one at the left barely visible) flank another plant in a pot.

In Tunisia and Algeria the fish are, it is true, widely used as amulets by Moslems. But in sections where there is a Jewish quarter the fish is preempted as a Jewish symbol. On the island of Djerba off the coast of southern Tunisia lives a very famous and very old Jewish community. Here the fish is almost omnipresent. A house with a fish over the door is thereby marked as being the residence of Jews. I photographed one such, fig. 33, where there is a central device which looks like a vase with three stalks growing from it but which may be a conventionalized hand.[145] Above this is a fish, and beside it, on either side, a dolphin. The Jewesses of Djerba have a distinctive headdress, a brimless hat which gives the effect of a turban, usually dark red; gold disks, as many as can be afforded, are attached to it; larger disks are on the dome of the hat, smaller ones form a fringe at the bottom. I was fortunate enough to be allowed to photograph one of these hats, fig. 34, and it can be seen that the design on the larger disks is that of fish, with a "round object" made up of a central boss and eight surrounding bosses, all within a circle. I strongly suspect that the fish is so much a favorite on the houses and as a device to be worn by women because it is not only generally protective but is by Jews, as by Moslems in Egypt, associated with fertility.[146]

In these connections we may ask: Was the fish carried over as a talismanic symbol from Punic and late Egyptian usage to the Moslems, whence it went to Judaism, or is the Jewish fish of modern times a direct descendant of the Jewish fish of antiquity which, along with much else perhaps, was taken over by Moslems from Judaism? I know of no investigation of the symbolic and ritualistic heritage from Judaism to Islam, and without a rather complete study, conclusions about any one symbol must be tentative. But we have seen reason to suppose that the use of water on Moslem graves might have been part of a Jewish heritage,[147] and a similar history of the fish is also possible. Certainly the Jewish fish lore antedates Mahomet. In any case, it is clear that the fish survives to the present as an active talismanic symbol among both Moslems and Jews.

2. *The Dolphin in Paganism*

IN PAGANISM dolphins were almost omnipresent on tombs and funerary inscriptions, where they survive, as Leclercq says, by the thousands, either alone or with the trident or anchor.[148] They are in many other places, such as decorative walls in Pompeii, or baths, where they have been supposed to be comparable to marine scenes in modern bathrooms. But it may safely be assumed that the burden of proof, not merely of assertion, rests upon anyone who would claim that a symbol thus universal in funerary ornament was, at least in that setting, "merely decorative." [149] It was obviously conventional, and many of

145. Cf. the drawings in *Ichthys*, III, plate XXIX. We should recall that early Christians used the fish monogram as a protection over the doors of their houses: *Ichthys*, I, 243–257.

146. See below, pp. 49 f.

147. See above, I, 109 f.

148. See CL, IV, 284.

149. Frey dismisses the problem in pagan art with a wave of his hand: *RAC*, VIII (1931), 304 f.

the professional artists who used dolphins may have put them in one place rather than another largely as they fitted into their designs. But the dolphin itself must have meant something or it would not have persisted in the crudest gravestone scratchings and in graffiti—where "convention" and "decoration" are alike strangers—as well as in highly artistic creations.

Although the tradition of the fish has led us especially to Syria and Palestine, and to North Africa where we may suppose Punic influence—that is, basically to eastern and semitic sources—the tradition of the dolphin seems just as characteristically Greco-Roman.[150] The study of E. B. Stebbins [151] makes it possible to review this material summarily. She thinks that in geometric art, indeed right back to Minoan art, many of the pisciform representations are intended to be dolphins, but from the sixth century on there is no mistaking that dolphins are often presented, and in hellenistic and Roman periods the creature is almost omnipresent. Miss Stebbins insists that this frequency is primarily due to two factors, that the dolphin symbolized the sea and that it could be used ideally, almost what we would now call impressionistically, from the amplification of its curves to fill spaces as desired. That the dolphin was a symbol in a sense closer to the way in which we are using the term she does not discuss systematically, though she has collected much material for such discussion.

This material falls into several groups. First, the dolphin was associated in many ways with Dionysus. One recalls at once the story which is found in a number of sources, most familiarly in the Homeric Hymn to Dionysus, of how Tyrrhenian pirates attempted to kidnap the young god. Dionysus turned the pirate sailors into dolphins and took over the ship himself.[152] The black-figure cylix by Execias, fig. 29,[153] is always, and properly, connected with this legend.[154] In the story of a Coeranus, who seems to be Dionysus, the hero saved some dolphins from being killed by a fisherman and in return was himself saved by dolphins when shipwrecked.[155] Melicertes-Palaemon also appears to be an alternative name for Dionysus. His mother Ino held him as a baby in her arms when she jumped from the Molivian cliff into the sea. He was carried to the Isthmus by a dolphin, where he seems to have come back to life and to have been worshiped, while he changed his mother into the sea goddess Leucothea.[156] Numerous stories of this kind were told of a great diversity of mythical persons, of whom Arion is perhaps the best known. Most frequently the stories tell of the friendship of a dolphin and a boy, who in the hellenistic period becomes Eros. The dolphin as the carrier of a person, dead or alive,

150. Two "dolphins" have been identified from early Mesopotamia, but I can see no reasons to call either of them dolphins: E. D. Van Buren, *The Fauna of Ancient Mesopotamia*, 1939, 82.

151. Earlier studies are listed in her introduction: see esp. Hermann Usener, *Die Sintfluthsagen*, 1899, 138–180.

152. For the various classical versions of the story see Stebbins, 61 f.

153. From FR, I, plate 42. Cf. also J. C. Hoppin, *A Handbook of Greek Black-Figured Vases*, 1924, 98.

154. See Stebbins, 9 f.

155. Ibid., 62 f. For the dolphin and fish in a bacchanalian riot see the Corinthian black-figure vase of the Louvre published by E. Pottier, in *CVA*, France 9, Louvre 6, plate 12, figs. 4 and 6; cf. p. 11.

156. Stebbins, 63–65.

lived on into Christian legends of saints.[157] All of these Miss Stebbins groups with Dionysus, and it seems with reason. Essentially we have in the stories the dolphin as savior, carrying a person to immortality. Arion with his lyre is in later art given the hat which at once associates him with Orpheus, and since he plays his lyre on the back of a dolphin, he evidently has power to soothe the sea monsters with his music. I suspect that the dolphin was the symbol of Dionysus in association with the sea.

Indeed I suspect that in the story of the Tyrrhenian pirates we have a profound myth of salvation. In Freudian terms much can be made of it: the god is taken on the ship (the human personality), is recognized by the helmsman (the ego), though the crew (the impulses of the id, what Paul calls the "flesh") try to use him for their own purposes. The god becomes the master, changes the crew (now in the water) into dolphins, and he and the helmsman thereafter sail together in a ship which has become the bower of Dionysus. The personality has been so changed that "for me to live is Dionysus" would exactly describe its new state. The impulses of the id have been not destroyed but saved: changed into dolphins beneath the ship, they have been transformed into what, as we shall see, Christians later called *pisciculi*. The whole is a picture of divinization. I should not like to say that this was all consciously in the mind of the writer of the Homeric Hymn, but it is quite the essential picture of salvation as presented by Paul. The suggestion throughout these stories is that the dolphin is the god, as the sheep or fish was later Christ. The great one is the Savior, through whom we come into immortality by ourselves becoming sheep of his pasture, or little fish. We should expect then that the dolphin would be presented with all the ambiguity of Christian use of the sheep, which on a grave would represent the faithful as one of Christ's flock, and at the same time as the Christ who had saved him. In such matters *either-or* yields completely to *both-and*. To this important hymn we shall return in Volume VII.

A similar group of stories and ritualistic observances connects the dolphin, who carries the soul, with Apollo, specifically Apollo Delphinius, whose cult was very widespread.[158] It appears that Delphinius is to be derived from dolphin rather than Delphi, itself presumably named from the dolphin. The dolphin, either swimming before the boat or leaping up into it, is said to have led Cretan mariners to the harbor of Cressa, whence they were directed to Delphi by the dolphin-god to found his sanctuary and become his priests. Or the dolphin-god brings Icadius there on his back for the same purpose. In many places there was a month called Delphinius, in which the festival of Hydrophoria, or water carrying—connected with the cult of the dead—was celebrated. In the ceremonies to Apollo of the quindecimviri at Rome the dolphin was used as a symbol. So the hellenistic representations of Eros on the dolphin, or the dolphin alone, had roots in the worship of Apollo quite as much as in that of Dionysus, and we begin to feel that the dolphin as the conveyor of the soul, common in funerary art from this time, has value as a symbol apart from its explanation in terms of either god. Indeed the dolphins have seemed to some scholars to represent also the water of the world beyond death, passing

157. Ibid., 65–77.

158. For this material and references see ibid., 77–83.

through which the soul is purified. We are close here to a symbolism which could easily be, and apparently was, reinterpreted for Christian (and perhaps Jewish) baptism.

The dolphin, especially in artistic representations, was of course frequently associated with Poseidon as his symbol and as a form that he on occasion assumed—particularly for amatory purposes, as when he wooed Amymone. The great amatory figure from the sea, Aphrodite, was similarly associated with the dolphin everywhere in art. Fish had been elaborately associated with Ishtar as early as the third millennium by the Sumerians.[159] Aphrodite was in one legend taken to Cyprus by a dolphin, so that the creature was especially connected with her as Anadyomene. The amatory value of the dolphin came to be expressed by Eros riding on one, or catching it, as already mentioned; this device also seems not to refer to a specific deity but to represent divine power generally.[160] Indeed what we have said about the symbol having value in its own right appears to be reinforced when the dolphin is observed with Mithra and with various pantheistic deities.[161]

Incidentally, Pliny [162] tells of dolphins who helped fishermen catch fish; in addition to their share of the fish they got from the fishermen some bread soaked in wine, a suggestion from paganism itself of the eucharistic possibilities of the dolphin.

It is surprising, therefore, after reviewing the material Miss Stebbins has collected, to see that she thereafter has systematically minimized any symbolic importance of the appearances of the dolphin on Greek vases,[163] shields,[164] and women's garments (possibly hieratic garments) [165] and speaks of them as space fillers, mere decorations, or simply as indications of the water of the sea.[166] The frequent use of the dolphin as a prop for a statue, in place of the more usual stump of a tree,[167] a convention especially associated with Aphrodite, impresses me as being a part of the symbolic tradition. As the dolphin becomes more frequently presented by later artists, it seems to Miss Stebbins to lose symbolic value and to become "a formal motif or literary ornament." [168] To Aulus Gellius [169] in the

159. H. Zimmern, *König Lipit-Ištar's Vergöttlichung*, 1916, 21; cf. 40–42 (Berichte, K. Sächsischen Gesellschaft der Wissenschaften, Leipzig, Phil. Hist. Klasse, LXVIII, v).

160. It is enough to see the recently discovered mosaics from Antioch, published by the Committee for the Excavation of Antioch and Its Vicinity, *Antioch on the Orontes*. There, in II, *The Excavations 1933–1936*, Princeton, 1938, plate 38, Secs. 1, 3, 5, Eros on a dolphin catches fish; and in Sec. 4 Eros catches the dolphin on which he is riding. See also plate 39, Sec. 1; plate 80, Sec. 3. Cf. in the same series, III, *The Excavations 1937–1939*, Princeton, 1941, plate 48, no. 105; plate 61, no. 128A; plate 66, no. 138; plate 69, no. 142; plate 79, no. 165, 2; plate 83, no. 170B. In III, plate 77, no. 161B, a fish, not a dolphin, has what may be a protruding tongue. Doro Levi, *Antioch Mosaic Pavements*, Princeton, 1947, discusses many of these mosaics. A. A. Barb, "Diva Matrix," *Journal of the Warburg and Courtauld Institutes*, XVI (1953), 200, has the interesting suggestion that the dolphin with Aphrodite was the uterus.

161. See Stebbins, 86, 120, 122.

162. *Natural History*, IX, 29–32. Stebbins, 89.

163. Ibid., 97.

164. Ibid., 101.

165. Ibid., 107.

166. Ibid., 109.

167. Ibid., 118–120.

168. Ibid., 60; cf. p. 123: "As the design was more and more used, it became a stock pattern, so that the symbolism must have receded behind customary usage and mechanical execution, and eventually have been forgotten." The same could be said, but not truly, of the cross or of the Shield of David. That the symbolism of the dolphin has now largely disappeared does not mean we can say that frequency of usage in late antiquity meant it had likewise disappeared at that time.

169. *Attic Nights*, VI, 8.

second century after Christ, on the contrary, the stories of the boy riders are still demonstrations that dolphins are *venerei et amasii* (even though the love in the story is homosexual), and show that these dolphins were "under the sway of Aphrodite." [170] It is a matter of personal judgment whether such a statement is to be read as purely formal literary ornament or as a literal reference to the goddess. But the active passion of the dolphin survives in either reading, and I cannot believe that Gellius would have seen dolphins on a sarcophagus without at least unconsciously feeling their significance.

The erotic symbolism found in the dolphin is an element which will recur with a great number of the symbols as we study them. Salvation, the coming into immortality, will everywhere be found in association with the idea of the love of the savior for human beings, and of their love for him. In the ancient world this could be expressed quite specifically in terms of Eros or Aphrodite, or the swan consorting with Leda on a sarcophagus. Christians had to soften such representation. They talked of *agapē* rather than *erōs*, and when it was a Christian saint brought to shore by a dolphin, the sexual symbolism of the figure was certainly not in the conscious mind of those who told the story. But the saving dolphin, in all probability, still represented a loving act of God. The difference between *agapē* and *erōs* is for metaphysicians, not historians, to argue. What we see clearly, keeping to plain English, is that the dolphin represented the kindly, loving, immortalizing aspects of deity, with reference to whichever deity it represented. In the course of transition the openly erotic was by no means entirely repressed. Indeed, Coptic Christians represented Aphrodite Anadyomene with her dolphins, holding a cross in a wreath above her head on what appears to be a eucharistic paten, fig. 35.[171] The distinction between *erōs* and *agapē* was certainly not clear here. I see no reason, accordingly, against supposing that the erotic value of the dolphin as a divine symbol, however much the specifically erotic had to be reinterpreted, went over to the Christian and Jewish monuments with the form.

The dolphin had been associated with so many gods that it was clearly a symbol in its own right, one which, as seen in its use with Mithra, Isis, or Pantheos, could be so interpreted that it was appropriate for any deity. It is an excellent example of the vocabulary of the symbolic lingua franca of the period.[172] It always carried its symbolic value with it, however, and in whatever association it was presented suggested the loving concern of deity to bring one into a happy life after death. As such it could be used freely on the graves or in the places of worship of both Jews and Christians and as a living symbol presumably carried this value with it into those religions. That it was also a very handy device to fill in odd places in a design in no sense indicates that it had thereby lost its symbolic value, any more than "red, white, and blue" ceases to have symbolic im-

170. This is a statement quoted by Gellius from Apion. Stebbins, 119, seems to me not to understand the passage so well as had J. J. Bernoulli, *Aphrodite*, 1873, 245, whose interpretation she rejects.

171. From a photograph published by courtesy of the Coptic Museum, Cairo, where the object is no. 5028. Aphrodite appears a number of times on Christian objects in this museum.

172. See above, IV, 36–38, 46 f.

portance in America because it is often displayed as festoons of bunting to decorate buildings. We do not know how Jews who used the dolphin would have expressed it, but it seems that overtly erotic symbolism would have been as distasteful to them as to Christians and that they would similarly have softened the symbolism, indeed have led the way in doing so for Christians. Such is certainly the impression of Philo's use of erotic imagery.[173]

When Leclercq concludes that Christians used the dolphin to indicate the Savior, he points out what seems only a continuation and adaptation of its pagan value.[174] Leclercq [175] thinks that in Christian art the dolphin twisted on the anchor or trident is Christ on the cross, and this seems generally presumed. There is little evidence for it, so far as I know, but it may well have been the rationalization of a symbol, dolphin with anchor or trident, to which Christians wanted to give specific *Christian* meaning because they wanted to use the symbol of the dolphin-savior in their own context. And as usual, if Leclercq's guess is correct about the meaning of the dolphin and trident, the Christian interpretation does not change the value of the symbol. The interpretation still follows the method ascribed to Paul at Athens: it gives a specific name to the Unknown God, saying in effect, "Christ is the true dolphin."

What could the Jews have called it? That we cannot say. But they did use the dolphin most conspicuously in their catacomb, in a design made up otherwise of religious symbols of their faith, and we may suppose that they too, in their own terms, saw in it a symbol of hope for themselves and their loved ones. It will appear that they may have called it Leviathan. More than that cannot be said with certainty; but two scraps of literary evidence are worth recalling. First, Philo [176] told a story of a boy loved by a dolphin, which died when the boy died; so it is clear that hellenized Jews were familiar with this lore. Secondly, without any context, the "rabbis" are quoted in the Talmud as follows:

> Dolphins are fruitful and multiply by coupling with human beings. What are dolphins? —Said Rab Judah: Humans of the sea.[177]

If even the rabbis had picked it up, the erotic symbolism of the dolphin must have been widely current indeed.

3. *Sea Monsters in Paganism*

THE GOAT FISH first appears to my knowledge in the Neo-Sumerian period, when it was the "distinctive attribute of Ea." [178] Such is recognized to be its meaning in fig. 36,[179]

173. See my *By Light, Light*, esp. pp. 145–148, 157–160.

174. G. A. Eisen and F. Kouchakji, *Glass*, 1927, II, 545 f., suggest that for Christians the fish is Christ, the dolphin resurrection.

175. In CL, IV, 285–287.

176. *Animal*, 67.

177. *BT*, *Bekoroth*, 8a (ET, 47).

178. Van Buren, "Fish Offerings in Ancient Mesopotamia," *Iraq*, X (1948), 111–121.

179. From Legrain, *The Culture of the Babylonians*, plate LIII, fig. 801; cf. plate XXXV, fig. 801, and his text, p. 330. The name of the owner is beside the device.

and it seems only an alternative for the god of the flowing bowl in fig. 37.[180] Both of these seals are from Nippur. The zodiacal figure is clearly this early Ea [181] and continued as a popular representation of Ea and his associates for millennia. It is probably as such that the goat fish is mentioned in two magical charms, where figurines of the monster in wood or clay are stipulated among other objects to be used with the charms.[182] Since in one of these an altar to Ea is also called for, the figurine of the goat fish may be presumed to represent that god. Ea was primarily the "Lord of the Watery Deep," from which comes all sweet water on the surface of the earth and later all rain from heaven. His water was that of purifying spells and rites. As god of the depths he was god of wisdom, him in whom all secrets were hidden.[183] It is impossible for me to trace this figure into hellenistic sources. It seems to have come from the East primarily with the zodiac.[184] But its import in its own right carried over, for stories of the monster were told in hellenistic times. Personalized, he was made the companion of Zeus in the war with the Titans, whom he terrorized by trumpeting on a shell.[185] The story has clearly conflated him with Triton, but also, in putting down the Titans, with Orpheus, who could scatter the forces of evil, tame the wild impulses with his music. The myth seems a Greek adaptation or explanation of the values of the figure which go back to its association with Ea. How many mythical explanations were given this figure in adapting its value as it passed through Syria and other eastern civilizations we cannot now reconstruct.

In iconography of the Roman period Capricorn appears only in sporadic cases. A curious drinking horn at Lyons has the horn in place of the tail, and Capricorn before it, fig. 38.[186] That it is Capricorn rather than a common goat is made highly likely by the typical position of the two front feet and by the impression of the object as a whole. So far as I know, the object is unique, and the conclusion that Capricorn was associated with ritualistic drinking, as we shall see the fish was, cannot be drawn from a unique item which may have been only a *jeu d'esprit* of the artist, though of course the possibility of

180. From ibid., fig. 804; cf. plate XXXVI, fig. 804, and the text, p. 331. The name of the owner also stands on this seal. Legrain calls the goat fish Ea but says that the god with the flowing bowl in this figure is the "fisherman . . . a symbol and servant of Ea." There is no indication that this is a fisherman and certainly none that it is a servant of Ea. For the Akkadian prototype of Ea, the god with the flowing bowl and fish, see also Van Buren, "Fish Offerings," 111–121, and her fig. 10.

181. H. Frankfort, *Cylinder Seals*, 1939, 156. Frankfort has a good collection of the appearances of the goat fish on seals: see esp. 165 f. and the index, s.v. On Cappadocian seals the goat fish as Ea became the dispenser of rain, ibid., 247. E. D. Van Buren, *The Flowing Vase and the God with Streams*, 1933, also presents many instances: see her index, s.v.

182. O. R. Gurney, "Babylonian Prophylactic Figures and Their Rituals," *Annals of Archaeology and Anthropology* (University of Liverpool), XXII (1935), 55 (cf. 57), and 71. For the first of these see also H. Zimmern, *Beiträge zur Kenntnis der babylonischen Religion*, 1901, 163, line 8 (Assyriologische Bibliothek, XII).

183. Van Buren, *The Flowing Vase*, 8–10.

184. For the acceptance of the zodiac by the Greeks see Cumont in DS, V, 1050 f.

185. Haebler in PW, III, 1550 f. The sources are Erotosthenes and Euhemerus and stories of "Egyptian priests": C. Robert, *Erotosthenis catasterismorum reliquiae*, 1878, 148–151; B. Bunte, *Hygini astronomica*, 1875, 49, 69 f.

186. From Reinach, *Statuaire*, IV, 451, no. 6. Reinach gives no reference for other publication of this horn, and I could not find one.

such association remains. Capricorn was the birth sign of Augustus, one which meant so much to him that he had it put on the reverse of many of his coins, and it appears beside his head on the great cameo of the Museum of Vienna, and probably on a relief from North Africa at the Musée Lavigerie.[187] The figure of Capricorn was a favorite symbol with the Roman legions, some of which used it alone or with other animals. Four, possibly five, of these legions were certainly created by Augustus, and a sixth was reorganized by him, so it has been supposed that they took the sign in his honor. There is no explanation why the other three legions did so.[188] It was used on coins other than those of Augustus, and Furtwängler recalls these, as well as a number of amulets from before the time of Augustus.[189] They seem to him lucky tokens. But in the marine mosaics of the Roman period Capricorn has no special place among the monsters of the sea.

Three of the monsters in the mosaic of the baths at Ostia are quite clearly Capricorn, as in fig. 40,[190] but various other animals are also represented with the long fishy tails. The animals turned into sea monsters in all these mosaics seem to me not chosen at random, however, for they are the animals especially familiar in Dionysiac association. The lion, leopard, ass,[191] horse, bull, and even in one case a marine deer, fig. 41,[192] are so common along with the goat that the impression is that of a bacchanalian orgy in the sea, with Poseidon, often the companion of Dionysus in classic Greek art, now taking his place at the center. The monstrous sea serpent and sea goat are often hard to distinguish, but the creatures with long necks are probably to be identified as sea serpents.[193]

We must conclude, accordingly, that Capricorn as such had no special importance in the religious life of the Roman empire and that the instances in the Jewish remains are to be considered along with the pagan sea monsters in general. These had divine attributes or were themselves attributes of divinities and hence indicated divine power and action, a power which seemed enhanced by their being features and creatures of the vasty deep.

It is then not surprising that early Christians represented the "great fish" of Jonah as a monster of this type. I show only one of a great number, fig. 39.[194] Indeed I suspect

187. Suetonius, *Octavius*, 94. For Capricorn with Augustus see M. Delattre, *Musée Lavigerie*, 1899, II, plate v, 6. (Description de l'Afrique du Nord, VIII, II).

188. C. Renel, *Cultes militaires de Rome: Les Enseignes*, 1903, 212, 217 f.; see also 200 f., 213, 215, 225, 229, 262.

189. A. Furtwängler, *Die antiken Gemmen*, 1900, 264, 296 f.

190. From G. Calza, *BA*, VI (1912), 200, fig. 2; see the whole mosaic in his fig. 1. His fig. 4 seems to show a marine sheep.

191. Ibid., 201, fig. 3.

192. From T. Ashby, "Drawings of Ancient Paintings in English Collections," *Papers of the British School at Rome*, VII (1914), plate v: cf. p. 15. The original seems to have been in the Palace of Titus.

193. They can be most quickly reviewed in Reinach, *Peintures*, 34, no. 1; 36, no. 3; 39, nos. 1, 5, 6; 40, no. 1 (cf. no. 3, which may be a goat); 42, nos. 1, 4, 5; 79, no. 4, is again dubious but is probably a goat.

194. From Wilpert, *Pitture*, plate 82, no. 2; cf. plates 26, 45, 47, 60, 61, 67, 85, 95, 109, 122, 156, 160, 189, all from catacombs. The sea monster could be used as a symbol by itself in the Christian catacombs: see ibid., plates, 11, 85. The sea monster swallows Jonah on a Christian patera: Garrucci, *Arte cristiana*, III, plate 169; and on a gold glass: ibid., plate 174.

that this conception of the "great fish" came over from Judaism and is represented to us in the amulets of Volume III, figs. 1042 f.[195] It is the great monster with special powers which, we shall see, swallowed Jonah in Jewish tradition and was probably identified with the Leviathan. To this we shall return.

195. Cf. above, II, 225.

CHAPTER TWO

The Symbolic Value of the Fish in Judaism

TO BOTH DÖLGER and Cumont it seemed that the Christians first adopted the fish symbol in Syria,[1] and certainly I agree that it is the oriental fish symbol which appears in John VI, the earliest explicit acceptance of the fish as a eucharistic symbol and as a symbol of the Savior who was eaten in the Eucharist.[2]

The fish, however, was frequently represented in the West as a substitute for wine in the scene of the Last Supper. The earliest of such scenes to my knowledge are in the Catacomb of St. Callistus in Rome; fig. 47 [3] is one of the scenes in that Catacomb. The baskets in these scenes show that the paintings interpret the Last Supper in terms of the miracle of the loaves and fishes, as does the Fourth Gospel. Fig. 42 [4] from the sacristy of the Cathedral in Salerno shows the multiplication of fishes above, and the Last Supper below, with only the fish and bread on the table. The Last Supper is a fish meal in Sant' Apollinare Nuovo, Ravenna.[5] A Coptic version of the same is shown in fig. 43.[6] The famous mosaic of the late fifth century in the church at Tabha, on the Sea of Galilee near Capernaum, is interesting also, fig. 48.[7] Tabha is the traditional site of the multiplication of the loaves and fishes, and the tradition is indicated by the mosaic, which shows a basket of bread flanked on each side by a fish and a lozenge. This stands directly behind the

1. *Ichthys*, I, 141, 443. It seemed to him adopted as a missionary device to oppose the cults of Atargatis and of the Cabiri and the "Thracian Rider." Christians, he said, could not have "borrowed the symbol out of any of the Mysteries," since the Christian fathers hated the Mysteries so thoroughly. Cumont in PW, IX, 848, followed Dölger in this.

2. See my "John a Primitive Gospel," *JBL*, LXIV (1945), 145–182.

3. From Wilpert, *Pitture*, plate 41, no. 4; cf. plates 27, no. 2 and 41, no. 3.

4. From *Ichthys*, III, plate LXXII. Cf. ibid., plate LXXI, 1, where this meal with bread and fish is conflated with the scene of the Miracle at Cana.

5. C. Ricci, *Tavole storiche dei mosaici di Ravenna*, 1935, IV, plate R1.

6. From a photograph, courtesy of the Coptic Museum, Cairo, where the plaque is preserved. See below, p. 81.

7. From Alfons Schneider, *Die Brotvermehrungskirche von Et-Tâbga am Genesarethsee und ihre Mosaiken*, 1934, 17, fig. 2 (Collectanea Hierosolymitana, IV). In other parts of the same church are mosaics devoted to scenes of water birds with plants and flowers; one bird is in the act of killing a snake, the pose familiar from amulets: see above, III, fig. 1071, and II, p. 242. Schneider gives an excellent presentation of the entire material but has no appreciation of its symbolism as a whole. On p. 63 he considers his fig. 22, a pair of geese at a chalice, as "ein beliebtes antikes Motiv (trinkende Pfauen oder Tauben), man möchte sagen, ins Humoristische umgebogen."

altar between it and the bench for the priests in the apse. The eucharistic significance of bread and fish, with no wine shown, again seems clear.

Both Dölger and Cumont assumed that the fish came into Christianity directly from paganism, however, though Cumont had an appreciative word for the suggestion of Scheftelowitz [8] that, originally pagan, it came in as part of the Jewish heritage of Christianity.[9] Dölger's rejection of this suggestion with more scorn than reason [10] is consonant with his general rejection of the symbolic importance of Jewish representations. Actually, out of the mass of Jewish remains he considered only the fish, a limitation which exposed him to the danger of studying these data piece by piece (or symbol by symbol) with an a priori judgment that Judaism was always halachic Judaism and that all true symbolism arose in Christianity. With the mass of Jewish symbols of the Greco-Roman period before us, we cannot thus summarily dismiss the particular problem of the Jewish fish. In 1911 Scheftelowitz developed the theory that the fish came into Christianity from Judaism, where it had early been popular and familiar. He did not know more than a fraction of the Jewish archeological instances now before the reader, and he wrote without reference to Jewish symbolism in general. His study was judged unconvincing at the time and has been largely neglected, or misrepresented. The fish symbolism he suggested seemed quite foreign to that religion which his readers, from the literary evidence of the rabbis, supposed Judaism to be. But there was much in his study which now appears freshly relevant, and accordingly I review his material, with considerable additions.[11]

Scheftelowitz discussed the fish under four heads: first, the faithful were themselves little fishes in Judaism as well as in Christianity; secondly, the fish in Judaism was the Messiah, as for Christians he was the Christ; thirdly, the fish was in both religions a sacramental food; fourthly, the fish was for Jews and Christians alike a symbol of the hope of immortality. For discussing the meaning of the fish to Jews, this arrangement is still useful.

A. THE FAITHFUL AS LITTLE FISHES

TERTULLIAN in a most important passage called the Christians little fishes: "But we little fishes, according to our *Ichthys* Jesus Christ, are born in the water, nor are we saved in any other way than by remaining in the water." [12]

8. "Fisch-Symbol." R. Eisler drew heavily upon this study for his chapter "The Sabbatic Fish-Meal of the Jews and the Banquet of the Last Days," in his *Orpheus*, 221–225, and for his "Fisch."

9. In *PW*, IX, 847.

10. *Ichthys*, II, 490–492, 540–544.

11. See also Beyer and Lietzmann, *Torlonia*, 19, n. 3; Cohn-Wiener, 116; Eisler, *Orph.-dion.*, 112.

12. *De baptismo*, 1. This statement comes out in sudden contrast to Tertullian's denunciation of the heretical teachings of a woman of the Cainite sect, who, because she denied the validity of baptism with water, says Tertullian, was a viper of the dry land in contrast to "us little fish" etc. See C. R. Morey in *Princeton Theological Review*, VIII (1910), 403–406. For other Christian passages connecting the fish with baptized Christians see *Ichthys*, V, 308–320. Mory assumed that Tertullian's reference to the "Ichthys," the Greek term in a Latin document, meant that Tertullian was acquainted with the Ichthys acrostic of the Christians. This seems very dubious to me. The symbol was itself the Ichthys, originating of course in Greek-speaking circles, and that it had already been given its Christian explanation in the acrostic is by no means indicated by Tertullian's use of the Greek word.

Parallel with this, Scheftelowitz quotes the following material: R. Samuel, of the beginning of the third century, explained Habakkuk I, 14 ("Thou makest men as the fish of the sea") as follows:

> Men are compared with fishes because just as fishes of the sea die at once when they come up on dry land, so does man also die as soon as he abandons the Torah and the precepts.[13]

A very important midrashic discussion is preserved of why Jacob said (according to some traditions at Genesis XLVIII, 16) "Let them increase like fish":

> As the [evil] eye has no power over fish, so will the eye have no power over them. . . . Just as fish live in water, yet when a drop falls from above they catch it thirstily as though they had never tasted water in their lives; so are Israel brought up in the waters of the Torah, yet when they hear a new exposition in the Torah, they receive it thirstily as though they had never heard a Torah teaching in their lives.[14]

Comparison of God to living water is familiar in the Old Testament,[15] but the rabbis tended to turn this figure into praise of Torah. So the "waters of the Torah" in which the fish lived in the preceding quotation are further described:

> R. Hanina said: Who dreams of a well will see peace; as it is said, "And Isaac's servants digged in the valley, and found there a well of living water" (Gen. XXVI, 19). R. Nathan said: He will find Torah; as it is said, "Whoso findeth me findeth *life*" (Prov. VIII, 35), and it is written here "a well of *living* water." Raba said: [It means] life literally.[16]

That the Israelites, especially those faithful to the Law, are little fishes swimming in the Torah, where alone they can live, must have been a very old conception. It was proverbial in the time of Akiba early in the second century after Christ, as the following shows:

> Our rabbis have taught: Once the wicked government [Rome] decreed that Israel should no longer occupy themselves with Torah. There came Pappos ben Judah and found R. Akiba attracting great assemblies and studying Torah. He said to him, "Akiba, art thou not afraid of the wicked government?" He replied, "I will tell thee a parable: To what is the matter like? To a fox who was walking along the bank of the stream and saw some fishes gathering together from one place to another. He said to them, 'From what are you fleeing?' They answered, 'From nets which men are bringing against us.' He said to them, 'Let it be your pleasure to come up on the dry land, and let us, me and you, dwell together even as my fathers dwelt with your fathers.' They replied, 'Art thou

13. *BT*, *Abodah Zarah*, 3b (ET, 11 f.). The passage goes on to other comparisons, for example that both are scorched by the sun and that, in the case of both, the larger and more powerful devour the smaller.

14. *MR*, *Gen.*, XCVII, 3 (ET, II, 940). This is an anonymous statement in the Midrash, perhaps from the fifth century but probably much earlier.

15. Ps. XXXVI, 9; Is. LV, 1; Jer. XVII, 13.

16. *BT*, *Berakoth*, 56b (ET, 369). Scheftelowitz, "Fisch-Symbol," 3, n. 3, has further references of the sort.

he of whom they tell that thou art the shrewdest of animals? Thou art not clever but a fool! For if we are afraid in the place which is our life-element, how much more so in a place which is our death-element!' So also is it with us: If now while we sit and study Torah, in which it is written, 'For that is thy life, and the length of thy days' (Deut. xxx, 20), we are in such a plight, how much more so if we go and neglect it!"[17]

The rabbis and students of the Torah, who were the representatives of Judaism par excellence, were of course fish par excellence. This comparison was made from very early times, according to the tradition. Scheftelowitz quotes from Chapter 40 of *The Aboth of R. Nathan*, a sort of tosefta to the talmudic *Aboth*. That it presents genuine second-century material cannot be asserted, but even if it was written somewhat later, its tradition is still interesting:

> On the subject of disciples Rabban Gamaliel the Elder [the Gamaliel in the New Testament] spoke of four kinds: An unclean fish, a clean fish, a fish from the Jordan, a fish from the Great Sea.
>
> An unclean fish: who is that? A poor youth who studies Scripture and Mishna, Halakha and Agada, and is without understanding.
>
> A clean fish: who is that? That's a rich youth who studies Scripture and Mishna, Halakha and Agada, and has understanding.
>
> A fish from the Jordan: who is that? That's a scholar who studies Scripture and Mishna, Midrash, Halakha, and Agada, and is without the talent for give and take.
>
> A fish from the Great Sea: who is that? That's a scholar who studies Scripture and Mishna, Midrash, Halakha and Agada, and has the talent for give and take.[18]

This is indeed an impressive group of passages to represent that Jews are fishes. In comparison, the unique Christian statement where Tertullian says that the Christians are little fishes, a passage to which scholars have given great attention, seems isolated and secondary.[19] Had we only this literary evidence we should conclude that Jews had proverbially compared the pious man to a fish who can survive only in his native element, that of Jewish legalism, and that this comparison had come over into Christianity with other Christian heritages from Judaism, come over with the necessity of reinterpretation, since obviously the water could now no longer be the Torah as the water of life. Inevitably this water in Christianity became the mystical water of baptism. The change did not work very well, for the baptismal water is something the Christian does not live in as the Jew lives in Torah. Dölger tried to avoid the difficulty by introducing the conception

17. *BT*, *Berakoth*, 61b (ET, 406 f.).

18. As translated by Judah Goldin, *The Fathers according to Rabbi Nathan*, 1955, 166 (Yale Judaica Series, X). Cf. Scheftelowitz, "Fisch-Symbol," 5.

19. The Christian as a little fish in the living waters appears also in Origen, *In Matt.* XIII, 10 (a dubious passage which Morey, op. cit., interprets this way); Jerome, *Epist.* VII, 3 (certainly a reflection of Tertullian); St. Severianus the Bishop, *Sermon*: "The fish consecrates fishes. For if Christ were not the fish, he would never have risen from the dead"—a statement sufficiently obscure. All of these are quoted and discussed by Morey, op. cit., 403–420. They tell us very little indeed about the Christian fish.

that the water of baptism was the Logos. But Tertullian makes Christ not the water but the *Ichthys*, another and greater fish. Tertullian's statement is best understood as an offhand reinterpretation of a *façon de parler* inherited from Judaism, where the conception that the pious were fish had consistent meaning.

B. THE FISH AS THE MESSIAH OR CHRIST

THE CONCLUSION is strengthened when we learn further from Scheftelowitz that the pious as little fishes were in Judaism likewise contrasted with a greater fish.[20]

We cannot stress a very cryptic passage in which Joshua was said to be qualified to lead the Israelites (themselves compared with fishes) to the promised land because he "was the son of him whose name was as the name of a fish.[21]" Much may have been behind the statement, but if so it cannot now be safely inferred. More explicit is the following, attributed to R. Ashi of the fourth century:

> If Leviathan by hook be hauled to land,
> What hope have fishes of a shallow strand? [22]

The rabbi has here contrasted the great Leviathan, who lives in the depths, with the little fishes in shallow water, who are human beings.

Leviathan, in Jewish tradition, is a monster fish that lives at the bottom of the sea over the spring or fountain which feeds the ocean with water.[23] The monster was originally one of several monstrous beasts of El, the supreme god of Ugaritic mythology. Its name was there Lotan (or Shalyat), and it was a great serpent with seven heads, which was crushed by Anath, the warrior goddess who helped Baal in his revolt against El.[24] But if Gaster [25] is right, as seems likely, that these powers are those of a seasonal ritual, Lotan would be alive the next year to be killed anew. All the later Jewish stories of Leviathan, of course, are based upon the references to that creature in the Bible, especially Job XLI and Isaiah XXVII, 1. In the longer passage in Job the great fish is mentioned as one of the instances of God's might in contrast to the insignificance of Job. It is impossible to catch him with a hook, or press down his tongue with a rope. His great size and power are described, and his inviolability, as well as his ability to spout fire from his mouth, make the

20. Leviathan and Behemoth were also discussed by R. Wischnitzer-Bernstein, "Die messianische Hütte in der jüdischen Kunst," *MGWJ*, LXXX (1936), 377–390; see esp. the plate facing p. 384.

21. *MR*, *Gen.*, XCVII, 3 (ET, II, 940 f.). The passage plays upon the fact that Nun, the name of Joshua's father, in Aramaic means "fish."

22. *BT*, *Moed Katan*, 25b (ET, 160).

23. I Enoch LX, 7 f. On the Leviathan, besides Scheftelowitz see Friedlander's notes in his edition of the *Pirke Eliezer*, 63, n. 11; 70, n. 4; 76, n. 3. G. H. Box, *Ezra-Apocalypse*, 90–92; *JE*, VIII, 37–39; J. Drummond, *Jewish Messiah*, 352–355; Paul Volz, *Die Eschatologie der jüdischen Gemeinde im nt. Zeitalter*, 1934, 389; I. Löw in *Judaica*, *Herm. Cohen Festschrift*, 1912, 338–340. But by far the largest collection of material on Leviathan is in Ginzberg, *Legends*, I, 27–30, 40 f.; V, 41–38. I have used material quoted by these without further acknowledgment.

24. See the translations by H. L. Ginsberg in Pritchard, *Texts*, 137A (D, 37–39); 138B (g, i, 1–3, 15–17).

25. T. H. Gaster, *Thespis*, 1950, 1–108.

deep boil like a pot, and make the sea like ointment. It is this fabulous monster who is killed in Isaiah xxvii, 1. "In that day"—an inevitably messianic phrase—God will punish him, slay him with the sword.

In later Jewish legend this material was much expanded. Statistics were of course invented for the monster. Its bulk stretches the imagination indeed. A fish three hundred parasangs in length proclaimed himself a minor creature of the sea, for he was going to swim into the mouth of Leviathan.[26] Leviathan was originally created male and female, the one "the slant serpent" the other "the tortuous serpent," so that apparently Jews thought of them often in the generally familiar sea-serpent form, which I see reflected in the sea horses or sea goats of the art. The sea serpent is old in Hebrew tradition, for in the cursing of the sinful Israelites in Amos ix, 3, God is represented as saying, "Though they be hid from my sight in the bottom of the sea, thence will I command the serpent, and it shall bite them." In view of the pictures it is interesting that Leviathan is a sea goat with horns according to R. Ashi,[27] or a sea gazelle,[28] as well as a serpent. He is aptly represented as Capricorn. Had the male and female

> mated with one another they would have destroyed the whole world. What [then] did the Holy One, blessed be he, do? He castrated the male and killed the female preserving it in salt for the righteous in the world to come.[29]

Jewish fancy liked to play with these conceptions; it also gave to Leviathan important functions in the Messianic Age. Presumably in that age (the passage says only "in the future") Gabriel will make

> a chase of Leviathan; for it is said: "Canst thou draw out Leviathan with a fish hook? Or press down his tongue with a cord?" And if the Holy One, blessed be he, will not help him [Gabriel] he will be unable to prevail over him.[30]

One reasonably concludes that this snaring of Leviathan is part of the Messianic Age. For at that time it is promised that the flesh of Leviathan will be distributed to the sur-

26. *BT*, *Baba Bathra*, 74a (ET, I, 294). In the passage of Job, Leviathan is described in such a way that the beast is universally taken to be a crocodile or alligator by modern commentators, though Jewish tradition made Leviathan always a fish or a sea serpent. One of the anomalies which anthropology brings to light was pointed out to me by my colleague George Kubler: the Aztecs in Mexico also had a great sea fish, important in myths of creation, whose name likewise meant alligator. See the anonymous account of an early Jesuit missionary (c. 1569), "Historia de los Mexicanos por sus pinturas, II," *Nueva colección de documentos para la historia de Mexico*, 1891, III, 230.

27. *BT*, *Baba Bathra*, 74a (ET, I, 294).

28. Ibid., 74b (ET, I, 296).

29. See ibid., 74b (ET, I, 296). In Enoch lx, 7 f., Leviathan is the female and Behemoth, a corresponding land monster, is the male. In this passage of the *Baba Bathra* Behemoth was also created male and female. See also *MR*, *Gen.*, vii, 4 (ET, I, 51). The two are to have a terrific fight at the end of the world, according to one tradition, and those Jews who have not gone to pagan animal fights will be allowed to watch it: *MR*, *Levit.*, xiii, 3 (ET, 167).

30. *BT*, *Baba Bathra*, 74b–75a (ET, I, 298).

viving remnant.[31] In anticipation of this banquet, apparently, the rabbis take care to assure the faithful that since Leviathan has scales and fins, its flesh is kosher.[32] The great event is described by R. Johanan:

> The Holy One, blessed be he, will in time to come make a banquet for the righteous from the flesh of Leviathan. . . . The rest [of Leviathan] will be distributed and sold in the markets of Jerusalem. . . . The Holy One, blessed be he, will in time to come make a tabernacle for the righteous from the skin of Leviathan. . . . If a man is worthy, a tabernacle is made for him; if he is not worthy [of this] a [mere] covering is made for him, for it is said: "And his head with a fish covering" (Job XL, 31). If a man is [sufficiently] worthy a covering is made for him; if he is not worthy [even of this], a necklace is made for him. . . . If he is not worthy [even of this] an amulet is made for him. . . . The rest [of Leviathan] will be spread by the Holy One, blessed be he, upon the walls of Jerusalem, and its splendour will shine from one end of the world to the other; as it is said: "And nations shall walk at thy light, and kings at the brightness of thy rising" (Is. LX, 3).[33]

Scheftelowitz quotes two additional statements,[34] one that the special prerogative of tasting the head of Leviathan will be reserved for those who have fulfilled the Law, and the other that Jonah wished the fish, in whose belly he then was, to swim to Leviathan, so that he could kill Leviathan and give this miraculous meal to the pious; but he was not allowed to do so. However, the *Pirke de R. Eliezer* [35] tells that the fish carrying Jonah took him to Leviathan, since it was its turn to be devoured by Leviathan. When Jonah thus came alongside Leviathan, he said to the great fish, "On thy account I have descended to see thy abode in the sea, for, moreover, in the future will I descend and put a rope in thy tongue, and I will bring thee up and prepare thee for the great feast of the righteous."

As a variant, Jews told the legend of a final duel between Leviathan of the sea and Behemoth, a similar monster of the land. In this connection the sources are again clear: the flesh of both will be distributed to the faithful at the great day of the coming of the Messiah.[36]

31. In II Baruch (Syriac), XXIX, 4, both the male and female are thus given as food. See also IV Ezra VI, 52. There was great variety in the legends about the final killing of Leviathan: see Ginzberg, *Legends*, V, 43–46, for an amazing collection of this material.

32. See esp. *BT*, *Hullin*, 67b (ET, I, 364). His scales are of course mentioned in Job XLI, 15.

33. *BT*, *Baba Bathra*, 75a (ET, I, 299).

34. Op. cit., 7: he refers to *Yalkut* to Job XL, and *Yalkut* to Jonah I.

35. Quoted from the edition of G. Friedlander, 1916, 70; at this speech of Jonah, Leviathan swam hurriedly away and so the fish carrying Jonah was saved. For the daily food of Leviathan see ibid., 63 f.

36. II Baruch (Syriac), XXIX, 4; cf. IV Ezra VI, 51 f.; *MR*, *Levit.*, XIII, 3 (ET, 167); *Pirke Eliezer*, p. 75 f. For other rabbinic material see Scheftelowitz, "Fisch-Symbol," p. 39, n. 2, and on p. 40 where he quotes the late (eleventh century) but most interesting poem *Aqdamut:* here the pious, in eating this meal, sit about tables of jasper and carbuncle, etc. Box, *Ezra-Apocalypse*, p. 92, quotes from *Palest. Targum* in Gen. I, 21: "Leviathan and its female . . . are prepared for the day of consolation." On Behemoth see above, n. 29.

> That man who observes the prescription about the Feast of the Tabernacles, will the Holy One, blessed be he, allow to live in the future world in the tent of Leviathan. . . . In the hour when the just shall be in the tents of the skin of Leviathan will the Holy One, blessed be he, say: Let each man who has fulfilled the ordinary commands come at once and eat of his head.[37]

Jewish tradition, then, has very clearly the idea that the faithful are little fishes swimming in the water of life, the Torah, and doomed to instant destruction if they get out. It also contrasts these little fish with the great fish, Leviathan, which from being merely a terrible monster has become also a symbol of the glory of the Messianic Age. For it will then be caught and its kosher flesh will be given the faithful in a special eschatological banquet, and will, when smeared upon the walls of Jerusalem, give it cosmic glory.

This conception of Leviathan marks an important change from that in the Bible. There Leviathan is a terrible monster; now he is still terrifying, but as he is *eaten*, he is to become a blessing to man, the ultimate reward of the most righteous. This change seems to me deeply significant. For fish eating has come to symbolize the hope of Israel, an eating of the greatest of all fishes. In no case is the Leviathan who is eaten himself the Messiah; but a midrash assures us that the "mystery" of Leviathan is comparable to the "mystery of the chariot," [38] and I feel that much more lies behind this eating of Leviathan than appears in our records. For one thing, there is the coming into Judaism of a ritualistic fish meal, which had to be Judaized to be acceptable. The method of Judaizing, as in all syncretism, is to give to the newly accepted rite or god a name traditional in the religion adopting it or him. So the fish that was now newly eaten and which would be eaten in the future may have been called by the fanciful name from *Jewish* mythology, Leviathan. Nothing in the Old Testament references to Leviathan would have suggested such elaborations as we have seen the rabbis made, and the probability is that when we have elaboration not warranted by an original text it means that new, presumably foreign and syncretistic, ideas are being read back into the old text. This is the basic method of all syncretism by allegory, in Judaism and paganism and Christianity alike. The question before us is whether in the early years of the Greco-Roman period (perhaps still earlier) such a fish meal did come into Judaism.

We may now mention a passage generally overlooked in this connection, one to which we shall frequently recur, since its importance seems guaranteed for us by one of the pictures in the Dura synagogue. Judaism fostered a highly important tradition of a wandering spring or fountain which followed the Israelites through the desert. It was with them on the occasions when Moses was commanded to strike the rock and seems to have been constantly available to them. Details of this tradition will be discussed below,[39] where it will appear that when Philo called this spring and its water Wisdom or the Logos

37. A later work, *Neue Pesikta*, translated by A. Wünsche, *Aus Israels Lehrhallen*, 1910, V, II, 34 (I have translated his German).

38. *MR*, *Song of Songs*, I, 4 (ET, 48).

39. See below, VI, 199.

and Paul called it Christ, each was identifying its mystic flow with his particular name for the source of the fluid of life. Gaining access to this spring, especially in the name of the Water of Marah, or in the Scene at the Well, is what Philo represents as the highest mystic achievement of the Israelites and so for all mankind. It is accordingly curious, as we shall see, that at Dura the triple representation of the Exodus ends in a scene where the Israelites with Moses stand beside a pool of water which Moses is apparently producing with his rod. The spring itself teems with leaping fish. I mentioned this scene in *By Light, Light* [40] and shall return to it. Why the fish should figure thus prominently I did not understand until by chance I read in the *Sifre to Numbers*, one of the very old midrashim, a statement attributed to Akiba, of the end of the first century or beginning of the second. Akiba is explaining a remark made by Moses to God. The Israelites had complained that they were surfeited with manna, and God had promised to help by giving them flesh to eat, a promise later fulfilled by the remarkable flight of quails. Moses was aghast at the idea of providing meat for so large a company and asked (Numbers xi, 22) whether all the fish of the sea were to be collected to satisfy them. Akiba comments:

> Even if you should collect for them all the [fish in the sea would that suffice them? But I say: Have they perhaps murmured because they had no] fish to eat? Indeed a spring was brought out with them into the wilderness which yielded them fat fishes, more than they needed.[41]

Kuhn notes that this legend appears no place else in rabbinic literature, but it seems equally clear in a statement the context of which we shall present shortly,[42] attributed to a "Master":

> When the Israelites were drawing water, the Holy One, blessed be he, prepared for them in the water little fish for their pitchers.

So the fish in the well at Dura are of great importance: first because they connect the Dura well with this mysterious wandering source of life in the desert which had so great a history in Jewish and Christian traditions; and secondly because they show the active notion that the function of the well could be thought of as supplying fish to eat quite as much as supplying water to drink. Indeed from the sacramental point of view we shall come increasingly to feel that the two are variant symbols for the same thing and that to eat the fishes, or the great fish, was a way of taking into oneself the fluid which embodied the life or being of the Savior. The same identification probably lies behind the statement we have already encountered that Leviathan lives over the great well or spring of the sea. An early, if not the earliest, account of the founding of the Christian Eucharist represented the Savior as giving bread and fish to a large company in the waste land beside

40. Page 222.

41. *Sifre to Numbers*, Sec. 95; see the edition with notes, *Sifre zu Numeri*, by J. Winter, H. Windisch, and K. G. Kuhn, 1934, II, 254 (G. Kittel, *Rabbinische Texte*, Ser. II, *Tannaitische Midraschim*).

42. See below, p. 49. The passage is in *BT, Yoma*, 75a (ET, 361).

the Sea of Galilee and then explaining that what was given was his flesh (the bread) and his blood (apparently the fish), a story that makes sense in terms of this body of ideas as in no other way. But it implies that in pre-Christian Jewish circles there was a generally practised fish meal which must have had mystical importance, else the cryptic story in the Gospel of John would have conveyed no meaning. A principle not yet adequately applied in New Testament interpretation, one which would apply also to the interpretation of rabbinic writings, is that a causal allusion implies reference to a generally familiar notion. If the unexplained transition in the Gospel from the eating of fish to the taking and drinking of the blood of Jesus was intelligible at the time, we must assume familiarity with the idea that to eat fish was a sacramental communion with Deity.

Meanwhile we trace the great fish on into Christianity. Tertullian's reference to the little fishes in contrast with the big fish has been clarified, as it appeared to be a ready adaptation of the Jewish conception. The same is true of three other famous Christian passages where the great fish comes into question.[43]

The first of these, the inscription of Abercius, Scheftelowitz quotes. The pertinent part of the inscription reads:

> Everywhere I had companions, Paul. . . . Faith was everywhere my guide and ever laid before me food, the fish from the fountain, the very great, the pure [fish] which the holy Virgin seized. And this she ever gave to the friends to eat(?), having a goodly wine and giving it mixed with water, and bread also.[44]

Scheftelowitz [45] seems to me justified in connecting the "great and pure" fish at the "fountain," whose flesh is given to the faithful in this inscription, with the similar Jewish fish at the fountain, likewise given to the faithful to eat in the rabbinic tradition. His conclusion would have been strengthened if he had also used two other Christian passages, for another inscription, that of Pectorius, from Autun, reads:

> Divine race of the heavenly Fish, keep thy heart holy, since thou hast received among mortals the immortal fountain of divine water. Cheer thy soul, O friend, with the everflowing water of Wisdom, dispenser of riches. Take the honey-sweet food of the Savior of the saints, eat it with desire, holding the Fish in thy hands.
>
> Fill thou (me) with the Fish,—this is my longing, O my Lord and Savior! Soft may my mother sleep, I beseech thee, O light of the dead! Aschandius, my father, beloved of my heart, together with the dear mother and my brothers, in the peace of the Fish remember thy Pectorius.[46]

43. See also Christian material quoted by Ginzberg, *Legends*, V, 45.

44. As translated by Morey in *Princeton Theological Review*, IX (1911), 272. The inscription has been very much discussed. See the review of the literature by Morey here, and by Leclercq in CL, I, 66–87; also *Ichthys*, I, 8–12; 87–112; II, 454–486; V, 218.

45. "Fisch-Symbol," 7.

46. As translated by Morey, 283, who says, "The inscription has been variously dated from the second to the sixth century." See *Ichthys*, I, 12–15; II, 507–515. For a discussion of the text see Otto Pohl, *Das Ichthys-Monument von Autun*, Diss., Berlin, 1880.

The third passage comes from a strange document, half pagan, half Christian in imagery, *Narratio rerum quae in Perside acciderunt*. In the passage in question the Greek Hera is identified with the Virgin and with the fountain. She bears a child who is to be "the beginning and the end." Suddenly, with no reference to anything else in the passage, the statement appears:

> For the fountain of water flows ever with the water of the spirit, having the one and only Fish, taken with the hook of divinity, which feeds the whole world, as if dwelling in the sea, with its own flesh.[47]

All three of these passages are sufficiently obscure in themselves. By stressing the water and fountain, some scholars wanted to make the whole a reference to baptism. Morey seems to me quite right in calling attention to the really central theme in all three —the eating of the fish—and the eucharistic setting. What Morey did not know is that the three passages, with their mystic fountain, gain clarity at last, and only, when we see behind them the Jewish Leviathan in legend and picture which, like the Fish in the *Narratio*, is to be caught by the hook of divinity and given to all men (the pious) to eat. The Christian passages seem to me to be obscure precisely because they are attempts to appropriate this Leviathan from Judaism into Christianity. In Judaism and Christianity alike the Fish, the fountain, and the miraculous fisher are the constants, as well as the saving power of the Fish's pure flesh to those who eat it. The fisher is in the Christian adaptation not the angel Gabriel but the Virgin,[48] and the giving of the flesh has begun with the incarnation, since the Christian Messiah has already come and the Eucharist is available. So the allegories make the awkward fountain now into a suggestion of baptism, now into the flow of water which was to Philo and the early Christians the flow of the Logos. The huge size and ceremonial purity of the fish survives in the inscription of Abercius; [49] the sea survives in the *Narratio*. The Christian fish is certainly the "eucharistic fish," whatever that means, but it is also still the Jewish fish.[50]

C. *THE FISH AS A SACRAMENTAL OR EUCHARISTIC FOOD*

THE QUESTION begins to thrust itself forward: does the parallel not go farther, and was there not a Jewish sacramental fish meal which was the vehicle to carry the fish

47. As translated by Morey, *Princeton Theological Review*, VIII (1910), 428; see pp. 426–429.

48. Whether she is Mary or the Church (for both interpretations have been suggested) is indifferent to us.

49. Eisler, *Orpheus*, 253, also takes this word "pure" to come from the original Jewish conception that Leviathan was kosher.

50. Most discussions of these passages (such as that of *Ichthys*, I, 87–112; II, 454–515) begin where this leaves off—that is, with the Christian adaptations of the basic elements: the great fish itself, the fisherman, the fountain, and the fish meal. The chief collection of inscriptional evidence for the fish as symbol of the saving Christ is that of Leclercq in CL, VII, II, 2012–2045, s.v. ΙΧΘΥΣ. It shows how vital the symbol was in early Christianity. One of the most interesting inscriptions is that of Maritima, which we may translate: "Saint Maritima, you have not left the sweet light, for in all [the contingencies after death] you have with you the immortal Fish; for your piety precedes you everywhere." In the inscription two fish with an anchor between them take the place of the word "fish": a true rebus. See no. 9 in ibid., 2018 f.

symbol on into the new faith? To this the answer must be uncertain. Nothing conclusive indicates a meal with such a meaning in Judaism, but the inconclusive hints at the possibility cannot be dismissed merely with a gesture, as Dölger, we said,[51] thought he could dismiss Scheftelowitz.[52] These hints it will be convenient to marshal.

(a) It is still remembered in Judaism that fish should be eaten of a Friday evening in honor of the Sabbath. The custom is very old, for while it is not actually commanded by the Talmud, it is so mentioned as to make it apparent that the stricter the Jew, the more likely he was to eat fish Friday evening.[53] One delights in the Sabbath by eating beets, fish, and garlic, said the talmudic rabbis: "Even a trifle, if it is prepared in honor of the Sabbath, is a delight. What is it [the trifle]?—Said R. Papa: A pie of fish-hash." [54] Here and elsewhere [55] the Talmud gives us the impression that fish are eaten on the Sabbath to make the day pleasant, to do it honor. This is the current explanation still: it was given to Dölger by what he called "ein einfacher Jude," and Dölger leapt to the conclusion that "in these words lies the whole solution" of the Jewish fish.[56] But those who know the Talmud at all (and the Jews who know it best are quickest to admit it) are aware that the Talmud is a savagely edited document, in which what in Judaism was displeasing to the later rabbis was not only prohibited, but, just as often, ignored or suppressed. The rabbinical statement that the Sabbath fish simply honors the Sabbath has, of course, become proverbial among orthodox Jews, who now know only this explanation of the Friday evening fish. That, however, by no means limits the possible meaning of the fish in the first centuries after Christ. It is interesting that since the end of the Middle Ages, at least, it has been obligatory for the orthodox to have fish, meat, and wine at each of the three chief meals of the Sabbath,[57] and that the three articles were and are important to them.[58]

(b) Really a continuation of the foregoing, but so important that we must mark it by itself, is the much quoted passage of Persius: [59]

51. See above, p. 32.

52. Dölger disposes of Scheftelowitz' evidence without quoting or discussing it: he simply pronounces that the conclusions are absurd. See *Ichthys*, II, 490 f. (n.), 536–544. With less emotion Frey likewise mentions Scheftelowitz, but he also considers none of his evidence. He admits that in talmudic and cabbalistic writings the fish had considerable importance, but then asserts that in the earlier age the fish meal was only a symbol of festivity, a statement for which he has not a particle of evidence. See Frey in *RAC*, VIII (1931), 306–308.

53. The story of R. Joseph in *BT*, *Shabbath*, 119a (ET, II, 586), who bought a fish with a pearl in its belly for the Sabbath evening meal, is so told as to imply that he usually bought a fish for that occasion. See below, p. 44.

54. *BT*, *Shabbath*, 118b (ET, II, 581).

55. See the references in Scheftelowitz, pp. 19–21; also M. Grunwald in *UJE*, IV (1941), 319.

56. Loc. cit., 540 f. In ibid., V, 139–142, he shows evidence that fish in pagan representations also referred to an unusually good meal. To this he returns at great length, pp. 327–610, where he collects a large amount of material for pagan and Christian feasts to show that fish were a symbol of luxury on such occasions. He seems to me to be carried into special pleading by it all when he concludes that the Christian fish meals had at the beginning no eucharistic association or reference.

57. *Shulchan Aruch*, Orach Chajim, 250–252 (GT, I, 47).

58. Abrahams, *Jewish Life*, 100, 166.

59. *Satire*, v, 180–184.

> But when Herod's birthday is come, and the lamps, put in the greasy windows along with violets, emit their unctuous clouds of smoke; and when the tail of a tunny floats curled round in a red dish, and the white jar is bulging with wine, you move your lips in silence and turn pale at the circumcised Sabbath.

Whether the tunny's tail here indicates a fish meal or a ceremonial accompaniment of other food on the red dish, and whether the meal happens only on Herod's birthday or regularly on the Sabbath, cannot be concluded from Persius' confused statement. But all scholars have connected the passage with the *cena pura* of the Jews, the meaning of which term has been very widely discussed [60] and still presents difficulties. In Judaism the approach of the Sabbath or of a Festival is attended with careful preparation, so that in Greek the day before the Sabbath was specifically named the *paraskeuē*, "preparation," or "the day of preparation." [61] This preparation must have consisted primarily of a meal, for in Latin translations the Greek word was rendered directly by *cena pura*, which can only have meant "pure supper," for in Latin *cena* was a dignified word for an evening meal. Tertullian lists the *cena pura* among Jewish Festivals along with the Sabbath, the ceremonies of the lamps, fasts of unleavened bread, and the "littoral prayers." [62] The term was generally used but came to mean especially the Sabbath-evening (Friday evening) meal, the most important single meal of the week.

But why was it *pura?* Schürer [63] and Dölger [64] protest that the reference could not be to "kosher," since every meal of a Jew was kosher. They insist that somehow, anyhow, the word must have meant "festal," an interpretation which ties in well with the "festal supper" of the Jews on Friday night from then to the present. But Bacher was not satisfied with thus ignoring the meaning of the word *pura* itself. He suggested, as a possibility: "The Roman Jews indicated with the epithet '*pura*' the holiness and consecration of this festal meal, in contrast to the luxurious character of meals, often degenerating into debauchery, as they were conducted in imperial Rome." [65] This is a step in the right direction, for it at least tries honestly to recognize the word *pura* itself. Bacher appears, however, to suggest a strange motive for the adjective. The Jews, it seems to me, would much more likely have called their festival *pura* because of something distinctive in the Sabbath evening meal. They must, if they spoke Latin, have used the word *cena* for all their own daily evening meals, and we should most naturally assume that it was in contrast to their own ordinary suppers, not to those of the Romans, that they would have named their Sabbath Eve meal.

Now there are several ways one can think of in which *pura* may have suggested itself to the Jews: First, the Roman Jews may have found it extremely difficult to keep strictly kosher all the time, and have made this meal kosher by special effort. Secondly, the meal may have been kosher par excellence, as Good Friday is the *good* Friday par excellence,

60. See esp. W. Bacher, "Cena pura," *ZNW*, VI (1905), 200–202; *Ichthys*, II, 536–544. The most important passages are all quoted by Dölger.

61. Mark xv, 42; Luke xxiii, 54; John xix, 14, 31.

62. Tertullian, *Ad nationes*, I, xiii.

63. In *ZNW*, VI (1905), 8, n. 1.

64. *Ichthys*, II, 536–544.

65. Op. cit., 201 f.

not because all other Fridays are bad; it is the especially good Friday. The Day of Atonement does not mean to the Jew that atonement is possible only on that day. Similarly Jews have always made great point that their food must be kosher: it is not at all impossible that the Jews may have called their most important festal meal of the Sabbath evening the "kosher supper," meaning the supper which is kosher par excellence. Thirdly, the word may have referred to some article of food eaten at that meal, which was "pure" in some sense so important that it gave its name to the whole meal, made it kosher in a special sense.

This brings us back to the one distinctive thing which, we know from both rabbinic and pagan testimony, was eaten at that meal, namely the fish. Rabbinic sources have let us see that casually as the fish is mentioned, people were regarded as especially praiseworthy in the eyes of God if they, at any cost, got fish for sacred occasions. The story of R. Joseph has already been mentioned.[66] It tells how a rich gentile was warned that R. Joseph, who honored the Sabbath, would some day eat up all his possessions. To safeguard himself the gentile sold all he had and bought a single pearl. Unfortunately he then lost that pearl in a lake. A fish swallowed it, which was later caught and sold to Joseph, "who honored the Sabbath," we understand, by eating fish at the Friday evening meal. Joseph found the pearl in the fish and sold it for a fortune. The moral of the story is pointed out: "He who lends to the Sabbath is repaid by the Sabbath."

The story reminds us of the Christian parable of the "pearl of great price," and all the more so as a second story brings out the same moral: [67]

> A pious man in Rome held the Sabbaths and festal days much in honor. On the eve of the Day of Atonement he went to the market to buy something, but found only a fish, which the servant of the prefect also wanted to buy. They bid against each other, until finally the Jew got the fish, but at a gold denarius per pound. When the prefect, at dinner, heard why no fish came to the table he had the Jew, who he presumed was wealthy, called before him. The Jew came, and represented himself as a tailor.
>
> "And a tailor eats fish at a gold denarius per pound?"
>
> "My lord, permit me to speak!"
>
> "Speak," said the prefect.
>
> "We have a day which is more precious to us than all days of the year. All the sins which we have committed during the whole year are forgiven us on this day. Therefore we honor this day more than all the days of the year."
>
> Then said the prefect: "You have justified yourself and are free."
>
> How did God repay the man who thus honored the Festival? He had him find a valuable pearl in the fish, from the sale of which he supported himself the rest of his life.

66. See above, p. 42. n. 53; from *BT*, *Shabbath*, 119a (ET, II, 586). The story was very popular, for it is found in the Yiddish collection of haggadoth, *Ma'aseh Book:* see the translation by Moses Gaster, 1934, I, 9, no. 6.

67. The story is translated as told by W. Bacher in *Die Agada der palästinensischen Amoräer*, III, 339 f. It is retold in abbreviated form in a fragment published by M. Gaster, *The Exempla of the Rabbis*, 1924, 81, no. 118.

The Jewish gold-glass fragments, which depict a banquet bolster with a table on which a fish is ready for eating, have generally and I think correctly, though with no evidence whatever, been taken to represent the cena pura, the Friday evening meal, or the formal meal before a Festival, at which fish was eaten.[68] I am sure that the cena pura was pre-eminently a fish meal and that the distinctive food, fish, and the distinctive name, *pura*, went together. For this I have no more evidence than exists for the general identifying of the gold-glass fish with the cena pura—that is, none at all. But for some reason entirely lost the great fish which was to be eaten in the Messianic Age, the fish which until then lives over the fountain of the ocean, was especially said to be "pure," though if Gabriel was to give it to the Jews to eat, that might have been assumed. It was not assumed. And in Christian tradition the fish, which is still properly Friday's food, is eaten, we know not why, as a specially pure food appropriate for holy days.[69]

A custom from the later Hasidim, as told by Buber, is in point, since this group preserved many ancient traditions otherwise lost. Buber says that at the end of the eighteenth century in Poland, at the third meal of the Sabbath, only one course was served and that was fish. The custom, he says, was regarded as a "mystery," and the local explanation was that "the souls of the righteous who have not yet completed their pilgrimage enter into fish." When one eats such a fish piously the soul within it is redeemed. But there was also a tradition that a "higher soul" comes into every devout Jew when the Sabbath begins, and remains with him all through the Sabbath. So the souls in the fish have a "holy communion, before, at the end of the Sabbath, they wing their way back to Heaven." [70] Buber also tells how, when at this meal the rabbi desired to honor one of those present, he sent him a piece of fish from his own plate, which constituted what Buber calls a "special meal shared with the Rabbi." [71] The distinctive power of fish is again represented in Jewish antiquity by the story of Tobias, who took a fish at the command of Raphael and with its viscera first killed a demon and then healed his father's blindness. We have no Jewish Tobias in the art of the Greco-Roman period, but the survival of three fishes on Christian gold glasses suggests that there was real significance in the fish's power to kill demons and give light to darkness, both of them ways of expressing the victory over death which it is usual to associate with these glasses as eucharistic vessels.[72] It seems to me

68. For example by Dölger, *Ichthys*, II, 536–544.

69. The association of fish in Christian tradition is, of course, with asceticism. The Christian is not required to eat fish. The definite command is to avoid meat on a fast day, and fish is accepted as the traditional substitute. I am only suggesting in what I say above that this present "explanation" may not at all exhaust the "value" in the Christian's fish of a Friday, or account for the origin of the custom.

70. Martin Buber, *For the Sake of Heaven*, 1945, 40.

71. Ibid., 41. See also a mysterious story of the purchase of fish in ibid., 51, a story which seems to have little point except to heighten, in some way, the "mystery" of the fish. A haggada in which the importance of honoring the Sabbath is brought out in various ways ends: "Therefore a man should honor the Sabbath in the very best way he can, with good fish and good meat and good wine. And God will repay him more than double. Moreover he will also merit the second soul and be able to rest": M. Gaster, *Ma'aseh Book*, I, 306.

72. Tobit VI, VIII, and XI. For the gold glasses see R. Garrucci, *Vetri ornati di figure in oro*, 1858, plate III, 4–6.

significant that Tobias, after taking out the gall, heart, and liver, "roasted part of the fish and did eat, and left part thereof salted." [73]

The evidence forms no chain but presents itself as a series of arrows all apparently pointing in one direction. Jews ate "pure" fish, a big fish (the tunny is the biggest edible fish commonly caught), at a meal called the "pure supper." To get it they were ready to make great sacrifice, and their sense of God's reward for doing so was expressed in the tradition that they found the pearl of great price in the fish. That is, I think there is more reason than Scheftelowitz himself made clear for believing that on Friday night and other sacred times the Jews ate a fish meal, ate it with bread and wine (as Persius and the art suggests and as the kiddush on Friday night still perpetuates), and that this fish meal prefigured the messianic meal, which itself was the symbol of the hope of immortality, the same hope as that which the "pearl of great price" still represents in Christianity.[74]

The Jewish meal of immortality appears also in a talmudic story of a rabbi and his wife who were poor to the point of starvation:

> Once his wife said to him: "How long shall we go on suffering so much?" He replied: "What shall we do?" "Pray that something may be given to you," [she replied]. He prayed and there emerged the figure of a hand reaching out to him a leg of a golden table. Thereupon he saw in a dream that the pious would one day eat at a three-legged golden table but he would eat at a two-legged table. Her husband said to her: "Are you content that everybody shall eat at a perfect table and we at an imperfect table?" She replied: "What then shall we do?—Pray that the leg be taken from you." He prayed and it was taken away.[75]

The reference can be only to the figure of the meal at the Judgment which typified immortality to pagans and Christians and, as the meal of Leviathan, also to Jews. Upon this three-legged table in pagan and Christian funerary art a fish was ordinarily found.[76] In the two fragments of gold glass discussed above where the table with the fish is preserved in Jewish remains, the one glass [77] is so broken that no legs are left on the table, but the other shows a three-legged table.[78] The convention is clear. The impoverished rabbi and his wife had rather starve in this life than be unable to have a perfect tripod for the meal of immortality in the next life. The tripod, we must conclude, was as proverbial in Judaism as in paganism and Christianity. Hence, in spite of the fact that Scheftelowitz' evidence by no means supports his conclusion, it seems quite likely that the rabbi and his wife hoped not only that they might have a tripod with the meal of immortality on it,

73. Tobit VI, 6. See above, II, 163 f.

74. On immortality in talmudic writings as a banquet see *BT*, *Shabbath*, 153a (ET, II, 781 f.); *Aboth*, IV, 16 (ET, 53). In the latter passage the word in Hebrew is the Latin *triclinium*, which at once suggests the "bolster" of the Jewish gold glass.

75. *BT*, *Taanith*, 25a (ET, 128 f.). See Scheftelowitz, "Fisch-Symbol," 22.

76. Sufficient evidence will be found in *Ichthys*, IV, plates 236, 240, 242, 246 (bis), 251 f., 259, 263 (bis).

77. See above, III, fig. 973; cf. II, 112.

78. See III, fig. 974; cf. II, 112. It has curious diagonal braces for each leg, so that at first it is not apparent that the table is actually a tripod.

but that upon the tripod, as in pagan, Christian, and Jewish representations, would be a fish to eat. Please God the rabbi and his wife were not disappointed.

D. THE FISH AS A SYMBOL OF THE HOPE OF IMMORTALITY

THE FISH in Christianity as the symbol of immortality is beginning to emerge as possibly having its prototype in the Jewish fish and to be connected with the fish meal of the cena pura.[79] More specific material for this connection is found first in the cabbalistic *Zohar*, a late work, indeed, but one which, as has long been recognized and we shall increasingly see, has preserved from the early period much of the Judaism of nonrabbinic Jews which rabbis saw fit to suppress. In the *Zohar* [80] the fish, by comparison with the one which swallowed Jonah, was taken to represent the grave and resurrection. The story of Jonah is elaborately allegorized, so that Jonah's going into the ship represents that descent of the soul into the body which was ultimately "Orphic" in origin. The tempest that struck the ship is the summons to heavenly judgment for the sinful acts which result from this combination of soul and body, and all struggle against it is vain. So the soul is cast out into the sea, the grave, the place of judgment. "For the fish that swallowed him is, in fact, the grave." Here he stays through putrefaction and its horrors. After thirty days the soul leaves the body to continue decomposing

> until the time when the Holy One, blessed be he, will awaken the dead. . . . It is of that occasion that it is written: "And the Lord spoke unto the fish, and it vomited out Jonah upon the dry land"; for as soon as that voice will resound among the graves they will all cast out the dead bodies that they contain.

This is not true of all the dead, for

> some of them will rise and others will not. Happy is the portion of Israel, of whom it is written, "My dead bodies shall arise." Thus in the narrative of that fish we find words of healing for the whole world. . . . In a similar way the Land of Israel will in the future first be stirred to new life, and afterwards "the earth will cast forth the dead."

If this allegory of the fish of Jonah is old, it is quite possible that a Jewish Jonah existed in art as an antetype to the Jonah so early and commonly found on Christian

79. The best work in early Christian archeology has been done by Catholics, whose great learning in the field gives a totally undeserved importance to some of their judgments. So in discussing the Christian dolphin with trident, Frey, without either preparation or later justification, asserts: "And thus is solved another question, that of the derivation of the Christian fish, and more precisely of the dolphin with trident, from Jewish art. Such a derivation does not exist, and I add that the Christian symbols do not even derive from analogous classical representations": *RAC*, VIII (1931), 309 f. Apparently to justify this statement Frey goes on to show that the Christians made early use of the fish as metaphor in writing and as symbol in art; but he seems quite unaware that this has no relevance whatever to his assertion that the Christian fish was derived from neither Jews nor pagans. The a priori behind such writing is that what is early in Christianity must have come by revelation, not derivation, a premise which eliminates all scientific approach to the problem.

80. *Zohar*, Vayaqhel (Exodus), 199a, b (ET, IV, 173–176). See Scheftelowitz, p. 10.

graves. Indeed one amulet, possibly two, showing Jonah and the fish [81] seems more probably Jewish than Christian, and with exactly this value of giving immortality. Scheftelowitz sees a continuity between these statements in the *Zohar*, especially its speculation about the three days in the fish's belly,[82] and the prophecy of Jesus' resurrection put into the mouth of Jesus himself [83] in terms of Jonah. This continuity he supposes was within a very old Jewish tradition which Christians took over for Jesus but which survived to the *Zohar* in Judaism itself. This seems to me, while wholly undemonstrable, by no means improbable. From some source the story of Jesus' empty tomb came very strongly to emphasize the detail that Jesus was there only three days, and nothing which we know is more likely to have suggested this than an already established allegory that the three days of Jonah in the fish's belly, followed by his release, symbolized the resurrection from the dead. Be that as it may, we are at least beginning to see that the fish on the grave may have had much the same background in Jewish symbolism as in Christian. That is, it may have suggested a meal of immortality, a hope of immortality as symbolized in the cena pura, with its fish (and wine). Jews ate the fish in expectation and symbol of the great heavenly banquet, which pagans and Christians also used to represent the future bliss.[84] Hamburger has collected an interesting mass of material to show the importance of the messianic meal in Judaism and in early Christianity, especially in parables of the kingdom. The meal in both religions has striking similarities.[85] He insists that these hopes are only figurative and that Jews did not expect literally to eat in the future world. This we may allow while we suggest that the Christian Eucharist, which was from the first an anticipation of the Christian heavenly meal as specified in the very words of the institution, was itself a literal meal looking toward the future immaterial reality. So the Jews may well have had an actual fish meal which lay behind their hope of a future fish meal in some spiritual sense. The continuity of symbolism of the fish meal from paganism to Judaism and to Christianity strongly suggests the continuity of a value with the symbol, or even a rite. Such a meal could have been carried over into Judaism and Christianity only on condition that it could be reinterpreted to give it first Jewish, then Christian, meaning. Whether such a Jewish meal was the source of the Christian Eucharist or whether the Eucharist, arising from other sources, only later came to use the Jewish fish symbol is a question the answer to which, in the total lack of evidence, will depend upon our preconceptions. We may notice [86] that the fish meal persisted into Islam as a symbol of immortality. The Jews themselves seem to me to have been enriching the fish symbol with *ex post facto* interpretation when in later writings they joined it with the zodiacal Pisces,

81. See above, II, 225–227; III, figs. 1042 f.

82. I have omitted this in summarizing the passage.

83. Matt. XVI, 4.

84. The soul which falls and is received in the water by divinities may be suggested on a pagan gem, which represents, in a setting of the zodiac and other astral symbols, the fall of Phaethon. Phaethon falls into the water between a god of the sea and a swan. See Max Sommerville, *Engraved Gems*, 1889, 361. Lehmann has suggested that this Phaethon gem may have had a Mithraic association: see Friedrich Behn, *Das Mithrasheiligtum zu Dieburg*, 1928, 16–22 (Römisch-germanische Forschungen, I).

85. Hamburger, *RE*, II, 1312–1315.

86. With Scheftelowitz, "Fisch-Symbol," 38, n. 3.

in ascendance in the month of Adar, the last month of the Jewish year and so, they said, the symbol of the last age, that of the Messiah.[87]

At the same time the explanation which makes the fish a fertility symbol may go far back.[88] For as Scheftelowitz points out,[89] not only was it associated with the various *deae matres*, who were all originally sources of fertility: as a symbol connected with the mystery of the Thracian Rider also it probably had old fertility significance.

Eisler has collected interesting material on this from Judaism.[90] An important passage is a statement by R. Bar-Kappara that a maiden should be married on the fourth day of the week and that intercourse should take place on the fifth day because on that day the blessing for fishes was pronounced.[91]

Still more important is a very confused discussion in the Talmud [92] which must be quoted at length:

> *We remember the fish which we were wont to eat in Egypt for nought.* Rab and Samuel [were disputing its meaning], one said: [Fish here means] real fish; the other said: Illicit intercourse. One who said it means real fish [explains it so because of] "*which we were wont to eat*"; the other who interprets it as "illicit intercourse," does so because the term "*for nought*" is used. But according to him who said it means "intercourse," does not Scripture read: "*Which we were wont to eat*"?—Scripture uses an euphemism, as it is written: *She eateth and wipeth her mouth and saith: I have done no wickedness.* What does "*for nought*" mean according to him who says they were real fish?—They were brought to them from public property, for a Master taught: When the Israelites were drawing water, the Holy One, blessed be he, prepared for them in the water little fish for their pitchers. According to him who said "real fish," but with regard to illicit intercourse [he holds] they were not dissolute, it will be quite right that Scripture said: *A garden shut up is my sister*, etc. but according to the view that fishes mean "illicit intercourse," what "*fountain sealed*" is here? —They were not dissolute with regard to forbidden relations. It will be right according to him who interprets it as "illicit intercourse," hence Scripture said: *And Moses heard the people weeping for their families*, i.e., because of the families [relations] with whom they were forbidden to have intercourse; but according to him who interprets it as "fish," what does "*weeping for their families*" mean?—Both are implied.

From this passage we may draw two inferences. First, fish were proverbially a symbol of intercourse for the rabbis, and are here "forbidden intercourse" because it is the fish of Egypt which are mentioned in the proof text. The discussion of the text with this Egyptian element gets so involved that it can end only in a question mark. Secondly the baraita of a "Master" is quite independent, namely the tradition that when the Israelites were drawing

87. Ibid., 47 f.

88. Ibid., 376–382. Probably the idea is implicit in Hab. I, 14, and the rabbis so interpreted the דגו, of Gen. XLVIII, 16; see Scheftelowitz, "Fisch-Symbol," 376.

89. Ibid., 378–380.

90. See Scheftelowitz, p. 377, and Eisler, "Fisch," 175 f.

91. *BT*, *Kethuboth*, 5a (ET, I, 15).

92. *BT*, *Yoma*, 75a (ET, 361 f.).

water, God prepared little fishes for them to draw out with the water in their pitchers, a statement we have already discussed.[93]

In both interpretations of the fish in the talmudic passage, whether as real fish or as intercourse, the symbolism of the fish seems to be that of life, in the sense of the life produced in intercourse or of the higher life given men in the extraordinary spring of water.

The association of the fish with fertility continued late in Jewish life. Polish Jews celebrated a hymeneal banquet up to the sixteenth century which was called the "fish meal" because fish was the most important food included.[94] Fish played an important part in marriage celebrations of Jews in Morocco, where the seventh day of the seven-day wedding feast is called the "fish day" because then the groom sends the bride a lot of fish which she has her mother or some other woman throw at his feet. Eisler presumes that the fish are then eaten, though there is no report of this.[95] The sephardic Jews in Sarajevo in Bosnia have a "customary fish dance" at betrothal ceremonies. After the exchange of rings the relatives come one after another before the bride and lay at her feet one or more fish whose heads are decorated with flowers, their bellies with tinsel. She must hop over each fish. The report ends by saying that this custom is strictly observed and that it "symbolizes the desire for fertility." [96] The guess that the Jewesses of North Africa wear fish amulets for a similar purpose [97] is by no means without foundation. But the life produced by begetting and birth and the life which we desire after death are in our emotions very close, to the point that having a family has often replaced all desire for personal immortality, as it seems to have done for Jews throughout what we call the Old Testament period. In the Roman period, and probably before it, desire for personal immortality obviously came again strongly to the fore.

E. THE FISH MEAL

IN ALL OF this material, accordingly, I see as the really basic continuity a meal the value of which was that it gave life and was pre-eminently a foretaste and guarantee of immortality; so it was figuratively represented as a heavenly banquet in paganism, Judaism, and Christianity alike. Why always, in all of these, does the meal consist primarily of fish? This the evidence does not explain, but the very repetition of so arbitrary a symbol powerfully suggests a lineal continuity of the symbol, even of a rite, from one milieu to the next. We lack the pagan explanations, though we have abundant instances of the symbol itself in paganism. The Jewish explanations are of course Jewish, and the Christian explanations are Christian—but in both the faithful are little fishes and the Savior is, or is related to, the big fish.

93. See above, p. 39.

94. Eisler, loc. cit., infers from *Semahoth*, 8 and 14, that fish were similarly at the bridal banquet in much earlier times, but this passage refers to usage of fish and other articles of food with the dead.

95. Loc. cit.; Scheftelowitz, p. 377.

96. Eisler, "Fisch," 184. On p. 189 he refers to a custom among the same Jews of having the bride step over a fish net and gives abundant evidence to suggest that to catch a fish in the net symbolized becoming pregnant. On fish meals in marriage, see Schauss, *Lifetime*, 178, 218.

97. See above, p. 22.

Dölger's [98] protest against this point of view is entirely an emotional one. Leviathan could not have been an antetype of the Christian *Ichthys*, he argues, because Leviathan is in the Bible an evil monster—which completely ignores the fact that in the talmudic writings this terrible monster becomes a source of special messianic food. Dölger feels that the *cena dominica* of Christianity was developed in *contrast* to the cena pura of the Jews and that if so, "it is quite possible that the Christians contrasted Christ, the food of the Eucharist, as the true mystic fish, with the actual fish of the *cena pura*." In preparation for this, ignoring, as we have indicated, all the evidence of Scheftelowitz, he has asserted that the cena pura was simply the "splendid" meal. But even so he gives himself away, for in the very contrast which he suggests there was definite continuity: the contrast was not in the fish itself, which was a constant from the one religion to the other, but in the explanation of, the name given to, the fish. Dölger parallels Paul's "cup of blessing," [99] which is in contrast with the "cup of blessing" of the kiddush, and Christ the Lamb of God, who is in contrast to the Paschal Lamb.[100] All of these "contrasts" of Dölger and of the early Christians were, it must be apparent, only reinterpretations of symbols held over from the one religion into the other, from Judaism into Christianity, and strengthen my argument that the new grew out of the old largely by reinterpretation, by new explanations of old symbols which kept their original value throughout. Did the Jew eat the fish at that time (as in some explanations he still does) as a symbol of Leviathan and the meal of immortality in the Messianic Age? Positive proof, let me repeat, has not been adduced. But Dölger's insistence that the Jewish cena pura was simply an unusually good meal leaves utterly unexplained the fish on the gold glass and in the synagogues and graves. As he interprets the Jewish fish it would correspond to the American turkey, the food canonized from long tradition for Thanksgiving Day, Christmas, and any other especially festive American meal. But we do not put the turkey on our graves, nor indicate it, along with the most holy symbols of our religion, upon anything comparable to the ancient gold glass. Dölger has quite failed to take this material seriously (he knew, in fact, but a fraction of it), and so he could all the more readily reject a misrepresented Scheftelowitz.

Another dimension in the term is suggested by the Hermetic tract *Asclepius*, a highly mystical document ending in a prayer which Festugière says "contains the ordinary themes of Hermetic gnosticism." [101] That is, it is a prayer to the hermaphroditic God of Life, himself eternally pregnant, asking that we may be kept in his love. But the last sentence reads: "After making this prayer we turn to a *coena pura*, one without the flesh of animals." [102] Festugière has a number of references in which we learn that such vegetarianism was suggestive of Pythagoreanism. But we are at once arrested by the fact that here the mystic meal was a cena pura, and this, I suspect, was the meaning in all we have been discussing. For although the Hermetics celebrating the mystic meal had it consist of Pythagorean vegetables and the Jews had a fish, both meals seem to reflect the desire for

98. *Ichthys*, II, 536–544; cf. 490 f.

99. I Cor. x, 16.

100. I Cor. v, 7.

101. *Asclepius*, 41. See NF, II, 401; cf. 355, n. 359.

102. The prayer is quoted below, VI, 86. Much will be said of hermaphroditism in this volume and those following.

spiritual impregnation and, with this, spiritual rebirth or revival. Since the Jews have borrowed so much from the Greeks, I strongly suspect that they borrowed this mystic term along with the fish meal itself and that in doing so they consciously compared their meal with the mystic meals of the pagans. Again we have a hint that the Jews of the Greco-Roman world really celebrated a meal which was to them a mystic meal—that is, a sacrament of divine participation.

The Jewish material on the fish taken together, then, and set in its place among the other symbols, suggests very strongly that the fish meal was a fact and that it had come into Judaism as something of great significance. It had come into Judaism itself, clearly, from the outside, and to account for it, to justify what it meant to them, the Jews had reinterpreted passages in the Bible about Leviathan so that the slaying of the great fish, the drawing out of its tongue with a rope, was a messianic portent, and the eating of it was the supreme blessing. In reverse the fish was itself the grave, and the symbol, as Jonah had been, of resurrection. None of this literary material comes from the Jews who made the gold glass and put the fish on their graves and synagogues. But in view of the ways in which we have seen the fish, dolphin, and goat fish represented in Jewish archeological remains, it is hard to believe that the fish which was eaten did not represent to the Jews of the period a mystic sharing in the divine power which would be fully manifest in the Messianic Age and in which each loyal Jew hoped for resurrection and future life. Christians continued the meal and the symbol—certainly the symbol—to express the same hope and faith. They too, like the Jews, were little fishes, although they swam not in the Law but in the water of baptism, in Christ.[103] Similarly, they but changed the name, made Ichthys mean their particular Savior, to justify their taking the fish with them to the grave and to heaven.

At the relation of the Eucharist to the fish and to this material in general we can only guess. The problem is that according to the tradition of Paul and the Synoptics the Eucharist goes back to an institution of bread and wine by Jesus at the Last Supper. Yet the Synoptics tell the story of the multiplication of the loaves and the fishes, a miracle which in the Fourth Gospel [104] is the institution or figure of the Eucharist, in that Gospel to the exclusion of any reference to its institution at the Last Supper. The incident in which Jesus after his resurrection offers fish and bread to the disciples, as told in an appendix to that Gospel,[105] seems another legend of the institution of the Eucharist in terms of fish and bread. Further, the art and later literary tradition in Christianity, as Morey's article shows, present fish, bread, and wine—all three—as the symbols of the Eucharist. These contrasting suggestions may perhaps be harmonized if we suppose that the earliest Christian Eucharist was a development (a contrast if Dölger prefers) from the Jewish cena pura, which originally used, as the evening meal of the Jewish Sabbath still does, all three: fish, bread, and wine. By this the Christian Eucharist proper came into

103. I am paraphrasing the famous statement, quoted above, p. 32, of Tertullian, *De baptismo*, 1: "Sed nos pisciculi secundum ΙΧΘΥΝ nostrum Jesum Christum in aqua nascimur, nec aliter quam in aqua permanendo salvi sumus."

104. John VI, 1–59.

105. John XXI, 9–13.

being as the Christians gave new and specifically Christian interpretation to the elements of the meal. All three, bread, wine, and fish, became Christ. It was Paul who "received of the Lord," presumably in a revelation,[106] that the bread and wine were especially marked out by Jesus at the Last Cena, and it was the Pauline Eucharist which, in some way we shall probably never be able to trace, became dominant, and as it did so displaced the fish. Still the fish lingered on long in Christian symbolism. It continued to represent immortality, as it had for Jews and probably many pagan cults; as such it could survive especially on Christian graves. Its connection with water early suggested allegorizing the fish in terms of the flow of Logos and Sophia, of Light, in the Christian baptism. The *pisciculi* who live now, according to Tertullian, in the water of baptism are an easy adaptation from the Jewish *pisciculi* who live in the Law. And of course the great messianic fish of Judaism became Christ for the Christians. The point is that the symbol, the thing, the fish itself, seems to have come into Christianity so early that it could suggest the stories of the miraculous multiplication of fishes in the Synoptics, and that the constant throughout was not explanation but the fish itself, given men to eat. The same constant appears in the consecutive usage of fish in Jewish Sabbath evening meals and in Jewish, then Christian,[107] symbolic representations in art. The obvious, and only plausible, hypothesis to cover these scattered facts is that the Christian fish and the Jewish fish had the same value and that it was from Judaism that Christians got the symbol which, never fully appropriate, they had by the fifth century largely dropped even from their art.

Even if this be granted, however, one cannot read Christian symbolism too readily back into Judaism. But we have seen at least striking suggestions that the Christians from the very beginning took the symbol over because in Judaism the fish was at least associated with the Messiah, if it was not the Messiah himself, and was certainly the food of the Messianic Age, the life-giving hope of immortality. Christians, we know, were everywhere telling men that the Jewish Messiah, who was to bring men life and hope, had already come in the person of Jesus. If the Jewish messianic fish whose flesh all were to eat was a current conception and was prefigured in the Friday night fish meal, it is not surprising that Christians should have identified Jesus with that fish; nor is it surprising that after they had indicated this identification by the famous acrostic, they soon forgot the fish's Jewish origin. Yet Jews still eat the fish of a Friday night and at Seder: they too have forgotten the fish's meaning; but, as with all good religious symbols and acts, it is the deed, the thing, that matters, not the explanations. Catholics and Jews still stand together to buy fish of a Friday, though neither knows what the eating of fish meant sixteen hundred years ago.

106. A. D. Nock, "Hellenistic Mysteries and Christian Sacraments," *Mnemosyne*, Ser. IV, Vol. V (1952), 193, said, "certainly Paul's account of the Last Supper was what he had been taught by early disciples." Since Paul denied that he had received anything from them, and says directly that he received this "from the Lord," the certainty of Nock is strange to say the least.

107. I cannot see any point in arguing that since the Christian usages of the fish are in some cases earlier than any we have found in Judaism, we must follow that time sequence for history. The discoveries of archeology are too random for anyone to argue that the earliest Jewish fish we have found is the earliest case where Jews used it.

F. SYMBOLS APPEARING WITH THE FISH

THE FISH scenes in Jewish art themselves have more that is interesting to tell us. Perhaps enough has been said of the identity of design of the Jewish cena pura with the Christian eucharistic presentations, and the pagan representations of the meal of immortality. But the other scenes, which have always been treated separately, show combinations from a fixed vocabulary of emblems to a degree never yet pointed out. The simplest is that of the stone fragment from Acrae,[108] where what we have of the design shows "round objects" which are presumably bread, a wine jar, a fish, two ducks or geese, and a palm tree with pendant fruit. This is the complete vocabulary of what we may call the fish groups of symbols. The group reappears, incompletely, in a painting in the Catacomb Vigna Randanini. Here, as was pointed out,[109] is a band with eight compartments. Four show baskets of bread, two show ducks, and two show fishes. Wine is represented by the goddess in the center, a goddess of life who as such bears the cornucopia; she pours a libation of wine. At Hammam Lif [110] are two great fish, one actually a dolphin, being "drawn out with a fish hook," or with their "tongues pressed down with a cord," as Job [111] said was to happen to Leviathan. Beside the fish, as before, stand two ducks, and a wheel which seems to have its own line of tradition and which here perhaps meant bread, as we shall see. The whole is directed toward the Elysian Fields and drawn above a mystic scene of a fountain. The fountain is identified with the chalice (kiddush or the wine), while the birds beside it, the peacocks, and the trees of life—again palm trees with pendant fruit—show that the fountain represents the Fountain of Life or immortality. Leviathan has become the fish above the Fountain of Life. So the vocabulary continues basically unchanged, presumably because of a recognized symbolism.

The group partially reappears on the wall of a Roman catacomb, where the fish stands beside two large palm trees.[112] The fish is shown at Beth Alpha [113] with the wine symbol—a bunch of grapes—and is here drawn with its tongue out. The fish on the lamp with the two "eyes" recall the statement quoted that Jews are little fishes because the evil eye cannot hurt them.[114]

The Jewish use of fish in art, far from being arbitrary, then, appears to follow a definite pattern which, as far as we can explain it at all, is reflected in the talmudic tradition. To the ducks in this tradition we shall return in a later volume, where they also will be discussed as symbols of immortality.

It is interesting that only parts of this vocabulary went over into Christianity. Leclercq published several designs in which the fish appears with a bird. I show only two,

108. See above, p. 5.
109. Above, p. 9.
110. Above, p. 4.
111. Job XL, 25; XLI, 1.
112. Above, p. 5.
113. Above, p. 4.
114. Above, p. 7. The identification of fish and wine in III, fig. 376, although not certainly Jewish, expresses the same idea.

figs. 45[115] and 46.[116] But I have found the fish with a duck in only one of his examples, a Christian lamp, fig. 44.[117] Lehmann has suggested that the lamp may actually be a Jewish piece. Why the fish here eats the duck, if that is what is represented, I cannot say. In this type of symbolic art the one who is saved, the antelope or the hare, is often being devoured by the savior, the lion, or the eagle, as we shall frequently notice in later volumes. As a matter of fact it may be that the fish is here not eating the duck, but that the duck was simply put in the small space because it belonged with such a fish. In Christian symbolism the duck seems to have been replaced by the dove.[118]

Of the fish above the chalice I find two Christian instances, one of which is the lamp shown in fig. 50.[119] While nothing in this Christian lamp suggests a fountain, as does the Hammam Lif chalice, it is noteworthy that both cups have a gadrooned lower half and both have a peculiar round ball at the bottom which would make it impossible for the vase to rest upon anything. This is explained, perhaps, by the Jewish chalice, which has a base attached beneath the ball. The Christian chalice would seem to be an abbreviation of some such chalice as appears in the Jewish picture. The Christian fish with it may well mean the fish above the "Fountain," since, as we have seen, the Christians appropriated that convention. The same interpretation is possible for the mosaic from San Vitale at Ravenna in fig. 52,[120] where we see two of a band of portraits of saints on the intrados of an arch. At each end is a chalice which does not have the peculiar base of the two we have been discussing but is a cup upon a stand, and is flanked by doves like the Jewish cup. Above it are the saints, each with a pair of dolphins and a scallop shell of mystic birth and immortality, as we shall understand it in the next volume. The saints whose memory the mosaic celebrates, and who are depicted in wreaths above all these objects, are indeed marked as having achieved eternal life. The simpler representation of fish with grapes appears in fig. 51,[121] where the fishes, since they face in two directions, are the Pisces of the zodiac; but one of them eats a wafer, the other grapes, an explicit representation of the Eucharist.

115. From Edmond Le Blant, *Nouveau recueil des inscriptions chrétiennes de la Gaule*, 1892, 156. Cf. Leclercq in CL, VII, 2044. It is a fragment of an inscription found at Saint Romain-d'Albon, dated A.D. 631, last reported in the Girard Collection.

116. From de Rossi in *BAC*, Ser. II, Vol. VI (1875), plate XII, 3*a;* cf. p. 168. It is a graffito painted in red on top of a stone dedicated to three martyrs. The inscription itself is incised, but there seems to be no question of the antiquity of the graffito. It was found at Ain Regada, in North Africa. See Leclercq in CL, VII, 2046, and fig. 6079, col. 2044.

117. From de Rossi, Ser. II, Vol. I (1870), plate IV, 9. He discussed it in Ser. I, Vol. V (1867), 88 f. It was then in the possession of Baron Visconti, its origin unrecorded. Cf. Leclercq in CL, VII, 2075. De Rossi thought the design a symbolic fragment from a marine scene. He dated the lamp in the fourth century.

118. See *Ichthys*, III, LXXXV, 1; XCVII, 6, 10; IV, 173, 1. The dove carries a bunch of grapes in ibid., IV, 183, 1. See also Leclercq in CL, VII, 2073, fig. 6108. At ibid., 2040, no. 76, Leclercq suggests that the design he reproduced more fully at IV, 2112, fig. 3975, is a fish with a dove.

119. From [J. A.] Martigny, *Dictionnaire des antiquités chrétiennes*, 2d ed., 1877, 772; cf. Leclercq, op. cit., 2079, fig. 6115.

120. Photo Alinari: no. 18211. For the whole intrados see C. Ricci, *Tavole storiche dei mosaici di Ravenna*, San Vitale, 1935, III, VI, plate *L*.

121. From *Ichthys*, IV, 186, no. 2.

A striking element common to Jews and Christians is the convention of putting a wheel, either a spoked wheel or a "round object," beside the fish, though in Jewish art the wheel could stand alone.[122] The Jewish examples of "round objects" are usually identified with the mazzoth of Passover, but if I am right in seeing the Friday evening meal in this symbolism, they are the *hallah*, the newly baked bread which is still blessed, broken, and distributed with the wine at that time. When the fish meal was celebrated at the Passover or Seder, the loaves would become mazzoth, but were not such ordinarily.[123] It has already been mentioned that this "round object" with fish was on a tombstone which Frey took to be Christian,[124] and the design now appears to have been so common that in itself it, and this inscription with it, might have been either Christian or Jewish. The Christian usages where these round "loaves" appear with fishes can most rapidly be surveyed again in the illustrations of the article by Leclercq, or in Dölger's *Ichthys*. The combination appears also on a lamp at the Cyprus Museum, fig. 53,[125] which is presumably Christian. Artistically, I suspect that in Jewish-Christian tradition the "wheel" form preceded the "loaf" form. The wheel appears with the fish abstractly as in fig. 58 [126] but in many cases the fish was put with the wheel in various ways to suggest different interpretations of the combination. In fig. 54 [127] by the fish's being woven through the wheel the two seem completely identified. The wheel could also be associated with the five loaves of the Christian miracle, as was done in at least two instances by drawing five of the wheels, figs. 56 [128] and 57,[129] along with a pair of fishes; the extra diagonal line in fig. 60 shows that they were still, in form, wheels. Much more commonly the wheel was changed into a circle containing the ☧ monogram; the fish could be drawn beside that device,[130] but more often the word ΙΧΘΥΣ was spelled out under the monogram, which in fig. 55,[131] as shown by the extra transverse line, is still a wheel. The symbol could be further abbreviated by putting the letters ΙΧΘΥΣ around in the interstices of the monogram, fig. 59.[132] On the cover of one sarcophagus a "loaf" is on either side of

122. See above, III, fig. 68, for an instance of the wheel in the Jewish catacomb at Sheikh Ibreiq.

123. Eisler, *Orpheus*, 223.

124. See above, p. 10.

125. No. D.2807. Published by permission of the Director of Antiquities and the Cyprus Museum.

126. From de Rossi in *BAC*, Ser. II, Vol. IV, 1873, plate VIII, no. 1; cf. p. 106. It was found at Ravenna near St. Apollinare in Classe. I follow de Rossi and Dölger in calling the stone Christian, but the two fish may be Pisces, and the stone may be pagan. Cf. *Ichthys*, IV, 180.

127. From *Ichthys*, I, 333. A carnelian from Asia, at the Bibliothèque Nationale, Paris. This identification is, I am sure, what is meant by the design, rather than, as Dölger explains, a making of *Ichthys* itself into a monogram.

128. From C. Rohault de Fleury, *La Messe*, IV, plate CCLXVII. An inscription from Modena.

129. From *Ichthys*, III, plate XCI, 1; it is at the Kircher Museum, Rome. See also ibid., V, plates 298, 301.

130. As in CL, VII, 2023, fig. 6056; and *Ichthys*, IV, 181.

131. From *Ichthys*, I, 233, fig. 25*a*. It is a drawing by G. Marini of an alabaster fragment as originally found at Roma Vecchia. Cf. CL, VII, 2033, fig. 6072; 2038, no. 64; 2040, nos. 74 f.; 2041, no. 79.

132. From de Rossi in *BAC*, Ser. II, Vol. IV (1873), plate IV/V, figs. 1–4; cf. pp. 77–80. It is a lead sarcophagus from Saida in Phoenicia, then reported in private possession in France. On the top, and on one end, the monogram with Ichthys is marked for its sanctity by being put under an arch, and the vines in the margin, with gadrooned cup, and birds drinking in the interstices, show how

a fish in the fish meal, fig. 61.[133] One of the loaves has the simple cross which indicates bread; the other is still a wheel. The history of the design is a clear instance of new explanations being associated with a symbol, which had such emotional value that it was retained, even though the old explanations were rejected, supplemented, or forgotten.

In view of this development of the wheel-wafer it is interesting to compare the fish designs in Vigna Randanini with the eucharistic fish in the Catacomb of St. Callistus (Lucina), fig. 60.[134] The baskets of loaves in the Christian representation are the same as those which appear in the Jewish design between the medallions of fish and ducks, but the peculiar bending of the fish about an object and the presence of the basket of loaves in both cases show that while the designs themselves are different, the elements which went into the two are the same.

* * *

If we take this combination of elements back into paganism, some new light is thrown on the origin of the symbol for Judaism. We must again anticipate our discussion of the water birds, especially ducks and geese, to say that they, like other originally erotic symbols, had become popular devices to put on graves.[135] It is here of direct interest that in the Book of the Dead [136] the snaring of fish and water fowl in a net is a definite part of the eschatological experience. Here the deceased is a little fish or duck who escapes the divine (malicious) fowlers, or fishermen, because he knows their names and the names of the net and its parts. Naville was perplexed that the fowling and fishing should have been confused in a single chapter of the Book, but the confusion, if such it was, was general, since in a design of the Roman period the net holds fish and fowl crowded together.[137] The fowl are of course water birds. In connection with water birds it will appear in a later volume that Egyptian influence of some sort was likely in the assortment of waders and divers at Hammam Lif and Beth Alpha, though there is no ground to conclude any special symbolism in the selection. But nothing in Egypt which I have seen suggests the origin of the repeated connection of fish and duck in Judaism and Christianity, or throws

---

much this design is in the general tradition of symbols we are discussing. The monograms on the front are also impressive, and all was designed to help into immortality the gentleman figured in a niche at the other end. See also *Ichthys*, I, 236, and Leclercq in CL, VII, 2066.

133. From *Ichthys*, III, plate LXI, 1. Dölger says it is from the "catacombs of Rome" but gives no other information.

134. From a photograph published by courtesy of the Pontificia Commissione di Archeologia Sacra, Rome. The catacomb shows a pair of these: cf. Wilpert, *Pitture*, Tavole, plates 27, 28. In the original the wine is represented by a red patch in the square at the front of the basket. Cf. above, III, figs. 742, 748 f.

135. To be discussed in Vol. VIII of this series.

136. *BD*, 339 (chap. CXIII, 3–7); 510–517 (chaps. CLIIIA and CLIIIB).

137. C. R. Lepsius, *Denkmäler aus Aegypten und Aethiopien*, 1849–1856, IX, iv, plate 88*b;* cf. VIII, iii, plate 278. Incidentally the Egyptians occasionally drew fish in their hieroglyphics with a long snout or "tongue" in a way to suggest the convention at Hammam Lif: F. Guilmant, *Le Tombeau de Ramsès IX*, 1907, plate XCVI (*Mém.* Inst., XV). The same sort of snout appears in a painted tomb in Palestine, where Egyptian influence, especially in the animals represented, was strong: PT, 26 f., plate XI.

any light on its meaning.[138] For all the importance of fish symbolism in Syria, to which Dölger ascribed the origin of the Christian fish and which would be just as likely a source of the Jewish fish, that region shows us nothing, so far as I know, to suggest putting the fish with ducks, or with bread, or with the cup or other wine symbols.

It is in Greek and hellenistic sources that these elements appear, though so scattered and unconsecutive that conclusions are difficult. Oddly, the appearances of the ducks and fish, and of the fish and "round objects" which are most like the Jewish and Christian instances, are found on Minoan-Mycenean and primitive Greek remains. I give one example, fig. 63,[139] but there are many others.[140] Interesting are the numerous scenes where a boat is rowed between fish and water birds. These are especially prominent on fibulae, alongside a heavily drawn central rosette, the outer ring of which suggests a wheel. I show a single example, fig. 62,[141] the famous sherd from a geometric vase at the Louvre. It is usual to say that the fish represent the water under the boat, but while such designs are common on fibulae from that period, the fish and water bird often appear on them without the boat, where it cannot be supposed that the artist was attempting to represent a seascape; see fig. 64.[142] On a Laconian vase from a somewhat later period, fig. 65,[143] a fish devours a "round object," the earliest instance of this form that I know. Above it, Polyphemus is represented having his eye pierced and at the same time being given to drink from a cantharus. At the top is a snake. Making Polyphemus drunk and then

138. On the fish in Egypt in general, see *Ichthys*, II, 49–160. By the presence of a bird beside the fish we are reminded of the Jewish tradition which said that a bird, the "ziz," was prepared along with Behemoth and Leviathan to be eaten at the final banquet. See *JE*, VIII, 39. But this bird in Jewish tradition was a monster of the air as the others were monsters of the sea and land, and I cannot assume that these small ducks in Jewish art refer to it.

139. From *Mon. Ant.*, 1891, I, ii, plate 1; see p. 207 f. It is a funerary urn from Crete, at the Museum in Candia. See Anna Roes, *Greek Geometric Art: Its Symbolism and Its Origin*, 60 f.

140. See, e.g., PC, *Histoire*, VI, 920, fig. 474; *MDAI, Ath.*, LVIII (1933), 98, fig. 40 (a "round object" is before one of the fish in a band of fishes, and a water bird is on the upper level). The fish with "round object" may go back to Egypt, where fish occasionally have lotus flowers in their mouths: *JEA*, XIII (1927), 11 f., plate VII, no. 5958. Cf. H. G. Evers, *Staat aus dem Stein* [1929], plate 129. For a discussion of fish and birds see Roes, 60–65. She supposes that the device was originally Persian. The "round object," like virtually all the symbols of geometric art, she treats as solar, which undoubtedly they often are. But in trying to explain in this one way the whole vocabulary of symbols, she seems to me to break down. She does not like the use of psychology in historic studies of symbols and quotes two unfortunate instances on pp. 124–126. But her method leaves her helpless when the solar symbols become marine symbols also. She has, however, given an excellent record of the forms, and her work, even if it does not go far enough, is rich in suggestion.

141. From O. Rayet and M. Collignon, *Histoire de la céramique grecque*, 1888, 29, fig. 20. These scholars here discuss the boat as one of numerous representations of war ships on such vases, but a funerary pageant is above this one, and I suspect that with birds and sacred signs of all sorts (and since the boat itself is marked with the wheel) we have here a funerary boat. The fish seem to me to indicate more than water. See also PC, *Histoire*, VIII, 254, fig. 129; E. Pottier, *Vases antiques du Louvre*, 1897, I, 23, no. A517.

142. From Furtwängler in *AA*, *JDAI*, IX (1894), 116, fig. 2. See also fig. 1 and H. B. Walters, *Catalogue of the Bronzes, Greek, Roman and Etruscan . . . in the British Museum*, 1899, 372, 374.

143. From P. Ducati, *Storia della ceramica greca*, 1922, 170, fig. 133, now at Paris, Bibliothèque Nationale.

piercing his eye is definitely traditional from Homer, but the snake and fish seem to create another dimension which reflects much earlier symbolism. At a still later date a cantharus was put between two fish on a Greek gem of the fifth century B.C.,[144] and Pausanias tells the story of a Dionysus Phallen who was honored at Methymna and whose figure some fishermen had drawn out of the sea.[145] We know that in 200 B.C. fishes [146] with cakes were part of an offering for the dead in Thera.[147]

One of the unexplained but recurrent peculiarities of our material, which we have already noticed, is the repeated similarity between Jewish and Etruscan remains. It is in Etruscan remains in this case that the early Cretan groupings of fish, ducks (or other water birds), trees, and wine symbols appear, in mystic or funerary setting. One mirror shows Aphrodite with Eros (there is no duck, but a dove is on her shoulder) fishing under the shadow of a palm tree: the fish to be caught is plainly shown.[148] On another mirror two women confront each other on either side of a palm tree: behind one woman is a duck, and in the foreground fish, dolphins, and a duck swim; above that part of the scene which is on the dry land arches a border of grapes on the vine.[149] Even more striking are the funerary designs in which a boat is rowed on water between fish and water birds, recalling the similar designs from early Crete. This motif is especially elaborated in the tombs of Tarquinia, from which I reproduce fig. 66.[150] Here above the scene of birds, sea, boat, and fish is the funerary banquet, or the meal of immortality, where of course the jars for wine are stressed, balanced by crowns and little birds (ducks?) at the other end. From the same tomb comes fig. 69,[151] showing a diver almost the exact replica of the diver in the Jewish tomb at Sheikh Ibreiq.[152] The boat, fish (here only the dolphin), and water birds appear in a highly stylized representation on an Etruscan sarcophagus, fig. 68.[153] In one scene on the sarcophagus Odysseus (impersonating the dead person?) is in the underworld, and a view through an opening in the cave shows the Styx with the boat of Charon, a dolphin, water birds, vegetation, etc., all of which strikingly suggests that these elements had symbolic power—symbolic, we guess, for the future life, since all the instances come from funerary art. Galli, who published the sarcophagus, was aware that the fish and water birds suggested Cretan parallels, and he published two interesting examples; [154] but he did not indicate that the boat quite as distinctly looks back to Crete. To me the re-

144. A. Furtwängler, *Die antiken Gemmen*, 1900, I, plate XXXI, 14.

145. Pausanias, X, XIX, 3; from Roscher, *Lex. Myth.*, I, 1063, lines 26–31.

146. The same word, *opsaria*, is used for the fishes in the miracles in John VI, 9, 11, and XXI, 10, 13.

147. P. Boyancé, *Le Culte des muses chez les philosophes grecs*, 1937, 339; and *Ichthys*, II, 381.

148. Gisela M. Richter, *Greek, Etruscan and Roman Bronzes*, 1915, 280 f., no. 814.

149. E. Gerhard, *Etruskische Spiegel*, IV, 1867, plate CDXXI.

150. From *Monumenti della pittura antica scoperti in Italia*, Sec. I, Fasc. II, 1937, p. 12. It is beautifully reproduced in color in ibid., plate B². Cf. G. Q. Giglioli, *L'Arte etrusca*, 1935, plate CXIII, 2.

151. From *Monumenti*, p. 11; cf. plate B¹ for color; see Giglioli, plate CXIV. On these see also Jan de Wit, *JDAI*, XLIV (1929), 31–85; *Historia*, IV (1930), 110 f.

152. See above, III, fig. 70.

153. From *Mon. Ant.*, XXIV, i (1917), 99, fig. 48. The whole sarcophagus is shown on an unnumbered plate at the end of the volume, with this detail in fig. D.

154. Ibid., 106, figs. 51, 52. See his discussion, pp. 103–107.

appearance of the three elements, fish, water birds, and boat, suggests very strongly that some symbolic tradition came over, however indirectly, from early Crete to the Etruscans. Lehmann told me that he suspected Egyptian influence in such scenes, and this may have been the ultimate origin of the tradition. The differences in the presentation in the three sources suggest, however, a continuity of symbolic tradition rather than artistic imitation.

The Etruscan material introduces us to another use of the fish, which will appear increasingly important as we go on. On the base of an Etruscan lamp, fig. 67,[155] appears, eight times repeated, the ithyphallic figure of Pan, squatting down and playing his pipe; under his feet is a dolphin. This figure alternates around the edge of the lamp with eight female figures, all with human head and upper body, and the lower parts of a bird—that is, with the conventional representation of a soul-bird or Siren. In the center is a Medusa head. The soul-bird figure as well as the Medusa head and the phalli as symbols of the fluid of life will all be discussed later in this study. Phallic and ithyphallic figures were used to ward off evil spirits as Dölger rightly observed, while, as he recognized, the Medusa head likewise suggests apotropaic significance in the design. But he has nothing to say of the soul-bird figures, which apparently he did not recognize as such; hence he stops again with a partial explanation. He seems to me to be right in associating the fish with the phallus [156] and in pointing out the apotropaic value of each. But in the setting with soul-birds and in the fuller meaning of Medusa, phallus, and fish, it would appear that the design looks beyond the merely apotropaic to a total representation of the source of immortal life, in which the identification of the fish with the phallus is an important part. The fish as an alternative figure for the fluid of the god in the Eucharist, as shown in the explanation of the miraculous feeding in John vi, would seem to belong in this association of symbols. To this we shall have to return.

Quite different from these Etruscan remains yet in many things reminiscent is the grave painting near Ascalon in Palestine, which no inscriptions or decisive symbols mark as pagan, Jewish, or Christian, fig. 70.[157] Here on the roof is a vine with various scenes in its interstices. On the south wall below it is a scene of two water nymphs beside a pool in which fish are highly active. Various animals are at the water, but perched on flowers in the most artificial way also sit two ducks beside the nymphs. It is striking that this too is funerary art.

In Roman art proper we have scattered hints, as in Greek art, of this group of symbols, but nothing connected. In all pagan art, that is, I see no definite suggestions of the immediate inspiration of either the Jewish or Christian combinations of ducks, bread, and wine, with fish as symbols of immortality. What may prove to be the reason why Etruscan

155. From Giglioli, plate ccxxx; cf. his p. 42 for description and bibliography, to which add *Ichthys*, III, plate xxx, 1; II, 404 f.; V, 136–138.

156. In *Ichthys*, V, 138, n. 45, Dölger gives only one parallel, in a work not accessible to me. But he often refers to the identity of fish and phallus, and his material, when collected, is quite overwhelming: see I, 109; 429, n. 2; II, 65, 134, 154, 225, 322, 376, 444; V, 43 f., 186–188. We have encountered the phallic association of the fish frequently: see above, pp. 18 f., 22, 49.

157. From J. Ory, "A Painted Tomb near Ascalon," *QDAP*, VIII (1939), plate xxvii; cf. p. 40. See also fig. 2.

and Jewish designs so often recall each other I cannot suggest: nothing we now know justifies assuming any direct connection. But the very strangeness of the vocabulary as found in Jewish and Christian designs makes it quite unlikely that the combination was worked out independently by pagans, Jews, and Christians. There was no "local pagan art," [158] so far as we know, which Christians or Jews without effort could have been taking over, as might possibly be assumed was the case with designs of the fish in the *fractio panis*, or meal of immortality. What seems the most likely guess is that Jews, for some reason or other, had come to associate the Messianic Age and their hope of personal immortality with a great fish, and to symbolize that hope in a fish meal, in connection with which water birds played some as yet unexplained part, and bread and wine were also significant. Whether this was a Jewish "sacrament" or not is a question which takes us very far indeed from the direct evidence of the pictures, though it may be recalled that Jews themselves have not been afraid to use the word in speaking of their table in general and of this meal in particular. Hence I. Abrahams wrote, "Some Jewish customs still prevalent are based on the idea that the meal—especially the Sabbath meal—is a sacrifice and a sacrament." [159] In any case, the pictures strongly suggest that the Christian fish usage followed the Jewish usage and was an adaptation of it.[160] And the Christian usage was sacramental.

Indeed, until most recent times at least the fish has been a favorite form for the boxes which hold the spices for Habdalah. We saw reason to suppose that such spices were descendants of ancient incense burning.[161] We may well close this chapter with such an eighteenth-century box, fig. 71,[162] and with the recollection that long ago Caylus published a bronze fish from Roman times, fig. 72,[163] which is an incense burner. The base is broken away, but the upper half could be removed so that hot coals could be put inside and then sprinkled with incense. This upper half is pierced with holes to permit the fumes of the incense to escape. A question remains finally in our minds, one which each reader, with the evidence before him, must answer for himself. Since the spices of Habdalah are thought to give spiritual strengthening to carry the faithful through the secular days of the week, what has it meant to Jews through the centuries as they inhaled their aroma from a box in the form of a fish?

158. See Calder in the *JRS*, XIV (1924), 82.

159. In *JQR*, XIX (1907), 628 n. Cited there by J. H. A. Hart in a treatment of "Jewish Sacramental Meals" which is quite disappointing.

160. When Eisler, *Orpheus*, 221, says, "we know for certain" that Christians took the fish meal from Jews, he is prejudicing the case by overstatement.

161. See above, IV, 195–208.

162. From a photograph, by courtesy of the Jewish Museum, New York, where it is no. M–126. It was made somewhere in western Europe in the eighteenth century. M. Narkiss told me he still regards the fish as a fertility symbol.

163. From Caylus, *Rec. d'ant.*, VI, plate XCIV, 1; cf. pp. 296 f. Dölger has reproduced this in *Ichthys*, III, plate XVI, 1; cf. II, 210. Caylus shows on the same plate the inside of the fish with its arrangement to receive coals. Its origin was unknown to Caylus but was judged to be "Roman." There is no indication where it now is; probably it is in Paris. Could the object have been Jewish also?

CHAPTER THREE

Bread

IN DISCUSSING the fish, symbols of bread and wine had also to be mentioned because they frequently appeared beside the fishes. Without forgetting that the fishes led us to suspect a sacramental Jewish meal, where the fish was eaten as a foretaste of the Messiah and his gift of immortality, we must now begin afresh and without prejudice examine the bread symbols, for they are represented in great numbers in the Jewish art, with usually no suggestion of fish beside them.

Bread symbols appear in two forms. The first is that of what I call "round objects," which have often been recognized as loaves. The second is that of baskets of loaves. The representations and associations of each must be discussed separately.

A. BREAD AS "ROUND OBJECTS"

THE FORM in which loaves of bread or cakes (the two are indistinguishable) are represented is what I have been forced to call by the neutral term "round object" because, as we shall see, the same shape is used to represent a considerable variety of things. Our chief difficulty will be in determining which of the "round objects" are intended to indicate bread. But since the form seems definitely at times to represent bread, we must stop at this point to go into its various meanings and ask what is implied by the fact that it could have such diversified reference.

Under the term "round objects" I have included all designs of disks which emphasize the circle, rather than the rays from the circle, as is usually the case in what we call the rosette.[1] The "round object" is often drawn as a larger circle with a smaller concentric circle inside it, though the inner circle may become simply a dot at the center. Such a design is frequently found on places where we should have expected a rosette, and it often alternates with the rosette on the same object.

1. In Judaism

"ROUND OBJECTS" were used from early times in Palestine as marks on jar handles, interchangeably with rosettes. They were presumably potters' marks but may well have

1. The rosette will be discussed in a later volume.

been chosen by the potters not only for identification but for a talismanic value. Duncan [2] points out that they largely disappear from the pottery of the Maccabean period proper, but they return everywhere soon afterward. They appear on twenty-seven of the ossuaries published in our third volume, on eleven of the sarcophagi, on what seems to be a ritualistic plate of some kind, in eight tombs, on four tombstones, on two glasses, on forty-nine of the lamps, twenty-six times in synagogues, in one of the Roman catacombs, and nine times on gold glasses from Rome.[3] They were indeed popular but have been regarded by archeologists as mere decorative space fillers unless they seemed actually to represent bread.[4] For example, in the last scene of the Ezekiel cycle at Dura, fig. 73,[5] the "round objects" occupy so conspicuous a place on top of the altar that they have seemed to be showbread, though what the showbread was doing on the altar of burnt offering has not been clarified. Since Ezekiel, just to the left of the part of the painting shown in our illustration, is clinging to the horns of the altar, and since the altar of incense is to be seen on a table immediately behind the loaves, while a little tent is over the whole, I should suppose that the objects together are an abbreviation of the Temple furniture (the Temple here as the Tabernacle) to indicate that Ezekiel was captured by soldiers when he was in the Temple and then executed (in the scene following). There are only two loaves, as contrasted with the proper twelve of showbread, and they are round, not rectangular, as the Talmud prescribes.[6] It seems by all means the best assumption that in this case the "round objects" are bread. It is perhaps worth suggesting that each of the two represents a pile of six loaves, for it was in two piles of six that the loaves were to be put on the table. Philo [7] makes a point of this, and in terms of his cosmic explanation of the Temple service sees each pile as representing one of the equinoxes, six months apart. But I think it safer to suppose that the artist limited himself to two loaves because that was all he had space to present effectively. When they are painted flanking the incense burner, however, the whole takes the form, beloved in all our representations, of a central ritualistic object flanked by two others.

So it becomes likely that such a pair of "round objects" under the menorah in the synagogue at Nawa are loaves,[8] while the same assumption is likely when the "round

2. In PEF, *QS*, 1926, 38. A good example of the early jar handle with "round object" is to be seen in [C. W.] Wilson and Warren, *The Recovery of Jerusalem*, 1871, 474. Another very early instance is a plate from Gezer in Macalister, *Gezer*, II, 272. And see below, p. 66.

3. References to the figures which show "round objects" in Vol. III will be found classified in the index to that volume, s.v. "Round object."

4. For example, Frey recognized them as bread in his *CIJ*, nos. 343, 361, 519, 653*a;* i.e., in Vol. III, our figs. 710, 724, 856, and 969, respectively.

5. Courtesy of the Yale University Art Gallery. This is from the restoration of the scene made by H. J. Gute.

6. The biblical, extrabiblical (except the Philonic), and rabbinic material on the showbread is collected by E. G. Hirsch in *JE*, XI, 312 f.

7. *Spec.* I, 172.

8. See above, III, fig. 624. They may be the ends of Torah scrolls, as on the stone from Priene (III, fig. 878), but on this stone the scroll is clearly represented as a spiral, not a "round object," so that I think the "round objects" at Nawa are bread. Yet one cannot be sure, for the ends of scrolls are "round objects" on three gold glasses (III, figs. 965 f., 974) and are spirals on two (III, figs. 967, 973). See the rolls simply as circles in III, figs. 706 f., 710.

object" has a cross at its center as in a design from the synagogue at Chorazin,[9] or within a wreath of acanthus on the same synagogue, fig. 75,[10] or under a ceremonial table at Dura.[11] It may well be bread, also, when put beside the menorah in the synagogue at Eshtemoa,[12] on Palestinian lamps,[13] on two tombstones from Rome,[14] and on a gold glass.[15] The crossed "round object" within a wreath raises the question whether all "round objects" within wreaths may not have been loaves, since the objects within wreaths all seem to be marked thereby as sacred objects or symbolic forms. So on three of the ceiling tiles at Dura the "round object" is within a wreath, as in fig. 74.[16] From one of the three the paint had chipped off so that a synagogue inscription beneath it could be seen: obviously the over-painted symbol could not have been "manufacturer's stock." [17] In the following section, when we see the "round objects" in baskets, we shall have a further instance of them as symbols of bread.

Many times, however, the menorah itself is made of "round objects," [18] or is covered with them; [19] in one case it is made of what I have called "cursive round objects." [20] That these represent bread seems very dubious, since the lights on the menorah itself can be "round objects," [21] or the dominating central light may be emphasized in that form.[22] That is, the "round object" can represent light or especially characterize it, a usage we shall see justified from paganism, so that it can by no means be assumed that the form always represents bread. Hence when "round objects" are used to make designs of all sorts on clay lamps,[23] it seems to me that they characterize, or sanctify, the light of the lamp. The sanctity of the "round objects" appears to be deliberately emphasized when they are put under arches [24] but becomes much more dubious when they are used for designs of floor carpeting in mosaic.[25] Yet I suspect it is as symbols of light that they are clustered on or about representations of shrines,[26] since we saw that light symbolism was very close to that of the Law as light.[27] This was strikingly brought out when little circles of glass were used to reflect actual light from the shrines in the funerary plaques,[28] and

9. See III, fig. 485.

10. Published by courtesy of the Palestine Archeological Museum. It is the same stone as the one in III, fig. 496; cf. III, fig. 493.

11. See below, figs. 117 f., and p. 103. Pearson and Gute disagree whether this was originally a simple "round object" or had a cross within it. In either case it seems to me bread.

12. See III, fig. 609.

13. See III, fig. 316, 334, 342.

14. See III, figs. 710, 724.

15. See III, fig. 969.

16. Courtesy of the Yale University Art Gallery, where the photograph is numbered Dura 1933, 265.

17. For other instances of "round objects" within a wreath see III, figs. 245, 250, 464, 468, 500, 556.

18. See III, figs. 434, 603, 651 f., 929 f., 932, 937, 964, 967.

19. See III, figs. 335, 440, 646, 814, 817, 925 f., 928, 942, 946, 966, 974.

20. See III, fig. 643.

21. See III, figs. 332, 335.

22. See III, fig. 621. I have guessed that the tying of the top of the menorah to the actual light on lamps has this meaning: see I, 158 f.

23. See III, figs. 263, 268_2, 269, 274, 277, 325, 356. This seems only elaborated in III, fig. 349.

24. See III, figs. 299, 305.

25. See III, figs. 657, 666, 884.

26. See III, figs. 282, 286 f., 602, 646, 817, 965 f.

27. See IV, 78, 94, 136.

28. See III, figs. 440–442, 446; cf. I, 174–177; IV, 122.

in a mizrach.[29] In what sense they were used so commonly on ossuaries,[30] on sarcophagi,[31] on a doorpost in the cemetery of Sheikh Ibreiq,[32] on the reveal of the smaller door in the Dura synagogue,[33] and even to indicate the hair on a lion,[34] it is impossible to say.

In view of the fact that the "round object" is often a symbol of light, it is well to assure ourselves that it can definitely be bread as well. In fig. 78,[35] part of a mosaic from Antioch showing a great banquet, the loaves as "round objects" are as recognizable as the fish, while fig. 80 [36] shows in a modern photograph that bread is still made in this way in the Near East. We saw a considerable number of such loaves with fishes in the previous chapters, where there was no doubt that they were bread.[37] This power of double implication in the symbol, by which bread and the divine light are equated or identified, will seem important as we continue.

2. *In Paganism and Christianity*

A BRIEF GLANCE at the historic appearances of the symbol gives no occasion to dispute that these might often be cakes or loaves but indicates again that such an explanation could not be expected to apply to all the cases.

In Mesopotamia the object is rare, but it is on a very early seal [38] and covers the royal chariot of Tiglath-Pileser III,[39] and so far as I can tell from the photograph it alternates with the royal rosette on the robes of a later king.[40] A tier of "round objects" is to be found on a Syro-Hittite seal, with a sun symbol above it: the tier seems here to take the place of the sacred tree.[41] A group of these objects can apparently represent bread,[42] and on one seal it seems to be at once the sun or a star and to be used for the head of sacred animals, probably to indicate their sanctity.[43] One "round object" is certainly the sun; see fig. 77,[44] a Syro-Hittite seal. In early Cyprus, seals show the object beside the sacred tree, or with the lunar crescent in a way to suggest that it is solar.[45]

29. See IV, fig. 49; cf. p. 124.

30. See III, figs. 130 f., 136 f., 141 f., 144–147, 151, 153, 160–162, 167 f., 172, 185, 189, 209, 221.

31. See III, figs. 231, 233 f., 236, 243, 245, 247, 250.

32. "Two disks cut in relief, one concave with a knob in the center, the other flat and smooth" were reported by N. Avigad, *Israel Exploration Journal*, IV (1954), 9.

33. See III, fig. 546.

34. See III, fig. 523, and below, Vol. VII.

35. From a photograph published by courtesy of the Department of Art and Archeology, Princeton University. See Doro Levi, *Antioch Mosaic Pavements*, 1947, II, plate CLIIa; cf. I, 135.

36. From G. Dalman, *Arbeit und Sitte in Palästina*, IV, 1935, fig. 27; see also p. 132.

37. See above, pp. 56 f.

38. Of the "archaic-Sumerian period," Osten, *Newell*, fig. 71.

39. H. R. Hall, *La Sculpture babylonienne et assyrienne au British Museum*, 1928, plate XXV (Ars Asiatica, XI).

40. Ibid., plate LVII. For rosettes on the royal robe see also ibid., plate XXVII.

41. *AASOR*, V (1923/4), 55. Cf. Ward, *Seal Cylinders*, 275 f., fig. 832; see also fig. 831. Tiers of three "round objects" are on either side of a tree on the seal published in Osten, *Newell*, no. 361, and there called (p. 12) "Hittite" ("Cypriote").

42. Dougherty, *AASOR*, V (1923/4), 54; H. Frankfort, *Cylinder Seals*, 1939, plates XXXVIIIg, *l;* XLIIg, *o;* XLIII*i*.

43. Frankfort, plate XLIII*f;* cf. *c*, *e*, *g-i*.

44. From Ward, *Seal Cylinders*, 319, fig. 1015. Ward calls this seal "peculiar."

45. Ibid., 349, figs. 1192, 1194 f., 1199 f., 1204.

Erman points out that in the form ⊙, the simplest representation of the sun, the "round object" was for millennia the hieroglyph for the sun god Ra.[46] It is probably with double meaning of sun and bread that this became the form of Egyptian ceremonial cakes for burial offerings, fig. 81.[47] Sayce [48] and Macalister [49] may have been right in implying that the "round objects" on jar handles and images came into primitive Canaanite syncretism from Egypt; Sukenik called the form on jar handles a "degenerate form of a solar disk." [50] From Palestine itself, near Jerusalem, came fig. 76,[51] a headdress on a bull or cow, where the sun disk is a "round object," though the acanthus below it indicates a hellenistic or Roman dating.

A peculiar usage of "round objects" in the Near East of the Greco-Roman period puzzled me when I published the first volume of this series, but since then it has been clarified by my colleague Harald Ingholt. The Jewish instance of this usage there published is a column of six "round objects" with a wedge above and below them, carved on the stone door of a Palestinian Jewish tomb.[52] Also, without the wedges, the same six "round objects" in a column are painted on each of the reveals of the smaller doorway into the Dura synagogue.[53] A pair of similar tiers of seven "round objects" are on the lamp of Mrs. Schloessinger, fig. 5.

Ingholt has shown [54] that in the early centuries of the Christian era the disk, as he calls the "round object," had come in the East to represent light so definitely that symbols for the gods were made in the form of standards with a varied number of disks upon them, very similar to the standards of the Roman legions. There might be as few as three of these disks, but the proper number seems to have been seven, because they represented

46. Erman, *Relig. Ägypt.*, 115.

47. From A. M. Calverley, *The Temple of King Sethos I at Abydos*, 1933, I, plate 7; see also F. W. von Bissing, *Denkmäler ägyptischer Sculptur*, 1911, III, plate 32; *BD*, 209 (the vignette to chap. LXIIIB); Stephen Thompson, *British Museum Photographs from the Egyptian Collection*, 1872, nos. 268 f.; E. A. W. Budge, *The Egyptian Heaven and Hell*, 1905, I, 50–52, says that they are the eye of Horus or Ra, but this is probably the same thing. The "round object," later replaced by the rosette, was commonly put on the base out of which grew the lettuce of Min, a base which originally represented irrigated fields. I should guess that the mark still represented the sun, whether as "round object" or rosette, and that the sun's place in the fertility of the fields was being suggested. See H. Gauthier, *Les Fêtes du dieu Min*, 1931, 167–171, figs. 8, 10 f., 13.

48. In PEF, *QS*, 1893, 30; but in ibid., 1900, 67, he says that the object was of Canaanite origin taken down to Egypt. His earlier idea seems to me much more natural.

49. In ibid., 1924, 138.

50. In *JPOS*, XIV (1934), 184. But Sukenik was not sure whether these devices are solar disks or "some indication of the measurement." For the jar handles see also Bliss in PEF, *QS*, 1899, 184–187, plate VI; and Duncan, ibid., 1925, plate VII, fig. 21.

51. From PEF, *An.*, IV (1923–1925), 159. For other similar objects see the pages following in that publication.

52. See above, III, 44; cf. I, 85 f. In this passage I said merely that the suggestion of Dussaud that the tier of "round objects" constituted a Roman standard was unacceptable, and that the man buried within had been a soldier in the Roman army. As this volume was in press I learned that a second stone door with this design has been found in Israel: B. Sappir, "A Door Fragment with a Menorah from Ibillin" (in Hebrew), *Yediot, Bulletin of the Israel Exploration Society*, XVII (1953), 153. It will be published below, in Vol. VII.

53. See III, fig. 546.

54. *Parthian Sculptures from Hatra*, 1954, 20–27, 32, 34 f., 37–43, 46 (Memoirs of the Connecticut Academy of Arts and Sciences, XII).

the seven planets. As a whole, then, they were usually and properly dedicated to the supreme deity as God of the Heavens. The name of this god apparently was definite in any one locality, and Ingholt has shown that in Hatra it was the emblem of Samayya, because that was what the god of the heavens was called there. But it was so generally used as a symbol for the supreme God that Jews could use it in the places mentioned and understand that their own "Heaven," a common name for the Jewish God, was indicated by it. Such, I now believe, was the meaning of the tiers of "round objects" in Jewish usage.

It is in Greece and Italy, however, that we find material which explains other uses of the "round object" in late Syria and, I believe, in Jewish representations of our period.

Concentric circles were frequently used on early Greek geometric vases, where they seem to represent the sun and to be part of the heritage from the East and Egypt.[55] Roes calls them "filling-ornaments," though she herself agrees that they are solar symbols.[56] While they certainly fill space, I doubt if they were ever used merely to do that. When put with [57] or on [58] an animal, they may well have declared the solar quality of the animal. In the same way "round objects" of all sorts are most common on all Greek, Etruscan, hellenistic, and Roman art. A review of them and an exact appraisal of what they represent in each case would be a major work in itself, one which would, I am sure, still leave many of the identifications uncertain. I must content myself here with a few examples, which without such a review will have to be somewhat at random but which will give one not acquainted with the material as a whole some notion of its varieties.

The most common single use of the "round object" is to represent a patera, a flat bowl with a raised center, used for libations on all sorts of occasions, fig. 79.[59] The patera could be quite plain or could be ornamented with what look like varieties of rosettes, so that even circles enclosing rosettes are often pateras.[60] These, however, appear to have been used interchangeably with rosettes not set in a circle,[61] rosettes which, drawn in this way, seem more like solar or astral symbols than pateras. How one should distinguish between them I shall not attempt to suggest. Another variant shows the larger circle containing a ring of four to twelve or more little circles, with another little circle at the center. This too may well have been a patera, as in fig. 82,[62] or a tympanum,[63] since such a ring of circles appears as decoration on both of these (though at other times the same device may represent a cake crusted with seeds).[64] Indeed, fig. 82 is a good example of our

55. They are most easily to be seen in Roes, *Greek Geometric Art*, figs. 1, 6, 19, 38, 49, 57–59, 68, 88, 90.

56. Ibid., 10.

57. E.g. ibid., figs. 19, 57, 88, 90.

58. Ibid., fig. 68.

59. From Reinach, *Vases*, Millingen, plate 23. This patera is in the Vatican Museum. I can see no reason to challenge Reinach's identification (p. 104) of these objects as pateras when, consecrated by fillets, they hang over the altar. What scene is represented on the vase is disputed.

60. For examples see *BA*, III (1909), 413, fig. 6; 419, fig. 14.

61. Reinach, *Vases*, Millingen, plate 11.

62. From *Hesperia*, IV (1935), 493, fig. 15, no. 101 (cf. p. 519). It is an Attic red-figure lecythus of the fifth century, found in the Agora at Athens and presumably still in the collection in the Agora.

63. Reinach, *Vases*, Millin, I, plate 7. Cf. J. D. Beazley, *Etruscan Vase-Painting*, 1947, plate XXXVI, 1.

64. So Reinach understood a pair of such objects in a bacchic scene: *Vases*, Millin, I, plate 60; cf. p. 37 and see also plate 67 and p. 40; but on page

difficulty, for while the object is presumably a patera, it may be a cake which, along with the little one below, is being put on the altar. The same problem, more abstractly presented, arises in the identification of the variously drawn "round objects" in fig. 83,[65] which Bendinelli called pateras. They may have stood for any of these other things, including bread. But the object with little circles, presented with birds (ducks?), appears to be a talismanic device on a brooch from the temenos of Locri Epizephyrii, fig. 84 [66]—that is, to imply direct potency as a symbol. When the line of the circumference is absent and only the central circle and the ring of little circles remain, we cannot be sure that we have not gone over again to a solar or astral symbol. At the same time a very similar representation must be understood as a crown.[67] Frequently the "round objects" seem definitely to be shields,[68] though when they are over a warrior's head they may equally well represent the patera making libation for him, fig. 85.[69]

In classic and post-classic Hellenism, when they are not pateras being used at a sacrifice, or in a funerary rite,[70] such objects are most commonly shown in Dionysiac scenes.[71] A century ago they were often taken to be the little loaves used in Dionysiac rituals. In the modern reaction against symbolism they are often just as arbitrarily called "filling ornaments." So Beazley says [72] of the "round object" fig. 87.[73] In describing most of the vases on which they appear [74] Beazley ignores them entirely. This seems to me rather an escape from the problem than a solution. That as pateras or cymbals [75] they would have had ritualistic reference would not be disputed. Deonna's suggestion is still valid that sometimes a "round object" is the rhombus or solar disk. The rhombus was a toy, a sort of ball, offered the infant Dionysus as a lure by the Titans and used in some way in Dionysiac ritual.[76]

52 he calls the identical forms pateras, as they appear in his Vol. II, plate 16; on p. 94, with reference to Millingen, plate 3, the identification with cakes is uncertain, as it is on p. 99, with reference to Millingen, plates 14 f. Jane Harrison, *Prolegomena*, 591, 602, called these objects wheels. She recalled the lost book of Dionysius, *The Interpretation of the Symbolism That Has to Do with Wheels*, and in many cases she may be right.

65. From G. Bendinelli in *Mon. Ant.*, XXIII, ii (1916), 639, fig. 2; cf. p. 635, no. 43. It is a scyphus, found at Todi, on the border of Umbria and Etruria. It is now at the National Museum of the Villa Giulia. The scene of panthers and the duck or goose seems to me both bacchic and symbolic.

66. From Orsi in *BA*, III (1909), 476, fig. 47.

67. Reinach, *Vases*, Millin, II, plates 23, 57; Millingen, plate 45.

68. As when one is represented between a pair of greaves, ibid., Millin, II, plate 37, p. 65; cf. ibid., Millingen, plate 19.

69. From Reinach, *Vases*, Millin, I, plate 41. At the Louvre.

70. See Nike pouring a libation on a funerary altar on a lecythus, A. Fairbanks, *Athenian Lekythoi, with Outline Drawing in Glaze Varnish on a White Ground*, 1907, plate I, 1; cf. his *Athenian Lekythoi with Outline Drawing in Matt Color on a White Ground*, 1914, plate XXI, 1 (University of Michigan Studies, Humanistic Series, VI and VII).

71. They were especially favored by Etruscans in bacchic scenes: cf. Beazley, plates XVIII, 3, 5, 8, 10; XXIV, 4; XXV, 5, 6; XXXIV, 1; XXXV, 4, 6; XXXVI, 1, 2.

72. Page 61.

73. An early red-figure stamnos at the Boston Museum of Art, published by courtesy of the Museum. Beazley, plate XIV, 2. Cf. his plate XIII*a*, 2.

74. See above, n. 71.

75. Lehmann, *Baltimore*, 50, takes "round objects" within the gable of a Dionysiac sarcophagus lid to be cymbals. This is a likely guess, but they may also be bread.

76. W. Deonna, "Rombe ou roue solaire," *RA*, Ser. V, Vol. IV (1916), 252–256.

It is quite likely that the older suggestion was right and that they were often loaves of ritualistic bread or cakes. When they are marked with crosses or merely formed of concentric circles, the chances that they are meant to indicate bread seem to me very high. So in fig. 86,[77] a vase last reported in a private collection at Naples, it is reasonable to suppose that the "round objects" are cakes or loaves for the sacrifice. Polybius says, "They [the Roman soldiers of an earlier time] had a shield of ox-hide very similar to the navel-centered *popana* (loaves or cakes) which were put upon sacrifices." [78] This is a passing allusion in a description of Roman arms and there is no indication of what sacrifices Polybius had in mind, but the very casualness of the reference suggests that such cakes were a byword in connection with sacrifices of all sorts.

Unfortunately, so far as I can discover, there has been no systematic study of the use of loaves or cakes in Greek and Roman rituals, and such a study is quite beyond our present task. Greek literature has a great number of references to cakes or loaves, and it is probable that most or all of these cakes were used in sacrifices in one region or another. The place to begin would be the discussion of bread and cakes in Athenaeus,[79] where a bewildering list of terms for them is given, in many cases with recipes for their preparation.[80] Athenaeus' interest is more gustatory than religious, but he does mention statues in Boeotia to a Megalartus and Megalomazus, deities whose names mean Great Bread and Great Barley Cake, and says that loaves were offered to them.[81] A "penny cake," *obelias*, was reputedly invented by Dionysus and so was presumably associated with him in ritual.[82] Athenaeus quotes Trypho and Nicander as saying that in Aetolia the loaves made for the gods were called *thiagones*, but that they were called *dramices* and *araxis* by the Athamanes.[83] There is, he continues, a sort of loaves called "*blōmiaioi artoi* with divisions in them, loaves which the Romans call *quadrati*." These would seem to be the crossed loaves that later in Christian usage are properly taken to be the Host but which appear on both pagan and Jewish monuments.

Later in the same treatise Athenaeus returns to give an even more elaborate list of cakes.[84] At Rhodes, he says,[85] a woman sacrificed to Artemis with a libation and a cake called *amphiphōn*. This cake, surrounded by torches, was brought not only to the temples of Artemis but also "to places where three roads meet, on the day when the moon is overtaken at its setting by the rising of the sun; and so the heaven is *amphiphōs*," or doubly illumined. The reference of this cake to light is indisputable. The Delians sacrifice to Isis by offering a cheese cake called the *basynias*.[86] Several kinds of cakes are mentioned as part of the bridal ceremony,[87] one of which, the *kribanai*, is shaped like a breast, again recalling our "round objects."

77. From Reinach, *Vases*, Millingen, plate 58.

78. Polybius, *Histories*, VI, XXV, 7. The Jewish "round objects" were taken to be shields by Dussaud, *Monuments*, 89.

79. *Deipnosophists*, III, 13–83; 100.

80. Athenaeus assures us that his list is by no means complete: ibid., 82.

81. Ibid., 73.

82. Ibid., 76.

83. Ibid., 80 f.

84. Ibid., XIV, 51–60.

85. Ibid., XIV, 53; for other references see LS s.v.

86. Ibid.

87. Ibid., 53 f.

Diomedes reported a festival at Syracuse for Artemis where the people brought, among other things, a *panis magnus* on which figures of animals were stamped.[88] Such animals of bread, Nilsson explains, were a substitute for animal sacrifice. *Daratai* were cakes offered at weddings and at the introduction of new-born children into a phratry.[89]

In a fragment from a lost play of Menander [90] sacrifices are described, presumably those offered Pan and the nymphs in the deme of Phyle. Here it is said that one offering sacrifice brought wine and an animal of sacrifice, along with chests which apparently contained a popanon and frankincense. Menander protested that some sacrificants actually gave the gods only the inedible portions of the animal and ate the rest themselves. But the frankincense and the popanon they did not dare tamper with: the frankincense was a "pious thing," and the popanon was put whole on the fire.[91] To Aristotle is ascribed the statement that at Delos there was a horned altar to Apollo as the Giver of Life, on which no animal was sacrificed, but only "flour and meal and popana without fire" were put on it.[92] This seems to me highly significant for the meaning of the loaves: they were appropriate for the "Life Giver" as victims were not, and presumably carried the sense of a sacrifice which brought life, in whatever sense, to those who made the offering. The solar association of the loaves, which we shall encounter increasingly, would probably also have been felt in an offering to Apollo. Porphyry quotes Clearchus describing the sacrifices he made to various gods, where Clearchus says his offering to them was frankincense, *psaista* (another word for cakes or loaves), and popana.[93] The Ichthyophagi showed their submission to Nearchus, the general of Alexander, by bringing out to him popana dates, and tunny baked in pans.[94] Even Osiris, says Juvenal,[95] could be bribed not to punish those who had intercourse on days sacred to him if he were offered a goose and popana, where the Greek word has come directly into Latin. The goose and popana recall fig. 82. Aristophanes describes an offering to Demeter and Persephone which consists of a popanon brought to the altar in a basket.[96] An inscription [97] of the fourth century B.C. discovered at the Pireus describes offerings which should be made apparently for recovery from illness:

88. H. Keil, *Grammatici latini*, I, 486. It is quoted in full by M. P. Nilsson, *Griechische Feste*, 1906, 200, n. 1. Cf. 202 and 224.

89. They were offered especially at Delphi: Nilsson, 465.

90. Fragments, *The Peevish Man* (F. Allinson, in Loeb ed., 346).

91. It is not said whether such people used the wine properly as a libation, or, robbing the gods, drank it.

92. Frag. 447; ed. V. Rose in the ed. of Aristotle by the Academia Regia Borussica, V, 1870. It is from Diogenes Laertius, *Lives of Eminent Philosophers*, VIII, 13.

93. Porphyry, *De Abstinentia*, II, 16 (ed. J. de Rhoer, 1767, 129 f.). De Rhoer's notes, ad loc., have interesting material on the nature of these cakes. Psaista were made of ground barley mixed into cakes with olive oil and wine. Popana were round, flat, light cakes. I should guess that when the "round objects" are bread or cakes they are usually popana, since that has appeared to be the commonest word for cakes in religious usage. On frankincense and a popanon as offering see also Lucian, *De Sacrificiis*, 12.

94. Arrian, *Indica*, XXVIII, 1. The word for pan, *kribanos*, is the regular word for an earthern bread pan, so that the fish, too, were presented as loaves or cakes.

95. Juvenal, *Satires*, VI, 540 f.

96. Aristophanes, *Thesmophoriazusae*, 285.

97. *IG*, II, 1651.

Gods! Make your offerings in this way: To Maleatas, three popana; to Apollo, three popana; to Hermes, three popana; to Iaso, three popana; to Akeso, three popana; to Panacea, three popana; to the Dogs, three popana; to the Hunters, three popana.[98]

Euthydemus of Eleusis, priest of Asclepias, set up the stelae by the altars, on which he for the first made a likeness of the popana which must be offered.

To Helios, a honey cake;[99] to Mnemosyne, a honey cake; three altars on which wine is not used;[100] three altars on which wine is not used; no wine.

Unfortunately the stelae by the altars on which likenesses of the sacrificial popana were put have not, so far as I know, been preserved. I fancy they were our "round objects" with the umbilical center as Polybius described them and if found would have been described as "space fillers."

Fragmentary as is the foregoing list of instances, enough has been cited to show that cakes or loaves by many names, but especially called popana, played a most important part in Greek ritual of all sorts. They were particularly significant in mystery religions, however, especially with the Thesmophorian goddesses, Demeter and Kore.[101] We return for these to Clement of Alexandria's[102] oft-quoted description of the contents of the chest used in the Eleusinian mysteries: *sesamai*, or round sesame cakes;[103] *pyramides*, cakes of barley and honey whose shape is unknown; *tolypai*, globular cakes; *popana polyomphala*, which would appear to be our cakes with multiple circles; *phthoides*, a kind of cheese cakes with honey and other ingredients.[104] With these cakes were several symbolic objects. Athenaeus mentions other kinds of cakes used in the Thesmophorian festival at Syracuse.[105] It also appears not by chance that "round objects" were to be seen so often in bacchic scenes. While they may frequently stand in these for libations of wine or for cymbals, many times they presumably are loaves or cakes.

All of these meanings are likewise possible when the "round object" appears on hellenistic and Roman monuments. It is hardly necessary to document the very frequent usages of a dead person holding one up, apparently to pour a libation from it, as he reclines on the couch that is at once the funerary couch and the banquet couch on which he feasts at the heavenly banquet;[106] in such a case the object is a libation bowl. It is usually with this association—as an instrument of libation—that the "round object," sometimes "umbilical" and sometimes not, appears in a great variety of positions on funerary monuments.[107] Likewise it is held everywhere as a libation (or cake?) over altars, or is carved

98. Maleatas is one of the epithets of Apollo: see Roscher, *Lex. Myth.*, 2302 f. Iaso, Akeso, and Panacea were daughters of Asclepias. By the "Dogs" reference is made to demonic attendants, here presumably of Asclepias. The "Hunters" (*kunēgeteis*) were also demons.

99. *Arestēra kērion.* How this cake would have differed in appearance from a popanon I do not know.

100. *Nēphōlioi bōmoi*, literally "altars without wine."

101. Nilsson, *Griech. Relig.*, I, 439 f.

102. *Protrepticus*, II, XX, 4 (ed. Stählin, 17).

103. Athenaeus, *Deipnosophists*, XIV, 56.

104. Ibid., XIV, 57.

105. Ibid., XIV, 56.

106. It is sufficient to cite a single example: *AAL, M*, Ser. IV, Vol. IV, ii, plate XIV at p. 268.

107. See, for example, *Mon. Ant.*, XXXI, ii (1926), plate facing p. 403; *AAL, N*, 1899, 340, fig. 2; *AA, JDAI*, XLVIII (1933), 133, fig. 17.

on altars,[108] and this libation scene is especially appropriate, it would seem, for funerary ornament.[109] It also occurs on the mystic doors of such ornament.[110] That all of these "round objects" stand for a single thing we can now see is not true. Some may be shields, some cakes, some pateras, or whatever. On doors they are often taken to be knobs. But as one begins to notice their constant repetition in pagan art and their proud place especially on pagan funerary scenes and architecture,[111] they increasingly impress one with the notion that they meant something in themselves to the pagans who used them. For example, there are the "round objects" on the back of a little hermaphroditic figure from Roman Gaul, fig. 89.[112] There the Syrian design of a large rosette with little ones around it is portrayed in "round objects" instead of rosettes. Perhaps this was an image left in Gaul by a Syrian soldier. The stars within the "round objects" make astral significance almost inevitable here.

This takes us back again to Syria, and here we find "round objects" very prominent and important. North Africa, which by its Punic tradition has many survivals from the Levant, used the "disk" or the "solar rosette" interchangeably for the sun, fig. 90.[113] There was a tendency in this region similar to that in Gaul to fill all possible places with "round objects," as we have already seen done on a late Punic stele.[114] It is noteworthy that Toutain classes with these the small ossuary-like box from Algeria,[115] on which is the typical rosette decoration and a middle row of "round objects" as well. "Round objects," whether as simple disks [116] or concentric circles [117] or umbilical designs,[118] are abundantly familiar also from Roman Syria. One is carved on the gable of a votive tablet to Anaitis and Helios published by Cumont,[119] and the object could take the place of the rosette on

108. Presumably a sepulchral cippus in the form of an altar is shown in Arthur H. Smith, *A Catalogue of Sculpture in the Department of Greek and Roman Antiquities, British Museum*, III, 1904, 383, where it balances, and seems to be an alternative for, a wine pitcher. See also W. Altmann, *Die römischen Grabaltäre der Kaiserzeit*, 1905, figs. 68, no. 43; 74, no. 54; 76, no. 60; 143*a*, no. 235; 145*a*, no. 242. But in fig. 138, no. 225, the same forms represent tympana in the hands of maenads.

109. An instance in *AAL, N*, 1908, 324, fig. 2.

110. *Mon. ined.*, V, plate VIII. See the small door at the bottom.

111. A case of a "round object" on an official stele where the names of the city officers are listed is worth mentioning. Here above the list, in the gable of a pediment in relief, is carved a large "round object" flanked by two small vases. At least the association with wine is thereby kept: *Hesperia*, II, iv (1933), fig. 17 at p. 507.

112. From A. Blanchet, *Etude sur les figurines en terre cuite de la Gaule romaine*, 1901, Supplément, plate II, fig. 32.

113. From J. Toutain, "Les Symboles astraux sur les monuments funéraires de l'Afrique du nord," *Revue des études anciennes*, XIII (1911), 166, fig. 1. The illustrations throughout the article are very interesting for our purpose. See also Punic "round objects" in *CR, AIB*, 1916, 29, 32.

114. See above, IV, fig. 104; cf. p. 138.

115. See above, III, fig. 174; cf. I, 123.

116. For example, see Butler, *Architecture*, 1889, 287.

117. Ibid., 300.

118. *JRS*, XVIII (1928), plate XVI, no. 51; see p. 176. See also the interesting sarcophagus decorated only with large "round objects," from a pagan cemetery in Sebastya in Samaria, *QDAP*, VIII (1939), plate XXXIX, 2.

119. *CR, AIB*, 1915, 270–276. Here Anaitis is the same as the "Ephesian Artemis," and on the robe of Helios, as on other images, the rosette is prominent. See R. Tonneau in *RB*, XXXVIII (1929), plate X and p. 326.

the robe of Helios himself,[120] as we saw on the robe of Aaron at Dura.[121] They were especially popular for the symbolic lead sarcophagi of Syria.[122] The object, even in its umbilical form, is indisputably solar (and astral) on a gravestone from Nîmes, fig. 88,[123] to which Cumont gives us several parallels.[124] But when the "round objects" appear balancing wreaths on a Nabatean tomb at Petra, fig. 92,[125] we feel we may have returned to the bread or libation pateras on tombs, and we recall that with probably the same meaning, whatever it is, the object appears within the wreath on synagogues.[126]

The symbol leads us into Christianity, where we know from its frequent appearance in eucharistic baskets,[127] and with fish, that it represents bread. Two striking conventions show how important it could become. In Coptic art we have scores of tombstones on which the "round object" is at the head of a cross, fig. 91.[128] A glance shows what has happened: the Egyptian ankh, ☥, symbol of life, especially of life as it flows in the divine Light Stream, the most beloved of all symbols of Egyptian hopes, has been Christianized, become the Christian cross, and in place of the loop the Christians are drawing the "round object," itself long the symbol of food and light-life in Egypt.[129] The natural assumption, one that few will reject, is that there was a deliberate adaptation of the ankh into the cross—or the crucifix, for Christ is represented on it in the form of the holy wafer of the Eucharist. Actually the Copts may well have had in mind also the solar meaning of the disk, since Christ as the Logos was Light in Christian thinking. No symbol ever lost religious value by having plural implications.

The association of the "round object" with the cross continued at least through the Middle Ages. In fig. 94 is shown an early cross of unknown provenance and date which

120. *RA*, Ser. IV, Vol. I (1903), 350, fig. 11 (at the side, right).

121. The design on the robe is disputed.

122. See, for example, *AA*, *JDAI*, XLIII (1928), 465. See also the Syrian tomb in R. E. Brünnow and A. von Domaszewski, *Die Provincia Arabia*, 1904, I, 156.

123. From Cumont, *Symbolisme*, 226, fig. 47.

124. Ibid., 210, n. 3; 225 f. See also the lamps with "round objects" found in Beit Nattif in Palestine, published by Baramki in *QDAP*, V (1935/6), plate VII. Some of the objects found together in this place are Jewish (plate X, 24) but many are pagan, and so we cannot claim these lamps as Jewish. Two of them show "round objects" with swastikas (nos. 1, 2); two others show "round objects" at the ends of the tail feathers of peacocks (nos. 7, 8), and several others have "round objects" in more conventional designs (nos. 3–6).

125. Courtesy of the Palestine Archeological Museum. It is the so-called Lion Triclinium.

126. See above, III, figs. 464, 468, 493, 495 f.

127. In Wilpert, *Pitture*, plates 28, 196, the loaves in the baskets are clearly "round objects" with the central dot. In his plate 237 they have the cross at the center as in Dura under the mystic table.

128. From W. E. Crum, *Coptic Monuments* (Catalogue général des antiquités égyptiennes du Musée du Caire, V), plate XXVI, no. 8551. Many others of the same sort are shown on the adjoining plates. The "round object" is otherwise often used in Coptic art: Oskar Wulff, *Altchristliche und mittelalterliche byzantinische und italienische Bildwerke*, 1909, I, nos. 294 f., 299, 309, 345, 350 f., 517, 519, 600, 1129, 1430, and many others. See above, IV, fig. 98.

129. See above, p. 66. For a collection of crosses—most of them consisting of the ankh and "round object"—from Coptic chapels see A. Fakhry, *The Necropolis of el-Bagawāt in Kharga Oasis*, 1951, 36–38 (Service des Antiquités de l'Egypte, The Egyptian Deserts).

I photographed in the Museum of the Pontifical Biblical Institute at Jerusalem, Israel.[130] Here the cross is itself made of the "round objects," as—we saw above—were many of the menorahs. Figure 93 [131] shows a lamp from Cyprus of perhaps the fifth century, where the "round objects" are put in at random on and about the cross, as well as in the outer border. In fig. 95 [132] can be seen a Byzantine cross, again of uncertain date, where the little "round objects" are stamped on it with no sense of artistic appropriateness. Such Byzantine crosses are very familiar. The same convention was very popular in Christianity of the early centuries in North Africa.[133] The "round objects" again seem to have a talismanic value of their own, an impression confirmed when they appear in much the same way on magical beads, as in fig. 99.[134] But in Byzantine and Coptic Christianity the symbol definitely had special meaning with the cross. That the Jews of the late Roman empire commonly made the menorah similarly out of a series of "round objects" seems now equally significant.

The second Christian usage is one to which we have just referred, the eastern custom of presenting the eucharistic wafers as "round objects." Figure 101 [135] shows the matter clearly, for here, in a mosaic from San Vitale in Ravenna, the Host is elaborately marked to make it a "round object" in the form of a rosette. A little stone bread stamp, presumably for the Host, is preserved in the Palestine Archaeological Museum, fig. 98,[136] from an undisturbed grave of A.D. 396. Pressing this on the dough would produce the umbilical bread with the ring of little circles we have seen. The custom of stamping eucharistic bread in some such way has continued to the present in many eastern sects.[137] This marking of bread survives with us only on hot cross buns.

That the "round object" could stand as a symbol of both light and bread no longer confuses us. The form was applied to bread or (I presume) to libation vessels, because it sanctified them. Sometimes we see the "round object" on ancient monuments apparently

130. I publish the photograph by courtesy of the Institute.

131. Published by permission of the Director of Antiquities and the Cyprus Museum, where the lamp is no. D.2869.

132. My photograph of the cross, which is the property of Miss Esther W. Boyer, American College for Girls, Istanbul. Miss Boyer has no knowledge of its origin. See also the so-called cross of St. Angelo at the Cathedral of Ravenna: C. Ricci, Ravenna, 1906, fig. 115.

133. See A. Delattre, *Musée Lavigerie de Saint-Louis de Carthage*, III, 1899, plates VII, 1, and XI, 2, 4, 12 f., 16 (Description de l'Afrique du Nord: Musées et collections archéologiques de l'Algérie et de la Tunisie).

134. From A. Ashik, *Vosporskoe Tsarstvo*, Odessa, 1848, III, plate at p. 210; cf. S. Seligmann, *Der böse Blick*, 1910, I, 305. The necklace was found in Kerch, Crimea, and is presumably in one of the Russian museums.

135. From C. Ricci, *Tavole storiche dei mosaici di Ravenna*, 1935, VI, *San Vitale*, plate LVI. Cf. the feeding of Abraham's three visitors, ibid., plate LVIII, and the eucharistic presentation of the sacrifice of Isaac in ibid., VII, *San Apollinare in Classe*, plate LXX.

136. Published by courtesy of the Palestine Archaeological Museum, where it is no. 32.2890. It is of friable local limestone. See Iliffe in *QDAP*, III (1933), 90 and plate XXIV, 3. Iliffe thought it a bread stamp, the most likely assumption, though it could have been used to stamp the center of plates.

137. E. S. Drower, *The Mandaeans of Iraq and Iran*, 1937, 232, says that the Parsis mark their sacred loaves with three rows of three little circles, while saying, "Good thoughts, good words, good deeds," and that the Nestorians have a similar custom with sacred bread. She has a rich collection of such instances in an unpublished manuscript I had the privilege of reading.

a motif in itself; at other times it seems to stand for bread or a patera. As a basis for judging what object one of these forms is supposed to represent, we usually have only the context in which it is drawn or carved. To the "round object" as such we shall return when we discuss rosettes in a later volume. But we now begin to feel that since Jews used the form so commonly as a sanctifying device on so many kinds of objects, the fact that they used it, like pagans before them and Christians later, to represent their bread strongly suggests that Jews of the time had a sense of sanctity about bread, if not solemn rites with it, beyond what has survived in orthodox Judaism.

Indeed it seems likely that Jews had a stamped ritualistic bread comparable to the marked bread of the Eucharist, since we have what appear to be Jewish bread stamps from antiquity. I published several metal stamps in an earlier volume,[138] which may have had various uses. But one,[139] at the Museum of Haifa, is of wood and seemed to Roche of the Museum to be a bread stamp. I should say the same of fig. 96,[140] a wooden stamp from Coptic Egypt with a menorah flanked by unidentifiable objects.[141] One in bronze just published reached me while this volume was in press. It is a seal with two separate stamping faces attached by a bar, fig. 97.[142] The first face has a menorah with what Naményi takes to be a shofar and lulab, and with *Dei gratias* in the border. The other reads *Utere felix.* The round stamp is so constructed as to make it a "round object." Naményi notes that Reifenberg thought these stamps were used "to mark foods that were prepared according to ritualistic prescription"—that is, they would mark the food as kosher. But he himself surmises that "Use it, happy one," or as he wrote me he would prefer, *soit heureux qui s'en servira*, was a formula of good wishes, that it was used to stamp vessels made without the use of molds, and that these vessels would have been used as kiddush cups. He compares it with the inscriptions on gold glasses. Naményi's guess is definitely better than Reifenberg's, but the seal could also have been used as a stamp for ritualistic bread, which made one who ate it *felix* in a mystic sense. Such words, including the inscriptions on gold glasses, were discussed at length in earlier volumes, and this object seems most intelligible in such a context.[143]

We have seen that the ceremonial significance of bread offerings had a great history. Throughout Greco-Roman antiquity bread or cakes had deep sanctity, and we must presume that the element of communion, at least in the sense that the gods eat with the sacrificants, was usually felt. This was probably of especial importance in the Eleusinian

138. See above, III, figs. 1012–1017.

139. See III, fig. 1018.

140. From Oskar Wulff, *Altchristliche und mittelalterliche byzantinische und italienische Bildwerke*, I. *Altchristliche Bildwerke*, 1909, plate XII, fig. 316; cf. p. 99.

141. Wulff suggests that the objects flanking the menorah are the letters iota and sigma (round), and that the device is thus adapted for Christianity. I have not seen the original, but the photograph by no means warrants such an identification of the objects. The stamp seems entirely Jewish to me.

142. From photographs kindly sent me by E Naményi. See his "Vestiges juifs dans les musées de Paris," *Le Revue du F[onds] S[ocial] J[uif] U[nifie]*, IV (1955), 20. He says the diameter of the round seal is .075 m., the length of the rectangular face 0.78 m. He dates it in the third to the fifth century A.D. It is exhibited in the room of Christian antiquities in the Louvre.

143. See above, II, 114–119, 140, 146 f. In the mystic or eschatological banquet at Ostia, III, fig. 637, each participant has such a name; one of them is Felix: cf. I, 245.

mysteries, where the goddesses themselves tended to become the fruit of the ground as well as the ground from which the fruit came, so that taking the cakes from the chest and presumably eating some of them was one of the high points of the initiatory rites. The values of the Eleusinian mysteries were appropriated by a great many of the others. As we shall see, Jews did not need to learn from Greeks that God wanted to share their bread with them, and that he must meticulously be given his portion. But we have learned that Jews, from their hellenistic environment, came to represent this bread as did Greeks, and later Christians, and that in this form there was a suggestion of divine power even of divinity, which nothing in the older Jewish offerings of bread had carried.

The sanctity of Jewish bread is further indicated by the device of presenting it in baskets, and this device we must now consider.

B. BASKETS OF BREAD

BASKETS OF BREAD must be discussed together with baskets of fruit. It is often hard to distinguish the contents of the baskets represented, and the meaning of showing the bread in baskets can appear only as we begin to see the significance of the baskets in general.

1. *Baskets on Jewish Monuments*

IN PALESTINE the earliest Jewish representation of a basket is on the coins of Simon Maccabeus, where a pair of these, filled, are beneath a date palm.[144] Over a doorway in one of the tombs at Sheikh Ibreiq a band of leaves is cut, at the end of which is a basket of fruit.[145] A Palestinian lamp, whose border is a grapevine, has a menorah on the handle and a basket of what seems to be fruit at the spout.[146] In the synagogue mosaic at Beth Alpha two baskets appear in the border. The first contains bread but has a little bunch of three grapes attached to it and is the companion piece to a large bunch of grapes.[147] The contents of the second basket are indistinguishable.[148] Baskets and grapes were reported in a similar border at the synagogue of Naaran.[149] In the synagogue at Beth Alpha one of the Seasons, Summer, conventionally holds a basket, presumably containing fruit.[150]

In the west, in Jewish as in pagan art, baskets are among the regular attributes of the Seasons. They appear with Seasons on four fragments of sarcophagi found in Jewish catacombs,[151] in the first of which a basket of fruit is also between two Seasons. Indeed, on one sarcophagus found in the Catacomb Torlonia the Dionysiac basket appears with the snake emerging from it and Liber pater and a boy performing a rite over it.[152] While I consider this a sarcophagus used by a Jew, it goes so far beyond the ordinary vocabulary

144. See above, III, fig. 690; cf. I, 276.

145. See III, fig. 82; cf. I, 97.

146. See III, fig. 348; cf. I, 159.

147. See III, fig. 633; cf. I, 244.

148. It is to be seen in III, fig. 632, in the upper part of the border at the left. Sukenik guessed that it contains fruit.

149. See I, 254. Sukenik called these "baskets of fruit," but I have not been able to see a photograph of this border, and his description of the contents of baskets is not always reliable. They may have contained bread.

150. See III, fig. 640; cf. I, 249.

151. See III, figs. 733, 789, 796, 824; cf. II, 13, 26, 29, 41.

152. See III, fig. 833; cf. II, 43.

of Jewish symbolism that I do not include its decorations as Jewish symbols. But on another sarcophagus fragment from the Catacomb Vigna Randanini a basket of fruit is under a portrait bust.[153] This seems to me by no means beyond the range of Jewish symbolism, even though portrait busts are rare in Jewish art. Baskets of fruit and flowers with confronting birds flanking them are on the ceiling of one of the painted rooms in Vigna Randanini, and in another room such baskets alternate with designs of fish and ducks.[154]

The basket is represented on three Jewish tombstones at Rome. The first of these Frey describes but does not reproduce.[155] The stone as he describes it bears an inscription to Asterius the gerousiarch and Lucina his wife, with a menorah at the top, a palm branch (or lulab) at the right, and at the left a bird, above which is a "basket of fruits, *sans doute* first fruits." How these objects are drawn in this case I have no way of knowing. But the two stones which he reproduces by no means justify his definite identification. Of these, one [156] bears a simple inscription of a wife to her husband, with an ethrog on one side and the basket on the other; the contents of the basket are indicated only by dots. On the second [157] there are two such baskets, with a stemmed leaf beside one of them. Such leaves are common on inscriptions of all religions of the period, but the emphasis here upon the stem is unusual and suggests that an ethrog may have been intended. In any case the contents of the baskets are indicated again by dots. The suggestion of Graziosi [158] and Müller [159] that these dots represent grain and accordingly that the baskets are filled with offerings of the first fruit of the grain harvest is much more likely than that of Frey,[160] who insists that in each instance the dots represent fruit in the strict sense of the term, not grain. But all agree that it refers to the Festival of First Fruits. Such a conclusion might be strengthened by the fact that the baskets are balanced in one case, possibly in two cases, by the ethrog, and in the third probably by the lulab, both of which symbols come from the Feast of Tabernacles, an alternative harvest Festival.

At Hammam Lif in North Africa two baskets appear,[161] one containing fruits with stems (apparently pomegranates) and the other "round objects," presumably loaves of bread or cakes. We shall see reason to suppose that these two baskets together represent the basic offerings of first fruits. Again in North Africa the Jewish catacomb of Gammarth near Carthage shows the remains of a vintage scene where there were rows of wine jars and of baskets.[162]

That these baskets are merely representations of market baskets used in everyday life the very circumstances of their appearance have made most unlikely. The tradition of such baskets in pagan and Christian art strengthens the impression that baskets thus shown are probably ceremonial baskets or are in some way symbolic.

153. See III, fig. 802; cf. II, 29.

154. See III, figs. 743 f., 749 f.; cf. II, 18.

155. A photograph of the stone was kindly sent to me by the Terme Museum, Rome, where it is no. 72.884 recto. I do not publish the photograph because it shows a patchwork of fragments from which the basket and bird are now gone. Cf. Frey, *CIJ*, no. 95.

156. See III, fig. 702.

157. See III, fig. 784.

158. *NBAC*, XXI (1915), 23.

159. Müller, *Monteverde*, 83 f.

160. *CIJ*, at his no. 213.

161. See above, III, figs. 904, 906; cf. II, 96.

162. See III, fig. 870; cf. II, 66.

2. Baskets in Pagan Art

R. DOUGHERTY [163] has shown that basket symbolism was extensively used in cults of the ancient Near East and that the corresponding usage in Greco-Roman religions was probably derived, or enriched, from them, since seal cylinders and biblical passages indicate that the basket had cryptic meaning, to some extent at least, among the Babylonians and Hebrews before it became a *cista mystica* in the classical world.[164] Dougherty quoted a number of cuneiform documents which indicate that the basket (*sellu* in Babylonian) was used by the king in Babylonia as the object wherein taxes and offerings for him were collected; this basket was sacred and was important in religious rites. These passages are supported by seals and other iconographical evidence. To the Old Testament passages which suggest a ritualistic use of baskets we shall return.[165]

Dougherty omits Egyptian material on the basket in general, though he does cite the legend in Plutarch [166] that, like Moses, Osiris was floated out to sea in a chest. The Egyptian use of the basket may actually have been important in the formation of our Jewish usage, for it is in ancient Egypt that we first see those rows of baskets which appear once in Judaism and many times in early Christian art. But I have found no traces of especial basket symbolism in Egypt, since in that country, for all their artistic resemblance to later designs, fig. 100,[167] the baskets seem quite utilitarian: they contain offerings of food for the dead or are being used in vintage scenes which I can find no reason to think were symbolic.

In Greece the basket was a symbol with various associations, and it almost always contained the most vital symbols of life and redemption.[168] Baskets were used in classical tradition with almost every god in Greece, but rarely in Rome except under Greek influence, and they had various forms. The cista mystica, a tall covered basket, was usually pictured with the snake of Dionysus emerging from it, as we saw on the sarcophagus from the Catacomb Torlonia in Rome,[169] but it actually contained the secret objects of the mystery, including some cakes. To look inside this basket and taste the cakes was the high point of the Dionysiac ceremonies of initiation.[170] The Eleusinian mysteries used both the cista and the calathus, which was an uncovered basket of the sort used in Jewish and

163. "Cuneiform Parallels to Solomon's Provisioning System," *AASOR*, V (1923/4, published 1925), 23–65. To this now add the basket of fruit in the grave painting discussed below, p. 80, and the baskets of fruit on the sarcophagus fragments from Tourmousaya, reported in *RB*, N.S., X (1913), 108 f.

164. Basket symbolism must have first appeared in Greek regions very early, for G. W. Elderkin, *Kantharos*, 1924, 26–28, has traced the device back to the Minoan age.

165. See below, p. 84.

166. *On Isis*, XIII–XV (356C–357A).

167. From Giulio Farina, *La Pittura egiziana*, 1929, plate CXI. The more usual type of representation appears in ibid., plate CXXI.

168. On Greek baskets in general see L. Deubner, "Baskets," *HERE*, II, 433–435, and Dougherty in the same volume, 34–40; articles in DS, I, ii, 812–814, 877, 890 f., 1205–1208, 1211–1213; in PW, III, 2591–2606; X, 1548 f., 1862–1866.

169. See above, III, fig. 833; cf. II, 43.

170. On the *cista mystica* in general see C. Lenormant in DS, I, ii, 1205–1208; A. Mau in PW, III, 2591–2593. A phallus in the cista is mentioned by Clement of Alexandria, *Protrepticus*, II, XIX, 4 (ed. Stählin, p. 15); and the contents of the cista of Eleusis are enumerated in ibid., XXI, 2–XXII, 6 (Stählin, 16 f.); Arnobius, *Adversus nationes*, V, 26. The *kistē* was defined by ancients usually as a basket for food or clothing: see Suidas, Hesychius, and Apollonius Sophista, s.v. *kistē*; Pollux, VI, 13.

Christian art, and to take things out of the cista and put them into the calathus, and then back into the cista, was the "token" (*sunthēma*) of those mysteries. The *cana* was a flat basket which similarly contained mystic objects as well as instruments of sacrifice. It is from a cana that the phallus or snake of Dionysus usually emerges in representations, though the cana may show the god as a baby boy instead.[171] The ramifications of all these forms and uses of baskets, which are indeed very complicated, need not be described. The calathus, as the type which appears in Jewish and Christian art, in any case is the basket of most importance to us. It was frequently put into the hands of a god or goddess to indicate fertility: calathi in the hands of the Seasons, as we have seen them represented in several Jewish examples,[172] are stock attributes of the Seasons. All the forms of the basket were definitely associated with fertility, and Farnell was right when he said that the usual symbols of fertility employed by Greek art language are the calathus and the cornucopia,[173] since the phallus soon became too literal for many people.

The calathi were used in pagan grave inscriptions. A maiden who brings to a funerary stele a calathus, shown on an Attic lecythus,[174] suggests a classic Greek funerary meaning for the basket, and the strange plaques from Locri Epizephyrii indicate something of what that meaning was.[175] For in these plaques the calathus is held by the enthroned goddess, fig. 102; [176] it is brought with other offerings to the grave, fig. 103,[177] or brought to a goddess, fig. 105; [178] it is carried by Victory, apparently carried down to men, along with a cock, fig. 104; [179] it appears on the shelf over some sort of holy cabinet, figs. 106 [180] and 108; [181] it is presented to the young god (Dionysus) appearing from the opened cista or *liknon*, fig. 109,[182] and is used for gathering fruit from a tree, fig. 110.[183] Above all, the calathus appears in the rape of Kore, who, as she is seized, drops it and spills its contents, figs. 107 [184] and 111.[185] This last pointedly suggests again that the basket represents fertility and that the rape of Kore ends the fruits of the earth. She takes a cock to Hades with her, promise of returning crops, but her capture means the end of the fruits of that year. The full calathus must then, both inherently and from its context, mean full fruition and, in funerary art, the full fruition of personal immortality. It is interesting that on Roman sarcophagi centuries later the capture of Persephone meant the spilling of the basket.[186]

171. See, for example, Quagliati, in *Ausonia*, III (1909), 193.

172. See above, II, 18.

173. Farnell, *Cults*, V, 244.

174. Walter Riezler, *Weissgrundige attische Lekythen*, 1914, plate 86.

175. P. Orsi in *BA*, III (1909), 406–428, 463–482. Cf. Quagliati, 136–234.

176. From Orsi, 413, fig. 5.

177. From ibid., 420, fig. 16.

178. From ibid., 428, fig. 27.

179. From ibid., 422, fig. 19.

180. From ibid., 423, fig. 20.

181. From ibid., 425, fig. 23.

182. From ibid., 469, fig. 41. One recalls the phrase of Plutarch, "The holy ones offer a secret sacrifice in the shrine of Apollo whenever the devotees of Dionysus awaken the god (Liknites) of the mystic basket" (*On Isis*, XXXV).

183. From Orsi, 470, fig. 42.

184. From ibid., 465, fig. 32.

185. From ibid., 466, fig. 34; see also Orsi's figs. 33 and 35. In both the figures shown the basket contains fruit, so there seems no justification for L. Deubner's statement, *HERE*, II, 435, that the basket "must be regarded as a flower basket only."

186. See Robert, *Sarkophag-Reliefs*, III, iii, plates CXX–CXXXI.

But she is shown with a full basket on a pagan tomb in Palestine, fig. 112,[187] or rather a dead woman is given the goddess' dignity and attributes to show that the woman has become immortal.

There is no indication that the basket has a different meaning when it appears everywhere in the vintage scenes, both the very early ones where the crude satyrs or sileni harvest the grapes and those of the hellenistic and Roman periods where cupids fill baskets with grapes from the vines. The vintage scene is a motif to which we shall often return in the following volumes; [188] it is common in wall paintings, mosaics,[189] and especially in funerary art. So standardized is this ornamentation that one is inclined to feel that the calathus, when it appears alone, is often an abbreviation of the vintage scene and represents the final product of the vine available for the appropriation of man—that is, it represents immortality again, deification, from a slightly different approach but with the same meaning as for Demeter and Kore.

It is Demeter or the Mother of the Gods or the Syrian Aphrodite, the "Female Principle" by whatever name, associated with Dionysus in a single symbol of hope for immortality, to which reference seems to be made when the basket appears alone or with a mass of other symbols on hellenistic and Roman gravestones. This was especially true during the Roman period in the East. A number of instances may be seen together in the monuments from Cotiaeum in Asia Minor.[190] Here the basket appears alone [191] or with a small bird (a dove?) perched on it.[192] The publishers called these "baskets of wool" in their descriptions, but with no visible justification. These baskets are often presented on stones, which also show an eastern solar eagle [193] or various other symbols.[194] I offer only

187. From a photograph kindly sent me by C. C. McCown. See his "A Painted Tomb at Marwa," *QDAP*, IX (1939/42), 1–30. It is a representation of a man and wife, identified with Hades and Persephone. The contents of Persephone's basket are not certain. McCown says (p. 18) that they may be "a fruit of the color of apricots or *mishmish* . . . red grapes . . . even a basket of flowers . . . possibly poppies." From the leaf in the center the one thing they cannot be is loaves of bread or cakes. The leaf, which is long, suggests grain to me more than anything else.

188. The motif can be adequately seen in a single volume, Billiard, *La Vigne*, figs. 7, 9, 64 f., 67, 95 f., 123, 133, 136 f., 145, and plate xv.

189. A mosaic floor from Sousse in North Africa shows the counterpart of the Hammam Lif baskets within coils of the vine. Other objects, as at Hammam Lif, especially birds, are in other coils. The whole is a border round a Bacchic procession. See P. Gauckler et al., *Musées et collections archéologiques de l'Algérie et de la Tunisie, Musées de Sousse*, Paris, 1902, plate vi, 1 (Description de l'Afrique du Nord, XI).

190. See W. H. Buckler, W. M. Calder, and C. W. Cox, "Asia Minor, 1924. II. Monuments from Cotiaeum," *JRS*, XV (1925), 141–175, with plates xix–xxiv.

191. Ibid., 153, fig. 77; 166, fig. 88; 175, fig. 93; 171, no. 162 (plate xxiii).

192. Ibid., 146, fig. 66; 156, no. 144 (plate xxi); 158, no. 145 (plate xxi); 159, no. 146 (plate xxi). Cf. S. Reinach, *Voyage archéologique en Grèce et en Asie Mineure*, 1888, plate 135, no. 2; *JÖAI, Beiblatt*, XXX (1936), 54, figs. 30, 31. A dove is on either side of the basket in *AA, JDAI*, XLVIII (1933), 138, fig. 21.

193. Buckler et al., 153, fig. 77; 159, no. 146 (plate xxi); and, as I should guess, 165, fig. 86. Here, what the authors suggest may be "a flaming altar(?)" looks to me more like a basket. The "flame" may well be the foliage from fruit or grain as we saw it above in III, fig. 906.

194. *JÖAI, Beiblatt*, XXX (1936), 56, fig. 33; 62, fig. 37; 63, fig. 38. *Annual of the British School at Athens*, XIII (1906/7), 308, fig. 12, *JRS*, XVIII (1928), 31, fig. 8.

one example, a basalt tombstone from Roman Syria on which the basket and solar eagle stand below the husband and wife, fig. 114.[195] It is a stone reputedly found in Marash. In Cumont's sketch the eagle has a tiny wreath in its mouth like those in the mouths of the eagles at the synagogue of Yafa,[196] but the wreath does not appear on this stone. The baskets themselves most commonly were indicated as containing a "means of grace," a holy food of some kind which promised greater life both here and hereafter. Jewish and Christian usage appears to have carried on this value unchanged.

3. *Baskets in Early Christian Art*

ONE OF THE first things encountered in early Christian art is the association of the basket of bread with the Eucharist. This was done abstractly by presenting the fish and basket, with the red of the wine smeared upon the basket, fig. 60.[197] The same idea seems represented by the fish and basket in the church at Tabha, fig. 48, beside the altar. In the early eucharistic scenes Christ beside a table touches a number of baskets with his rod: the rod shows that Christ is here an adaptation of a Moses figure.[198] The same idea again was expressed simply by putting baskets on either side of a eucharistic scene [199] or, more commonly, by showing Christ multiplying the loaves in baskets (usually seven) with his rod, without the eucharistic setting.[200] When the baskets become wine jars which Christ touches with his rod beside the eucharistic banquet,[201] the idea is still before us that Christ founded the Eucharist. And when the baskets appear in vintage scenes in the catacombs,[202] it is not a stretch of imagination to suppose that the early Christians who saw them took their implication to be that the Erotes in the vine were plucking no ordinary

195. From a photograph published by courtesy of the Department of Antiquities, Israel. It appeared in *Israel, Life and Letters*, 1953, 82, where it was supposed, from the eagle, to be the stone of a Roman centurion and his wife. There is no inscription on the stone, and nothing indicates that the people represented were Romans. It is much like the stones at Cotiaeum, though it is even more deeply eastern in feeling than they. F. Cumont, *Etudes syriennes*, 1917, 48, fig. 24, published a sketch of the stone, or a very similar one, and properly recognized that the basket and eagle alike had reference to immortality. He even suggested (p. 49, n. 3) that the basket with the eagle, several examples of which he shows (pp. 42–48), represents the lunar divinity beside the solar eagle. This is possible, but I know no evidence to confirm it.

196. See above, III, fig. 569.

197. See above, p. 57. It is the convention of years' standing to prove that the Christian calathus is eucharistic by quoting Jerome, *Epistle*, CXXV, 20 (*CSEL*, LVI, 141): "No one is richer than he who carries the body of the Lord in a wicker basket (*canistro*) or his blood in a glass (*vitro*)." But the generalization is very dubious from the context, which tells how an extraordinary Bishop of Toulouse, Exuperius, gave himself and his goods exclusively to feed the poor, and carried such a basket in his ministrations. That the basket was used sacramentally in general may be true but cannot be concluded from this one passage.

198. Wilpert, *Pitture*, plate 57, 115, 120, 265. The transition of the Moses figure with the rod to that of Christ was mentioned in my "Early Christian and Jewish Art," *JQR*, N.S., XXXIII (1943), 409, and will be discussed further in a later volume.

199. Wilpert, *Pitture*, plates 15, 41.

200. Ibid., plates 54, 92, 115, 120, 139, 165, 196, 199, 212, 216, 226, 228, 237, 240. It may be that the earliest relevant literary reference to sacramental baskets is that in Mark VI, 43. The same convention often appears on Christian gold glass: R. Garrucci, *Vetri ornati di figure in oro*, 1858, plates VII, 1–5, 16 f.; VIII, 1.

201. Wilpert, *Pitture*, plate 57.

202. Ibid., plates 33 f., 52, 148, 245.

fruit but the eucharistic gift of the True Vine which divine love had made available. Christians could put the basket in the interstices of a vine much as the Jews had done in Hammam Lif and Beth Alpha. Figure 113 [203] shows a mosaic from a Christian church at Jerusalem. In the center Christ as Orpheus tames the wild natures typified not only by the animals and birds but by Pan and Heracles as a centaur. Round this runs a vine made of acanthus leaves as at Hammam Lif, within whose loops are, for the most part, animals and birds, as in the synagogues. But in the second opening from the top, right, is a basket whose contents the excavators could not identify.[204] We may well conclude that baskets were profoundly symbolic in Christianity at the time when Jews were drawing their baskets in almost the same forms. In fact, the Christian baskets seem to me to stem from Jewish prototypes, since it is hard to believe that the Jewish baskets were derived from the Christian eucharistic ones. Furthermore, the baskets as used in Judaism itself naturally would suggest that they had meaning in connection with grapes, especially the one in Beth Alpha which, though containing bread, not only balances a bunch of grapes but actually has a few grapes attached to it. The designs in themselves, in short, would suggest a ceremonial use of bread with wine in Judaism which much resembled that in Christianity.

C. *SYMBOLIC VALUE OF BREAD*

IT SEEMS an innovation of Jews and Christians that the baskets represented in such places should contain bread. For though we have seen that pagans often brought bread in baskets or chests to sacrifices and mystic rites, I have not been able to find a single calathus of bread represented in pagan art outside Egypt and must conclude that common as were the pagan ceremonial baskets with bread, the Jewish symbols of calathi with bread (followed by the Christian calathi) could not as such have been borrowed from pagan art types. While the baskets themselves are pagan, to represent them as being filled with bread must be presumed to reflect some Jewish usage of bread, or of bread in baskets. The baskets seem to sanctify the bread they contain and to indicate its "value."

But what was that value? The appearances of loaves of bread, with fish and in baskets, in Jewish synagogues and on Jewish tombstones suggest that the bread was at that time something sacred. The symbol, like the Jewish fish and, as we shall see, the Jewish symbols of wine, was taken over by Christians to represent the Host. Christianity and Judaism alike used the "round object" to represent both bread and mystic light as the source of

203. From a photograph, courtesy of the Archeological Museum, Istanbul, where the mosaic now is. See the first publication by the excavator, Vincent, in *RB*, X (1901), 436–444, esp. for the basket, 439.

204. Another striking parallel between this and the Beth Alpha mosaic is a strange medallion in each: in the Orpheus mosaic it appears just above the basket; at Beth Alpha it is the fourth medallion above the basket, In both cases it is filled with odd-shaped objects lying loose. At Beth Alpha they lie within a circle which Sukenik (*Beth Alpha*, 42) took to be a "vessel" (see his plate XXIII, 2) holding fruit. Clearly there was a common symbolic tradition behind the designs of these various borders. It was a tradition probably preserved later in carpets or tapestries, as Sukenik assumes, and Strzygowski illustrated: *ZDPV*, XXIV (1901), 139–171.

life. When such loaves were put in baskets, they appear to have been marked thereby as sacred bread. And I cannot imagine that sacred bread had any use but as sacred food. The bread was presumably eaten, and eaten under such circumstances that the life-light it brought would be valuable even on a grave or among the symbols in the vine in a synagogue. The symbolic form, however, has come over from paganism, and such direct transition of a symbol is beginning to suggest to us a continuity of value, although new explanations contradicted the old. The bread offered the gods in sacrifice, or eaten in a mystic meal, was a form of communion with the gods, a way of sharing their life to the extent that one shared their divine immortality. Of the Christian Host the same could be said, however much the Christian Eucharist surpassed any pagan rites in depth and feeling. Between the pagan and Christian usages of bread and baskets stand the Jewish "round objects," and it was bread in baskets in the Jewish form which became the favorite way of representing the bread of heaven for Christians.

The natural conclusion one draws from the Jewish "round objects," accordingly—a conclusion we should at once come to in any other religion—is that corresponding to the symbol there was an actual bread or cake in Judaism the eating of which brought divine life or salvation. This salvation, by analogy, would have consisted in escape from the body, or sharing in divine nature, in terms of a bread which was Light, or in terms of astral or solar mysticism. In any case the bread would have brought life here and in the life to come, since that seems to have been the meaning of the symbol for both pagans and Christians. With this would harmonize the frequent other appearances of the "round object," those on tombs—where it corresponds to the similar object on Christian tombs—within wreaths, and under the mystic table at Dura. To call these simply mazzoth explains nothing, for no Jew trained only in Jewish halacha would ever dream of representing mazzoth in such ways: he did not desire to be buried with one and would not think of representing a mazzah on his menorah. If the "round object" on Jewish tombs at that time was a mazzah, the mazzah meant something which it does not mean now. That is, the bread symbols, in baskets and simply as "round objects," suggest strongly that we must look beyond the usual rabbinic tradition of mazzoth to explain them.[205]

It is to biblical proof texts and to ancient usages of bread that the Jews of the Roman world must have looked to justify their symbolism. Dougherty [206] recalled in his discussion of oriental baskets that at the consecration of priests a basket (Hebrew *sal*) was used which contained unleavened bread and unleavened cake mingled with oil, and wafers anointed with oil. At the ceremony one each of the loaves, cakes, and wafers were to be taken from the basket, waved, and then burnt on the altar; after the sacrifice the new priests were to take the unleavened bread to the door of the tent and eat "those things whereof atonement was made to consecrate and sanctify them: but a stranger shall not eat thereof because

205. The custom in the East of hanging a mazzah in the synagogue throughout the year (*JE*, VIII, 396; *UJE*, VII, 414) may recall the "round objects" on the menorahs and carved on synagogues. But if any such origin of the modern custom existed, it is entirely forgotten by the Jews who do it, for they say only that it is to remind them throughout the year of the deliverance from Egypt.

206. *AASOR*, V (1925), 23–65. See above, p. 78.

they are holy."[207] A very similar rite, including a basket of the same foods, was used in the ceremony in which a Nazirite was released from his vow; and when Gideon presented an offering to the angel of Yahweh, he placed the flesh of a kid in a basket of the same type.[208] From all of this Dougherty concluded that this basket had "mystic significance." These baskets of bread in the Old Testament appear to me indeed to represent a holy food, a "thing whereof atonement was made." That the bread could be eaten only by the priests or, in a probably older ceremony, by a Nazirite who by his vow had made himself at least temporarily a peculiarly sacred person, strengthens this impression. The function of the baskets was to indicate the sanctity of the bread, if not directly to consecrate it. But these were Temple ceremonies from which the Jew of the diaspora was in practice shut away even before the Temple was destroyed. They seem to me of little direct importance for explaining the symbols we are discussing.

1. *First Fruits*

OF MUCH GREATER relevance appear to be the practices associated with First Fruits. For the basket is mentioned also in the Old Testament as the vehicle of the first fruits. Dougherty did not discuss this basket because it had another name in Hebrew, but we are following objects and symbols, not words, and the Festival of First Fruits seems very important to me here.

First Fruits was from the beginning an important matter for all Jews,[209] as it was among the Babylonians and Canaanites, and indeed is found to be almost universally so among savages.[210] In the earliest legislation the reference is to a "feast of harvest, the first fruits of thy labors," which was apparently to be observed twice, once for the summer harvest and once for the autumn.[211] The first fruits were to be brought into the "house of Yahweh."[212] This seems to me an addendum to adjust a primitive offering at shrines to the later centralization of the offering in the Temple in Jerusalem. In Deuteronomy[213] it is stipulated that the first fruits be brought to the Temple in a basket which the priest is to put before the altar, and the person who makes the offering is to recite the story of the coming of the Israelites from Egypt to the land of milk and honey. After this he, with Levites and sojourners, is to "rejoice" in God's gifts, which Peake takes to mean that he is to celebrate a feast. In what is perhaps a later addition[214] this offering is made the portion of Levi, and in Ezekiel[215] it is the portion of the priests, here including specifically the first fruits of the dough. In the Holiness Code[216] there is mention of the offering of a sheaf of the first fruits, which should be waved; sacrifices of a lamb, of meal, and of wine

207. Exod. XXIX, 2, 3, 23, 32–34; cf. Levit. VIII, 2, 26, 31.

208. Num. VI, 15, 17, 19; Judges VI, 19.

209. An outline of the material from the Old Testament will be found by W. Nowack in *JE*, V, 398; by A. S. Peake in *HDB*, II, 10 f.; and by J. Strahan in *HERE*, VI, 46 f.

210. J. G. Frazer, *Golden Bough*, 3d ed., II, 48–168; J. A. MacCulloch in *HERE*, VI, 41–45.

211. Exod. XXIII, 16.

212. Ibid., 19; cf. XXXIV, 22, 26.

213. Deut. XXVI, 1–11.

214. Deut. XVIII, 4.

215. Ezek. XLIV, 30.

216. Levit. XXIII, 10–14, 17–21.

were to follow. Until this was done nothing from the new harvest might be eaten in any form. Specifically there were to be two "wave-loaves," made of fine flour and with leaven. The Priestly Code [217] makes it even more clear that the first fruits were the property of the priests, and they have become not merely the first but "all the best." By this time all trace of the earlier popular feast seems to have disappeared, and the offering comes very close to, if it does not merge into, the tithe.

The Talmud gives no indication of the continuance of First Fruits as a popular Festival. The treatise *Bikkurim* [218] in the Babylonian Talmud, for example, describes the processions carrying the baskets to the Temple with flute playing. "Even King Agrippa would take the basket and place it on his shoulder and walk as far as the Temple court." The baskets of the rich were inlaid with gold and silver, while those of the poor were wicker baskets of peeled willow branches, and the priests were given the baskets along with their contents. Nothing, however, is said of a feast in which any but the priests would share on these occasions. Indeed, the talmudic rabbis treat First Fruits throughout in an antiquarian spirit. Their discussion concerns only the proper laws for the offering in the Temple, as concluded from the various commands in the Torah. But they admit that with the destruction of the Temple the law in practice became a dead letter,[219] and in several places they suggest that now as a substitute adequate in God's sight Jews contribute to the support of rabbinical scholars.[220]

First Fruits in its original form of celebration and in rabbinical tradition, accordingly, gives us no help with our baskets and loaves on the Jewish monuments we are considering, to say nothing of the two baskets beside each other at Hammam Lif, one filled with bread, the other with fruit. And yet it still seems likely that there was some connection, since it is only in the Festival of First Fruits that bread and baskets appear together. If this is so, it means that the bread of First Fruits had received an entirely new interpretation, one that connected it with spiritual salvation and immortality.

The idea suggested to us by the Jewish representations is found fully formed in the New Testament and in early Christian tradition. We get it there not with any exposition but only in passing references; yet as compared with the laws of First Fruits in the Old Testament and rabbinical sources, we are clearly in a new world. In view of my conviction that passing allusions imply common knowledge, the references to First Fruits in the New Testament become highly significant.

The term by which the Hebrew word for First Fruits was translated in the Septuagint

217. Num. XVIII, 12 f.

218. See esp. III, 1–8 (ET, 399–401).

219. *BT*, *Shekalim*, VIII (ET, 36): "[The laws of] the shekels and of the first fruit have force only during the existence of the Temple."

220. As in *MR*, *Levit.*, XXXIV, 13 (ET, 439). In this sense First Fruits went over to the Christian church and became its financial basis. In the *Didache*, 13, the true prophet is to be given first fruits of various foods, clothing, and money, and from this can be traced the regular support of bishops and clergy, to be transformed, as in Judaism, into the tithes. See J. A. MacCulloch in *HERE*, VI, 45. I suspect that this obligation for regular support was one of the factors most important in the superiority of the Christian church organization over that of the pagan religions.

was *aparchē*, which originally in classical Greek seems to have referred to preliminary offerings before a sacrifice, such as hairs cut from the forehead of a victim.[221] This was broadened by Plutarch's time,[222] at least, so that the term indicated the banquet held at sacrifices and the organized ceremonial feasts, ceremonies of almost sacramental participation. At the same time the term meant the offering to the gods of the firstlings, much as in Israel, so that in this sense the Greek word was a literal translation of the Hebrew.

But in the New Testament, Christ is himself the first fruit of those who sleep.[223] The immediate impression given by this passage is that Christ was the first dead man to come to life again, and that he is the example par excellence of those who will rise from death to immortality. Such a use in the sense of firstling seems justified by the fact that Paul called the first convert of Asia [224] and the first of Achaia [225] each the first fruit of his own district. But Christ as the first fruit of the dead was more than the first one to be raised; he was the means of this immortality for others, and this deeper meaning of the term is assured by other statements of Paul. For "first fruit" seems in itself to indicate Christ when Paul says [226] that we who have the first fruit of the Spirit within ourselves groan until the consummation, when we shall receive our final "adoption," that is, fully be made "sons," by the redemption of our bodies, an event which presumably will occur at the resurrection when our bodies will be transformed to something spiritual.[227] The first fruits in this passage must be Christ himself, or what Paul calls the spirit of Christ, working for our salvation within us. As the fish and lamb could be now the Savior and now the Christian, so the convert could be called first fruit, as we saw in Asia and Achaia, with more implied than that they were firstlings.

Strangely enough, the idea, essentially mystical, is directly stated in the hard-headed epistle of James,[228] where it is said that we are the first fruits of his creatures, since God, the Father of lights, has brought us forth by his Logos of Truth, a statement which seems to imply the second birth of Christians through the Logos, who is the truth and the instrument of Creation, as set forth in the Fourth Gospel. The author of the epistle assumed that he was writing to people who knew this way of thinking so well that he could refer to it in passing as a commonplace. The Israelites as a group seem to be the first fruit to Paul [229] as, we shall see, they were to Philo, while in the Apocalypse [230] the word is reserved as a title for those saints in glory who have not been defiled by women.

When now we suddenly see symbols of first fruits on Jewish tombs, the conclusion seems to me inevitable that these passing allusions in early Christianity were all intelligible to readers of the New Testament, as they have not been since, because the conception was already proverbial in Judaism that first fruits was a symbol of immortality, if not a

221. On first fruits in Greek tradition see W. H. D. Rouse in *HERE*, VI, 45 f.; P. Stengel in PW, I, 2666–2668.

222. Plutarch *De recta ratione audiendi*, 6.

223. I Cor. xv, 20, 23. "Those that sleep" are literally those who are in the *koimēsis*, the sleep of burial. This is the word we have met constantly on Jewish tombs, the word which has become our "cemetery."

224. Rom. xvi, 5.

225. I Cor. xvi, 15.

226. Rom. viii, 23.

227. I Cor. xv, 35–44.

228. Jas. i, 17 f.

229. Rom. xi, 16.

230. Rev. xiv, 4.

symbol of some special saving principle or Being, the Light-Logos, which Christians came to identify with their own Savior and which brought immortality. The idea, we saw, was not to be found in the rabbinical writings, as far as I know; so we turn to the tradition of First Fruits in Philo.

Philo at first disappoints us, for he gives no exact equivalent to the conception used in the New Testament. I should guess that this was because Philo himself had very little interest in personal immortality.[231] But Philo says much about the institution of First Fruits which helps a great deal in the problem.

He uses the term in a general way for contributions to the Temple, such as the mirrors contributed by the women for the brazen laver,[232] spoils dedicated after a conquest,[233] and the gifts sent to Jerusalem by Jews of the diaspora.[234] The priests, he says, offer first fruits when they make libation of the blood and burn the fat in the sacrifices,[235] and when out of the offerings they themselves take some of the grain, mix it with oil into cakes, fry them, and then burn them on the altar.[236] Still more figuratively, he says that young men should offer the first fruits of their minds to culture (*paideia*).[237]

Of the ancient ritualistic requirement to offer first fruits Philo has, of course, much to say in a variety of connections. We may well begin with his more legal treatise, the *Special Laws*, where he explains for gentiles the custom in his day still practised in the Temple.

Within the Festival of Unleavened Bread, on the second day of that Festival, Philo says, it is required that a sheaf of barley be brought to the Temple as a first fruit not only of Palestine but of the whole earth.[238] For in making this offering the Jews act as priests for all humanity, since they alone properly recognize the one and true God. So their offerings, Festivals, and prayers are "a means of supplication for the human race in general." This suggests at once that First Fruits represents more than an offering of thanksgiving, one which will insure future crops. It is a "means of supplication." For such ceremonies Philo's collective term is "eucharists," offerings of thanksgiving.[239] Philo uses this term for almost all the Festivals[240] but does so constantly in discussing First Fruits. The sheaf is given in thanks for the fertility of the past, but as God sees our gratitude he rewards us by fertility in the future, as we learn explicitly elsewhere.[241]

231. See my "Philo and Immortality," *HTR*, XXXIX (1946), 85–108.

232. *Mos.* II, 137: This was the first fruit of their modesty and of the marriage relation.

233. *Mos.* I, 316–318.

234. *Legat.* 156 f., 216, 291, 311 f., 316 f. In *Spec.* I, 77 f., Philo says that the donors gladly give these first fruits in every city, "expecting that the payment will give them release from slavery or healing of diseases and the enjoyment of liberty fully secured and also salvation in all respects." Colson here translates *sōtēria eis hapan* as "complete preservation from danger," but I suspect Philo used the word with more than physical security in mind.

235. *Spec.* IV, 125.

236. *Spec.* I, 255 f. Philo seems to have Levit. II, 14–16 in mind.

237. *Prob.* 15.

238. *Spec.* II, 162–175.

239. Ibid., 168, 171.

240. See my "Literal Mystery in Hellenistic Judaism," *Quantulacumque, Studies Presented to Kirsopp Lake*, 1937, 237 f.

241. *Virt.* 159. Here *eucharistērion* is shortened, as often, into *charistērion* without change of meaning. Cf. *Decal.*, 160.

The sheaf is a great offering, but another follows it fifty days later (the number is of course made portentous) when the Festival of First Fruits proper is celebrated.[242] For this Philo prefers the term "feast of the first begotten," a biblical equivalent of First Fruits.[243] In an earlier discussion [244] Philo mentions the offering of the first begotten of the flocks, but in this passage his central emphasis is upon the offering of the first wheat in the form of two loaves of leavened wheat bread.[245] The leaven typifies the deepest meaning of the rite, he says, for the possession of adequate provision for future food brings joy, and this is in the rite itself, which is a "eucharist celebrated with joy." [246]

It seems to me highly significant when Philo goes on to explain that the eucharist celebrated in material (*aisthētēs*) form with the leavened loaves is really a eucharist of the invisible exaltation (*eupathia*) in the mind.[247] Philo's terms in this statement, as Colson points out,[248] are from Stoicism, but he has given an amazingly accurate description of this eucharist as what Christians later called an outward and visible sign of inner and invisible grace.

The Feast of First Fruits, Philo says, is properly celebrated in the spring with the wheat harvest and the young animals born at that time.[249] But actually it continues as long as there are fresh crops, "from early summer to late autumn," [250] since the first fruit of each sort of crop is to be put into baskets and given the priests, who before eating will set the baskets before the altar while the donor sings a canticle of dedication. The provision for this is familiar in the Bible,[251] but Philo considerably improves on the canticle for the occasion as he paraphrases it. The basket to him then could have been a sign of first fruits, and it might contain offering of any sort. These offerings of baskets, or of first fruits in general, he explains, do honor to God and in restraining our acquisitiveness lead us into the virtues of piety and humanity.[252]

Philo, of course, could not stop with this. The basket, or first fruits, symbolizes to him that we should offer to God "the first fruits of the *euphoria* [there is a pun here, since this word in Greek means both a high state of mind and fertility] of the fine things which the soul made to flower, develop, and bring forth fruit"—that is, the "harvest of the mind." [253] The highest intellectual products are the gift of God no less than are the products of the field, a fact, Philo points out, which was made clear especially in the offerings of Cain and Abel.[254] The real trouble with Cain's sacrifice was that he kept the first fruits for himself and gave only from what ripened afterward, which involved, Philo

242. *Spec.* II, 179–187; cf. I, 131–140.

243. The term *heortē prōtogennēmatōn* is made the direct synonym of *aparchē* in *Spec.*, I, 183, from Exod. XXIII, 16.

244. *Spec.* I, 183–185. The loaves are discussed here in Sec. 185.

245. See also *Spec.*, I, 132.

246. *Gegēthotas eucharistein*, *Spec.* II, 185.

247. Ibid.

248. In his note to this passage in his translation of Philo, VII, 628.

249. *Spec.* II, 214–222.

250. Ibid., II, 220 f.

251. Deut. XXVI, 1–11.

252. *Virt.* 95; *Spec.* IV, 98 f.

253. *Som.* II, 272. The canticle of consecration is here much reduced and obviously refers not to worship in the Temple at Jerusalem but to the cosmic temple, where the fruits of the mind could alone be offered.

254. *Conf.* 124–127.

tells us, failure to recognize that the conceptions in our minds are showered down upon us by God. The figure is that of rain rather than Philo's more usual Light-Stream, but here as in the epistle of James, where the figure is that of light, God is the source of every good and perfect gift. It is also notable that in this passage of Philo the first begotten has been called by that word of great importance, *prototokos*,[255] a fact which suggests that much of the meaning of the term in Christianity has its background in this developing significance of first fruits.

Our proper offering of first fruits, Philo tells us, is in our righteous conduct and virtue,[256] and in offering these we offer a *logos eucharistērikos*,[257] which may be translated as "address of thanksgiving," though it is hard to see how righteous conduct could be described as an "address" and I suspect that much which lay behind this "address of thanksgiving" also lay behind Paul's obscure *logikē latreia*.[258] In an allegory which we need not try to unravel Philo explains this experience as consisting of four stages. First we should recognize the inadequacy of even the lore of the ancients and should have "the sudden beam of self-inspired (*automathēs*) wisdom" shine in us, spring up within us as young shoots, so that we become God's disciples.[259] This grain is secondly to be roasted into firm loaves by the Unconquerable Logos,[260] and the loaves, thirdly, must by analysis and study be sliced into all sorts of parts and woven into a harmonious whole.[261] I gather that Philo means by this that we must take the insights of mystical revelation and work them into what we would now call a coherent system.[262] The fourth stage is one of contemplation and self-discipline in this system.[263] The man who can do all this is the one who can fully offer first fruits. Such an achievement is utterly beyond the mass of Jews, Philo is aware, but God nevertheless took the Jewish people to be his own. For the Jews, Philo says, not only offer first fruits for all men but are themselves the first fruits of men in God's sight. The Jews, he says,[264] have been set aside as the first fruits of the human race to the Creator and Father, a prerogative they attained, however imperfect individual Jews may since have been, through the righteousness and virtues of the Patriarchs, "which endure like immortal plants bearing an everblooming fruit that for their descendants is saving and profitable in every way." That is, in the virtues of the Patriarchs Jews have a first fruit which has made all Jews into first fruits, the especial symbol of which could, we now see, be baskets filled with fruit of any kind or with grain or with loaves of bread. The double implication of Christianity is already here in Philo. Just as the Christians become first fruits through the merit of Christ, the Jews had become first fruits through the merits of the Patriarchs. Christ as the saving first fruits has his prototype in Philo's Jewish saviors, the Patriarchs who are also first fruits.

255. Philo had it, of course, from the "first-born" in Exod. XXII, 29 (28 in LXX) and Num. XVIII, 15, 17.

256. *Sacr.* 73; cf. 109.

257. Ibid., 74.

258. Rom. XII, 1. It is notable that this in Paul is also an offering up to God of our bodies, presumably in keeping them virtuous.

259. *Sacr.* 78 f.

260. Ibid., 80 f.

261. Ibid., 82–85.

262. Ibid., 86.

263. Ibid., 87.

264. *Spec.* IV, 180 f.

In one of his most deeply mystical passages,[265] Philo explains how we may share in the virtues of the Patriarchs: it is, Philo says, through intercourse (*sumbiōsis*) with cosmic Virtue, who was especially represented in Sarah though also in the other wives of the Patriarchs.[266] Like Abraham, Philo in his youth was not ready for her but bore bastards by other mistresses—that is, by lower forms of intellectual activity—which distracted him from the true ideal. We should pray that we may be worthy to beget a child by Virtue herself, as Abraham finally did. So do we get her full virtues in ourselves. We may do so only as we become identified with God as Abraham did, for "she is accustomed to bear for God alone, and she offers up in Eucharist the first fruits of the good things she bears to God who, as Moses says,[267] opens her womb which never loses its virginity." Philo, I said, does not link this with immortality, since mystic elevation and union seem to have made personal immortality unimportant to him. But the popular version of mystical exaltation has always been to hope for it in the next life, and we may well suppose that most of the Jews whose funerary symbols we are studying thought of this final achievement in eschatological terms. It was there that they too would become, or have in themselves to offer, the true first fruits of the spirit.

We have come by a devious way, but now we can see that first fruits, whether shown as baskets of fruit, baskets of loaves, or just as loaves, would be a very meaningful thing to represent on tombstones. They marked the true Jew, the accepted Jew, the Jew who had *sōtēria*, salvation or security, even in the face of death. Incidentally, the Christian use of the figure, that Christ is the true first fruits born of a Virgin and that we can share in his nature so that we ourselves become first fruits, now seems natural and meaningful for the first time. The Christian passages could all be quite passing allusions because, I am sure, this wealth of significance in First Fruits had grown from the ancient offering in the Temple to be one of the deepest symbols of the Judaism of the diaspora.

First Fruits, I am further convinced, was originally one of the important inspirations of the Christian eucharistic bread. The tradition all goes back, presumably, to the strange story about an incident in the life of Elisha:

> There came a man from Baal-shalishah, and brought the man of God bread of the first fruits, twenty loaves of barley, and fresh ears of grain in his sack. And Elisha said, "Give to the men, that they may eat." But his servant said, "How am I to set this before a hundred men?" So he repeated, "Give them to the men that they may eat, for thus saith Yahweh, 'They shall eat and shall have some left.' " So he set it before them and they ate, and had some left, according to the word of Yahweh.[268]

Here, in the marvelous power of the loaves of the first fruits is the clear prototype of the feeding of the multitude in the Gospels. Fish had become so meaningful a food, as we saw in the previous chapter, that to make the New Testament story they were added to

265. *Congr.* 5–7.

266. For a fuller exposition of this notion in Philo see my *By Light, Light*, 139 f., 146.

267. Where Philo got this from Moses I cannot discover. Wendland and Colson both refer to Gen. XXIX, 31, but that passage seems to me quite irrelevant.

268. II Kings IV, 42–44.

the bread of this incident of Elisha, along with the quite relevant detail that what was "left" was gathered into baskets. So it is bread in the basket, as shown both in the Christian catacombs and at Tabha, which with fish represents the Eucharist.[269]

2. *Manna*

THE ASSOCIATION of First Fruits with the miraculous feeding and the Eucharist suggests another line of thought which, we know from the Fourth Gospel, was early a part of this complex, namely the bread of heaven, the manna, with which as heavenly food Jesus is made directly to identify himself: or, more accurately, the manna was a lesser manifestation of the bread of heaven which is now made fully available in the body of Jesus.[270] The result of eating this heavenly bread, which is Jesus, is that one gets immortal life. The basic idea is likewise made clear through Philo's treatment of manna.

In Philo also the fact that the Israelites got physical nourishment from the manna is of slight moment. In his most important passage on the subject, manna is made directly into the heavenly food of the soul.[271] It consists of the *logoi* that God pours out like rain. Only a day's supply of such food was given at a time, and for several reasons, chiefly because man is not capable of receiving the grace of God in a single torrential rush and because by daily rationing we are constantly reminded of our dependence upon God. He that would try to have God's grace in some other way lacks hope, faith, and sense. The food is also described as lights and heavenly understandings. All of these plurals, including *logoi*, mean the great Light, Sophia, or Logos, in partial, daily portions.[272] Indeed, in another passage [273] Philo insists that the Rock, Sophia, the manna, and the Logos are all synonymous but goes on to say that from this food come two cakes, one of honey that sweetens life, the other of oil, spiritual illumination. As Colson points out,[274] these two cakes are suggested by the fact that the manna in Exodus XVI, 31, tasted like a cake of honey, and in Numbers XI, 8, like a cake of oil. But any Jew would recognize at once a parallel to the two loaves of First Fruits.

This conception of the divine food by which the believer is nourished, food which could be called manna but is better understood to be the Logos itself (or himself), is the one which is directly expressed in the Gospel of John. Here the conception is advanced to the point that Jesus calls himself the true manna, the bread of heaven, the bread of life, or the living bread, which is his flesh. The revelation of this was, according to John, in the miracle of feeding the five thousand, a miracle which itself seems closely akin to the miraculous feeding of the multitude from the basket of bread of First Fruits.

D. BREAD IN LATER MYSTIC JUDAISM

THE PIECES do not completely fit together, but they do suggest a very definite picture. Christ for the Christians was the first fruits who made his followers into first fruits—that

269. See above, p. 81.

270. John VI, 25–58.

271. *LA* III, 162–176. See my *By Light, Light*, 208.

272. Cf. *Fug.* 138; *Mut.* 259 f.; *Congr.* 170–174; *Heres*, 191.

273. *Det.* 114–118.

274. Loeb ed. of Philo, II, 495.

is, conquered their evil nature and gave them immortality. The supreme symbol of this was that as the Logos he was available as a heavenly food, his very body, which the Christians could take into themselves as *logoi*, eucharists, or mystical illuminations, in the Philonic sense, but which was represented in the actual bread that was Christ's body. All of this is attested for Judaism except the last stage, the physical sacrament which can still for Christians be described in Philo's words about First Fruits, that the Eucharist celebrated with material loaves is really a Eucharist of the invisible exaltation of the mind. For Christians such bread is medicine of immortality.

Did Jews of the time, hellenized or rabbinic or both, have any literal feeling about the bread of First Fruits, or of any bread—that it was a bread of heaven which, when properly blessed and eaten, brought such a spiritual benefit? Was this whole body of ideas, which we shall see persisted on into Cabbalism, always with Jews only a mystical allegory of Old Testament texts, or was there a Jewish ritualistic concomitant of eating bread, or first fruits, to which the conception of the body of Christ could easily be applied to make the rite Christian? We cannot, I feel, answer the questions finally either way. Though much suggests it, nothing proves that the Jews ever had a sacrament of the bread of heaven which brought immortality. Yet we must not forget the great vine of the Dura synagogue. As originally drawn there was beneath it on one side a crater flanked by panthers, and on the other a table, on top of which was a banqueting bolster, while a wafer of bread was under the table. We shall discuss this whole design more fully in connection with wine.[275]

To prevent our denying that Jews ever had rituals with bread there comes before our eyes again the bread—with fish, with symbols of wine, with grapes, and in baskets—as it appears in synagogues and on graves. Obviously I myself would like to think that there was such a Jewish bread rite, indeed a rite of fish, bread, and wine, and that the Christians only adapted it for their purpose. I cannot explain the monuments otherwise. But those who with scholarly caution wish to suspend judgment, as in reality I do myself, must never forget these Jewish representations of the bread.

Perhaps a residue of such a Jewish ritualistic use is to be found in a prayer quoted in a former volume,[276] but so striking that it must be repeated here:

> *The Prayer of the Bread.* The Lord God spoke to the Patriarch Abraham: "Arise, take thee bread, wine, water, and an iron vessel, go up upon Mount Tabor and call three times, "Man of God!" When Melchizedek comes out to thee, then cut off from his hair, his nails, and the edges of his lips [his beard], and eat [these clippings]! And do thou give him from the vessel all thou hast with thee that he may eat." Then Abraham the Patriarch arose, took the bread, the wine, the water, and the vessel of iron, ascended Mount Tabor, and called three times, "Man of God!" Melchizedek came out to him. Then he took clippings from his [Melchizedek's] hair, nails, and the edges of his lips

275. See below, pp. 103–111.

276. See above, II, 165. It is from a Coptic ritual published by S. Gaselee, "De Abraha et Melchisedec," *Parerga Coptica*, Cambridge, 1914, II, 2–13.

[his beard], and ate them; and gave him from the vessel all he had with him, and [Melchizedek] ate it. Then Melchizedek blessed Abraham by the inbreathing of his spirit, while he said: "This sign will be effective for all coming generations."

So now again, O Lord, be thou the one who blesses this bread, and give it to thy servant as [a token of] marriage.

This prayer is part of a marriage ritual, which opens with an invocation asking God to bless oil that is to be used as an unguent. Then God is called upon to bless a "crown of justice" with which the bridal pair is to be crowned. The third prayer again blesses oil, a prayer which is perhaps an alternative for the first. In this one the story of the anointing of David is told, and it is made definite that the bride and groom will be anointed with the oil when it has been blessed. The "Prayer of the Bread" follows, and the whole closes with a "Prayer over Wine," which opens with telling how God called upon Michael—but the text breaks off, only to begin again telling how Abraham, at God's command, took bread and wine to Melchizedek. Here Melchizedek blesses the wine in a way to recall the Eucharist: he lifted his eyes to heaven, gave thanks, blessed the bread and wine, sanctified them, broke (the bread), imparted a blessing upon Abraham and his servants, and gave them his peace. This blessing of the bread and wine, however, reflects much more closely the story of Jesus feeding the five thousand in Mark than it does the eucharistic language, and I have repeatedly indicated that the miracle, which seems the earliest eucharistic story of Christianity, appears itself to have grown out of the Jewish practice with First Fruits. The specifically Christian traces in the entire liturgy are so incidental that, as with the synagogue liturgy which I previously published,[277] I suspect that we have here a Christian reworking of a Jewish marriage ritual, in which bread and wine, along with oil and a crown, were blessed and given the bridal couple to be a means of their spiritual blessing as well as the seal of their union. Of this only the blessed wine is now left in Jewish marriage. There are so many uncertainties that no weight can be put upon the liturgy as direct evidence for Judaism. But if in itself the evidence is only a straw in the wind, it may help us to see how the wind was blowing. As we continue we shall feel increasingly that with the rise of Christianity both those Jews who were under rabbinic leadership and the Jews of the diaspora who came later to accept the Talmud repudiated much of the more mystical Judaism which the monuments of our period will increasingly seem to attest. Survivals of the older rituals, though stripped of their mystical implications, have appeared with the fish and will appear much more abundantly as we go on to discuss wine. Such a survival for bread, I suspect, is to be seen in every orthodox meal as the head of the house comes to the table with freshly washed hands, pronounces the blessing, and breaks and eats a piece of bread.

The idea seems almost to become explicit in the *Zohar*. One passage discusses the show bread on the table in the Tabernacle.[278] This bread made "nourishment emanate to the whole world." The table in the Tabernacle was never empty of bread: "In the same manner the table over which a man pronounces blessings for food must not be empty, for

277. See *By Light, Light*, 306–358.

278. *Zohar*, Terumah, 155a (ET, IV, 42).

blessing cannot rest on emptiness." The show bread was the "bread of the Countenance, because all the nourishment and sustenance of the world emanated from this supernal Countenance. . . . Man must cherish the mysteries connected with his [own] table, in all these aspects of which we have spoken on account of that Table [of the Tabernacle]."

Another passage goes on from a discussion of the cup of benediction which is drunk after grace has been recited at the conclusion of a meal:

> The Cup of Benediction is blessed by the very benediction which man pronounces over it to the Holy One, blessed be He, because it is the mystery of Faith, and therefore man must guard it with the utmost care, as the very essence of the King's Majesty, since for its sake is the table blessed. Also, when grace is recited, the table must not be empty, since "no blessing can rest on an empty table." . . . In a word, the heavenly blessings come to rest only on a place that is complete. Esoterically this is expressed in the words . . . "He giveth wisdom to the wise." The symbol for all this is the table of the "Bread of the Countenance," for it is written: "And thou shalt set upon the table bread of the Countenance before me always." [279]

The same idea of the bread upon the Jews' table seems to me to lie behind another passage in which it is said that the manna nourishes and crowns the tree of life so that the community of Israel

> is fed therefrom by the hand of the Righteous One, the sacred grade of the sign of the covenant. In the book of Rab Hannuna the Elder it says that the bread mentioned here is the Sabbath bread, which is double in quantity, as it is written in connection with the manna: "They gathered double bread"; that is to say, bread from heaven and bread from earth, the one being "bread of luxury," the other "bread of poverty." For on the Sabbath the lower bread was united with the upper bread, and one was blessed for the sake of the other. He further said that the Sabbath receives from the celestial Sabbath which flows forth and illumines all, and in this way bread is joined with bread and becomes double.[280]

I strongly suspect that the Jew who wrote these passages, and the multitudes of Jews who, to the present time, have read the *Zohar* almost as canonical writing, actually have felt that their daily table, and especially the Sabbath table, was one from which, by the blessing of the bread and wine, they got more than physical nourishment and that their bread could and did for them become the "bread from heaven." We have for this Jewish usage no such vivid explanation as the Christians evolved when they identified the bread and wine with the body and blood of their Logos. But we do have amazingly similar values in the two religions, and from all the evidence it seems to me much more likely that the early Christians adapted for the Eucharist an old Jewish usage than that mystic Jews, in spite of their abhorrence of Christianity, came to put Christian values upon their own bread and wine. Certainly it now sounds to us very Jewish that at the last supper

279. Ibid., 157b (ET, IV, 52 f.).

280. *Zohar*, Vayehi, 246a (ET, II, 380 f.).

Jesus took the bread and cup, blessed them, "eucharistized" them,[281] and after breaking the bread gave them to his disciples as a means of mystical and eschatological fulfillment. The bread, may I finally repeat, was carried over with the fish and wine in Jewish synagogues and Jewish tombs. The interpretation of one of the three must be incomplete without the others. It is in the study of wine that we will find the strongest confirmation of our position.

281. Mark XIV, 22 f., and Matt. XXVI, 26–28, have *eulogēsas* for the bread and *eucharistēsas* for the wine, but Paul in I Cor. XI, 24, and Luke XXII, 17–19, use the latter term for both blessings, and it is clear that the two are here completely synonymous.

PART VIII

WINE

CHAPTER FOUR

Wine in Jewish Archeology

THE MATERIAL on Jewish cult food, both iconographic and literary, has already led to strong presumptions of a genuinely mystic sacrament among the Jews. To the evidence of this for fish and bread must now be added the constant evidence of the importance of wine; indeed, in the art remains the wine is far more often represented than either of the others.[1]

In Jewish art remains, wine is presented in purely pagan forms, those same pagan forms which reappear as the most important group of symbols of early Christianity, surpassed later only by the cross itself. Judaism, like Christianity, never reduced the wine symbols to a single one: wine could be represented as the vine, the cluster of grapes, the cup, a wine jar, baskets of grapes, vintage scenes, and the wine press. In Christianity the holy drink was further portrayed in Old Testament scenes of Moses bringing water from the rock, or of Melchizedek offering bread and wine to Abraham, scenes which, we shall finally conclude, probably had their origin also in Jewish art.

As before, we must begin by getting clearly in mind how universal these wine symbols are in the Jewish remains of the period, what form they took, and in what settings they appear.

The symbols of wine are among the earliest which we may be sure Jews were using. The decoration of objects from what may be called the years of Pharisaic dominance—that is, from the early Maccabees to the fall of Jerusalem in A.D. 70—was extremely reserved, as we saw on the coins, tombs, ossuaries, and lamps which seem to have been made at this time. Here were no human or animal figures, and no symbols from Jewish cult.[2] Only a very few symbols appear which Jews had borrowed from their neighbors: the "round object," the wreath, the rosette, the acanthus, the cornucopia. Among these were wine symbols of various sorts. A bunch of grapes was the most common presentation

1. Unfortunately this whole question as to the ancient form and meaning of wine in Jewish ritual is usually solved by begging it. I need refer, for example, only to the remark of Bishop W. H. Frere (*The Anaphora*, 1938, 7), who said of the kiddush: "The Jewish Prayer-book of today may be taken as evidence of what was customary in a Jewish home of our Lord's time." Although I doubt that the Prayer Book "may be taken" as such evidence, ordinarily it is so taken.

2. With the exception of the coins of Antigonus bearing a menorah. See above, III, figs. 674 f., and I, 273.

of the symbol on tombs,[3] but the jar or vase also appeared.[4] The first grapes on Jewish coins were on those of Herod Archelaus (4 B.C.–A.D. 6).[5] Wine symbols were common on the coins of the procurators, who were obviously trying much harder than the Herodians to use emblems which would be pleasing to the Jews.[6] Coins minted during the First Revolt and under Bar Kokba almost invariably carried some sort of reference to wine, by means of a wine pitcher, a triple bunch of grapes, a cup, a wine jar, or a grape leaf.[7] On several of the coins the bunch of grapes is shown on one side, a lyre on the other, as in fig. 115,[8] a combination which will later seem significant to us.

On lamps from Palestinian tombs wine motifs appear very commonly,[9] often as a vine growing from a vase,[10] while the wine jar or cup is equally frequent, either by itself[11] or with birds at either side.[12] Many of these are later than the Pharisaic period, but the dating of them is very uncertain. The ossuaries, however, are almost all from this period, and while the vine is not usual on the ossuaries, four of them show a drinking cup so prominently that the symbol was certainly pertinent.[13] Indeed, that the vine growing from a cup was a potent symbol with eschatological reference may be firmly concluded from the fact that an amulet with this design was found between the thighs of a Jewish woman's skeleton in an undisturbed grave in Palestine.[14] She was presumably buried with it on her vulva. The vase appears on another amulet that has the "reaper" on the other side.[15] The vase here is between two palm branches (lulabs?) with *Sabaō* written beside it.[16] A design on an amulet always presupposes belief in its active power.

From this evidence we can only conclude that wine was already a deeply symbolic element for Jews by the time of the early Maccabees and continued so throughout the years of Pharisaic dominance. The vine as such was thus symbolic, as was also wine drinking. While the vine used as a scroll to decorate a lintel could be taken as a merely decorative motif, the cups and the vines growing from cups, as well as the bunches of grapes, suggest much more a symbolic drinking of wine. Their frequent representation in funerary ornament seems to indicate an eschatological implication of such drinking, while this interchangeability with the vine could point to a notion that to drink the wine was to partake in the Vine in some special sense. The symbols on the coins of Herod Archelaus

3. See III, figs. 31 f., 87.

4. See III, figs. 36, 43 (probably later, since it shows also a bull and a lion).

5. See III, fig. 677.

6. See I, 274 f. Cf. III, figs. 680 f.

7. See III, figs. 685, 687–689, 693–699.

8. From Reifenberg, *Coins*, plate XIII, no. 177. See below, p. 105.

9. See above, III, figs. 296, 317–319, 330.

10. See III, figs. 286 f., 320, 322–326, 340.

11. See III, figs. 288 f., 309, 314, 321, 376.

12. See III, figs. 311, 313, 329.

13. See III, figs. 153, 155, 157, 173.

14. See III, fig. 381; cf. I, 166; II, 235.

15. See III, fig. 1207; cf. II, 289.

16. Vases are not common on amulets, but their talismanic importance can be inferred from a famous bust found in Spain, "The Lady of Elché," which has often been discussed for its Greco-oriental quality. Dating from the fourth century B.C., it shows a woman in an unmistakable oriental headdress, with a double-stranded necklace from which hang seven little vases as pendants. See Georges Contenau, *Les Antiquités orientales: Monuments hittites, assyriens, phéniciens, perses, judaïques, chypriotes, araméens*, n.d., plate 39; cf. p. 21 (Musée du Louvre).

and, even more, of the two great Jewish revolts would suggest that such drinking also represented the very existence of the Jewish people as a group.

After the middle of the second century the wine symbols were put everywhere. A tomb door, probably from early in this period, has drinking cups on either side of a menorah,[17] and one sarcophagus shows a vine growing from a vase,[18] two others simply a grapevine.[19] Wine is strangely absent from the rich symbolism of Sheikh Ibreiq [20] and is not usually represented among the Jewish symbols on the blown glass,[21] but it is almost omnipresent in synagogal decoration as the cup or vase,[22] as the vase from which the vine grows,[23] as the vine,[24] or as the bunch of grapes.[25] These are presented in every way, from the border designs, which might in themselves be pure decoration, to starkly isolated objects, as when a bunch of grapes is the sacred object within a wreath,[26] or the vase is between animals.[27]

In the diaspora these symbols were not so commonly used, but they appear often enough to indicate that they had the same reference throughout the Judaism of the Greco-Roman world. The vine as such is much less common in the West than in Palestine. It is represented perhaps as only a formal scroll in the Catacomb Torlonia [28] and on a tombstone from Pannonia.[29] But to take its place the symbols of wine drinking are common. To a Dionysiac vintage scene on a synagogue in Palestine, where grapes are being pressed,[30] corresponds a similar scene on a Jewish sarcophagus at Rome,[31] while there was also a vintage scene on the walls of a Jewish tomb at Gammarth Hill.[32] On the walls of Palestinian synagogues birds are shown eating grapes,[33] as they do at Rome on a tombstone,[34] a sarcophagus,[35] and a catacomb.[36] A cupid plucks grapes on a Roman sarcophagus,[37] and a bunch of grapes stands isolated on a tombstone fragment from Alexandria.[38] The vase or jar of wine appears on four tombstones of Rome [39] and on the peculiar stone we have often referred to from Sicily.[40] It is a lively spouting symbol flanked by doves and peacocks in the synagogue of Hammam Lif,[41] and it is probably represented with two cornucopias

17. See above, III, fig. 44. The same is shown on a lamp, ibid., fig. 310.

18. See III, fig. 250.

19. See III, figs. 238 f.

20. Two wine jars are crudely scratched with two menorahs on a wall in one place (see III, fig. 80), and a little inlay was found in the form of a vase, probably from a wooden coffin, III, 982. But the general contrast to Jewish ornament in this respect is striking.

21. It is shown in the design sketched in III, fig. 401 (cf. I, 172), and perhaps in the design in the upper right of III, fig. 443.

22. See III, figs. 460, 509, 556, 621.

23. See III, figs. 470, 477, 511, 516, 537, 550, 564, 616, 619 f., 628.

24. See III, figs. 460, 469, 487–489, 492, 502, 521, 526, 549 f., 559, 563, 604, 607, 610, 633, 635, 654.

25. See III, 528, 600, 633.

26. See III, fig. 473.

27. See III, figs. 460, 470, 536.

28. See III, figs. 807, 815.

29. See III, fig. 857.

30. See III, fig. 488.

31. See III, fig. 789.

32. See III, fig. 870.

33. See III, figs. 487, 654.

34. See III, fig. 729.

35. See III, fig. 736.

36. See III, fig. 813.

37. See III, fig. 820.

38. See III, fig. 863.

39. See III, figs. 714, 778, and 846 f.; perhaps also on fig. 783.

40. See III, fig. 856.

41. See III, figs. 887 f.

holding fruit on a Roman sarcophagus.[42] It appears among the Jewish cult objects on the Roman gold glasses.[43] It seems to me quite obvious that the drinking of wine and the symbolism of the vine were everywhere an important part of Jewish observance and thinking.

Indeed from various sources we know that the vine was magnificently represented in Herod's Temple itself. Josephus describes a cornice, below which was a series of doors and embroidered curtains the exact nature of which is not clear in the text. Below this cornice, but above the doors,

> had been put a golden vine with pendant bunches of grapes, a creation which was a marvel to those who saw it for its size and craftsmanship, as well as for the costliness of its material.[44]

In the *Jewish War* [45] he adds that each cluster of grapes was as tall as a man (*andromēkeis*). Tacitus [46] notes that this vine was found in the Temple and was one of the reasons why many thought the Jews worshiped Dionysus (Liber); but this was absurd, Tacitus commented, since the Jewish worship is so lugubrious. When in addition to these testimonies it is recalled that the Mishnah [47] mentions this vine in the Temple, there can be no doubt that such a vine was actually there. The Mishnah tells that offerings of leaves or grapes were brought and hung upon this vine, while its great size is recorded in the story that three hundred priests were needed to carry it.

It is a guess, but a good guess, that this vine in Herod's Temple took the place of another golden object worth five hundred talents, which Aristobulus gave as a bribe to Pompey. Strabo reports [48] that he saw this "vine or garden, called a thing of delight (*terpōlē*)" bearing the inscription "The gift of Alexander, the King of the Jews." [49] The inscription, which celebrates the object as a gift of Aristobulus' father, Alexander, could have had nothing to do with its being given to Pompey by Aristobulus, since, when Pompey was given the object, Alexander had been dead fifteen years. So it is to be presumed that the inscription celebrated Alexander's original gift of the object to the Temple. It is hard to think where such a gift would have been put if not in the Temple. The presence in the Temple of some object at least associated with the vine seems to go back, then, to Alexander's time.

We shall see reason to suspect in the case of the eagle that the Temple was by no means free of the sort of ornament which is perplexing us in the synagogues.[50] Why the

42. See III, fig. 802.

43. See III, figs. 964–967, 969 f., 974.

44. *Antt.*, xv, 395 (xi, 3). Schürer mentions this vine in his *Jüd. Volk.* (ET, II, ii, 292 f.), with the evidence here cited.

45. Bk. v, 210 (v. 4).

46. *Hist.*, v, 5.

47. *BT*, *Middoth*, III, 8 (Danby, *Mishnah*, 595). See F. J. Hollis, *The Archaeology of Herod's Temple*, 1934, 319 f.

48. Ap. Josephus, *Antt.*, XIV, 34–36 (iii, 1).

49. W. Wreszinski in *Orientalistische Literaturzeitung*, XXVIII (1925), 570–573, and XXIX (1926), 961–963, connects the word τερπωλή with ancient objects from Egypt which were a sort of stemmed vase with a structure in the center that might well have been called a "garden"; but it is hard to see why it should have been called a "vine," as Strabo does. I confess I do not know what Alexander's gift looked like.

50. The eagle will be discussed in Vol. VIII.

eagle was upon the Temple, and why the vine, we cannot say because our knowledge of Herod's Temple and its ornament is so inadequate. If we could recover it, it might surprise us as much as the decoration of the synagogues has done. All we can conclude from the golden vine in the Temple is that by the time of the construction of the Temple (that is, shortly before the birth of Christ) and probably at least a half century earlier, the vine had already been accepted in Judaism to the point that it was thus lavishly represented. It is very difficult for me to believe that this great object was in the Temple merely as decoration. That Josephus does not hint at a Jewish meaning or at any meaning for it by no means precludes the possibility that it had a meaning, since his exoteric account of Judaism is in general so superficial. I must myself connect this vine with the chalice on the coins and conclude that the natural reference of both would be to a ritualistic drinking of wine which was of great importance in Judaism from at least the middle of the first century before Christ. This, may I repeat, would be the immediate conclusion from such evidence in any other religion of the day and environment.[51]

The last important manifestation of the vine in Jewish art of the period is that at Dura. This vine, the most important single one of all, is preserved in a highly unsatisfactory condition, and experts in ancient painting who have examined the original by no means agree on its history or reconstruction. The difficulty is that it was twice painted and that almost instantly upon its exposure to the sun the underpainting came out to blend with the overpainting in a way to make a satisfactory reconstruction of either quite impossible. Indeed, from hearing the technicians who have examined the painting discuss it, I am not at all convinced that there are not more than two layers of painting in some parts.

H. F. Pearson, who worked with the painting after it had been finally cleaned, reconstructed the original vine as in fig. 117,[52] where it is more like a tree than a vine. It has at the left of its base a table with some peculiar thing upon it, a "round object" beneath it; on the right, heraldic felines face each other over a strange device.

H. J. Gute, who worked with the painting in earlier stages, when it had not been cleaned but when, as he put it, "more of the original paint was still there," reconstructed the first stages of the painting as in fig. 118,[53] where the vine grows from a vase at the bottom [54] and opens at the top to make room for a king enthroned, wearing the oriental trousers of all the royal figures at Dura, and with two little throne guards at the front in white Greek dress. Within the vine he saw at the left an Orpheus figure in conventional cap playing the lyre, a spread eagle of the Syrian type behind him, a large lion in the center of the vine facing him, together with a duck and a smaller bird. Under the vine are the table and lions as in Pearson's drawing. The table Gute saw as Pearson did, but under it,

51. We shall find below, VI, 128, that the vine was often a symbol of Israel in the Old Testament and with the rabbis, but, it would seem, not in a way to inspire the usages of the vine which we are here pointing out.

52. From an original drawing by Pearson reproduced by permission of the Yale University Art Gallery.

53. From an original drawing by Gute reproduced with his permission.

54. All that is left of the vase is a very clear fragment of its upper right corner. If Gute saw this detail correctly, his reconstruction of the rest of the vase is unavoidable.

where Pearson saw the "round object," he has drawn a round crossed cake of the sort familiar from Mithraism and Christianity alike. The cross has here presumably no significance other than to indicate that the object is a little loaf of bread,[55] and this we should have supposed was meant by the "round object" also, so we may say the two experts agree upon a bread symbol under the table. Upon the table as Gute draws it is a quite unexplained object; one guess would be that it is a bowl of some kind. Pearson has added a detail, however, which is most important, for he shows it with the vertical stripes which distinguish the semicircular banqueting cushion or bolster we have already found twice on Jewish gold glass behind the table of the fish meal, as well as upon pagan and Christian sacramental and eschatological holy meals.[56] The bolster is to be viewed here not as an object on the table but as actually arched behind the table in the way it usually appears. The table is thereby definitely marked, along with the bread symbols, as being of ritualistic, or at least of mystic, reference.

Opposite the table is the pair of rampant leonine animals as Pearson drew them. In Gute's drawing a large vase or crater is between them. What is above their heads seemed to Gute to be a pair of snakes, with heads toward each other. All of this belonged, according to Gute, to the earliest painting: but since the corner of the large central vase beneath the vine in his drawing overlapped the lion on the left, the two could not originally have stood in the same design, a fact which suggests, at least here, three attempts at painting something acceptable, since still another design, we shall shortly see, was afterward painted over this. It may well be that Gute's data should be interpreted to mean that the throne group at the top of the vine was not in the first painting, since he himself shows vine leaves overlapping the white robes of the throne-guards. But du Mesnil agreed with Gute that these vine leaves on the robes suggested that the guards, like the Orpheus group below, were standing within the vine in the original painting.

Of this much we are reasonably sure, however: the first painting seems to have begun with a vine, with the table and the rampant lions over the vase, or over Pearson's peculiar filigree design. Whether this earlier stage of the design contained Orpheus and the animals in the vine, with the throne group above, or these were added only in a secondary stage of the earlier design, I shall not attempt to say. But Gute has convinced me that at one time the painting looked very much as he has sketched it. At this stage it was the only large painting in the room and stood directly above the niche which served as the Torah shrine, with the small symbols painted upon it.[57] This vine must be considered of the greatest importance, then, and while Pearson thinks that Orpheus and the throne group were not in the original picture, Pearson and Gute agree that the mystic table on one side and the lions rampant on the other were both there. Gute has further drawn two large bowls, one at the base of the vine, one beneath the rampant lions, and it seems incredible that he is wrong in both cases, as Pearson would have us believe. But we do not need them, for even in Pearson's drawing of vine, bread, table, cushion, and

55. See above, pp. 62–76.
56. See above, p. 10.
57. See above, III, fig. 602; cf. I, 230 f.

lions we have a design which would again in any religion but Judaism have been taken as direct proof that the cult which used the room celebrated most importantly a sacrament of bread and wine and that the cult had such historic relation to Dionysiac celebrations that the Dionysiac vine and lions were in keeping there. It must be recalled, also, that this painting was before the eyes of the worshipers above the Torah shrine at a place where in other cults the most sacred symbols were commonly represented. Here in a Mithraeum would be the slaying of the holy bull; here in a Christian church would, if possible, be the most impressive picture in the room for stimulating devotion. And here, in the synagogue, are a vine and a table equipped with bread and a banqueting cushion, with, presumably, at least one great wine bowl. "Decoration" seems to me an impossible retreat before its almost speaking symbolism.

The history of this picture confirms such an impression, for to it was added an Orpheus and a throne scene. Whether these were added to an originally complete design, as Pearson says, or were part of the first drawing as Gute and Kraeling believe, is unimportant. The fact is that soon, if not from the first, the vine was felt to be inadequate in itself. To explain its meaning Orpheus and the throne scene were included. Orpheus is quite undeniable, playing a lyre to the lion, duck, dove, and eagle. What connection there could be between Orpheus with his lyre and the throne group is by no means at once apparent but will become clear, I believe, from Jewish traditions.

I have not seen it recalled in this connection that during the Second Revolt of A.D. 132, when Judaism seemed to be expressing itself in the most direct symbols, a lyre appeared on nine of the coins preserved, and on four of these a bunch of grapes appeared on the other side, as in fig. 115.[58] The lyre is thus by no means unparalleled in Jewish symbolism, and we now see that its conjunction on the Jewish coins with a wine symbol is likewise probably meaningful. That the lyre on the coins was thought to be the lyre of Orpheus, or that the player at Dura was ever called Orpheus by the Jewish worshipers, is the least likely explanation. Borrowings were not made that way unless religions were avowedly being fused, which there is as little cause to suspect at Dura as in the fanatical Bar Kokba revolt, or in Christianity. But the lyre with grapes was actually on the coins, and an Orpheus figure plays the lyre in the vine to the birds and lion at Dura. In early Christian art, where Orpheus frequently appears playing to animals,[59] this design would mean the saving presence of Christ or of the Logos within the eucharistic dispensation of grace. Everywhere it seems to have meant the power of the spiritual (or of a Savior) to calm the turbulence of our material natures. It is hard to suppose that the Orpheus at Dura meant anything essentially different, though he would certainly have been given some Jewish name like David. But it is useless to argue about the name, since when we had agreed upon a name, or even determined from some lost source his identity, it would still not be the David of the Old Testament who was represented, but a new David within a great vine who had power to charm the animals—that is, it would be a David who

58. Cf. Reifenberg, *Coins*, nos. 172, 178, 188, with grapes; 176, 184, with name inscribed within a wreath; and 192, 199, 205, with palm branch (lulab?) within a wreath.

59. For a review of Orpheus in Christian art see Leclercq in CL, "Orphée," XII, 2735–2755.

was the spiritual equivalent of, or who had the qualities associated by others with, Orpheus and Christ.

Clearly we must stop just a moment to ask what qualities Christ and Orpheus had in common, for it would be a Jewish adaptation of those common qualities, not necessarily the peculiar qualities of either, which we should expect in the Jewish Orpheus. That is, we should expect that the Jews, since they borrowed Orpheus, borrowed him for what we are calling his inherent value. The greatest difference between Orpheus and Christ was the total absence in Orpheus of the personal quality of Christ. Orpheus was a legendary figure, of little importance in himself, so little that it is now impossible to determine that he ever existed at all. "The legend was real, if Orpheus was not." [60] It was not Orpheus the person but the hymns that through the years accumulated about his name which were of such great importance, especially in later Greek tradition. He was the mythical (disputed, even in antiquity) author of certain poems; he was given the honor of having founded certain *teletai*, or mysteries, usually dedicated to Dionysus but sometimes to other gods as well, if indeed he was not thought to be the founder of all mysteries in general. But he was himself never the one worshiped in the mysteries, so far as we have any knowledge. As such his figure could be appropriated for Christ, as Dionysus or the object of a pagan cult could not, for he represented that inspiration by which mysteries were founded: "Christ is our Orpheus," the Christian pictures could say, precisely because Orpheus was himself so nebulous. The identification meant for Christ that Christ had founded the Christian mysteries and that his teachings too had power to tame the animal in man.

The connection in Judaism seems to have been more direct, for while Orphic hymns had originally sung of many gods, and in particular of Dionysus, in later times Neoplatonism and a higher type of monotheism in general were developing, and new "Orphic" and "Sibylline" poems were forged, which expressed the point of view of these new groups. Long before Philo's time the "Orphic" point of view in this new sense, along with the specific Orphic poems, was altered and claimed for Judaism and made to teach the basic principles of the Jewish Mystery. In *By Light, Light* I quoted an Orphic poem of the cosmic throne of God in its original pagan form and then the same passage as it was adapted to Judaism by Aristobulus the Jew.[61] The pagan version describes the universal God whom no human eye can behold; the other makes an exception of Moses, who did see God. In both versions there is a road to the throne of God which is God's own Stream of Light, or his Logos, and to ascend it is to achieve perfection. Orpheus the poet, in the pagan version, himself got from God his information about the path; in the Jewish version he apparently learned it from Moses, for he does not speak otherwise, he says, than as is taught in Moses' Law, just as Philo later insists that Plato got all his philosophy from Moses in the Torah. A third fragment, "Jewish Sibylline" [62] in character, is clearly another reworking of the same Orphic original but has become an impassioned plea to men to renounce darkness and tread the path of Light to this God. Judaism does not specifically

60. I. M. Linforth, *The Arts of Orpheus*, 1941, 167. I find myself in thorough general agreement with this book.

61. *By Light, Light*, 279–281.

62. Quoted in ibid., 285 f.

appear in this version, but it would seem to be taken from a Jewish context none the less.

It is in the vision of Moses as recounted by "Ezekiel the Tragic Poet" that the fullest adaptation of the idea is made.[63] For there the throne of the Orphic God appears to Moses in a dream: it rises to heaven from Mount Sinai, and the God upon it beckons to Moses to approach, then seats him upon the throne in his place, with the royal diadem on his head, the scepter in his hand; the host of stars are doing him obeisance when he awakens. This is almost certainly the Throne which came to play so great a part in the mysticism of later Judaism. Whether the Throne was originally eastern or Greek it is not necessary to debate, since we can see that it came directly into Judaism through Jewish adaptations of the Orphic hymns. Another Jew, Artapanus, of the second century B.C., gives us further suggestion when he insists that Moses was Musaeus, the "teacher of Orpheus." [64]

Orpheus, then, is by no means a surprising figure to appear in Jewish art. He and his lyre were both thoroughly Judaized, and we now see that Jews in the synagogue might have identified him with Moses even more probably than with David. But I doubt if he would have appeared in a synagogue without conveying some meaning, without in fact indicating that Judaism had in its teachings the true Mystery.

This much the vine with the mystic sacrament under it and Orpheus within it has suggested. It at once becomes striking that whether in the repainting or in its original form the vine grew up toward a great throne at the top. But for this too we are already prepared, since we have seen in the fragments of Eusebius that the Jews were so attracted by the Orphic concepts that they Judaized Orphic poems by making direct Jewish insertions into the originals, and that the Orphic poems which most impressed the Jewish writers were those that had as their center of interest the Throne of God. Is the throne here in the painting the Throne of God? The Jewish a priori that no Jew could have represented God on his throne makes us hesitate to take that logical step; but such is the logic of the design itself, for no other throne could so readily be taken to be at the top of the vine in this way. We shall return to this shortly.

Whether there ever was a stage when all of this, and only this, was upon the wall of the Dura synagogue we again need not dispute. The point is that at the final repainting of the wall this picture was reorganized a second if not a third time. The table and the rampant lions were covered with a red paint which was to serve as the base for new painting. The vine was cut horizontally in two, corresponding to the new divisions of the whole wall into tiers of paintings, but the vine was left above and below the new bar of division, so that in this final form the vine was still the object of central interest. According to Pearson it was at this time that the Orpheus and the throne group were added; according to Gute they were already there. In any case they were there in the final design, fig. 119.[65] In place of the table on the left was now painted a man reclining upon a couch, with twelve smaller figures behind him. In place of the rampant felines on the right was

63. See Eusebius, *Praeparatio evangelica*, IX, xxix, 5 (440A–C). Cf. *By Light, Light*, 290.

64. Eusebius, IX, xxvii, 2 f.

65. From a painting by Gute, photograph courtesy of the Yale University Art Gallery. This is a copy of the Dura painting as it now appears. It represents the final design, with much of the underpainting showing through it and blurring it.

painted a scene in which appeared the same couch and its occupant, who with crossed hands blessed two little boys before him, boys brought in by a larger figure on the right. The identification of these scenes has never been disputed from their first discovery; the scene on the left is Jacob on his deathbed blessing the twelve tribes, and that on the right shows Joseph bringing in his sons Ephraim and Menasseh for the special blessing which made the tribes thereafter really thirteen; for the tribe of Levi was always an extra tribe, one which in the journey through the wilderness guarded the tabernacle and Ark while six tribes went before and six tribes walked behind.

In the upper register the throne with its guards either was put in for the first time now or was enriched by the addition of a number of small figures about it, a number which Gute has convinced me was thirteen.[66] As du Mesnil saw, the vine was by no means eliminated but seemed freshly painted over some of the figures. Du Mesnil thinks that this was done to obscure a painting which for some reason was considered objectionable to the Jews.[67] The much more likely explanation is that the spattering of vine leaves was to indicate that this group too was still within the vine, a part of the vine symbolism, just as was the Orpheus group below. In the final painting, that is, even with the new bar across to mark the two registers, the continuous vine shows that we have a continuous picture which must, top and bottom, still be considered as a whole.

In trying to identify this scene of the throne we may begin, I am confident, by recognizing the two little throne guards in Greek costume. They had been painted in with the throne itself before the other small figures about them were added, according to Gute; and in any case we know from two other scenes at Dura, as du Mesnil pointed out, that these two are the conventional accompaniment of a throne, to mark its incumbent as being a king. The thirteen figures in their Persian trousers surrounding this group, however, seem explained by the two scenes below in which the tribes were established as thirteen in number. The picture is not, I am sure, the apotheosis of Moses but the apotheosis of Israel, whose tribes are established as a unit at the foot of the vine. Then they rise through the vine and the mystery symbolized by Orpheus and come to stand about the throne. It may be Moses who is there enthroned, not because he was in Exodus XVIII the judge of Israel [68] but because in the Orphic sense he is sitting upon the throne of God. It may be the throne of God himself, what du Mesnil calls a bolder hypothesis. My own impression is that the symbolism is much more fully developed than in the simple Orphic dream of

66. Du Mesnil, *Peintures*, 43–45, discusses this scene as "L'Apothéose de Moïse(?)." He says that he could count ten or eleven of the accompanying figures, but that the symmetry suggests at least twelve of them. Gute's thirteen seem to me to come from a closer examination and to fulfill du Mesnil's sense of the necessary symmetry. Carl Kraeling told me he thought he could discern traces of fifteen, but these seem to include the two throne guards in Greek dress who were part of the original throne scene. All three, then, seem to agree.

67. *Peintures*, 45. Du Mesnil actually discusses how the enthroned figure at the top, whether "Moses" or "God," the two alternatives he mentions, must have been displeasing to the congregation, and hence was "recouverte." But that is precisely what was never done with that figure. At whatever stage it was put in, it remained thereafter in spite of other alterations.

68. This is the rather desperate suggestion of du Mesnil, 44.

Ezekiel the poet nearly four centuries earlier, and that the figure upon the throne at Dura is from the more elaborate mysticism of later Judaism, which I am convinced bears more relation to Orphic mysticism than has been yet suggested. Metatron is one who comes at once to mind, but he is a most dangerous figure for an amateur in Jewish mysticism to use indiscriminately. Scholem [69] can dismiss with a wave of the hand the elaborate accumulation of evidence and arguments of Odeberg,[70] which show that Metatron is essentially, in function and so in name, the occupant of a throne second only to that of God. The disagreement between these two seems chiefly to be on whether the name Metatron refers to his being the occupant of a throne: there is no disputing the fact that Metatron does occupy a throne, is a "little Yahweh," or "Yaho" (to the scandal of the rabbis), and that he came to be par excellence the "Throne," in the sense of a divine being as mentioned by Paul.[71] But it would be extremely dangerous to insist that the majestic ruler at the top of the vine was Metatron. For the throne was so much a symbol of Jewish mysticism in this period that Scholem could say, "The earliest Jewish mysticism is throne-mysticism." He continues in the following paragraph to introduce his review of this literature:

> Its essence is not absorbed contemplation of God's true nature, but perception of His appearance on the throne, as described by Ezekiel, and cognition of the mysteries of the celestial throne-world. The throne-world is to the Jewish mystic what the *pleroma*, the "fullness," the bright sphere of divinity with its potencies, aeons, archons and dominions is to the Hellenistic and early Christian mystics of the period who appear in the history of religion under the names of Gnostics and Hermetics. The Jewish mystic, though guided by motives similar to theirs, nevertheless expresses his vision in terms of his own religious background. God's pre-existing throne, which embodies and exemplifies all forms of creation, is at once the goal and the theme of his mystical vision. From the fourteenth chapter of the Ethiopic Book of Enoch, which contains the oldest description of the throne in the whole of this literature, a long succession of mystical documents of the most varied character leads to the ecstatic descriptions of the throne-world in the tracts of the Merkabah visionaries to which we must now turn our attention. From the interpretation of the throne-world as the true centre of all mystical contemplation it is possible to deduce most of the concepts and doctrines of these ancient mystics.[72]

It would be very much in point to incorporate here the entire chapter of Scholem in which he goes on to discuss this *Merkabah* or throne mysticism, for it was at just the time of the Dura synagogue that the Merkabah was at the height of its popularity. The rabbis as a group did not like it and did all possible to repress it in the interests of halachic Judaism, although many individual rabbis succumbed to its lures.[73]

With this mysticism of the throne in mind, it for the first time becomes completely

69. *Jewish Mysticism*, 66–69.
70. *III Enoch*, 1928, 79–146.
71. Col. 1, 16.
72. Scholem, 43.
73. Scholem rightly says (p. 46) of the Merkabah mystics: "The original religious impulses active in these circles came, after all, from sources quite different from those of orthodox Judaism." Cf. p. 64.

appropriate that such a picture should rise above the Torah shrine at Dura in the place where pagans and Christians alike put their holiest symbols. One cannot suddenly begin to select details from the very complex and often contradictory Merkabah tradition, as it survives in fugitive documents and later quotations, and use them at random to explain the presence of the throne at Dura thus surrounded by the patriarchs of Israel. Furthermore, before any such detailed application could be made, the origin of this literature, of whose study Scholem is making only a beginning, must be traced in directions in which he has not looked at all, especially as regards the relation between this speculation and Orphic, Philonic, and Gnostic ideas. The Greek ancestry of the ideas expressed in the Dura picture is clearly indicated in the Dionysiac felines over the Greek vase and in the Orpheus, to say nothing of the Greek robes on the throne guards and the Greco-Roman bolster at the table. But this Greek heritage can hardly be evaluated offhand, probably can never be evaluated at Dura with any precision.

All we can now say of the picture is, therefore, that it seems to represent Israel at the culmination of the experience of the "throne." This experience, which was at first more abstractly represented by the sacramental vine and table, is now presented specifically as an "Orphic" mystery of Israel's foundation, a triumph which Israel achieves as, in and through the vine, it rises to the throne. We recall Philo's frequent allegory of Israel as the race which sees God and is accordingly a royal priesthood for all mankind.[74] Even if Pearson is right that the throne itself was lacking in the earlier form of the painting, it seems unwarranted to insist that the new details in the painting of Israel and the throne appreciably altered the meaning of the picture and indicated a change in the ideas of the congregation. For the constant in all is the vine. The second painting seems to me to have made the symbolism of the vine more explicit, and more definitely Jewish. By its very presence in the synagogue the vine had earlier been Jewish implicitly. The early form of the painting may well have been quite as mystic as the later. But the early painting as both Pearson and Gute restore it did not have a single distinctive Jewish detail about it and would have been as much in place if set before any pagan *thiasos* as in the Jewish synagogue.[75]

The constant in all the versions of this picture, I say, is the vine, which with the cup appears by now to be universal in the Jewish art of this period, from Rome to Dura. Simply on the basis of its archeological appearances it may be best explained as suggest-

74. See esp. *Abr.*, 56–59, and compare the Jewish liturgy quoted in *By Light, Light*, 310 (Frag. II, 2); 329 (Frag. X, 7); 353.

75. The foregoing discussion by no means excludes all that Grabar adduced to show that here is the Messiah on the throne. But Grabar leaves Orpheus as a postscript at the end of his discussion because he mistakenly supposed Orpheus to have been put in later as an afterthought. Kraeling assured me that Orpheus was in the first painting along with the animals, and so the Orphic orientation of the vine and throne must be basic, not the few references to Israel as the vine that Grabar can quote from the Old Testament. But my mystic explanation of the throne and Grabar's eschatological Messiah are by no means mutually exclusive, as any one who understands mystical Christianity and Judaism will recognize. See A. Grabar, "Le Thème religieux des fresques de la synagogue de Doura," *RHR*, CXXIII (1941), 142–192, esp. 159–171. This was accepted by H. Riesenfeld, *Jésus transfiguré*, Copenhagen, 1947, 61 (Acta Seminarii Neotestamentici Upsaliensis, XVI).

ing at once a mystic symbol and a reference to an actual sacrament, just as was the vine in Christianity later. We have encountered vines, grapes, chalices, wine pressing scenes, chalices from which a vine grows or a fountain flows, upon Jewish remains of every sort and place, along with the actual gold glass cups, which it is natural to think were used for ritualistic drinking by Jews, as such objects were by pagans and Christians. One simple hypothesis, and only one, is at hand to explain all this material, namely that a wine-drinking ritual was at that time of great importance in a mystic hope for the experience of God and for immortality. If such a rite existed it would probably have been interpreted very differently by different Jews, for we must never forget that at this period there was not even such an approximate standardization of Judaism as the Talmud later effected. The pictorial representations finally are so close to the pictorial symbols for the Christian Eucharist that one would expect the rite as celebrated by Jews to have some resemblances, in form or meaning or both, to the Eucharist, though just what these would have been we cannot prejudge. The purpose of the following discussion of wine and fluid will be to enable us to come closer to an appraisal of their value in Judaism.

CHAPTER FIVE

The Divine Fluid in Mesopotamia and Syria

THE PROBLEM POSED by the archeological remains has come out very clearly. Was there a Jewish sacramental drinking of wine in this period which symbolized (or realized) mystic achievement and brought immortality? The first step would seem to be to look at the Jewish literary remains and the traditions of Jewish ritual to see at once whether they support this suggestion of the monuments. But the reader will not be ready to consider this evidence until he has come to appreciate what in paganism created and perpetuated this sort of symbolism and what were the values which steadily accompanied its use in both paganism and Christianity. The values, we shall see, were at once highly complex and deeply unified. We shall accordingly leave Judaism for a considerable journey into paganism.

In reviewing the pagan background, however, it will be necessary to follow out much more than the specific use of wine in religious rites or associations. The earliest drinking symbols in which the vase appears seem to refer to water or to the seminal fluid. Only much later does wine take over and become the sacramental fluid, or the means of imparting divine life, par excellence. Even in Christianity wine never displaced water completely as a spiritual vehicle. It is said that blood, another of the fluids, and water both flowed from Jesus on the cross, and the water of baptism and holy water still vividly witness the survival of symbolic water. While neither of these is drunk, holy water is a direct means of spiritual blessing or increment, and the water of baptism is the sacramental means of spiritual birth. That the desire for rebirth in more primitive and direct ages should have expressed itself in symbols of the fluid of the god's semen is not only what we should expect but what we shall abundantly find was true. Similarly, in feminine terms, the desire was for milk from the divine breasts, for here also was life for the infant which, before the gods, man always was. The desire for deity in the form of fluid naturally had its counterpart in the need for rain, or the great rising of the Nile, to give life to the crops. It was just as inevitable that the symbol in desert countries should often have been the drinking of cool water.

Much less to be expected but still everywhere encountered is the identification of this fluid of life with quite another fluid, the flow of light from the sun. The phrase "flow of light" is about all we have left of the ancient notion that light itself is a fluid. So the water of life and the light of life became interchangeable figures in a way entirely natural to the ancient mind, though it seems so strange to us.

Most of these symbols of fluid united in the later symbolism of the vine and of sacramental wine. We shall have it as our task in this section, then, to reconstruct from early times the persistent notion of the divine fluid as the source of life and to see how in the hellenistic and Roman period especially this fluid came supremely to represent itself in the sacramental cup of wine.

A. BABYLONIA AND ASSYRIA

IN REMAINS from Babylonia and Assyria the vine is often pictured, but not in a way to suggest that wine was a distinctively important element in the religions of the region. The literary evidence for the place of wine in the religion of Babylonia was reviewed not long ago by Lutz,[1] whose findings I would not pretend to challenge in a field so far from my own. He demonstrates that the peoples of that region consumed enormous quantities of beer and wine. The gods drank wine until "They were wholly at ease, their spirit was exalted." [2] And Ishtar, who seems to have been a goddess of wine as well as of love,[3] bade Assurbanipal "Eat food, drink strong wine, make music, [and] exalt my divinity," [4] a command which he and his wife may well be obeying in the famous scene of their feasting. In this scene Assurbanipal celebrates his victory over Te-Umman, fig. 116.[5] The head of the enemy hangs from a nearby tree not shown in our reproduction; the king reclines on a divan, his queen sits on a chair at his feet, a table is between them, and each is drinking from a bowl. Symbolic as this sort of scene will appear to be in later art, here it is extremely dangerous to conclude that anything is represented but the actual event, a "scene from daily life." Though wine and beer were both offered at sacrifices to the gods,[6] and libations were important,[7] nothing marks the wine offering as of unique significance. Lutz points out that especially among the Sumerians there were various wine gods and that the chief one, the goddess Geshtin, or Ama-geshtin, "the mother vinestalk," early ceased to be this and became Nina, "the lady of the waters." [8] Lutz forgets his own demonstration of the frequency of the use of wine and beer and explains the change by which the vine goddess became the water goddess on the grounds that in a desert country water is a more appropriate drink than intoxicants. But we shall observe frequently how short

1. Lutz, *Viticulture*, 115–133.

2. Closing line of the third tablet of the Babylonian creation series quoted in ibid., 117. Cf. Charles-F. Jean, *La Littérature des Babyloniens et des Assyriens*, 1924, 99.

3. Lutz, 130.

4. Ibid., 118 f.

5. From Stephen Thompson, *British Museum Photographs from the Assyrian Collection*, 1874, nos. 522*b*, *c*. Cf. Billiard, *La Vigne*, plate III at p. 56; H. R. Hall, *Babylonian and Assyrian Sculpture in the British Museum*, 1928, plate XLI, 2.

6. Lutz, 125.

7. B. Meissner, *Babylonien und Assyrien*, 1920, I, 275. Wine was especially important as an offering for the dead; ibid., 429.

8. Lutz, 131. On this goddess see H. Zimmern, "Der babylonische Gott Tamūz," *Abhandlungen, k. sächsische Gesellschaft der Wissenschaften*, Leipzig, XXVII (1909), 712–715. For further references see G. Furlani, *La Religione babilonese e assira*, I, 1928, 283, and notes 36 f.; S. Langdon, *Tammuz and Ishtar*, 1914, 7, 43.

is the step from wine to "fluid in general," especially to sap and water, so that it is interesting to see thus early a wine deity changing into the deity of waters.

Instead of looking specifically at wine and beer in this locality, it is much more profitable to follow "fluid in general" as represented especially by the vase. Actually, the vase is a frequent symbol in ancient Mesopotamia. It is often shown as an attribute of Shamash,[9] but more often the flowing vase characterized Ea.[10] These representations are found earlier than the Dynasty of Agade (about 2450 B.C.) but came into their own at that time and were at their height two or three centuries later. Ea was the third person in the highest triad, with Anu and Enlil. He was "Lord of the Watery Deep," who lived in the "House of Wisdom" in the Heavenly Ocean. He was lord of unfathomable and hidden knowledge, counselor of men and gods, god of dream oracles, magician, and exorcist. His was the purifying water used in spells and magical rites; he was lord of brooks and springs, who gave fertility to the crops.[11] So he is early pictured as a god from whose body flow streams of water, with fish often swimming up the stream to the god, or at the bottom of the stream, fig. 120.[12] More commonly the streams flow from a vase which he holds to his breast, fig. 121,[13] or which he holds out to a king, to a devotee, or to priests. The symbolism is well illustrated in two representations of Gudea, ruler of Lagash in the late third millennium B.C. The remains from Gudea show an almost complete preoccupation with figures of the flowing vase, but I discuss only two instances.[14] The first of these is a seal, fig. 128,[15] marked "Gudea, Ruler (Ensi) of Lagash." Gudea is the central figure in the seal; he is led by Ningizzidah, his patron god, to the great god on the throne, presumably Ea. Ea holds a flowing vase to his breast with streams rising and falling to six smaller vases, themselves flowing to the ground. But he also holds out a flowing vase with the tree of life in it to Ningizzidah, presumably as a gift of kingly power for Gudea. In the second, fig. 122,[16] Gudea is himself represented as the ruler, holding the vase; streams from it go down to four little flowing vases on the base beneath his robe.

9. G. Contenau in *RB*, N.S., XIII (1916), 537. What the vase meant with Shamash I do not know.

10. In calling the god with the vase Ea I am following the traditional identification, though it has been protested, most recently by S. H. Langdon: see his *Semitic Mythology*, 1931, 395, n. 21 (*The Mythology of All Races*, V). Langdon (p. 95) prefers to take the god "to be Anu with the waters of eternal life." It is interesting that the meaning of the water and vase is constant in all the mythological identifications.

11. Van Buren, *The Flowing Vase and the God with Streams*, 9.

12. From Christian Zervos, *L'Art de la Mésopotamie*, 1935, 258, a seal at the British Museum, no. 89115; cf. Van Buren, plate II, fig. 6. For a discussion of the divine figures on the seal, see ibid., 27–30.

13. From Porada, *Morgan*, plate XXXI, fig. 202E; cf. Text, 26. See also her figs. 195E, 197, 198E, 199, 201–206, 517, 979E. Cf. Contenau, 530; Van Buren, passim; Ward, *Seal Cylinders*, 214–218.

14. Van Buren, 62–75.

15. From L. Delaporte, *Catalogue des Cylindres*, I, 1910, 12, no. T108; cf. plate 10, fig. 8 (Musée du Louvre). It is numbered AOT.3451–52. The original seal is lost. It has frequently been reproduced. Fragments of a large relief with what was probably the same essential design are at Berlin; Van Buren, plate VIII, fig. 31; cf. pp. 63 f. In the description I have followed Van Buren in naming the gods. For further bibliography of the seal, see ibid., 65 n., and for a similar seal, ibid., plate XII, fig. 42.

16. From V. Scheil in *Revue d'assyriologie et d'archéologie orientale*, XXVII (1930), plates I and II at p. 164; cf. pp. 162 f.

One of these can be seen in the profile of the statue. The fact that in fig. 128 Ea has two vases seems to me important. The one which he holds to his breast characterizes his nature, which is to give life, fertility, rain, to the earth. The other invests him like all Egyptian and Oriental rulers (including the emperors of China), with the divine prerogative of bestowing the blessing of fertility upon his country. Whether the seal was Gudea's own or was simply named Gudea and showed his divine rulership but was actually used by one of his servants or subjects, the seal itself does not tell us. But the seal and the statue together indicate the transmission of the divine power of giving fertility from the god through the ruler to the land and people.

Widengren [17] has recently written to show the significance of the king as the gardener who waters the tree of life and who is the tree itself. He does not ask, however, why it was so important that the king should have power thus to give the fluid of life, and by it to perpetuate the tree—itself, in mythical pleonasm, the source of life. The function of the fluid would appear to be the giving of life to crops and people, as a true king continued to do into Roman times.[18] The king as one who receives the flowing bowl from Ea and then holds it himself is the source of life to both the people and crops of his realm. It seems to me a relic of this ancient symbol when David takes from Saul the king's spear and flask of water.[19]

Likewise, winged figures bring the flowing vase to the king Ur-Nammu, fig. 124.[20] The genii may have been regarded as intermediate deities bringing to the king the water of life. These scenes appear to be alternate devices for the presenting of the vase by the god to a devotee, and the filling of small vases at the god's feet.[21] Or a naked hero may use the vase to water the sacred bull, fig. 126.[22] All mean that the fluid is received by the devotee. Langdon [23] quotes an ancient poem in which two female genii descend from heaven, one bearing a jar of oil, the other water, to anoint the body of the sacred cow,

17. *The King and the Tree of Life in Ancient Near Eastern Religion, King and Saviour IV*, 47 (Uppsala Universitets Årsskrift, 1951, IV).

18. Cf. M. Streck, *Assurbanipal*, 1916, II, 153, Cylinder D, lines 5 f.: "In meinem ganzen Land spross[te empor?] die Erde [und?] alljährlich in Uberfluss." Cf. *Odyssey*, XIX, 109–114: "An excellent king, one who, god-fearing and ruling among men many and mighty, upholds righteousness, and the dark earth bears wheat and barley, and the trees are heavy with fruit, and the flocks bear without fail, and the sea gives forth fish, out of (his) good leadership, and the people thrive under him." Cf. M. I. Finley, *The World of Odysseus*, 1954, 102; Philo, *Legat.* 8–22.

19. I Sam. XXVII, 11 f. See my "Kingship in Early Israel," *JBL*, XLIII (1929), 169–205.

20. From Van Buren, *The Flowing Vase*, plate XI, fig. 37; see her pp. 73 f.

21. Langdon, 96, says of these figures that the water from their bowls flows into tiny bowls held by the king. If this is so, my interpretation of the other tiny bowls is substantiated, but I can find no reproduction of the scene which clearly shows this.

22. From Louis de Clercq, *Catalogue méthodique: Antiquités assyriennes*, I, *Cylindres orientaux*, 1888, plate V, fig. 46. Cf. Contenau, *Manuel*, II, 689; Parrot, *Refrigerium*, 40–45; Van Buren, 61 f., with large bibliography. My colleague Ferris Stephens helped me with this seal. See also a representation of "the Great God and Great Goddess" on a seal, beside whom stand a pair of confronting Gilgamesh figures with the flowing vase arching its streams over each of the two. A tree grows from the vase, and a scorpion is below it. The seal is published by Contenau, *Manuel*, I, 207, fig. 125. For the scorpion, with what may be a conventionalized flowing bowl, see ibid., 397, fig. 298.

23. Op. cit., 97, see esp. lines 25–29.

Ishtar, on the occasion of her giving birth to the divine calf Amarga. If this is a correct association, as I see no reason to doubt, our water jar is indeed the vehicle of the water of life. It is possible that the many scenes in which the god gives a cup, or a human being holds one, are variant symbolic representations of the same giving of the fluid of the gods to the mortals.[24]

Labat [25] says of the seal of fig. 128, following the common idea of ancient royalty, that the idea of the transmission of such divine power "was very rapidly vulgarized, and lost thereafter its initial character of royal investiture." If this is true, I must add that of such vulgarizations were the later popular fertility religions made. But I am impressed with Gaster's protest [26] that we actually do not know that such an idea and ritual were first worked out for the king and then vulgarized. Gaster feels that it all began with prehistoric popular rites which centered in the divine king as representative of the people and came to be celebrated about his person as the vivid representation of divinity, while the people themselves continued to "die" and "revive" in the seasonal symbols and rites. In any case the popular feeling is to be discovered in the royal rites and symbols. If in early millennia the life given by the god or king was in this world and in terms of crops and physical fertility, it also came to be (perhaps from the beginning it always had been) the hope of life after death—for the king first and then for his people. I see no way to determine at what point this eschatological function began. With it, of course, the royal life that as divine could survive death became possible for all the king's subjects. But the process and time of this expansion or transfer are lost to us.

While speaking of the king, I must digress briefly to mention that there is another figure of the deification of the king which has appeared in the liturgies but not on the monuments, the figure of receiving divine nature by nursing at the breast of the goddess, whatever name she may be given. So two kings of Lagash who lived before the first half of the third millennium ascribed their divinity primarily to such nursing.[27]

> A little one thou art, O Ashurbanipal, whom I confided to
> the goddess, queen of Nineveh.
> Weak wast thou, Ashurbanipal, when I satiated thee on the
> lap of the queen of Nineveh.
> Of the four teats which were put into thy mouth, two didst
> thou suck and with two didst thou cover thy face.[28]

It is strange that the act is not represented, since we shall see that it was a very important part of the Egyptian symbolism, one which continued down for ordinary people into the Greco-Roman period.[29] It was again a way of coming into divine life by drinking a divine fluid.

24. See, for example, Porada, *Morgan*, plates XVII, 105E; XXXIX, 250E, 252; XLV, 291; XLVII, 296, 302; XLVII, 305; XCIX, 674, 676.

25. R. Labat, *Le Caractère religieux de la royauté assyro-babylonienne*, 1939, 89.

26. See esp. T. H. Gaster, *Thespis*, 1950, 33, n.

27. Contenau, *Manuel*, I, 288.

28. Quoted by Langdon, 56. Cf. pp. 60, 64, where the goddess is addressed as "Mother of faithful breast."

29. See below, pp. 183–186.

As we return to the flowing vase, we must notice that it is not always Ea who holds it: various other gods or goddesses may do so. The most succinct abbreviation of the symbol that I know appears in fig. 129,[30] the imprint of a cylinder seal which shows four types of vessels, among them the flowing vase. I should guess that these are four symbolic forms, each of which referred to some definite cultic object. Since this seal (from Susa) is dated "toward 3,000 B.C." it would seem likely that the vase as an independent symbol was prehistoric and that it could be put into the hands of various gods or goddesses because it had meaning in its own right and was a sign of divine power, which in later civilizations could be appropriated for strange deities, such as Tammuz.[31] What the vase and its flow implied has been summarized by Mrs. Van Buren as follows:

> The subject of the vase from which streams of water bubble up and overflow on each side is so intimately connected with that of the god from whose body streams gush forth that in reality they form an indissoluble whole, a single conception, that of the beneficent deity who pours the waters of life and fertility upon man and nature. The flowing vase is merely an abbreviated symbol of the more complete composition, an outward and visible sign of the wondrous blessings bestowed by the divine munificence.[32]

It is not surprising that while the flowing vase seems basically a masculine symbol and is held by a god, it is also held by female figures.[33] At ancient Mari, capital of the Middle Euphrates destroyed by Hammurabi (now dated about 1800 B.C.) was found a remarkable statue of a goddess, five feet tall, fig. 123.[34] She holds a vase with its mouth forward from her waist, and down her robe the two traditional streams are drawn, with fish swimming up the center. The figure is constructed with conduits so that actual water could flow out of the vase, perhaps to be caught and drunk by the devout. To say that the female with this generally masculine symbol is a hermaphroditic representation is to go quite beyond any evidence, but not beyond possibility. One commentator very aptly recalled the statement in John (VII, 38), "He who believes in me, even as it is written, rivers of living waters shall flow from his bosom." [35] To be oneself the source of the fountain of life is the prerogative of deity, and the passage in John goes so far as to say not only that the believer will drink of the water, as in Isaiah and the Apocalypse,[36] but that he will be so exalted as to become a source of it. Mystic identification can go no farther. We shall see reason to suspect that such identification was very old.

That the flow from the ancient vase or god was a flow of the water of life has long been generally recognized, and in the case of the Babylonian god this is revealed by several details. First, a palm tree, more or less conventionalized, often grows from the bowl, standing above and between the two dividing streams, as we saw in fig. 128. The flowing vase which fertilizes the tree was commonly represented in Mesopotamian art

30. From Contenau, *Manuel*, I, 399, fig. 300.

31. Van Buren, *The Flowing Vase*, 104.

32. Ibid., 1.

33. For instances of the female with the vase see ibid., 75, 84, 100 f., 103, 128 f.

34. From A. Parrot, *Mari*, 1936, facing p. 176.

35. Hugo Prinz, *Altorientalische Symbolik*, 1915, 137, n. 8. See also J. W. Jack in *The Expository Times*, XLIX (1937/8), 124.

36. Is. LV, 1; Rev. XXI, 6; XXII, 17.

after the Egyptian mode, the vase with the spout from which water is being poured on the tree.[37] A very primitive instance from Chaldea shows the full symbol, a vase with a palm tree growing out of it which is being watered by an attendant with the spouted vase.[38] A relief of the period of Ur-Nammu, the IIIrd Dynasty of Ur, fig. 125,[39] shows the king pouring water upon a palm tree with fruit which grows from an altar or tall vase standing before the god. The convention of combining the tree of life with the flowing vase only enriches the basic symbolism, which is more primitively shown in the figures where the god himself, without any vase, is the source of the streams.[40] It is interesting that Innini, the Sumerian Ishtar, prayed to the water god, her father, when she went to Sheol for Tammuz: "The plant of life thou knowest, the water of life thou knowest. This one restore to life for me." [41] It was the prerogative of the gods that they ate the bread and drank the wine of heaven, which gave eternal life. So Tammuz is addressed: "Eater of roasted cakes, baked cakes of the oven. Drinking the holy waters of the pouch." [42] While this meal of immortality was accessible only to the gods, it seems to me probable that the tiny vases we have repeatedly seen at the bottom of the flow are the chalices from which the devotees drank this same fluid in ritual. The vase flowing from above into vases below was a common convention.[43]

I must believe that in the flowing vase, the tree, and the other symbols associated with these we have a clue to that aspect characteristic of almost every fertility religion in the ancient world, the idea that what is sought from the god is not only fertilization of crops, but the life of the god, now and hereafter, for the devotee himself. Indeed Mrs. Van Buren seems clearly right in saying that the flowing vase and the flowing god are one and that the vase represents the potency and benefaction of the deity. Its flow to the devotee strikingly resembles the flow from the god in Egypt which will be considered below.[44] In Egyptian representations we shall see that such a flow may be from any part of the divine person, though always it will appear to be the spermatic flow. It is a cosmic, creative flow, while at the same time it is the hope of rebirth, deification, and immortality for the individual. That either Egyptians or Mesopotamians borrowed the notion from the other I do not suggest. The idea is so primitive and obvious that it could easily have arisen independently in both civilizations, though of course borrowing either way is not

37. The earliest appearance of this vase which I know is to be found in Van Buren, plate I, 2, but there the liquid is poured upon an altar, not a tree.

38. Carl Frank, "Babylonisch-assyrische Kunst," *Kunstgeschichte in Bildern*, neue Bearb., n.d., I, II, 42, no. 5. Cf. Parrot, *Refrigerium*, 33, fig. 6.

39. Courtesy of the University Museum, University of Pennsylvania. See Van Buren, 73 f.; see her frontispiece and plates X and XI.

40. Ibid., plate II, 3, 6; III, 7; IV, 13. Ward, *Seal Cylinders*, 40, fig. 102. In ibid., 387, no. 71*c*, the flow is from a goddess. Ward tried to distinguish the god of water, Ea, the source of this flow, from a "sun-god" similarly represented (op. cit., 374; see also pp. 96–107 with several illustrations). Whether he is right I cannot say, but in either case what is represented is the flow of the divine fluid to men.

41. Langdon, 328; cf. 333.

42. Quoted by Langdon, 35; cf. pp. 32–34.

43. See, for example, Van Buren, plates X, 34, 35; XVIII, 64.

44. An interesting parallel from Egypt are the two goddesses, each holding a vase from which a light-stream flows, on the papyrus vignette published by A. Piankoff in *Egyptian Religion*, IV (1936), fig. 5 at p. 66.

precluded. What impresses me more than the possibility of borrowing is the fact that it is basically natural for a fertility-creator god to manifest his power in a spermatic flow, the water of life, and that it would inevitably be the objective of the individual to appropriate this same flow to satisfy his personal desire, not only for human and agricultural fertility, but for salvation and immortality.

The little fishes which so often appear swimming up this stream may be the devotees in it.[45] This is perhaps supported by the fact that a merman, what Ward calls a "man-fish," is so often associated with Ea and his stream, though what the merman really stands for has not been determined.[46] The priests of Ea are themselves fishes.[47] A more natural symbol for the transformation of the devotee to a life which would be lived in the "Water of Life" could not be devised. The value of the flow for the devotee is also indicated, as Langdon points out,[48] by the fact that Gilgamesh, the deified hero who sought the plant of life, often holds the vase or receives its flow, as we saw in fig. 126. Such a myth was very likely the product of a primitive cult act. We shall soon see direct evidence that this symbol did correspond to ritualistic drinking.

The most important single representation of the flowing vase in Mesopotamia still remains to be mentioned. It is a large mural, figs. 127 and 131,[49] from Mari, whence came the statue already discussed. In the center are two scenes, presented in panels one above the other. The upper panel shows the investiture of a king by Ishtar, who gives him the symbols of royalty.[50] His dress is that of the First Babylonian Dynasty—that is, at the end of the third or beginning of the second millennium.[51] An unidentified goddess seems to present the king to Ishtar, while Ishtar is herself accompanied by a god and goddess. Ishtar's foot is on a crouching lion, which Parrot takes to represent justice and law, but she herself is armed, so that as a whole she stands to him for the necessity of military power to maintain the peace.[52] Parrot points out that for Ishtar thus to invest the king at all is unique, since the ceremony is elsewhere always performed by Shamash. He sees her brought in primarily as the goddess of war, and her armor bears him out. But no armor could take the place of Ishtar's basic value as the source of universal fertility and personal "life," and this the rest of the painting seems to me to bring out.[53]

Beneath this royal panel are two goddesses, each with the flowing vase, their very garments apparently transformed into streams, so that here may be a new convention to represent the deity as being personally a source of the flow.[54] The vases from which the

45. W. C. Graham and H. G. May, *Culture and Conscience* [1936], 86, suggest that these fish "symbolize the life imparted by the fructifying waters."

46. See the famous seal published by Langdon, 86, and by Ward, 214, fig. 649. See also Van Buren, plate xx, fig. 70, and Ward, 410.

47. See below, p. 121.

48. Op. cit., 98 f.

49. From *Syria*, XVIII (1937), plate XXXIX and p. 336, fig. 8. It was published and discussed there by André Parrot, "Les Peintures du palais de Mari," esp. pp. 335–346. The reader should refer to his careful description for details.

50. On these symbols see ibid., 337, n. 3.

51. In ibid., 346, Parrot dates the scene in the thirty-third year of Hammurabi.

52. Ibid.

53. For this many-named goddess in her double role as goddess of war and of love see W. F. Albright, *Archaeology and the Religion of Israel*, 1942, 74–79.

54. I cannot state this positively, since most of our pictures of Babylonian dress come from seals, where the medium is different. On the seals, lines

streams flow have the little trees growing from them, and fish everywhere swim up and down the streams; one even swims across the central stream at the top.

These two scenes were certainly put together with meaning. When we recall that the true king, according to all ancient theories of kingship, brought heavenly benediction to his subjects in terms of fertility and prosperity, as well as in more mystical and personal ways,[55] the meaning of the junction seems at once apparent. The king, divinely established, was to bring down showers of blessing in every sense upon his people from the gods, because he himself was essentially invested with the divine fluid.

Such an interpretation of the central panels seems enforced by their setting. On either side are two trees, one pair which Parrot justifiably hesitates to identify, the other certainly date-palm trees. The top of the palm at the left is lost, but on the trunk the feet of the men picking the dates are clear, while nearly the whole tree appears on the right. Between the trees on each side three animals, one above another, face the central panels, animals which Parrot identifies as on the top a winged and crowned sphinx; in the center "a sort of griffin," winged, with his tail ending in a four-spoked whirl-rosette which suggests a swastika in a circle; and at the bottom a bull with his foot on a mound—"bearded and *sans doute* human-headed," says Parrot, though the head is gone on both sides. All these animals, we shall see, represent divine power and beneficence, and the same value is conveyed by the goddess who stands at the extreme right and left, her hands raised in benediction. Parrot thought the whole a product of hieratic symbolism, except for the palm trees, which seemed to him altogether too realistic to harmonize with the rest. But the date palm was itself a very common symbol, especially with the bunch of dates at either side.[56] Its association with the god of the flowing vase is likewise attested.[57] Only one detail remains to be mentioned, namely the large bird—perhaps a dove—which may be flying past the top of the palm tree, or just alighting, but in either case clearly is flying toward the central panel. Presumably a similar bird was at the top of the palm tree on the left.

The elements of this scene are strikingly present in the synagogue mosaic of Hammam Lif.[58] Here is the flowing bowl as a spouting chalice, and the date-palm trees and doves flank it. Peacocks have taken the place of the animals, a hellenistic element, and the old gods have of course disappeared. Either there must be some lineal succession of art tradition here, or the symbols must be of such primordial significance as to have re-emerged in Judaism two and a half millennia later. In either case it is hard to think that there was not deep religious meaning in the design. In the old painting of Mari we have the perennially disappointed hope of the subjects of ancient monarchy, namely that the

---

running the length of the fabric are almost universal, but these broad, wavy stripes to the feet seem to me unique, though I would not press the point.

55. See my "The Political Philosophy of Hellenistic Kingship," *Yale Classical Studies*, I (1928), 55–102; "Kingship in Early Israel," *JBL*, XLVIII (1929), 169–205.

56. As we shall see in Vol. VII.

57. See Ward, *Seal Cylinders*, 109, fig. 302, where Ea holds out the vase as he sits beside a date palm. The vase here does not "flow," but that was not necessary: in ibid., fig. 301, the same god does not even have a vase, his identity being indicated by the two fishes swimming up the imaginary current before him.

58. See above, III, figs. 887 f.

king would, by virtue of his divine character and power, bring his people peace, prosperity, and fullness of life.

The connection of the god holding the flowing vase with the date palm is strikingly presented on a later stone reservoir into which it is supposed libations were poured, fig. 130.[59] It was found in Assur and is of the period of Sennacherib (705–681 B.C.). At each of the four corners and at the middle of each side is a minor deity with a tiara, who holds the flowing vase in the usual way. The flow from the vase goes up, but that flow is probably identical with the flow which goes down to the ground from the god's body. The upward flow is relayed by a series of inverted vases. At either side of the god are two priests of Ea, who wear the typical fish-shaped vestment. Each of these priests carries a little bucket in one hand and an object in the other in the gesture characteristic of those who fertilize the palm tree. Contenau may be right in calling the little object an *aspersoir*—that is, an aspergillum, more commonly called a holy water brush. It may indeed be a cup with which he is catching the flow. But the pose and accoutrements are so commonly used in Assyrian symbolism to show the fertilization of the palm tree [60] that we naturally suppose the priests, here notably as fish, show in a new way that the fluid is the fluid of life. Presumably this all was to indicate the value of the fluid of the libations poured into the reservoir.

The cult act of individuals drinking from the divine stream appears directly in Mesopotamian scenes where two persons (sometimes only one) drink from tubes extending at either side from a central vase, as on a seal from Ur of a very early period, perhaps 3,000 B.C., fig. 132.[61] Since we know that the people of Mesopotamia early learned to make beer, it is commonly assumed [62] that beer is the fluid being drunk in such scenes. This may have been the case, but I know no suggestion of evidence to support the assumption. Parrot has pointed out that the motif appears "infinitely later" on Syro-Hittite seals. To this we shall come shortly. That such drinking was a holy rite seems again indicated on another early seal from Mesopotamia, fig. 133,[63] where divinities in the form of a lion and an ass drink from the vase. Parrot [64] explains these as the dead quenching their thirst in the afterlife, which is one of the meanings the design may well have carried but, as he agrees, the fluid still seems to be the fluid of life, and I should guess that such a way of drinking was definitely practised in cult. Contenau makes one of the two figures a god and the other a human being; Parrot objects on the ground that no distinction between

59. From Contenau, *Manuel*, IV, 2249, fig. 1274, last reported as being at the Berlin Museum.

60. The ritual of fertilizing the palm tree will be discussed in a later volume in connection with the symbolism of the tree. For examples see Contenau, *Manuel*, I, 243, 255.

61. From C. L. Woolley, *Ur Excavations*, II: *The Royal Cemetery*, 1934, plate 194, fig. 33; for a description, see ibid., I, 339. Cf. II, plate 193, figs. 17, 20; 194, figs. 22–26, 29, 31; 195, figs. 34, 37, 40. See also A. Moortgat, *Die bildende Kunst der alten Orient*, 1932, plate I, 1; Porada, *Morgan*, plate XVIII, figs. 112, 115 f. These scenes are discussed by Contenau, *Glyptique*, 109–112.

62. As by L. F. Hartman and A. L. Oppenheim, *On Beer and Brewing Techniques in Ancient Mesopotamia*, 37; cf. plates I f. (Supplement to the *JAOS*, X, 1950). Parrot, *Refrigerium*, 39 f., assumes that the fluid is water—Frankfort, *Cylinder Seals*, 77, that it is beer.

63. From H. Frankfort, *Iraq Excavations of the Oriental Institute* [Chicago], *1932/33*, 1934, 37, fig. 33. On p. 38 he says that it is Sumerian of the time of the dynasty of Akkad.

64. *Refrigerium*, 39 f.

the two is indicated in the drawing. But Parrot does not explain why *two* figures are so often represented. Frequently it is the god himself who thus drinks, as does Bes in Egypt [65] and one figure (a Syrian?) on an Egyptian wall painting.[66] I feel that both figures are usually human beings, presented on either side of the vase in accordance with the universal convention of putting an animal or symbol on either side of a central figure or symbol. Whether there is one figure drinking or two identical ones makes little difference, then. The central fact is that in thus drinking from the vase man gets the fluid of the vase.

It is at least worth suggesting that a series of drinking scenes shows the communion motif in very early Mesopotamia. A large number of such seals are preserved, of which I show only figs. 134,[67] 135,[68] and 136.[69] It has been noted that "divinities or divine symbols do not appear" on seals of this type. But in a great majority of the cases such seals indicate a significant distinction between the upper and lower registers. In the upper registers the figures are seated and drink in complete serenity, while in the lower registers the drinking, or vases, are shown in a cultic setting such as with animals for sacrifice or with an altar. It is apparent on these seals that drinking from cups is interchangeable with drinking from tubes. It is perhaps worth suggesting that the upper register shows the god partaking of the fluid of life and the lower register shows the cultic reproduction of this for human beings so that they too partake of the fluid. Since the headgear usual to mark divine beings is not here represented, I take confidence in making this suggestion from the fact that Contenau has noted that symbols of divinity are often not shown with the gods at this period, a strange omission.[70]

In fig. 139 [71] this symbolism is tied back to the flowing vase. Here each of the two men in the upper right corner holds a small vase, and from the vase between them a stream rises, divides, and flows into the smaller vases of the devotees. The larger figures seem to be the three chief deities of this religion,[72] though Miss Porada calls the one on the right the weather god, and is content to call the center figure simply a nude goddess, and to suggest that the figure on the left may be a king. The goddess must be the usual naked fertility goddess of the region, and so it is conspicuous that she holds a ewer, and thereby seems to

65. Lutz, *Viticulture*, 115, fig. 25.

66. Gressmann, *AOTB*, II, plate XXXIV, no. 79. Gressmann, p. 28, says that the drinking of beer in this way is attested for the ancient Sumerians and Hittites, and for the later Thracians, Phrygians, and Armenians, with reference to Xenophon, *Anabasis*, IV, V, 26 f.; B. Meissner, *Babylonien und Assyrien*, 1920, I, Plates, fig. 110.

67. From Woolley, plate 194, fig. 22.

68. From ibid., plate 200, fig. 98.

69. From ibid., plate 203, fig. 138; cf. figs. 23–32, 34 f., 37, 99–105, 138; Frankfort, *Cylinder Seals*, plate XV*a*, *c*, *f*.

70. On these as communion scenes see Contenau, *Glyptique*, 109–112.

71. Courtesy of the Pierpont Morgan Library, where the seal is, and of Miss Porada, who published it in her *Morgan*, no. 968, as a cylinder from the Second Syrian Group of 1600–1350 B.C. See her *Text*, 129 f. See also Contenau, *Glyptique*, fig. 146; in his figs. 138 and 140, two similar figures seem to be getting something from the object between them, but what this object is is not clear. Cf. Parrot, *Refrigerium*, 41, fig. 16; Ernst Heinrich, *Fara: Ergebnisse der Ausgrabungen der Deutschen Orient-Gesellschaft in Fara und Abu Hatab 1902/3*, Berlin, 1931, plate 63, esp. *g*, *k*, *l*, *n*. See also Moortgat, plate X, 6. In ibid., 7, 9, the figures drink opposite each other but without the central vase as source. Perhaps it is here assumed to be between them.

72. Contenau, *Glyptique*, 106.

bring fluid also; this seems symbolically not unrelated to the getting of the fluid by the two "communicants." In any case, the flowing vase itself has moved from the god's hands and become a cult vehicle of communion.[73]

That this fluid is the fluid of divine life seems to me clear from the existence of several examples of a peculiar design in which a woman stoops over to drink from a vase through a tube, while a male has coitus with her from behind. Of these I publish two which are at Yale. The first, fig. 140,[74] reproduces a photograph of a modern cast made from an original clay mold. Fig. 141,[75] an ancient cast, shows a variant of the same conception, and since several other examples are known, we are safe in assuming that the design constituted a symbol which had popular appeal. Specimens of this type have been dated "between Dungi and Hammurabi," [76] that is, apparently about at the end of the third and beginning of the second millennium; but figs. 137 and 138 [77] show two "antique" representations of the same motif (though the woman holds the pots but does not drink from them). The animal heads of fig. 138 indicate that this is a divine, or at least ritualistic, coitus. The same idea is presented in fig. 143,[78] where the *hieros gamos* is again being vividly enacted, and the vase with its spouts, and three round bosses which may be bread, are beside the bed. Andrae gives no reason but may be right when he says that these scenes are directly connected with the cult of Ishtar; in spite of the fact that there is no evidence for the provenance of any of these casts, it is reasonable to suppose that in a religion where temple prostitution was notorious these figurines continued to have religious meaning. Frankfort [79] connects such scenes of intercourse with the marriage of the goddess Bau and the god Ningirsu at the New Year's festival which ensured the year's fertility. The festival was followed by a great feast and presumably cultic intercourse, in which the life-giving act of the gods was rehearsed by the people. Merely indecent representations such scenes cannot be called, for it is hard to believe that drinking fluid from a vase through a tube was ever a popular accompaniment of coitus. The whole scene is most naturally to be taken as a symbol, or a representation of a symbolic cult act. And certainly it must be connected with the other symbols of drinking from a vase through a tube. If that symbolism represented again one's getting the fluid of life, to heighten the

73. See below, p. 138.

74. From the Yale Babylonian Collection, no. NBC, 4476. Published by permission of the Curator.

75. From ibid., 2367. It was mentioned by E. Douglas Van Buren, *Clay Figurines of Babylonia and Assyria*, 1930, no. 1093 (Yale Oriental Series, Researches, XVI). Another example was published, and reference given to three others, by Julius Jordan, *Uruk-Warka*, 1928, 63, plate 84, i; for a fragmentary example see Walter Andrae, *Die archaischen Ischtar-Tempel in Assur*, 1922, 114, fig. 92. See also Heinrich, *Fara*, plate 74, fig. *f*, and the description on p. 144, where Heinrich suggests that the woman is pounding a pestle; but this seems quite unlikely.

76. Jordan, 63.

77. From L. Legrain, *Ur Excavations*, III: *Archaic Seal-Impressions*, 1936, plate 18, nos. 368, 369; cf. plate 19, no. 370. Legrain, p. 34, oddly calls these "marital scenes." In fig. 137 there seems another coitus scene in the upper left corner. The large "round object," it is now possible to say, also suggests a ritualistic setting.

78. From a seal impression of the third millennium B.C. at the Oriental Institute of Chicago, As. 32–934. See H. Frankfort, *Iraq Excavations of the Oriental Institute* [Chicago], *1932/33*, 1934, 48, fig. 42 (cf. p. 45, fig. 40, and the comment on p. 49). See also ibid., plate 15*l*, and pp. 75, 77.

79. *Cylinder Seals*, 75–77.

symbol by showing the woman as she takes it simultaneously in two ways is most natural. As an isolated guess this suggestion would have little force; as a part of the general symbolism, by which the water originally flowed from the god's body, it seems to me very likely to be the meaning intended. The water of life, we have come to suspect, is to be had in sacramental drinking and in sacramental coitus. The latter may well have been symbolized in those regions not only in traditional designs but in the almost universal act of cultic "prostitution." [80]

In all of this symbolism we are driven back to the deeper question: which came first, the god who streamed water from his body, or the ritualistic drinking from the vase? The general tendency to regard the god and his myths as later rationalization of a primitive cult usage seems to me quite sound, and I should guess that ritualistic drinking antedated Ea and his attributes and derivative deities, at least in any fully formed sense of their personalities and mythologies. But in such a realm we can only speculate. What is assured is that the early inhabitants of Mesopotamia developed a conception that deity is the source of the fluid of life, a conception which was probably from the beginning a part of the elaborate use of sex in their religious formulations. The symbols, at first sight so different from those of Egypt and Greece, are, as we shall see, really very similar in value.

Parenthetically, may I call the reader's attention to the fact that in this section I have spoken of the devotee rather than the mystic, but only because to many the term "mystic" is reserved for religion on an intellectual level, religion with a philosophy. I do not agree with that reservation of the term, for in the higher religions the mystic may lose all intellectual interest as he is himself lost in the raptures of the experience itself, and I see no reason why religion on that level could not have prevailed among very primitive people, as we know that it does among our so-called primitive contemporaries. There is no evidence of a formal or abstract mystic philosophy among the ancient inhabitants of Mesopotamia, so far as I know. But the symbols, and what we know of the cult of Ishtar, show that if union was on a low "magical" level, these peoples had the basic elements in their religion which in a more philosophic age were developed into what all must call mysticism. And it seems to me highly probable that many from earliest times were having the mystic's experience if they had not yet developed the mystic's more philosophical explanations of the experience.

B. THE HITTITES AND SYRIANS

THE RELIGIOUS tradition of the great region from Armenia down through eastern Asia Minor to Palestine and below it was never unified and is more poorly attested by

80. I have not attempted to canvas the subject of ancient temple prostitution with any thoroughness. The material is very well presented in *GB*, *Adonis, Attis, and Osiris*, I, 36–78, in spite of Frazer's digressions into other civilizations. He seems justified in standing his ground against the numerous scholars who criticized his seeing religious value in the practice (ibid., 57–61). Much more material on the subject has come to light since Frazer was writing, but historians of religion in the field say that no one cares to expound it!

documents than is the case for either Mesopotamia or Egypt. The Semitic people of this territory were for a while under the dominion of the Indo-European Hittites, but local customs and loyalties were probably diverse and stubbornly kept. Later conquests by Assyrians, Babylonians, Egyptians, Persians, Macedonians, and Romans all left their imprint upon religious myths and symbols and only add to the perplexity of a historian who would try to reconstruct the religious motivation of the people or the meaning of the figures or designs represented on their larger monuments or on their seals. Experts are content to label many of these remains "Syro-Hittite." We shall consider the evidence for these countries in two blocks, the material from the periods before the Greek conquest and the Greco-Roman tradition. Here we shall attempt in neither period to describe the religion of this region as a whole, but only to see what we can learn of the importance there of the symbols of fluid.

1. *Literary Evidence*

THE MOST IMPORTANT of the recently discovered fragments of literary evidence for Hittite and Syrian religions are now readily accessible in English translation.[81] The documents are fragmentary, and while modern philologians have done brilliant work in reconstructing the languages in which they are written, many words and even sentences are still uncertain in meaning. Even more difficult is it to infer what religious motivations and ritualistic practices lay behind them. None of the documents gives a direct discussion of the questions which interest us here. The literary documents must be supplemented by the archeological remains.

The Hittite material is preserved on a series of clay tablets which date from the fifteenth century to 1225 B.C., though the rituals they give may in many cases have originated centuries earlier. From them it is clear that offerings of bread and wine were the commonest made and that libations, usually of wine, were poured out on a variety of occasions. The gods needed these offerings, or desired them, and the strongest appeal man had for divine protection was to remind the gods that if they allowed the destruction of their worshipers, such offerings could no longer be made.[82] References to rites with wine are common in the fragments of ritual.[83] But it might be blood which was caught in the cup and then poured out as a libation in a "magical" rite.[84] Wine and bread, with other elements, were to be used in a ritual to cure a man of impotence.[85] They were offered that the gods might give the king and queen "life, good health, long years," [86] or were presented by the king to the war god [87] or to the storm god.[88] In the majority of passages these are

81. Pritchard, *Texts*. The Hittite material is translated by Albrecht Goetze, the Syrian by H. L. Ginsberg. For other bibliography see the references there given. See also Gaster, *Thespis*. E. Cavaignac, *Les Hittites*, 1950 (L'Orient ancien illustré, III), gives an excellent review of the Hittites in general, but the section on religion (pp. 72–80) has little for our purpose.

82. Pritchard, *Texts*, 124A (II, d); 349B (II, 10); 399B (III, 8–15); 400A (IV, 5–14).

83. Ibid., 347A (II, 10–15); 351A (I, 55; II, 5, 47–52); 351B (III, 15, IV, 1–6); 352A (10–47).

84. Ibid., 348B (IV, 15–18).

85. Ibid., 349A (I, 5–10).

86. Ibid., 353A (40–47); 356A (top); 358A (III, 1–10).

87. Ibid., 358B (16–22); 359B (III, 1–12); 360A (V, 1–14); 360B (VI, 30 to end); 398B.

88. Ibid., 398B (64 to end).

merely mentioned as offerings which please the gods, who are themselves pictured as feasting [89] and presumably on these offerings, since they are so destitute without them. The libations may have had reference to the desire for rain on the *Purulli* festival of the storm god.[90] In one passage the king leads in "the celebration of communion feasts," [91] but while Gurney [92] made this "a communion feast shared with the divinity," Goetze [93] is convinced that the expression means simply festivals where everyone ate together.

In another passage the king and queen stand and "drink the (god) Tauri" and various other gods.[94] Goetze has read me the full text, in which it appears that the king and queen stand when drinking the greater gods, sit when drinking the lesser ones. With this went chanting by choristers, pouring of a libation into a vase, and a ceremony in which bread was brought in, broken by the king, and then carried out. The literal statement is that the god, or various gods, were so represented in the fluid that one drank them in it, which seems to me to go with the drinking scenes and spouting vases that we shall see on the Hittite seals. In the same way the reference to libation as described corresponds to the libations depicted in the period. This seems to me to be the earliest literary reference to a practice which appears reflected in much earlier art and which we shall see became the basic motif of sacrament as it still is in Christianity: the practice of drinking the god in ritual.

I must say that I read these texts with Gaster's general theory in mind, namely that the ritual for the king is a surrogate for a primordial fertility ritual, and that statements such as the ones in question are mythical enlargements of cultic practices, translations of "the punctual into terms of the durative, the real into those of the ideal." These implications, though unformulated and probably largely unconscious, were, he thinks, aspects inherent in the sacral acts from the beginning.[95] The reduction of what is in such texts to the "merely" ritualistic or the "merely" mystical seems to me, as to Gaster, to rob them of their essential meaning for the people who composed them. With the popular rituals, as Gaster conceives them from the myths, the popular seals and symbols are in no conflict at all. Both show a craving to participate in the divine nature, as well as, by ritual, to guarantee rain and the return of the sun for the group. Gaster's interest stops when he has demonstrated that drama originates in ancient rituals performed with a background of mythology. The myths seem, in Gaster's phrase, the verbal "expressions of a parallel aspect inherent in them [the rites] from the beginning." But, we have seen, the myths as verbal expressions, which we are calling the explanations,[96] could change enormously with time and environment. What is important is the basic value of rite or symbol through the ages. In any one period, however, the symbol or rite, together with the myth, not only per-

89. Ibid., 122A (top).

90. Ibid., 125B–126A. This, Goetze thinks, was a New Year's festival, but like the Jewish Tabernacles it seems to be associated with getting rain for the year.

91. Ibid., 397A (14).

92. O. R. Gurney, in *Liverpool Annals of Archeology and Anthropology*, XXVII (1940), 62–70.

93. In a review of Gurney in *JAOS*, LXI (1941), 302.

94. Goetze in Pritchard, *Texts*, 360B (30–33). Cf. A. Goetze, *Kleinasien*, *Kulturgeschichte des alten Orients*, 1933, 155 (Handbuch der Altertumswissenschaft, III, I, iii).

95. Gaster, *Thespis*, passim, esp. p. 5.

96. See above, IV, chap. 2.

petuates the group which uses it but also strengthens the individual even to the point of his hoping for immortality. That the "late Hittites," at least, had associations of immortality with the grape seems to me assured by the tombstone of a married couple shown in fig. 49.[97] Here the man holds a bunch of grapes, the woman what Akŭrgal thinks is a mirror.[98] Such a clutching of the grapes is a custom which continued for many centuries and which we have seen on a Jewish tombstone. It seems to me altogether likely that both husband and wife hoped for immortality through the symbols they hold on the stone.

We are trying to get at the psychological urge which prompted the people to such ritualistic practices in the beginning and to the psychological gratifications they derived from the practices, gratifications so real that people continued them, basically unchanged, for millennia, and even to the present. The fluid and its uses will seem to indicate that the satisfaction lay, as it still does, in participation of the individual in the divine.

Literary evidence from the early Semites of Syria is confined almost entirely to the Ras Shamra poems. These are mythological narratives in a Semitic dialect now called Ugaritic, written on clay tablets of roughly the middle of the second millennium B.C. Illuminating as preliminary studies have been,[99] it is not for an outsider to draw any detailed conclusions from this material, since experts disagree deeply in interpreting it. Yet wine, a divine fluid, and the goblet are so often mentioned in the myths told in the poems that they seem to me to reflect popular ritualistic usages. One could not come to such a conclusion merely from the references to the feasting and eating of the gods, though these may be mythological projections of ritualistic acts.[100] Even when El gives bread and wine "the blood of vines," and says this is an act of his love,[101] and when Baal, the god of rain, reproduces this feast, along with many kinds of meat, to consecrate the palace El has ordered to be built for him,[102] there is no direct suggestion of the meaning of the feasting and drinking. Wine is also used in sacrifice to El,[103] libations are very prominent in the ritual of atonement,[104] and drunkenness seems important.[105] But the significance of wine

97. A tombstone from Maras, now at Adana. From E. Akŭrgal, *Späthithitische Bildkunst*, Ankara, 1949, plate XL (where the full stone is also shown); cf. pp. 116, 124 (Ankara Üniversitesi dil ve Tarih-coğrafya Facültesi Yayimlari, no. 60; Arkeoloji enstitüsü, no. 4).

98. Ibid. I doubt this identification. At a funerary banquet on another tombstone of the same kind a woman holds the same object in her hand, before a dead man drinking: ibid., plate XLI; cf. p. 28, fig. 18. The other things held by the woman on this last stone seem to be pomegranates. I guess that the object in question is some form of bread or cake in her hand, but I do so quite without foundation.

99. I shall not attempt a bibliography of this material. Most of the poems are most conveniently available as translated by H. L. Ginsberg in Pritchard, *Texts*, 128–155, where he gives references at the head of each fragment of text. See also Gaster, *Thespis*. A considerable body of the literature not included by Ginsberg is given in English by Gordon, *Ug. Lit.* Many suggestions still of value were made by Dussaud, Mythologie.

100. As in Pritchard, *Texts*, 141B (46 f.), 146B (IV, 5; V, 4–10), 147A (VI).

101. Ibid., 133A (31–39).

102. Ibid., 134B (37–59).

103. Ibid., 143B (72–74), 144B (165–167).

104. Gordon, *Ug. Lit.*, 109–115. These are ritualistic texts which Ginsberg does not include in his collection in Pritchard, *Texts*, though they seem to me very important for Israelitic and Jewish cultus. Animal sacrifices are important in this

and other fluids appears to be clearly in the line of our investigation when Anath (one of the names of the goddess more commonly known as Astarte) tries to lure the human being Aqhat into giving her the divine bow by saying to him:

> And Baal when he gives life gives a feast,
> Gives a feast to the life-given and bids him drink;
> Sings and chants over him,
> Sweetly serenad[es] him:
> So give I life to Aqhat the youth.[106]

Aqhat spurns this and says he knows he will grow old and die like everyone else, which implies that the "life" Anath promised through Baal's feasting and drinking was immortality. We may well suppose that Aqhat's skepticism was not universal and that by means of the divine feasts and drinking required by the ritual most participants hoped to escape death or to come into a divine life after death.

The cup and the fluid in several forms become most meaningful for us in the Legend of King Keret, a poem whose original intention is much disputed. At the beginning of the poem as we have it, King Keret, of uncertain or mythological date and place, who is the son of El, is in a bad way. His wife has left him, his kinsmen have died, and he is reduced to despair because he has no progeny. In a dream El comes to him and tells him to take heart. He must first sacrifice to Baal and then lead his people out in a great army and attack a neighboring kingdom, Udum. When he has conquered that country, he is to demand the king's daughter Hurriya, "whose fairness is like Anath's fairness." Keret does as he has been told and gets Hurriya, who not only is of divine beauty but is the benefactress of Udum. For the wedding the gods themselves assemble, the poem continues, and El blesses the union:

> [The]n came the companies of the gods.
> And Puissant Baal spake up:
> "[Now] come, O Kindly One [El Be]nign!
> Wilt thou not bless [Keret] the Noble,
> Not beatify the Beloved, Lad of El?"—
> A cup [El] takes [in] (his) hand,
> A flagon in (his) [right hand].
> Indeed he blesses [*his servant*].

---

ritual, with libations of wine a close second. A passage which Gordon prints with italics because the translation is uncertain reads: "When Astarte enters the *cavern* [ ] *in* the house of the king *Serve, serve (drinks)* [ ] in the house of the gods" (p. 114, Text 5, lines 1 f.). If the translation is correct, this would imply a special association of Astarte with the drinking of wine. A bird is specifically sacrificed for her (p. 113, Text 3, line 40).

105. Pritchard, *Texts*, 150A (32 f.). J. Obermann, "How Daniel Was Blessed with a Son," *JAOS*, LXVI (1946), Supplement, no. 6, p. 17, remarks that the references to Daniel's drunkenness may reflect an orgiastic cult such as that of Dionysus. He compares the drunken father motif with the stories of Noah and Lot (Gen. IX, 20–27; XIX, 30–38).

106. Pritchard, *Texts*, 151B (30–35).

El blesses Keret,
  [Beatifi]es the Beloved, Lad of El:
"The wo[man thou ta]k'st, O Keret,
  The woman thou tak'st into thy house,
  The maid thou bring'st into thy court,
Shall bear seven sons unto thee;
  Yea, eight she'll produce for thee.
She shall bear Yassib (*yṣb*) the Lad,
  Who shall draw the milk of A[she]rah,
Suck the breasts of the maiden Anath,
  The two wet nurs[es *of the gods*]." [107]

This passage is full of important statements. El holds a cup of wine in his hands as he pronounces the blessing, "beatifies" Keret. The blessing is that Hurriya will bear the king a son, Yassib, and seven others, so that it is clearly fertility which Keret is being given. It is directly implied that the fluid symbolizes semen. The persistent convention of holding a cup of wine when a blessing is to be given will appear throughout this section of our study, and one recalls at once that Jewish marriages are still performed in this way. To be sure, the Jewish bride and groom drink from the cup by which their union is blessed; while nothing suggests it in this passage, I strongly suspect that since wine is something to drink, it was understood that Keret and Hurriya likewise drank of El's cup of blessing. In any case their children, especially Yassib, were to be divine children, which is indicated by the fact that Yassib was to be nursed by both Asherah and Anath, the nurses of the gods, as the king of Egypt was nursed by Isis and Hathor. Why the double personality of the divine mother was kept in both civilizations I cannot say, but this first appearance of the transference of divinity to a mortal by the fact of his being nursed by a goddess will find many counterparts. The fertility given by the cup of El seems to imply divine insemination; the milk is the means by which the goddess can give divine nature. One suspects that here is an emergence of the idea of a divine fluid which is given in ritual to impart immortality.

Still more important for our purpose is the remarkable ritual in which El begets two pairs of children. It is basically a fertility ritual to guarantee a period of seven fertile years. Gaster seems to me plausible in suggesting that it was a New Year's ritual, but he calls it the prototype of the Israelitic Feast of Weeks (Pentecost), when the first fruits were offered. The text seems to me to identify the rite as one performed in the season of the pruning of the vine, which was in the winter, and so it may have been a festival of the winter solstice. As such it was perhaps the temple enlargement of a ritual carried out originally in more primitive form by workers in the vineyards. What we have is a ritual enacted in the temple apparently with actual intercourse performed by the priests or king, if not by the worshipers in general, since it is no novelty to suggest that ritualistic intercourse was one of the basic elements in worship in this region. Such intercourse may be presumed to have been a part of the agrarian rites in the field. The ritual has been translated by Ginsberg, Gaster

107. Ibid., 146A (II, 11–29).

and Gordon.[108] I reproduce Gordon's version,[109] which I break up with comments that are largely paraphrases or quotations from his introduction to the text, though I draw freely upon Gaster's much fuller expositions.[110] Gaster calls the ritual "The Poem of Dawn and Sunset," but there is so much beside this in the text that I prefer Gordon's "The Birth of the Gods." Its sections are divided by lines drawn on the tablet by the scribe himself.

Section I (lines 1–10) is a prelude in which the "gods good and fair," the king and queen, and the "choristers and servitors" are greeted, and the gods at least are told to "eat of the bread and drink of the liquor of wine," a ceremony which Gordon says is the "*leitmotiv*, the underlying theme of the drama to be fulfilled at the finale." I suspect that the others addressed also ate the bread and drank the wine. Thus, we are at once deep in the symbolism of bread and wine.

I invoke the gods good and fair
  Sons of *Šarru[ma*] and *votaries.*
Honor on high! [ ]
  In the wilderness, *hills* [ ]
to their head and [ ]

Eat of the bread, ho!
  And drink of the liquor of wine, ho!
Mayest thou have peace, O king!
  Peace, O queen!
    Choristers
    And servitors.[111]

Section II (lines 8–11) describes a ceremony in which Mt-and-Šr, which Gaster translates "lord and master," sits (probably, as Gaster makes it, "sits enthroned") with a scepter of privation and bereavement (perhaps there were two scepters). As he holds these symbols of the failure of his fertility he is beaten by branches pruned from the vinestalks. That it is actually the king who enacts this role seems to me rather doubtful. The person,

108. Gaster, *Thespis*, 225–256; idem, *JAOS*, LXVI (1946), 49–76; Gordon, *Ug. Lit.*, 57–65. H. L. Ginsberg, "Birth of the Gracious and Beautiful Gods," *Journal of the Royal Asiatic Society*, 1935, 45–72. Earlier literature is referred to in these works.

109. The only alteration I am making is that, in the interest of consistency for my readers, I spell the supreme god's name El, as does Gaster, in place of the 'Il of both Ginsberg and Gordon.

110. It is a great temptation to give an eclectic text by choosing at will from the three versions mentioned, but this would be fair to none of them and, since I do not read Ugaritic, would be too subjective a procedure on my part. Hence I arbitrarily give the text of Gordon. Stimulating as are Gaster's interpretations, I feel that for details he often draws upon his imagination or upon parallels and analogies from other civilizations, the suggested amplifications of which it seems to me dangerous to transfer to the Ugaritic ritual without direct evidence. On the whole Gordon's more conservative treatment, at this stage, is much safer for an outsider to use. I presume that he has incorporated all that seemed to him acceptable in Ginsberg's much earlier translation.

111. Gordon, *Ug. Lit.*, 58 f. In reproducing Gordon's text I have not followed his convention of indicating the length of lacunae or undecipherable passages by the spacing between square brackets.

whoever it was, represents the dying year and its vegetation, and the humiliation of his failure is what is castigated, all in hope of a new year and new fertility. Since the ceremony was performed at the period of pruning, it was, as I have said, presumably in the late autumn if not in the winter solstice and so may have had solar associations—those of the passing of the old waning sun in the interest of the coming of the new and growing one. It seems highly probable that the ceremony was a part of the general Near Eastern Adonis tradition.

Mt-and-Šr sits;
In his hand is the staff of privation
  In his hand is the staff of bereavement.
They prune him with the prunings of the vine
  They switch him with the switches of the vine
    He is felled in his field like a vine.[112]

Sections III (line 12) and IV (lines 13–15) first give directions for a sevenfold performance with instrumental and choral music and then tell us that the rite thus celebrated is the cooking by "heroes" or "sturdy youths" of a kid in milk and of a lamb in butter. This is to be done, according to Ginsberg and Gaster, in honor of the "breast of the Asherah and the Virgin" (a doublet for the Mother Goddess who was both mother and virgin), but according to Gordon it is to be done in the "field" of the goddess. Gaster concludes that the ceremony is in honor of the goddess' breast at which, we have seen, the gods are nursed, but without the agreement of other scholars I do not know whether he is overtranslating. In any case the connection of the rite with the Mother Goddess is clear. The time of the festival is by no means set by the reference to kids. Kids are thrown in Palestine at all periods of the year, the mother gives milk from three to ten months, and the age of the kids sacrificed is not given. I should guess that their sacrifice was in line with the tradition in these countries, still registered in Exodus XXII, 29 f., that the first born of both men and cattle shall be offered, and that the age of the cattle sacrificed was eight days:[113]

Seven times is it to be recited to the accompaniment
  of the lute and the choristers declaim:

———

And the field
  The field of the gods
    The field of Asherah-and-Raḥm!
By the fire, seven times the heroes

112. Ibid., 59.

113. The Ugaritic text does not say that the kid is to be boiled in milk from its own mother, but it is generally agreed that the rite is the one alluded to in Exod. XXIII, 19, with the usual assumption that the Old Testament law was forbidding Jews to practise the ritual here recovered. Morgenstern may be right, however, in saying that the Israelites were forbidden only to boil the kid in the milk of its own mother, while the sacrifice is otherwise assumed to be allowed. See Morgenstern in *HUCA*, XV (1940), 116; Gaster, 244 n.

Coo[k a *ki*]*d* in milk
A *lamb* in butter
And by the flame, seven times, the offer[ing.] [114]

Section V (lines 16–18) makes a cryptic reference to the Mother Goddess as going out to some combat, according to Gordon. Gaster translates this as the bringing in at this point of the statues of the two goddesses:

Raḥmaya goes and *roams* [ ]
She grapples with the goodly hero [ ]
And - - - the choristers [115] [ ]

Section VI (lines 19 f.) Gordon understands as a shift of the scene to the dwelling places of the gods; Gaster thinks that eight seats are set up for the images brought in and sees an astral reference in the eight seats. The section seems to me too cryptic for assured interpretation. In any case a sevenfold rite of some kind is enacted:

The dwellings of the gods, eight [ ]
seven times: [116]

Section VII (lines 21 f.) is still more cryptic than the preceding, since the reference and meaning of the last word is quite uncertain:

I have zeal for the names
of the sons of *Šarruma* [117]

Section VIII (lines 23–27) is "an invocation to the good gods sucking the breasts of the goddess(es); and a greeting of the choristers and attendants bearing a sacrifice," according to Gordon. Gaster, who makes a religious drama out of all such texts, sees this section as the prologue of the drama proper, lines spoken by a "presenter" who corresponded to the Greek leader of the chorus. In any case it is notable that both the sun and grapes are of great importance and that the milk of the supreme goddess is the source of divinity for the gods themselves. Three types of fluids, light, wine, and milk, are becoming apparently interchangeable representations of the divine fluid:

I invoke the good gods
[*Islanders*, sons of the s]ea,
Who suck at the nipples of the breasts of Asherah [ ]

Sun *illumines* their doors [ ]
and the grapes.
Peace, O choristers, servitors!
Going with a goodly sacrifice.[118]

114. Gordon, *Ug. Lit.*, 59.
115. Ibid.
116. Ibid.
117. Ibid.
118. Ibid.

Section IX (lines 28 f.) Gordon takes to mark a shift of the scene to the field of the Mother Goddess, while Ginsberg and Gaster make it into an apostrophe to her breasts. I have no judgment in the face of such division, but continue to give Gordon's text:

The field of the gods
  The field of Asherah-and-Raḥmaya
    [ ][119]

Section X (lines 30–76) is the main body of the poem or ritual, and here there is so much consistency that I reserve comment until the reader has seen the text itself:

[ ] the shore of the sea
And *roams* the shore of the deep.
[El takes] two kindlings
  Two kindlings from the top of the fire.
Lo she is at the bottom
  Lo she rises
Lo she cries "Father, father!"
  Lo she cries "Mother, mother!".
"Let El's hand be long like the sea
  Yea, El's hand like the *flood!*"
El's hand became long like the sea
  Yea, El's hand like the *flood.*
El takes two kindlings
  Two kindlings from the top of the fire.
El takes and *puts* (*them*) in his house.
El lowers his rod
  El *lets down* the staff of his hand.
He raises, he shoots heavenward
  He shoots in the heavens a bird
    He *cleans* and sets it on the coal(s).
El would tup the two women.
Lo both women shout:
"O husband, husband!
Thy rod has fallen
  Lowered is the staff of thy hand!"
Lo the bird roasts on the fire
  Broils on the coals.
The two wives of El, wives of El,
  Wives of El and his forever!
And lo the wives shout:
"O father, father!
Thy rod has fallen
  Lowered is the staff of thy hand!"

119. Ibid.

Lo the bird roasts on the fire
  Even broils on the coals.
The two daughters, daughters of El
  Daughters of El and his forever.
And lo the two wives shout:
"O husband, husband!
Thy rod has fallen
  Lowered is the staff of thy hand!"
Lo the bird roasts on the fire
  Even broils on the coals.
The two wives, wi[ves of El],
  Wives of El and his forever.
He bends, he kis[ses] their lips
  Lo their lips are sweet
    Sweet as grapes.
From kissing and conception
  From the embrace of childbirth
They go into tra[vail]
  So that they bear
Dawn
  And Dusk.
Word is brought to El:
"The wi[ves] of El have b[or]ne!
  What have they borne?"
"My two children
  Dawn and Dusk!"
Lift up, prepare for Lady Sun
  And for the stars [ ]
He bends, their lips he kisses
  Lo their lips are sweet.
From kissing and conception
  [From] embracing and childbirth
    They again [ ]
count(s) to five [ ] the combination of the twain
Go into travail
  And they bear
    They bear the goodly [gods]
      The *islanders*, sons of the sea,
        Who suck from the nipples of the [Lady's br]easts.
Word is brought to El:
"Both wives of El have borne
  What have they borne?"
"The goodly gods [ ]
  The *islanders*, sons of the sea,
    Who suck from the nipples of the Lady's breasts!"

A lip to earth
  A lip to heaven
And there verily enter into their mouth
Birds of heaven
  And fish from the sea.
And there proceed [ ]
Set(s) both right and left in their mouth
"The wives I have wed have borne my *satisfaction.*
O sons I have begotten!
Lift up, *prepare*
In the midst of the wilderness of Kadesh
There you would be a *client*
Of the stones
  And of the trees
Seven complete years
  Yea eight cycles
Until the goodly gods walk the field
  Roam the corners of the desert.
And the guard of the sown *meets* them.
And they call to the guard of the sown:
"O guard, guard, open!"
And he opens a crevice behind them
  And they enter [ ]
"If [there is] bread
  Give, that we may eat!
If there is [wine]
  Give that we may drink!"
And the guard of the sown answers them:
"[There is bread to eat]
  There is wine to drink in [ ]
[ ] - - - - for a *hîn*
A *lôg* of his wine [ ]
And his companions, full of wine [ ] [120]

This remarkable account apparently accompanied a ritual drama in which the deity, this time El, was given back the virility which he had lost. There is a fire on the seashore, and El is beside it with two wives. It may be that he creates these consorts out of the "two kindlings from the top of the fire." El attempts to have intercourse with these wives, but his "rod" lowers and he is unable to impregnate them. He then shoots a bird and roasts

120. Ibid., 59–62. The translation of this passage by Pope with commentary, reached me when this volume was in press: Marvin H. Pope, *El in the Ugaritic Texts*, Leiden, 1955 (Supplements to Vetus Testamentum, III), 37 f. He makes it clear that the "hand" in the early lines, which is "long as the sea," is a euphemism for the phallus. He called my attention also for this passage to René Largement, *La Naissance de l'Aurore*, 1949 (Analecta Lovaniensia Biblica et Orientalia, II, ii).

it on the fire, but it is not until the bird is thoroughly roasted that the wives cease to taunt him about his fallen rod. His potency now returns and he impregnates them so that one wife bears Dawn, the other Dusk. El hails their arrival with the apostrophe, "Lift up, prepare for Lady Sun and for the stars." The intercourse is then repeated, and two more children are born, "the goodly gods, the *islanders*, sons of the sea, who suck from the nipples of the [Lady's br]easts." Opinion is divided about this repetition. Is it mere repetition, so that the second two children are really themselves Dawn and Dusk, or does El here beget two new children? Or is there another setting altogether, in which a human father is begetting by human wives, and the progeny are divine because he has followed the pattern of El's begetting? These gods (presumably the second pair) wander in the desert but come to the "god of the sown," who lets them in, presumably into the sown fields, where they commune on bread and wine. The final eating and drinking seems to be a ritualistic pledge of fertility for the crops.

If, as appears likely, this corresponds to a ritual, it seems inevitable to suppose that it was a fertility rite primarily for the coming of Lady Sun. All things considered, I judge it most apt to have been a ritual of the winter solstice, when fertility was at its lowest but when the new Dawn and Dusk were born and the parallel new gods of fertility needed to wander but a relatively short time in the wilderness before the fields began to bear their crops and the gods came in to strengthen the yield. For our purpose it is important to notice the simultaneous presentation of the meal of bread and wine, the symbolism of light, the importance of the milk of the Mother Goddess, and the direct reference to divine sexual intercourse which was presumably mirrored in human sexual intercourse in the celebration of the rituals. Together these suggest very strongly that the basic drive was to life for men and crops through all of the fluids and that they had their common denominator in the sense of the supreme value of the divine fluid as such, of which each of the fluids was but a single manifestation and symbol.

How objectively this ritual was regarded—that is, how much it was merely a way of getting fertility for the fields and how far people had at that time gone in the process of subjective identification that was later so apparent in the mysteries of Adonis and the like—the ritual itself does not tell us at all. The only approach to that problem is through the seals and other representations for private use. These never show together all the highly complex symbolism of so complete a ritual. But elements from the rites do appear and, I believe, throw at least some light on the question.

In any case we must assume that the later forms of Syrian religion which seem to center so much in the Great Goddess and Adonis are descendants from the sort of religion we have been considering. Dussaud [121] has suggested that Adonis combined in himself the two roles of Aliyy, the fertilizing spirit of the rains and the rainy season, the rivers, etc., and of Mot, the divine son, who was the harvest. With the Aliyy aspect goes the myth told by Adonis' followers:

> Cronos, having waylaid his father Uranus in an inland spot, and got him into his hands, cut off his genitalia near some fountains and rivers. There Uranus was hallowed,

121. "Mythologie," 383.

and his spirit (or breath, *pneuma*) was separated from him, and the blood of his genitalia flowed into the fountains and the waters of the rivers.[122]

The fertility of the water flow in the Adonis tradition was thus definitely visualized as a phallic flow from the god. How far back this goes I cannot guess, but it would seem to be an interpretation of the rivers, the fluid of which not merely was the source of crops but represented a god who also was the savior and giver of immortality to men. It was this Adonis who, Plutarch tells us, "was considered to be none other than Dionysus" in hellenistic syncretism.[123] Not to go into Dussaud's details, his conclusion is important for us.[124] There existed in early Phoenicia (and in Syria in general, from his evidence) a religious teaching which, by means of agrarian rites, associated the individuals with the phenomena of nature and the rhythm of the seasons. By the seventh century B.C. these mysteries were concentrated in the person of Adonis (Eshmoun) and were still later identified with Dionysus; as such they were displaced only by Christianity.

It was Syrian religion in this form which surrounded the Jews during most of their history in Palestine, and it seems to me to be this religion as it was hellenized and correlated with Dionysus which appears on the Greco-Roman remains of Syria and, with some Jewish adaptation whose nature is the goal of this study, on the synagogues and graves of Greco-Roman Jews. We shall return to the Syrian adaptations after we have studied the Greek symbolism in which the Syrian religion came to express itself.[125]

2. *Iconographic Evidence*

THAT THE VINE was at least one of the important symbols among the Hittites from early times is attested by the frequently published figure of the Hittite fertility god, the enormous stele of about 1,000 B.C. from Ivriz, near Tarsus, fig. 148.[126] The god presents to the adoring king with his left hand a few grain stalks whose heads are above his hand, and with the right hand a bunch of grapes at the end of a branch from which hang two other bunches. The vine twines round his body and grows from the ground behind his right foot, while the grain stalks go down to the ground behind his left foot. That is, the god is himself the embodiment of the growing vine and grain, and it is this fertility which he is presenting to the king, who, by all oriental standards, was to bring it to his land and people. It is probably the same god, under the name of Sandan, the "Baal of Tarsus," who appears holding grapes on early (Persian Age) coins of Tarsus.[127] One Hittite seal, fig. 142,[128] shows a goddess being inundated by a flow of Egyptian signs of life and duration. Above her head is a little bird, which seems to me to identify her with the fertility goddess Astarte, by whatever name she may have been locally called. The figures with her, a bald

122. Ap. Eusebius, *Praeparatio evangelica*, I, x, 38b.

123. *Quaestiones convivales*, IV, V, 3; quoted by Dussaud, "Mythologie," 401.

124. Ibid., 406.

125. See below, VI, 69–71.

126. Photo published by permission of the Archeological Museum, Istanbul, where the stone is. See C. Picard, *La Sculpture antique*, 1926, 167, and Contenau, *Manuel*, III, 1127–1130.

127. PC, *Histoire*, IV, 727; E. Pilcher, in PEF, *QS*, 1910, 79 f.

128. From Osten, *Brett*, plate VIII, no. 88; cf. Osten, *Newell*, 118, fig. 12.

man, apparently a Hathor figure, a winged disk, serpent, and a lion, make the design too complex for me to try to decipher the meaning of the whole, but the flooding of the fertility goddess with the shower of life seems definitely to belong among our symbols of fluid. We shall see similar flows when we come to Egypt.[129] With this seal goes the one shown in fig. 144,[130] a Syrian seal where the attendant goddesses are in Babylonian dress and the figure under the flow of ankhs or life is male. The flow comes from vases in a way to suggest the Mesopotamian flowing vase. But the flow is the same as in fig. 142. It seems to me apparent that we are dealing with people who will draw on any vocabulary to express the very definite idea of the fluid of life.

The commonest way of showing this was to use the Mesopotamian god of the flowing vase, or god from whose person the streams come, as well as representations of drinking through tubes from a vase. An example of the first of these is fig. 145,[131] where the god holds the flowing vase, up whose streams fish swim. He stands upon a little boat. His supremacy seems marked by the sun and moon at either side of him. Three lesser divinities, marked only by the moon, approach him.

The convention of the king holding the divine attribute of the flowing vase, which we saw in the statue of Gudea,[132] is amazingly reproduced for Sargon II, the Assyrian king, 722–705, a millennium and a half after Gudea, fig. 147.[133] Here it is not the king but a deity in the same pose. Four streams go out from his vase, two falling down the front of his robe and two going over his shoulders and running down his back. The little vases at the bottom are replaced by marking the lower part of his garment all round with wavy lines which I am sure represent not a fringe but the water or fluid which the god provides for the earth. The more we see such variations in presenting an idea, the more confidently we can assume that the representations do not show a mere convention but that behind them is the living force of an idea.

That there was still a ritualistic concomitant to this flow seems indicated to me by such scenes. In fig. 146 [134] we seem to see the same deity as the one in fig. 145, for here also he is flanked by the sun and moon as he gives forth the streams, while again devotees approach him. At the right two little figures seem to mark the ritualistic concomitant of this flow as they catch in little vases the stream from a flowing vase between them. Contenau has discussed these scenes as representing "communion," [135] and it is hard to believe that they did not correspond to ritual drinking in which the fluid of the god as the fluid of life was consumed.[136]

129. See below, p. 186.

130. From G. A. Eisen, *Ancient Oriental Cylinder Seals . . . Mrs. William H. Moore* [1940], plate XIV, no. 142.

131. From Contenau, *Glyptique*, plate VI, no. 20. It is at the Louvre, no. AM1486. Cf. L. Delaporte, *Catalogue des cylindres orientaux du Musée du Louvre*, 1920, II, plate 125, no. 5*b*.

132. See above, p. 114, and fig. 122.

133. From Victor Place, *Ninive et l'Assyrie*, 1867, plates XXXI bis. These statues were unfortunately destroyed. Cf. Contenau, *Manuel*, III, 1253; IV, 2240, fig. 1264.

134. From Contenau, *Glyptique*, plate XXVII, no. 187; cf. pp. 107, 111. It is at the Louvre, no. A897. See Delaporte, plate 95, no. 24.

135. Contenau, *Glyptique*, 109–112.

136. The god with the flowing vase appears on another Hittite seal published by Contenau, *Manuel*, II, 946.

Even more clearly ritualistic is the design shown in fig. 149,[137] a Syrian seal of the second millennium B.C. Here the god enthroned on the right drinks through a tube out of a large vase before him. In the center a priest in a long robe pours a libation into the larger vase from a smaller one.[138] At the left a devotee also drinks from a tube which goes into the large vase. "Any explanation," says Moortgat, "but a communion is hardly possible." To this I would add that it is just as difficult to think that the scene does not refer to an actual ritual of libation and communion drinking, though in the ritual the tube for the god may have been only assumed (his place might have been taken by a priest). Therefore it is notable that among the symbols put into the spaces between the figures is a fish, for this seems to me to characterize the fluid again as the fluid of life. Whether the actual fluid used was water, beer, or wine appears by this time unimportant.[139] It seems only a variant when the god greets a suppliant by extending a cup to him.[140] We see here the "vulgarization" of the royal investiture on which Labat remarked in connection with the Gudea seal, where the ruler was given the flowing vase by the god.[141] So it is not surprising that on funerary steles of the Hittites and Syrians these motifs should reappear. On one, fig. 152,[142] the dead person sits enthroned, and on a tripod before her is a banquet consisting, among other things, of bread and fish. She holds a flower in one hand and a cup in the other. I must say that the scene seems to me to have meant that the deceased had become deified in immortality.[143]

The richness of the symbolism is emphasized by another Syro-Hittite seal, fig. 150.[144] We have noted that the god who is the source of the stream is often marked as the supreme god by the sign of the sun and moon beside him. In this seal above the vase between the two drinkers is the sun with streams in a way to recall the favorite device of Ikhnaton of Egypt.[145] The fluid here is identified with the solar stream.

It seems only another variant of the symbolism when on a *kernos* ring of about 950 B.C. the two drinkers at the cup become a pair of doves, as in fig. 151.[146] Here, with a gazelle

137. From Moortgat, *Vorderasiatische Rollsiegel*, 1940, plate 62, no. 526; cf. p. 132.

138. This sort of libation into a vase was referred to in the liturgy quoted above, p. 128. It is often represented: see Contenau, *Manuel*, II, 824, 1002 f.

139. The same ritual seems indicated on a Cappadocian seal at the Louvre where the god is enthroned with sun and moon above him, a fish behind him. The drinking vase with two tubes is before him and a libation is being poured. See ibid., 817, fig. 584.

140. Contenau, *Glyptique*, figs. 8–44, passim.

141. See above, p. 114.

142. From E. Pottier, *L'Art hittite*, 1926, 71, fig. 81; cf. Contenau, *Manuel*, III, 1145 f. It was found in Zendjivli, and Contenau dates it in the eighth century B.C. It was last reported as being in the Museum of Berlin. For a similar funerary stele from Neirab see ibid., 1366. The motif was accepted also popularly in Persia; see ibid., IV, 2171, 2175.

143. King Ahiram at Byblos is also represented on his sarcophagus as sitting on his throne before a tripod table. A funerary feast is on the table; he holds a lotus in one hand and is about to drink from a little cup held in the other. Pierre Montet, *Byblos et l'Egypte*, 1928, plate CXXX; Text, p. 228–232 (Bibliothèque archéologique et historique, XI).

144. From Contenau, *Glyptique*, plate XXVIII, no. 196; cf. p. 112. Contenau reports the seal as in possession of I. Dodd.

145. See below, pp. 148–150.

146. From a photograph published by permission of the Oriental Institute, The University of Chicago. See H. G. May, *Material Remains of the Meggido Cult*, 1935, plate XVI; cf. pp. 17 f. (The University of Chicago Oriental Institute Publications, XXVI).

head, two pomegranates, and two wine jars, there are, at the top, the two doves drinking from the cup between them. Such objects, of which a number are known, appear to have been carried, or worn on the head, by the priest or priestess in the temples of Astarte in Syria. They have been found in remains dating from 1411 B.C. to several centuries later. Archeologists have called them *kernoi*, from the very similar objects of this name used in the worship of Demeter in the Mysteries of Eleusis,[147] though Watzinger protested against using the Greek term.[148] Rowe also associates these with the Gardens of Adonis, little fertility charms consisting of vessels in which wheat, vegetables, and flowers were planted, exposed to the sun, and well watered, so that, probably like our hothouse beds for seedlings, they anticipated and hence magically encouraged the growth of seed scattered in the field.[149] But as to the Syrian kernoi he adds, "I believe there is some evidence to indicate that the apertures on the cylinders are meant to typify the female attribute." [150] What that evidence is he does not say, but in view of the undisguised use of sexual symbolism and ritual in the cult of the Near Eastern goddess of fertility this is by no means unlikely. The sexual reference of doves in this region will be discussed in a later volume, together with the continuation of the dove as a symbol for identification of the devotee with the divinity. The doves in Jewish and Christian vines come at once to mind, and in Christian symbolism it has long been recognized that they represent the souls of the devout seeking refuge in the loving protection and power of the vine. Doves also drink at the cups in Jewish and Christian art, and it is significant that the convention, later a representation of the soul getting the divine Life, is clearly of Syrian (or Cypriote [151]) origin. I cannot believe that it did not mean the same to the ancient worshipers of Astarte who used it.

147. For the Greek references and parallels, especially from Cyprus, see Alan Rowe, *The Four Canaanite Temples of Beth Shan*, Pt. I, 1940, 45, 51 f., 56; cf. plates XIX, 11; XX, 21; LIA, 3; LIIA, 3; LXA, 3 (Publications of the Palestine Section of the University Museum, University of Pennsylvania, II). Cf. May, loc. cit.; Gressmann, *AOTB*, II, 1927, 193 f.

148. Carl Watzinger, *Tell el-Mutesellim*, 1929, II, 48 f. His argument is that there are dissimilarities as well as similarities between the Greek and Semitic objects and that the proper Syrian word for the rings is not known. *Faute de mieux*, however, they will probably continue to be called *kernoi*. Watzinger has extended bibliography for the objects in both civilizations.

149. The garden of Adonis will be discussed in a later volume.

150. Op. cit., 32 f.

151. Cypriote symbolism was so largely derived from Asia Minor, Syria, and Egypt that I suspect the device of doves drinking from a cup, in which one may properly see a fertility symbol, originated in Syria rather than Cyprus. But I know no evidence to confirm or refute this suspicion.

CHAPTER SIX

The Divine Fluid in Ancient Egypt

IN APPROACHING EGYPT an amateur is frightened by many things, not least by the fact that from classical times there has been a sharp division of interpretation. A hundred years ago Creuzer [1] pointed out that the Stoic and the Platonic versions of Egyptian ideology were quite at variance with each other. The Stoic writers gave what Creuzer called a "materialistic" or "exoteric" interpretation and said that the people of Egypt, like the Stoics themselves, recognized no gods or principles beyond matter, so that the highest Egyptian gods were the material planets, the signs and other phenomena of the zodiac, the stars of the horoscope, and the material sun which was the creator and highest god. The myths of Isis, Osiris, and the rest were all, the Stoics said, nature myths, stories of the stars, sun, and seasons.[2] In opposition, Neoplatonists, headed by Iamblichus (though Creuzer saw the tradition continuous at least from Plutarch), understood Egyptian religion in an "idealistic" or "esoteric" sense. By their account, in Egypt, Mind (*Nous*) and Speech (*Logos*) were at the head, and beneath them were various grades of emanations of intelligence. Creuzer himself effected a compromise; he said that the immaterial ideology is a late, yet genuinely Egyptian, development of an original naturalism.

The modern schools of approach are almost as sharply divided as the ancient, and along essentially the same lines. That the hellenistic Greeks saw in Egyptian symbols, rites, and myths something parallel to their own mystic formulations no one would attempt to deny. The point of disagreement is whether the mystic conceptions were really in the Egyptian material (granted some adaptation by Greeks) or were read by the Greeks altogether anew into a symbolism which itself had spoken only of nature, personal survival after death, and the king.

Without agreeing altogether with Creuzer and his successors, I must confess that I cannot sympathize with scholars who can be so objectively interested in the symbols of Egyptian art and liturgy as not to feel that there is much more here than farmers' folklore and astral myth. How people could create religion of such majesty, a symbolism which both expressed and satisfied such abandoned longing and faith, without themselves feeling its power, is to me incomprehensible. It is obvious that the myth cycles are based upon

1. F. Creuzer, *Symbolik und Mythologie*, 3d ed., 1840, I, ii, 117–123, 268–276.

2. For example, Chaeremon. See the passages in Hopfner, *Fontes*, 179–184.

nature cycles and just as obvious that many people can be satisfied in religion with a myth which accounts for the world and a ritual they can perform mechanically to pay their respects to the cosmos and its forces. There must have been many such Egyptians. And it is true that with many people religion does affect the emotions, but the effect is from the outside, the effect of holy adoration produced by a sense of the majesty of overwhelming power and goodness. The incredible magnitude of Egyptian religious monuments and conceptions must have made that impression upon every sensible Egyptian, of whatever degree in society. With others religion springs primarily from deeper emotions, such as those of anxiety or terror before the grim cruelty of nature; for them religion is largely a matter of appeasement, surely a tremendously important element in ancient Egypt.

There are still other people, however, whose emotions arise as much from within as from without, the "sick soul" type, who come to abhor themselves, who cling to life and dread death, whose hearts are torn at the loss of loved ones, and who cry aloud for a share in the perfection of pure life, for power that will supplement their weakness. Of this type the mystics, not those who merely "carry the thyrsus," are made. And to this type Egypt spoke in the Greco-Roman world, as it still can speak, with a force and directness beyond that of almost any religion. That is why I cannot believe that Egyptian mystery was the creation of the hellenistic mystics. There is a freemasonry among mystics which cannot be explained: a mystic is rarely mistaken in recognizing mysticism in others, and that the unmystical Chaeremon saw nothing beyond the material symbols of Egypt is no proof that the mystics from Plutarch to Iamblichus were mistaken in what they claim to have seen. The test, of course, will always be not the a priori alignment with one or the other ancient school but the Egyptian documents themselves. Yet even in reading documents it seems to be inevitable that a natural Stoic will sometimes fail to see what a natural mystic says is before his eyes.[3]

Certainly the Egyptian question in general is one for Egyptologists to settle. Yet the sort of question we must ask, Egyptologists have seldom raised. In spite of the difficulty of studying the history of symbols of fluid, therefore, we must try for ourselves to discover what Egypt has contributed to the symbolism we are studying, or at least what light the Greek interpretation of Egyptian symbolism throws upon hellenistic religious motivation. We must begin with ancient Egypt itself.

A. WINE ON EGYPTIAN MONUMENTS

IN EGYPT representations of the vine appear from early times and continue on into the hellenistic period without interruption. The Egyptians were very apt to include vintage and wine pressing among the industrial scenes painted in the tombs. This custom can be traced back to the IVth Dynasty, the paintings in the *mastaba* tombs of Sakkara,[4] where the workmen first trample and then squeeze the grapes. A similar design appears in the

3. One recalls the sentence of Jane Harrison: "Each man is in the matter of mysticism peculiarly the measure of his own understanding." *Prolegomena*, 365.

4. Lepsius, *Denkmäler*, IV, ii, plate XCVI.

tombs of Gizeh, of the Vth Dynasty, with the addition of a scene in which the wine is being stored in a row of large jars, fig. 153.[5] This motif of the jars at vintage scenes is a regular convention. They may be represented as being filled with the fresh juice [6] or simply as rows of storing vessels beside a press, fig. 154,[7] or in storage rooms.[8] From early times baskets are shown for gathering the grapes, baskets which not only are in the hands of the pickers [9] but also appear in groups or rows beside the vine.[10] The row of baskets, filled with grapes or pomegranates, is often conspicuous at the meal of the dead,[11] where the frequent representation of jars may also indicate wine.[12] From the point of view of iconography these rows of jars and the baskets seem of the greatest importance, a matter to which we shall return.

One curious tomb, the "Tomb of the Vines" at Thebes, at first suggests that the iconography of the vine, with symbolism behind the iconography, was really of great significance to Egyptians. It is a tomb in which the drama of successive experiences in the afterlife is told in pictures and inscriptions, with the constant accompaniment of a vine motif. The ceiling of the inner room, fig. 155,[13] is elaborately covered with a conventionalized vine. In spite of this unusual use of the vine and the emphasis placed upon baskets of grapes in the meal offerings, the inscriptions in the tomb, so far as I can make out, do not mention them at all. Virey, who published the tomb, says in one place [14] that the

5. From ibid., III, ii, plate LIII.

6. See also the representation from the tomb of Khety (XIth Dynasty), Champollion-le-Jeune, *Monuments de l'Egypte et de la Nubie*, 1845, Planches, IV, plate CCCLXXX, 3. Cf. P. Newberry, *Beni Hasan*, II, 1894, plate XVI. See also Billiard, *La Vigne*, 60; Davies and Gardiner, *Paintings*, I, plate XLVIII.

7. From J. G. Wilkinson, *The Manners and Customs of the Ancient Egyptians*, new ed. by Samuel Birch, 1878, I, 385. Birch describes the little shrine at the top as "the protecting deity of the storeroom"; cf. Norman Davies, *The Tomb of Neferḥotep at Thebes*, 1933, I, 37, and plate XLVIII (PME, IX). See also Billiard, *La Vigne*, 345; N. and N. Davies, *Tombs of Two Officials*, 1923, plate XXX (TTS, III). Norman Davies, *Two Ramesside Tombs at Thebes*, 1927, plates XXX–XXXIII (PME, V); idem, *The Tomb of Nakht at Thebes*, 1917, plates XXII, XXIII, XXVI (PME, I).

8. Wilkinson, I, 388; cf. Billiard, 437. Norman Davies, *The Rock Tombs of El Amarna*, 1903, I, plate XXVI (ASE, XIII); Nina Davies, *The Tombs of Menkheperrasonb, Amonmose, and Another*, 1933, plate VIII (TTS,V).

9. Champollion-le-Jeune, on the plate cited in n. 6 above; also ibid., plate CCCLVII; Billiard, 345; Davies and Gardiner, I, plate XLVIII; Wilkinson, 380 f.

10. Wilkinson, 379, 383; reproduced in Billiard, 45, 290. *Mém.* Miss., V, 1889, plate III after p. 488. In a vignette in *BD*, ed. Renouf and Naville, plate II, they contain various fruits and cakes: see the translation of Renouf and Naville, plate II.

11. Lepsius, *Denkmäler*, V, plate 78; VII, plate 240*d*. Champollion-le-Jeune, II, plate CLIII. Norman Davies, *The Tomb of Nakht at Thebes*, plate XXV.

12. "Place me with vases of milk and wine, with cakes and loaves and plenty of meat in the dwelling of Anubis": *BD*, ed. Davis, LVIII, 4, 5, p. 100. "I receive food on the altar, I drink consecrated wine at evening-time": ibid., LXXIX, 8, p. 113. The offering of wine to the dead is conspicuously stressed in TTS, V, plate XXXVIII; cf. Mariette, *Dendérah*, Text, 238, and III, 1873, plate XVI*c*. For other vintage scenes in the Theban Tombs see Arpag Mekhitarion, *Egyptian Painting*, trans. Stuart Gilbert, 1954, 19, 61 (The Great Centuries of Painting, ed. Albert Skira).

13. Philippe Virey, "La Tombe des vignes à Thèbes," *RT*, XX (1898), 211–223; XXI (1899), 127–133, 137–149; XXII (1900), 83–97. The above figure is from the last installment of this study, p. 86. See also W. Wreszinski, *Atlas zur altaegyptischen Kulturgeschichte*, 1923, I, II, plate 309; Mekhitarian, 53.

14. Op. cit., XX, 219.

artist used the vine for its symbolism of life and resurrection and that since the vine has grapes on one side of the tomb but none on the other, by this contrast he made it represent death and mutilation, out of which the new plant will grow, as Horus comes from the mutilated Osiris. He may be right, of course, but I could not draw such large symbolic implications from so isolated an instance. It is possible that the vine may have been inspired here by the occupation of the deceased, who was Sennofri, Director of the Granaries, Flocks, and Gardens of Amon and whose special predilection may have been for the vineyard, though these agricultural titles are quite inconspicuous among his other, more general, titles.

Sporadic cases of special representation of the vine could be collected: Osiris sitting under a grape arbor,[15] a decorative band made up of alternate bunches of grapes and lotus blossoms,[16] and a few others cited by Lutz, especially the beer god Bes.[17] But these are only occasional. We have mentioned that the meal offering, or meal of the dead, often shows grapes among the heaped-up viands, in bunches or in baskets,[18] but the grapes seem to have no special significance, since many more meals can be found without them than with them. It is tempting to think that the asp in fig. 154 at no. 11, and in similar pictures,[19] indicates sanctity in the wine, especially since with the asp is a lotus, a libation jar with liquid pouring from the spout, and a table of offerings. But there is no reason for going beyond Wilkinson's interpretation that the asp is "the protecting deity of the storeroom." [20] In one Pyramid Text it is said: "Behold, he cometh to thee as Orion; behold Osiris cometh as Orion the Lord of Wine." [21]

Much later, Siamen of the XXXIst Dynasty, at the very beginning of the first millennium, is represented in his palace offering two jars of wine to "Ptah, lord of truth," and the scene has the inscription, "Making an offering of wine to his father, in order that he may give life." [22] Also from a Theban Tomb, that of Djeserkarasonb of the time of Tuthmosis IV, 1420–1411, fig. 157,[23] is a wall painting in which two slave girls adorn a woman. One arranges her hair and another stands by with necklace [24] and lotus. Before

15. W. Max Müller, *Egyptian Mythology*, 1918, 113, shows the drawing but gives no indication of its source or date. I could not identify it. Osiris, or the dead man now deified as Osiris, was addressed: "Thou art those four gods, the glorious spirits of(?) wine and milk, who acclaim and make dancing, and who bring water in the arms of their father (*sic*). O Osiris Neferhotpe, raise thyself upon thy left side; Geb openeth for thee thine eyes, he straighteneth thy thighs. Adjusted(?) for thee is thy heart of thy mother, thy breast of thy true self": A. H. Gardiner, *The Tomb of Amenemhēt*, 1915, 115 (TTS, I). This reference to milk is important; see the discussion of milk below, pp. 183–186.

16. B. Bruyère and C. Kuentz, *Tombes thébaines*, I, I, 1926, plate VI (*Mém.* Inst., LIV).

17. Lutz, *Viticulture*, 114 f.

18. The sanctity of the meal, with grapes unusually conspicuous, is especially emphasized by a libation in one tomb; see V. Scheil, *Tombeau de Rat'eserkasenb*, 1889, first plate after p. 580 (*Mém.* Miss., V).

19. Wreszinski, I, II, plates 256, 355; see above, p. 143, n. 7.

20. Op. cit., I, 385; cf. III, 4.

21. Quoted by Renouf in his and Naville's ed. of *BD*, n. 12 to chap. CXXVIII, p. 256.

22. W. M. Flinders Petrie, *The Palace of Apries* (*Memphis II*), 1909, plate XXIV, and pp. 19 f. (BSAE, XV).

23. From Davies and Gardiner, *Paintings*, I, plate XXXVI.

24. For discussion of this necklace see below, VI, 78, n. 91.

her are foods and four jars of wine marked with the sign of ankh (life) and *was* (prosperity) and with a vine above them to show that they contain wine. In the Pyramid Texts it is said, "The sky has conceived wine," [25] and Osiris is "lord of the wine at the inundation," [26] but such scattered references to wine show only that it was one of the many fluids and foods used in Egyptian cult as an offering to get divine life. There is still insufficient evidence for assuming an important wine symbolism in ancient Egypt comparable to that of Dionysus in Greece.

Further, there seems to me no reason to generalize too strongly from official warnings against drunkenness.[27] That people not only enjoyed wine but hoped for a heaven well supplied with the pleasures of both wine and love seems amply witnessed by other familiar scenes of wine and dancing girls in the tombs.[28] The "Song of Khai-Inherat" addresses the dead:

Thou righteous, thou just and true man,
Calm, friendly, content, relaxed,
Happy, not speaking evil.
Give drunkenness to thy heart every day
Until that day comes in which there is landing![29]

But this is only a part of one of many such songs, and in the whole collection drunkenness takes on no special place, is rarely mentioned. In the liturgy wine appears occasionally as a libation,[30] and rarely such a phrase as "consecrated wine" is used.[31] There is even trace of a "festival of wine." [32] But the Pyramid Texts from very early Egypt and the Book of the Dead from a much later time are alike representative of general ritualistic and inscriptional testimony in that they mention wine simply as one of the foods and drinks in a list of food offerings to the dead or to the gods, and omit wine from these lists so often that it obviously had no essential place or role in the religion. Wine, as a luxury, was common in offerings to the gods, but for the dead both milk and beer are more common than wine, and

25. Line 1082*a*. So Edgerton translated the line. Mercer, *Pyramid Texts*, III, 540, and Sethe, *Pyramiden Texten*, IV, 354, make the sky "pregnant with the wine juice of the vine," which seems to them a poetic reference to the red flush of the sky at dawn.

26. Line 1524*a*. Cf. 819*c*–820*a*, where Osiris is lord of the wine cellar: see Mercer's note in *Pyramid Texts*, III, 738 f.

27. Such sayings are collected by J. Fichtner, *Die altorientalische Weisheit in ihrer israelitisch-jüdischen Ausprägung*, 1933, 18 (*ZAW*, Beiheft LXII); kindly pointed out to me by Professor Robert H. Pfeiffer.

28. The second plate in V. Scheil, as cited above, p. 148, n. 18.

29. Miriam Lichtheim, "The Song of the Harpers," *Journal of Near Eastern Studies*, IV (1945), 201. The entire collection (pp. 178–212) is of great interest.

30. Nina Davies and A. H. Gardiner, *The Tomb of Amenemhēt*, 1915, 40 (TTS, I); Norman Davies, *The Rock Tombs of El Amarna*, IV, 1906, 30 (ASE, XII); V, 1908, 10 f. (ASE, XVII).

31. As in *BD*, ed. Davis, 113 (plate LXXIX, 8): "I receive food on the altar, I drink consecrated wine at evening time." Renouf translated it "sacred liquor."

32. Mariette, *Dendérah*, 120. The material is Roman, and Mariette discusses the festival as a parallel to Dionysiac celebrations. But see Mercer, *Pyramid Texts*, III, 738 f.

water is overwhelmingly the most common of all.[33] Evidence of a unique sacramental or mystical use of wine is not forthcoming from ancient Egypt, although a cup of wine is so often an offering to the gods or king [34] and although a deified priest of Osiris is given bread and beer in his heavenly state, according to one most interesting text,[35] and Horus himself supplies the dead man with bread and wine in another.[36]

It is traditional to treat the meals for the dead, with or without their grapes and wine, as being merely food for consumption in the next world, the sort of provision which anthropologists have found the world over. Gardiner distinguishes two kinds of banquets in the paintings,[37] one the daily ritualistic offerings at the tombs and the other a "frank and deliberate reproduction of a terrestrial feast." But that these two explanations are the only ones possible seems to me unlikely. The banquets may also represent a sacramental communion in the next world, through which the dead person comes into a share of divine nature. But to dispute Gardiner's "Stoic" judgment is beyond my power, and, for our purpose, irrelevant. Even if the meals for the dead did have special sacramental significance, we have found no evidence that among the foods wine had any unique and distinctive position. When the Greeks later, as we shall see, came to identify Dionysus with Osiris, they seem to have had no inspiration from a natively Egyptian association of Osiris with wine in a special sense.

B. *THE EGYPTIAN CONCEPTION OF FLUID*

As in Mesopotamia, however, the "universal damp," "fluid in general," will be found much more illuminating than wine for our purpose. For it becomes at once apparent that it was a necessity that the dead be furnished not necessarily a specific fluid like wine but a fluid of some sort, if he was to hope for immortality.

Two books have been dedicated in whole or part to the elucidation of this conception of fluid in Egypt. Preisigke [38] has presented the sun rays as this fluid. "The sun god extends his arms to the earth as rays and thereby causes to flow out of himself the life power which is stored up in infinite fullness within him, as (to use a humble figure) the stored-up

33. *BD*, ed. Davis, XVII, 81, p. 82; XX, 8, p. 86; LXVIII, 4, p. 106; XCVII, 3, p. 121; CII, 3, p. 125; CVI, 1–3, p. 126; CIX, 9, p. 128; CXXII, 4, p. 133; CXXV, 66, 68, p. 139; CXXXVI, 12, 14, p. 148; CXLIV, 29 f., p. 158; CXLV, 77 f., p. 164; CXLVIII, 19, p. 171. Cf. Breasted, *Records*, V, 1907, 170, s.v. wine.

34. F. W. von Bissing, "Eine Stele des Mittleren Reichs mit religiösem Text," *ZaeS*, XL (1902/3), 118–120.

35. W. Wreszinski, "Das Buch vom Durchwandeln der Ewigkeit nach einer Stele im Vatikan," *ZaeS*, XLV (1908), 115.

36. Another case which just misses the possibility of mystic interpretation is the offering of "fine wine" by the king to the rising sun, here Horus, who grants in return "des vignes fertiles pour son pays, et une ébrieté sans tristesse": Mariette, *Dendérah*, 238, and III, plate 16*c*. Cf. Hathor as mistress of the vine and drunkenness, ibid., 240, and III, plate 21*x*. In spite of the symbolism of the lotus in Egypt, it would be dangerous to infer symbolism for the grape in the lotus and grape borders from Thebes. For these see E. Mackay, "Theban Borders of Lotus and Grapes," *Ancient Egypt*, 1921, 39–41, with illustrations.

37. A. H. Gardiner, 38–40; cf. 70.

38. Fr. Preisigke, *Vom göttlichen Fluidum nach ägyptischer Anschauung*, 1920 (Papyrusinstitut Heidelberg, I) continued in the same series, VI, 1922: *Die Gotteskraft der frühchristlichen Zeit.*

liquid flows out from a container. And this stream of power, which is thus properly the living ego of the sun god—that is, the spiritual sun god stuff itself—flows through his arms and hands, to stream thence into the living creatures." [39] The most familiar representation of this symbol is in the form developed during the reign of Ikhnaton, to whom the sun reaches out rays which have hands at their ends holding ankhs to the nostrils of the royal pair, fig. 160.[40] That is, the sun (which in this figure, as often, is itself shown to be the source of life by having an ankh under it) is giving its divine life to them. The symbolism of the sun's arms, Preisigke rightly points out, is much older than this.

In thus streaming out his life to creation the sun god is not himself in the least diminished. The fluid flows in a special way into each thing which is created; hence plants, animals, man, and the king, while they all get their life from the same fluid, get a different amount and so become different grades of existence.[41] Preisigke goes on to show the presence of this idea in theories of kingship, of a magical power in the fluid to drive out demons who are themselves bad fluids, in magic of name, love, and vengeance, in radiant crowns and the nimbus, in the practice of laying on of hands, and in many other interesting aspects of Egyptian and even Christian religion. That the evidence for this, and its ideology, could have been indefinitely expanded from the Light-Stream philosophy of Philo, Plotinus, and the Jewish and Christian mystics in general is obvious. Preisigke has done us a great service in assembling the material he has brought together.

Parrot, in the second of these two books, has dedicated some space to Egypt in a general study of the religious value of water drinking, which he isolates from the sun-stream.[42] To him, water is the primary source of life.[43] He tries to bring Egypt into line with his general theory that water in the ancient world was a necessity for the dead principally in order to refresh their thirst, since fear of thirst haunted desert peoples. For Egypt, Parrot seems to have assembled little material to his point. The vignettes of drinking on which he puts much stress are certainly scenes of quenching thirst; but what thirst and why? The literary evidence, so far as I can see, never becomes explicit for his point.[44]

He does make it very clear, however, that the Egyptians regarded it as of prime importance that the dead man be able to drink some sort of fluid, usually water, in the next world. The material collected by Parrot to illustrate this could be multiplied indefinitely.[45] There is every reason to suppose that the libations at the tombs were cult acts by which the dead were provided with this fluid.

39. Ibid., 3.

40. From Norman Davies, *The Rock Tombs of El Amarna*, VI, 1908, plate IV (ASE, XVIII). Many similar designs will be found throughout this and the other volumes on El Amarna. The divine hands which end in the gift of life, in the case of the kings with the gift of royal life, are probably still reflected in the ecclesiastical ordination by laying on of hands. The genealogy of the rite from Egypt into Christianity is interestingly traced by W. M. Flinders Petrie, *The Palace of Apries* (*Memphis II*), 1909, 10 (BSAE, XV).

41. Preisigke, 3.

42. Parrot, *Refrigerium*, 84–130.

43. Ibid., 97, 103, 121.

44. On the "cool water" as seminal fluid see below, p. 153.

45. See for example the stress on water drinking, which, among other things, is the body fluid of the god, in *BD*, ed. Davis, LVII, 3; LIX–LXIII; LXVIII, 4, 5, 7, 8; CVI, 1–3; CIX,* 9; CXXXVI, 14; CLXV, 15.

What Parrot seems to me to miss is that like the fluids we have studied in other cultures, this Egyptian fluid was also a stream of life, a stream of divine life, which not only quenched the thirst of the deceased, and so reduced the horror of death, but actually made him come alive. And there is every reason to suppose that the stream of light which Preisigke discussed is, for all its apparent difference, identical with the stream of water of Parrot in actual religious value, since both are the streaming life of Deity in which man may hope for power and life here and hereafter. Certainly they were combined in later Egypt,[46] and in hellenistic and later mysticism. How old the combination is I have no idea.

As a matter of fact, by the Egyptians also the fluid was represented as the spermatic flow from the divine phallus, and it is in their treatment of this aspect of religion that the meaning of the divine stream becomes most clear in all these civilizations. In the language of Egypt "life" is *ankh*, ☥, and it was of the Light-Stream as an Ankh-Stream that Preisigke was writing. It was most impressively depicted under Ikhnaton, where the stream had indicated the coming into the king of divine life, which dwelt in him in a particular way.[47] We have seen the diagrammatic presentation of this, where indeed "It is the breath of life in the nostrils to behold thy rays." [48] The king had become himself the sun for mortals as well as son of the sun.[49] But essentially Ikhnaton's solar stream of life was not a new conception. The power of the king was elaborately described years before Ikhnaton in an inscription of Amenemhet III, of the XIth Dynasty:

Adore the king, Nematre [Amenemhet III], living forever, in the midst of your bodies;
Enthrone his majesty in your hearts.
He is Esye (Sy') in the hearts;
His two eyes, they search every body.
He is the Sun, seeing with his rays;
He illuminates the Two Lands more than the sun-disk.
He makes the Two Lands green more than a great Nile;
He hath filled the Two Lands with strength.
(He is) life, cooling the nostrils;
When he begins to rage, he is satisfied to [- -].
The treasures which he gives are food for those who are in his following;
He feeds those who tread his path.
The king is food (k'),
His mouth is increase.
He is the one creating that which is;
He is the Khnum of all limbs;
The Begetter, who causes the people to be.
He is Bast protecting the Two Lands.

46. See below, p. 186.

47. See also J. H. Breasted, *The Dawn of Conscience*, 1933, 290 f.

48. Ibid.

49. Preisigke, 10–14; Erman, *Relig. Ägypt.*, 124. Breasted, *Records*, II, 423: "Thou art Re, and thy emanation is his emanation," is said to Tutunkamen; IV, 65: "Thou art Re, shining like him," to Rameses III. These were later than Ikhnaton, but the idea is very old.

He who adores him shall [escape] his arm,
He is Sekhmet toward him who transgresses his command.
is [gentle] toward him who has [- - -].[50]

Here the king is, by virtue of his relation to the sun god, himself the sun for Egypt; and the radiation of his light means that he illuminates, gives life to the nostrils (as the sun did later to Ikhnaton), and fertilizes the land more than the great Nile.[51] In all three figures alike he is the Begetter.[52] It is this basic ideology of the stream of life, that the stream is one of begetting in that it gives the divine fluid in a creative way, which Ikhnaton has presented in a newly emphasized iconographic form. Still the sun god gives out a stream of life.

That people of the day who drew the streams of ankh in the symbolic drawings of Ikhnaton understood them in this way is made likely by the representations of the impregnation of Amosis, only a few generations before Ikhnaton. Here Amosis appears in intercourse with his wife, fig. 156.[53] What passes to the queen is an ankh to the nostrils (as so commonly with Ikhnaton), as well as an ankh and symbol of power to her hand or, past her hand, to her body. With this picture are the following texts, which I give in the translation of Breasted:

The Interview. Utterance of Amon-Re, lord of Thebes, presider over Karnak. He made his form like the majesty of this husband, the King Okheperkere (Thutmose I). He found her as she slept in the beauty of her palace. She waked at the fragrance of the god, which she smelled in the presence of his majesty. He went to her immediately, coivit cum ea, he imposed his desire upon her, he caused that she should see him in his form of a god. When he came before her, she rejoiced at the sight of his beauty, his love passed into her limbs, which the fragrance of the god flooded; all his odors were from Punt.

Words of the Queen. Utterance by the king's-wife and king's-mother Ahmose, in the presence of the majesty of this august god, Amon, Lord of Thebes: "How great is thy fame! It is splendid to see thy front; thou hast united my majesty (fem.) with thy favors, thy dew is in all my limbs." After this, the majesty of this god did all that he desired with her.[54]

50. Quoted by Breasted, *Records*, I, 326 f., no. 747.

51. Tuthmosis I, two centuries before Ikhnaton, was "Beautiful in years, who makes hearts live; Bodily Son of Re, Shining-in-Beauty." "Shining like Re." Breasted, *Records*, II, 37, 40. The king is a "brilliant emanation of Amon" (ibid., 128), and the people "live by the breath which he gives" (ibid., 107); "he giveth life forever" (ibid., 195). Instances of this sort of language could be multiplied indefinitely.

52. Tuthmosis I was "Keb, the divine begetter, whose name is hidden, reproducer, Bull of the divine ennead, chosen emanation of the divine members": Breasted, ibid., 30.

53. From E. Naville, *The Temple of Deir el Bahari* [1896], II, plate XLVII. See also plate LI, where the presentation of the ankh accompanies, most conspicuously, the subsequent birth of the child conceived in plate XLVII. See also Colin Campbell, *The Miraculous Birth of King Amonhotep III*, 1912. This conception that the divine king is really the son of the God, and only the attributed son of his father, insofar as the father is human, became applied to leaders and saviors in Mystery religions, and hence to Philo's patriarchs (see above, p. 90) and to Christ.

54. *Records*, II, 80.

That is, whether presented in terms of water or of the sun (as it is here solar coming from Amon), the stream of life is the stream of fertilizing divinity which produces a new life and birth. It may, as here, mean the impregnation of the queen. But in other connections, abstracted from any story of physical birth, as with Ikhnaton, or in baptism scenes, it would be a likely presumption that the stream of ankh meant divine life and birth for the devotee, the basis for eternal life. Clearly, then, while Egypt did not contribute especially to the symbolism of wine, it did contribute greatly to the tradition of the divine fluid.

C. *FLUID IN THE LARGER EGYPTIAN DOCUMENTS*

THE MATERIALS for the study of the divine fluid in ancient Egypt are twofold, literary and pictorial, with (rarely) immediate combinations of the two.

There are a great diversity of texts from Egypt, but three extended documents stand out as the most important. The first is the Pyramid Texts, so called because they are found on the walls of five pyramids at Sakkara, where were buried kings of the Vth Dynasty. That is, they were written down, where they were discovered, in the last quarter of the third millennium, but it is generally agreed that they were composed more than a thousand years earlier. The Coffin Texts seem to be from a quarter to a half millennium later, and the Book of the Dead is some half millennium younger still. The three together give us the most important single literary record of Egyptian religion.

1. *The Pyramid Texts*

THESE TEXTS, the earliest extended literary sources of Egyptian religion, are themselves a mature combination of a great many elements, behind each of which must lie a long and elaborate development. The great number of gods, the contradiction of their functions, their presentation of various ideas of the future life, each obviously with its own complicated mythology, make together a document which is very confusing to read.[55] The last word on the various elements in the Pyramid Texts has by no means been spoken. Our present purpose is only to point out that fluid and phallic imagery appear in these texts frequently and prominently.

55. A most interesting suggestion is that of S. Schott, "Mythen in den Pyramidentexten," in Mercer, *Pyramid Texts*, IV, 106–122, that the myths were still largely unformed when the Pyramid Texts were composed for the royal burials. The basic element was the dramatic ritual of royal burial, with the implements used, such as the coffin and the sacrificial cattle. These were then identified with this or that detail of one or another of the traditional gods. Certain functions and symbols of the gods were established: "Osiris must succumb without hope. Seth must sin and be punished. Isis must weep, Nephthys forsake Seth. Horus must avenge his father" (pp. 120 f.). These details were treated in the ritual creatively and freely, with no obligation to follow accepted narratives of the gods, since these did not yet exist. Hence inconsistency is everywhere. Schott's idea is very close to my more general theory, that in the history of religion the basic entities are the symbolic form and act, and that the mythical or other explanations are secondary. R. Anthes, *JAOS*, LXXIV (1954), 35–39, rightly calls Schott's suggestion "a new foundation to our understanding of these texts."

The Pyramid Texts are those very ancient hymns, rituals, dramas, whatever their purpose eventually proves to have been, which tell of the reception of the king among the gods and his complete deification, his absorption, really, into the person of the Sun God.[56] Not popular religion, they give us our earliest form of that royal posthumous deification which later, much altered and yet much the same, was "vulgarized" for all men and became the basic motif of the hellenistic Egyptian mystery. With this material, as with the Mesopotamian and Syrian, there is always the unanswerable question of whether the conceptions were invented for the king or were a concentration and amplification for his person of indefinitely old popular fertility rites. All we can now say is that our records begin with the royal forms and then go on into popularizations.[57]

As early as these Pyramid Texts the divine fluid is presented as water and sunlight, and in both senses it is the source of life. The essential meaning of the water is stated in Utterance 685:

> To say: The waters of life which are in the sky, the waters of life which are in the earth come.
> The sky burns for thee, the earth trembles for thee, before the birth of the god.
> The two mountains divide, a god comes into being, the god had power over his body.
> The two mountains divide, N. comes into being, N. has power over his body.
> Behold N., his feet shall be kissed by the pure waters,
> which come into being through Atum, which the phallus of Shu makes, which the vulva of Tefnet brings into being.
> They have come to thee, they have brought to thee the pure waters which issue from their father;
> they purify thee, they fumigate thee, N., with incense.
> Thou liftest up the sky with thy hand; thou treadest (lit. layest) down the earth with thy foot.
> A libation is poured out at the gate of N.; the face of every god is washed.
> Thou washest thine arms, Osiris; thou washest thine arms N.
> Thy rejuvenescence is a god.[58]

Here it is clear that the water from the earth and the heavenly water are a single thing which brings the god to birth. The birth of the king, or his rebirth in immortality, is a rehearsal of the birth of the "god." Atum, the god of the western sun, that is the source of

56. Ordinarily this identification is with Ra, but it is also with many other gods, including Osiris, who seems now to be in the underworld and now almost if not quite indentical with Ra in heaven. On the relation of Osiris to Ra in the Pyramid Texts see Mercer, *Pyramid Texts*, IV, 22 f., 123–139 (the latter by H. Kees). In the following references to the Pyramid Texts the edition of Sethe, *Pyramidentexten* [1935], is used whenever possible, but it includes Secs. 134–1101d only; otherwise Louis Speleers, *Textes des Pyramides*, and Mercer, *Pyramid Texts*, are followed. Most of the English translations are taken from the latter. See also Speleers, *Comment faut-il lire les textes des pyramides égyptiennes?*, 1934.

57. On traces of the popular concomitants to royal immortality see Mercer, IV, 3, 43 f. (by R. E. Briggs).

58. Mercer, I, 303 f.

light, had created the twins Shu and Tefnet by masturbating,[59] or by spitting,[60] two mythological forms of expressing the idea of the hermaphrodism, the double sexuality, hence the suprasexuality, of the Ultimate Principle.[61] As the sky and earth burn and tremble, the birth of the god takes place through the water of Atum, which must be the light of the sun, as it is reactivated in the intercourse of Shu and Tefnet. This water is still flowing, to be used as a libation at the gate and to wash the king's feet, face, and arms. That is, it is identified with the waters used in cult practices, here specifically in funerary rites. Mercer [62] thinks the whole refers to the rejuvenation of the land by the flooding of the Nile. This is possible but by no means excludes the ritualistic implications of the passage.

The same combination of the fluid as light and water appears in repeated allusions to the "water in the eye of Horus," which the king as Osiris is urged to take to himself. The phrase is usually followed by a "lifting of the offering," which is often water [63] or wine [64] but which may be almost anything, even a club.[65] The symbolism of the eye of Horus is so bewilderingly complex [66] that any single suggestion of the meaning of the water in the eye is impossible.[67] But the eye is so often a shining thing, a brilliant thing, that its later solar implications seem present here also.

59. Lines 1248 f.: "Atum created by his masturbation in Heliopolis. He put his phallus in his fist to excite desire thereby. The twins were born, Shu and Tefnut. They put N. [the king] between them." Cf. lines 1587*b*, 1818*a*. Cf. E. A. W. Budge, *Osiris and the Egyptian Resurrection*, 1911, II, 330, at Sec. 465; Hermann Kees, *Aegypten*, 1933 (Handbuch der Altertumswissenschaft: Kulturgeschichte des alten Orients, I), 323.

60. Line 1652*c*. Only one pictorial representation of creation of these two gods by spitting is known to me, that in the tomb of Rameses II. See Champollion-le-Jeune, *Monuments de l'Egypte et de la Nubie, Notices descriptives*, 1844, I, i, 423. A pair of figures stand behind this group, but when W. Max Müller published the drawing he reproduced only one, which seems to distort the scene as a whole. Müller appears to be quite wrong in identifying the "Two Mysterious Ones" who receive the flow with the southern and northern Nile. See his *Egyptian Mythology*, 1923, 47 f. One of the two minor figures to whom flows the stream from the mouth of "Nuu, the Father of the Mysterious Gods" has a beard, the other not, so the best guess is that here Nuu is producing his children, who are in other connections called Shu and Tefnet. As to the creative power of saliva in general, John Lewis, "The Mother Worship in Egypt," *Journal of the Manchester Egyptian and Oriental Society*, XI (1924), 51 f., makes the following interesting observation: "The creative power of saliva enabled Isis to call into being from the saliva of Re a venomous snake to compel the aged deity to reveal to her his secret name. The supernatural productivity and efficacy of spittle is seen not only in the Egyptian stories of creation; it is also evidenced in the Pyramid Texts, the gospel story of the healing of the blind man, the much coveted spittle of the holy man of the east, the belief among fisherwomen of certain parts of Britain that a weakly baby should be spat upon by 'a man of God'."

61. Langdon, *Tammuz and Ishtar*, 3–5, discusses a similar phenomenon in the religions of Mesopotamia and says that the original first principle, being both male and female, is "absolutely genderless, the masculine element perhaps predominating." This seems to me just to miss, and so to miss altogether, the meaning of divine bisexuality. The two sexes in one god make him not less, but more, the primordial figure of sexual potency.

62. *Pyramid Texts*, III, 917–920.

63. Lines 72*a*, *b*.

64. Lines 92*b*, 93*a*, *b*.

65. Lines 43*a*, 47*a*, *b* (a club); 43*b* (a sword); 88*a*, *b* (two pots of liver).

66. T. G. Allen, *Horus in the Pyramid Texts*, 1915, 47–63, lists 431 various sorts of references to the eye. One can find among these almost anything one looks for. A fine example is in lines 451*a*–454*c*.

67. Mercer, II, 11, seems correct but inadequate

In any case this getting of the eye of Horus is frequently associated with the king's equipping himself with the liquid which goes forth from him [68] and which seems identical with the "liquid which went forth from Osiris." [69]

The combination of this with ritualistic water appears in Utterance 436 (lines 788*a*–789*b*):

> To make a libation. To say: Thy water belongs to thee; thine abundance belongs to thee;
> the efflux goes forth from the god, the secretion which comes out of Osiris,
> so that thy hands may be washed, so that thine ears may be open.
> This power is spiritualized by means of its soul.
> Wash thyself for thy *ka* washes itself.[70]

Here specifically the water of libation and washing is the water of Osiris restored to the king to be the water which is the distinctive principle of his life. But line 1146*a* links this to the fertility of the field again: "N. is the pouring down of rain; he came forth as the coming into being of water." It may be the "cool water" which Parrot understood as the refrigerium, the quenching of thirst, "This is thy cool water, Osiris; this is thy cool water, O N., which went forth from thy son, which went forth from Horus," [71] a statement probably accompanied by a libation. But the cool water here is shortly identified with sweat.[72] Having this fluid, the king, or Osiris, has the names "God" and "Fresh Water." [73] We are not surprised that the king could get this same fluid of life, which becomes his own fluid, also from the breasts of his mother Isis,[74] it is the same idea presented in relation to the goddess, as we have seen it actively used in Mesopotamia:

> "Mother of N.," so said I,
> "give thy breast to N., that N. may suck therewith."
> "(My) son N.," so said she, "take to thee my breast;
> that thou mayest suck it" said she,
> "that thou mayest live again," [75]
>
> They of the long hair and hanging breasts,
> who are on the hill of *šḥšḥ*.
> They draw their breasts over the mouth of N.,
> but they do not wean him for ever.[76]

The basic figure seems to me very similar to what we encountered in the flowing vase of Mesopotamia and Syria, that the fluid which goes from the god comes directly to the

when he equates the eye of Horus with the offering itself.

68. Lines 39*a-c;* 105*a*–106*b;* 117*b*, *c*.
69. Lines 90*a*–91*b;* cf. 37*a*, 64*c*.
70. Mercer, I, 149.
71. Line 22*a*.
72. Line 23*a;* cf. 24*a*, *b*.
73. Lines 25*b*, *c;* cf. 589*a*.
74. In lines 1873*a–c*, 1883*b–d* his mother Isis nurses him; in lines 623*a*, 1427*c*, *d* it is Nephthys; in line 371*c* it is both Isis and Nephthys; in lines 381*a*–382*b* the nurse is 'Ipii, which Sethe, *Pyramidentexten*, II, 111, thinks is "my mother"; Mercer, *Pyramid Texts*, II, 176, believes it to be the hippopotamus goddess. See also lines 131*d*–132*c*.
75. Lines 911*b*–912*b;* cf. 1109*b*–1111*b*.
76. Lines 1118*c*–1119*b*.

land, but in a special way to the king, who mediates it to his land and people. For the king himself this special flow was the essence of his royal prerogatives and character. He needed it again applied to him in the funerary rites to guarantee his final divinization and immortality; and, popularized, the rite of washing the corpse before burial is still a special ablution, one familiar, as we shall see, even in Jewish burial requirements today.

A mingling of the same ideas is with relative clarity presented in Utterance 317:

> To say: N. is come forth to-day at the head of the inundation of the flood.
> N. is a crocodile god, with green feather, with vigilant countenance, with forehead erect;
> effervescent, proceeding from leg and tail of the Great (One) who is in splendour.
> N. is come to his watercourses, which are in the land of the flood, in *Mḥ.t-wr.t*,
> to the places of satisfaction, with green fields, which are in the horizon,
> that N. may make green the herbs in both lands of the horizon,
> (and) that N. may bring the green to the great eye which is in the midst of the field.
> N. takes his throne which is in the horizon;
> N. appears as Sebek, son of Neit;
> N. eats with his mouth, N. urinates, N. cohabits with his phallus;
> N. is lord of semen, which women receive from their husband,
> wherever N. wishes, according to the desire of his heart.[77]

In this Utterance the king is immortalized as the source of the inundation, here the inundation of heaven, but only as a counterpart of his causing the fertilizing inundation of the Nile. He is identified with the crocodile god, Sebek, a figure from the Nile but one which was also the sun god, who here is born from the leg and tail of the Great One, the heavenly cow. He floods now the fields of heaven as he had done the fields of Egypt and makes them green, and then he is enthroned. In this great state he still eats with his mouth, urinates and cohabits with his phallus, expressions to show that he is fully alive. But he is also "lord of the semen which women receive from their husband, wherever N. wishes, according to the desire of his heart." The "wherever N. wishes" is an uncertain translation, but the general statement is clear, that all the life fluid of semen, wherever given to women, is something which comes directly from the deified king. That is, the king is here the source of all life fluid—the sun, the Nile for the fields, and semen among human beings. He is the universal source of fertility and life. It is evident that the various fluids are a single fluid in variant forms.

The parents of the king are in one passage or another given almost every name in the pantheon. As father I have noted Geb,[78] Khepri,[79] Atum,[80] Shu,[81] Ra,[82] and the Great One;[83] in one place, with Ra, he is given seven other mysteriously named fathers, prob-

77. Lines 507*a*–510*d*.

78. Geb is the most commonly named of all N.'s fathers. He was the great earth-god who was head of the gods and the Ennead. See, for example, lines 1*c*, 3*a*, 277*b*, 655*d*, 675*a*, 977*d*, 1195*b*, 1513*b*, etc.

79. Line 1210*a*. On Khepri cf. Mercer, *Pyramid Texts*, II, 95.

80. Lines 140*b*, 151*e*, 207*c*, *d*, 213*a*, *b*, 380*a*, 395*b*, 605*b*, 997*a*, 1451*a*.

81. Lines 5*d*, 294*a*–*c*, 784*a*, 2053*a*.

82. Lines 390*a*, 726*b*, 915*a*, 1479*c*, 2035*b*, 2120*a*–2121*a*.

83. Line 1702*a*.

ably all sun gods.[84] As mother the most common name is Nut, the sky goddess,[85] but Isis,[86] Tefnet,[87] the morning star,[88] the uraeus on Ra,[89] and a great variety of more obscure names also appear.[90] The king is ordinarily addressed as Osiris [91] and as such he is the father of Horus,[92] but he is also Horus his own son.[93] This takes us into one of the highly complicated ideas, the son's begetting himself on his own mother. It seems that the function of the ritual was to restore his original fluid to the point where he could be born anew,[94] but also, possessing the life fluid, so that he could thus beget himself in this new birth. Thus he would finally be able to have intercourse with Isis.

> Your sister [Isis] has come to you, rejoicing because of the love of you. Place her on your phallus, that your seed may (go forth into?) her, piercing (into?) Sothis (*śpdt*), so that Horus the piercing (*śpd*) be issued from you, being Horus who [is?] in Sothis (*śpdt*).[95]

Perhaps some meaning can be made out of the last phrase when we recall that Sothis was the dog star, the star of Isis, whose shining in the east was the herald of the rising of the Nile. Osiris, here the king as a heavenly being, at the same time seems to be the Nile, whose fertile flow was in juncture with Sothis or Isis.[96] Such confusion is typical of the Pyramid Texts. But this passage is in the Texts not as a record of the mythical birth of Horus but as an experience of the deified king, since it is specifically to the king as Osiris that the passage is addressed.

Again, after identifying the king with Horus in a triumphant entry through the gates which recalls Psalm 24, another passage [97] tells how the king becomes the husband of the body of Nut, "bearing the divine seed which is within thee. [The king] is the divine seed which is within thee, Oh Nut." [98] A most important idea here appears, one found also in another statement that the king as Ra fertilized Nut with the seed which was within *her*.[99] For here the king, who in his deification has already appeared to be the son of Nut, becomes her mate and fertilizes her, but like Ra he fertilizes her with the seed which was in her. The king, child of Nut—his being the child is emphasized by his being Horus in this

84. Lines 199*c*–201*d*.

85. For example 179*a*, 580*c*, 638*a*, 756*a*, 883*c*, 941*a*, 1030*d*, etc.

86. Lines 734*b*, 1375*a*, 1703*c*, 1883*d*.

87. Lines 779*b*, 2053*a*.

88. Lines 935*c*, 1104*b*, 1707*a*.

89. Lines 1108*c*, 2204*a*.

90. On this birth of the king from various deities see Speleers, *Comment faut-il lire les Textes des Pyramides égyptiennes?*, 114–116.

91. For example lines 582*c*, 590*a*, 648*a*, 651*a*, etc.

92. For example lines 101*e*, 176*a*, 257*a*, 589*a*, 650*b*, 767*b*, 1636*b*, 1979*b*.

93. Lines 8*i*, 316*a*, 493*a*, 1331*a*, 2022*a*. On this matter of the confused parenthood and identification of the king, see Speleers, 111–118, 169 f.

94. Lines 344*b*, 353*c*, 732*b*, 1704*d*, 1705*c*, 1706*c*.

95. Lines 632*a-d*; cf. 1635*a*–1636*b*. As translated for me by William Edgerton. Sethe's and Mercer's interpretations are slightly different but not in a way to affect our point here. That it is the king who does this impregnating is apparent from the first verse of this Utterance, line 626*a*, where Osiris is given the specific name of the king.

96. Even in Greek times Isis and Sothis were identified: Erman, *Relig. Ägypt.*, 391.

97. Lines 1408–1420.

98. Line 1416. This follows the translation of Speleers. Mercer makes no sense out of the passage, and Sethe did not get this far in his translation. It is probably the king who sleeps on his mother Nut in line 741*a*.

99. Line 990*a*.

"saying"—is the divine seed which was within Nut, and at the same time bears this seed; with it he fertilizes her, again apparently begetting himself, since he is the child of Nut, although as Horus he was also the child of Isis. He begets himself on both mothers, and this constitutes the final act of his rebirth.

The idea continued on into later formulations, in terms of which I suspect we should read these cryptic passages. For later the mystic first presents himself to the divine stream as himself a female and receives the seeds. By this process he becomes the bearer of seeds (hence male) and can return to the same divine stream—which now becomes female in its relation to him—have intercourse with it (the stream female and he male), and in this act, taking the place of the supreme source of the stream, achieve complete deification.[100] Here the religious value of the hermaphroditic conception appears. The stream has itself both masculine and feminine potencies and can work upon any mystic according to his needs. As Philo indicates, ascent to deification implies both male and female attitudes in the mystic, and both needs must be met by the symbolism. Hence the stream is semen from the male or milk from the female quite interchangeably.

It is hard for me to believe that the intelligent priests who expressed themselves in the welter of mythological symbolism of the Pyramid Texts used the myths in their seriatim contradictions without some such harmonizing idea in their minds: the idea that the fluid of life can be expressed in sexual symbols but in being both male and female is essentially above either sex.

While phallicism with its attendant symbols is by no means the only figure for the king's deification, it is apparent that from very early times such symbolism was important and frequent. The stream of life-giving seed was the stream of life itself. But the use of this conception, to our literal minds, has appeared to be varied to the point of complete confusion, since nothing can be more alien to our thinking than the idea of a male who receives seed from a female, herself at this stage becoming temporarily male, in order with those seeds to be able to beget himself, a new creature, on his own mother, who first gave him the seeds.

When the complications that arise from associating self-begetting with a variety of gods and goddesses have been simplified into this general conception, the question still presses: Whence could such a conception have come, what did it mean to its devotees, and what prompted such a formulation? One cannot help being reminded of the Freudian Oedipus complex, since the son has completely taken the place of the father, and yet the value of filial relationship with both father and mother is retained. Here also is the desire for full potency satisfied, for in the experience the mystic is given the seeds of the gods, and, equipped with their potency, he is desired by the very goddesses. That is, here is proclaimed (at this stage of course only for the king) the complete resolution of those tensions which in Freudian terms are the source of most of our inner unrest because we harass ourselves with desires to take the place of the father and at the same time retain the advantages of sonship. But whether the Freudian conception is relevant here or not, the contradictions of the Egyptian myths are no more baffling and illogical than the contradictions

100. See my *By Light, Light*, pp. 18 f. For the idea in Philo see ibid., 139 f.

of our own inner warfare. In heaven the king was to be all things simultaneously, as the gods themselves are, and this achievement, symbolized in his becoming his own father by his own mother, meant the essence of divinity for him as for them. It was the achievement of the new birth, the true life; it was the consummation of life without death or defeat; and in it hope of future life gained basic power and conviction. Such symbolism seems so completely foreign to our religious formulations that its power can be appreciated only on reflection. But the power is there.

In the earliest texts we have from Egypt, then, a stream of fluid is presented which is at once solar and phallic, and in both is the source of life, agricultural, royal, and eternal. It would be fascinating to trace this conception through Egyptian remains, pictorial and literary, but the task is beyond my competence and would be too large to include here. It will be of value, however, to indicate a few of the high points of the tradition through the ages in Egypt, since without some grasp of that tradition the eagerness with which Osiris was later conflated with Dionysus must be quite unintelligible.

2. *The Coffin Texts*

THE NEXT great step in the development of the religion of Egypt after the Pyramid Texts is represented by the Coffin Texts, traditionally dated from the Middle Kingdom, 2000–1600 B.C. approximately. Here the first great step is taken in the popularization of the ideas we have been considering, for the subject of these texts is the future life of the great nobles, and it is described with almost exactly the same figures as those which were used for the king.

> I am the *ba* of Shu who is upon the Flame which Atum-Ra kindled with his hand when he masturbated; when the enemy was cut to pieces by his mouth; when he spit me, as Shu, with Tefnet my sister . . . I am the ba of Shu to whom Nut was given, she who is above Geb, who [in turn] is under her feet. I am between the two.[101]

In this procession there is the same confusion as in the Pyramid Texts. The deceased is Shu who is the self-begotten (Atum).[102] He is "the seminal fluid of Atum; Atum has made me with the fluid of his flesh." [103] This last expression is used very often, along with creation or the rebirth of the dead from the god's nostrils or the mouth (by breathing, spitting, or naming the names of what is created), and in the god's heart.[104] But in general the immortality sought is that of being born as the son of one of the gods or goddesses. As in the

101. My translation of part of Discourse 77 and the beginning of 78, from the French translation of Louis Speleers, *Textes des cercueils du moyen empire égyptien* [1946], 50. For this publication Speleers had only the first two volumes of A. de Buck, *The Egyptian Coffin Texts*, 1935, 1938 (The University of Chicago Oriental Publications, XXXIV). Two additional volumes have since been published. But de Buck gives only a critical edition of the Texts in Egyptian, so that I know only the part translated by Speleers. De Buck's volume of translations (promised in his Vol. I, p. xv) has not yet been published.

102. Speleers, *Textes*, 42 f.

103. Ibid., 48 (de Buck, II, 6, for Discourse 76).

104. In pp. xxxvii–xliii of *Textes*, Speleers has collected the relevant passages.

Pyramid Texts this birth is made to come from almost any divine being.[105] The most extended passage on the birth yet translated from the Coffin Texts is that which represents the deceased as born of the seminal fluid of Osiris. As Isis carries him in her womb she makes elaborate supplication that he be protected from the evil Seth, and when he is born he declares himself the enemy of Seth.[106] Indeed, the deceased is the *ba* (the shadow or soul) of Osiris, and with it Osiris fornicates, so that "Thy seed mounts for thee in thy living *ba*." [107] But immediately Osiris is said to have given the deceased "milk from the red cow, gone up from the horizon which gives daily birth to Ra, as it gives daily birth to me." [108] Ra seems identical here with the red cow giving milk to the deceased, while the deceased has identified himself simultaneously with Osiris and Ra, as in the Pyramid Texts. But as Osiris has intercourse with his own *ba* to give new birth to the deceased, we have the same idea that is basic to Philo: while the divine birth is our hope, it is reproduced in a mystical experience in which sexes and personalities are so blended that the human being is identified with the One. This is done primarily through the action of the divine fluid.

3. *The Book of the Dead*

THE BOOK of the Dead has material which dates its origin some half a millennium later than the Coffin Texts, but it was copied and used for many centuries thereafter.[109] It presents less of a definite mythology or consistent eschatology for the soul than do even the Pyramid Texts. The dead person could now come from any social rank if he could afford elaborate burial, and the texts are chiefly charms to keep away various bad spirits or to protect and give life to the deceased. Not that the old confusion of identifications of the deceased with gods or goddesses is clarified. But one feels that the tone is lowered to the more magical level, if I may still use the term, where the deceased is so concerned with his own security and continuity that his new divine environment only slightly arouses his curiosity. It is a contrast quite reminiscent of that felt by one brought up in the dignity and rational consistency of formal Christian worship when he is confronted with the egocentricity and loose thinking of extreme evangelicals. Both, it is true, want personal salvation, as do the deceased in the Book of the Dead and in the Pyramid Texts. But the second type wants it for his own security, while the first type wants the same security, to be sure, but wants it in a rational context.

But just as among the evangelicals a large part of the older theology is implied by

105. The passages are again collected by Speleers, *Textes*, pp. xx f.

106. Ibid., 80–82 (Discourse 148).

107. Ibid., 59 (Spell 96).

108. Ibid.

109. As an amateur I have found working with the Book of the Dead the most uncertain major task in the field. The text varies enormously with different manuscripts, and the latest translation is that of Budge in 1909 (the second edition of 1923 was virtually a reprint). The older editions and translations were made from other manuscripts and often differ radically in content from the text used by Budge. The improved mastery of the language during the past nearly fifty years has never been applied systematically to this text. Accordingly, while the general statements I make are probably correct, it is quite likely that some of my conclusions from specific passages are not justified. In spite of this situation, the Book can hardly be ignored.

allusion, so a great deal of what we have been discussing in the older literature can still be found in the Book of the Dead. It is clear that the immortality of the deceased is not merely a matter of his going to join the gods as one of them; [110] he is deified through rebirth, a rebirth which is an identification with the birth of one or other of the gods. His birth may indeed be identified with the primal birth associated with Khepera, the beetle who came into existence from unformed matter.[111] He is also Atem or Atum (spelled *tem* in Budge's translation, *tum* in Davis), and as such he not only is the setting sun but is associated with—is "the only one in"—primordial water.[112] So he was born of Atum and was, like Atum, "born of the goddess who is in the middle of the water," presumably this same water.[113] He is also very commonly Ra, and everywhere Osiris, or Horus son of Osiris.[114] The old confusion of maternity likewise persists. He is Isis, but he was conceived in Isis and begotten in Nephthys, and then two sisters are given him "for his delight." [115] He is hailed as the phallus of Ra; [116] indeed, one passage greets him: "Who then is this? It is Osiris; or (as others say), Ra is his name, or it is the phallus of Ra wherewith he was united with himself." [117] In the same chapter this is expanded so that the deceased is the divine soul which dwells in the divine Twin Gods; but then this is explained as something still deeper when it is said that the soul of Osiris and the soul of Ra embraced each other and the Twin Gods sprang from the union.[118] Two gods, Hu and Sa, obviously the same Twin Gods, sprang into being from "the drops of blood which came forth from the phallus of Ra when he went forth to perform mutilation upon himself." [119] This is a variant of the old procreation of the twins Shu and Tefnet, from masturbation. It is clear that Ra's having intercourse with himself or with Osiris are but alternate forms of expressing the ultimate union of divine principles, from which, or in which, the deceased has now his existence. Only in this union is divinity complete, and complete divinity implies, requires, creativity. It seems to be this same phallus which is the symbol of almost pantheistic creativity: "I am Osiris, the lord of the heads that live, mighty of breast and powerful of back, with a phallus which goeth to the remotest limits [where] men and women [live]." [120] From this we are quite prepared to find that the Nile is the phallus of Osiris, as we shall meet it below.[121] It is perhaps basically the same idea also when the deceased is able to announce that he is "the mighty one who created his own light," [122] for the giving of light, like the creating of life, is essentially a divine prerogative. To the mystics of the hellenistic period the coming into Light was the coming into divine Life, and the welter of figures of

110. *BD*, 412 f. (chap. CXXXVIB, 2–18, esp. 12).

111. *BD*, 134, 268, 273 (chaps. XXIV, 1; LXXXIII, 3; LXXXV, 4). In the first of these references the unformed matter is called the "thigh of his mother," but Khepera brings himself into existence then. On Khepera see below, pp. 172 f.

112. *BD*, chap. VII, 4 (ed. Davis, 72).

113. Ibid., chap. III, 1 (ed. Davis, 71).

114. For example *BD*, 56 f. (chaps. VIII, 3; IX, 3).

115. *BD*, 110 (chap. XVII, 134–138). He was conceived by the goddess Sekhet, but it was the goddess Neith who gave him birth: *BD*, 228 (chap. LXVI, 2).

116. *BD*, 288 (chap. XCIII, 2).

117. *BD*, 95 (chap. XVII, 24 f.).

118. *BD*, 102 (chap. XVII, 109–112).

119. In *BD*, 98 (chap. XVII, 60–63). Cf. E. A. W. Budge, *The Gods of the Egyptians*, 1904, II, 89.

120. *BD*, 234 (chap. LXIX, 4 f.).

121. See below, pp. 193 f.

122. *BD*, 473 (chap. CXLVII, 3). He gives birth to himself like Khepera, and as such is the lord of light in *BD*, 273 (chap. LXXXV, 4 f.).

divine birth which we are encountering, all in terms of a solar religion—that is, of a religion centered in the great contrast of light and darkness, life and death—seem to me to be certainly the origin of the mystic language which we shall see in later writers. I need only remind my readers of how common the notion is in Philo—making appropriate the name of my *By Light, Light*.[123] For just as to be light is to give light, so to live is to germinate. It is the same idea, then, when the deceased cries,

> I am the god Khepera, and my members shall have an everlasting existence. I shall not decay, I shall not rot, I shall not putrefy. I shall not turn into worms, and I shall not see corruption before the eye of the god Shu. I shall have my being; I shall have my being; I shall live, I shall live; I shall germinate, I shall germinate, shall germinate.[124]

It is only in another figure of speech that the dead man claims his full divinity in terms of light:

> I am Ḥem-Nu(?) who sheddeth light in the darkness. I have come to give light in the darkness, which is made light and bright [by me]. I have given light in the darkness, and I have overthrown the destroying crocodiles. I have sung praises unto those who dwell in the darkness, I have raised up those who wept, and who had hidden their faces and had sunk down in wretchedness; and they did look then upon me. [Hail, then,] ye beings, I am Ḥem-Nu(?), and I will not let you hear concerning the matter. [I] have opened [the way], I am Ḥem-Nu(?), I have made light the darkness, I have come, having made an end of the darkness, which hath become light indeed.[125]

The life-light which one receives to the point where one can give out life-light is often symbolized in the Book of the Dead by the other fluids. Much is made of the giving of life to the deceased in the form of air for his nostrils, but the chapters in which this is especially discussed [126] soon are combined with the motifs of "snuffing the air among the waters of the underworld" [127] or of "snuffing the air and of having the mastery over the water in the underworld." [128] In these chapters the vignettes show three of the chief ways in which the deceased, while he holds a sail—symbol of the air he is getting—also gets this water: he is inundated with it, fig. 158,[129] in what we shall see is the regular convention of baptism; he and his wife drink from the pool of the water of the underworld, while three palm trees, conspicuously with the pair of date clusters on the taller central one, stand beside the pool, fig. 159; [130] or he is with a bowl beside the sacred sycamore tree from which Nut or Hathor pours for him the divine fluid, fig. 162.[131] In a chapter which follows, he drinks from a spring of water and as a result inherits "indefinite time" or "eternity." [132] The water, it is

123. A summary of much I have been saying is to be found in *BD*, 516 f. (chap. CLIII, 13–19).

124. *BD*, 520 (chap. CLIV, 16–18).

125. *BD*, 262 (chap. LXXX, 9–11).

126. *BD*, 197–199 (chaps. LIV f.).

127. *BD*, 199 (chap. LVI).

128. *BD*, 200–205 (chaps. LVII–LX).

129. *BD*, 200.

130. From *The Book of the Dead: Facsimile of the Papyrus of Ani*, British Museum, 1894, plate 16, no. 2.

131. From ibid., plate 16, no. 3. Cf. *BD*, ed. Renouf and Naville, plate XVIII for a number of similar vignettes; and see below, p. 187.

132. *BD*, 207 (chap. LXII).

explained,[133] keeps him from being burnt by fire, but this, important as it is, seems essentially incidental in comparison with the positive divine prerogatives which the water brings.

In one of the most important chapters of the Book [134] the soul goes through fourteen domains in the lower world. In the thirteenth he finds a domain of water, but the water is of fire, so that not even the gods (surely not the great gods) can drink it to quench their thirst. A single god is in this domain, apparently himself the source of the fiery water, who keeps the other gods away from it. But the deceased can come and drink even this water. The section ends with a reference to the fertilizing power of the actual Nile, one of the numerous indications that the deification of the deceased is of importance for those on earth. In any case, drinking from this fiery stream is far from the cooling experience of a refrigerium.

The deceased not only drinks the water; he is washed in it. This has appeared in the baptismal representation. It appears in texts very clearly where the deceased declares that he has washed himself with the water used by eleven of the great gods in preparation for their greatest exploits, as, in one of the instances: "I have washed myself in the water wherein the god Ra washeth himself when he leaveth the eastern part of the sky." [135] This washing of the deceased is a ceremony of purification but clearly is also one of identification, as, incidentally, is the baptism of Paul [136] and subsequent Christianity in contrast to that of Judaism. In pagan religions we may be allowed to say that such identification is deification. The washing of the corpse, however, not only was an important ritual for the ancient Egyptians but is still important, we shall see, for the modern Jew.[137]

To the drinking as well as to the much less commonly stressed washing, there must have been a ritualistic counterpart, performed for the deceased. This we find clearly attested in the omnipresent references to libations and offerings of food and drink to the dead. If the deceased does not have these offerings, he will have to eat the filth of the lower world, one of the worst things that could happen. In one passage the deceased eats and drinks these offerings "under the sycamore tree of my lady, the goddess Hathor," [138] which seems to connect the value of the tree, from which he gets the divine fluid, with the funerary offerings. Such reference to the funerary offerings, sometimes very elaborate, could suggest that the family of the dead man did indeed provide him with every sort of wine and drink,[139] or, in the way familiar in ritual everywhere, the more elaborate could be represented by a single token, especially by the pouring of a libation.[140] The most important chapter on the libations gives sixty-two interpretations, mostly literary variants on giving

133. *BD*, 208 f. (chap. LXIIIA).

134. *BD*, 496 f. (chap. CXLIX, Sec. 13). The meaning is more clearly brought out by Renouf and Naville, 306.

135. These declarations are scattered through the text, *BD*, 448–455 (chap. CXLV, 3–39).

136. Rom. VI, 3 f.

137. See below, VI, 164.

138. *BD*, 194 (chap. LII, 4 f.). In *BD*, 266 (chap. LXXXII, 6) the tree of Hathor is a palm tree but serves the same function as the place where the deceased consumes the offerings.

139. As in *BD*, 639–643 (chap. CLXXXIX).

140. *BD*, 321, where is given an extended list of offerings to go with simple libation pouring. Apparently, all are represented in the libation.

the deceased power.[141] But one passage indicates that as a result of the libation the deceased will become "lord of the phallus and ravisher of women for ever," [142] while another indicates that he will "be endowed abundantly with *tchefau* food in the underworld." [143] These libations seem to have been primarily of "cool water," [144] and certainly one function of the cool water was "to do away with the thirst of him that keepeth ward over the Lakes," [145] and it was apparently with the same idea that the deceased prayed for "offerings of coolness." [146] But if the note of refrigerium is occasionally sounded, the prayer "let him not thirst" quickly becomes:

> Let him suffer neither hunger nor thirst . . . do away with his hunger, O thou that fillest hearts. O chiefs who dispense cakes [and ale], O ye who have charge of the water flood, command ye that cakes and ale be given unto Osiris Nebseni.[147]

Indeed, "the water of the scribe Nebseni is the wine of Ra." [148] For his comfort, that he may not be hungry or thirsty, he has been given sepulchral meals by the lord of eternity,[149] a sepulchral meal which is so commonly cakes and ale that I suspect another definite ritualistic concomitant.[150] The cakes and ale are getting close to the bread and wine in which all spiritual nourishment has been concentrated for so many centuries, especially since the Egyptian "cakes" seem to be "bread made of the finest grain." [151] The conception is carried on into a version of the Book of the Dead of about 1000 B.C.,[152] and in a version of the Greco-Roman period, where it is said "The water flood of the Prince cometh unto thee from Abu (Elephantine), and it filleth thy table with offerings of *tchefau* food." [153]

Water, or fluid, is thus the prime source of life, whether in terms of sex, air, or food. It seems quite likely that these were all united into the ritualistic food of immortality, which could supremely be represented by cakes and ale, or by the simple libation of water. In his version of the Book of the Dead the scribe Ani describes the next world, with its awful darkness, its lack of water and air, the impossibility of satisfying one's love urges in it, or of living in quietness of heart. But Ani goes on to pray:

> Let the state of the shining ones be given me instead of water and air and the satisfying of the longings of love, and let quietness of heart be given me instead of cakes and ale.[154]

Here we are back in our circle to the place where light has become the saving fluid, so that if Ani can come into the state of the "shining ones" all the rest is transcended. But it is

141. *BD*, 548–572 (chap. CLXVIII).

142. *BD*, 557, Sec. 15.

143. Ibid., Sec. 17. It is frequently suggested that the deceased will enjoy the pleasures of love in the next world: for example *BD*, 267, 324, 327, 331, 334.

144. *BD*, 291 (chap. XCV, 2).

145. *BD*, 293 (chap. XCVII, 4).

146. *BD*, 296 (chap. XCVIII, 8).

147. *BD*, 603 f. (chap. CLXXVIII, 4–6; cf. 11 f., 17).

148. *BD*, 605 (chap. CLXXVIII, 19–21).

149. Ibid.; cf. p. 606.

150. For example, *BD*, 481–483 (chap. CXLVIII, 3, 8, 10); 485 (chap. CXLIX, 2).

151. *BD*, 485, n.

152. The Papyrus of Nesi-Khonsu, published by Budge in *BD*, 655, 660.

153. The Book of Breathings, published by Budge in *BD*, 664.

154. *BD*, 597 (chap. CLXXV, 12 f.).

dubious that many Egyptians even momentarily transcended a ritualistic approach. For them in general the aspiration was to achieve what was said in the formula:

> Life is with thee, and offerings of meat and drink follow thee, and that which is thy due is offered up before thy face.[155]

D. *PHALLICISM IN LATER EGYPT*

TO TRACE these ideas of the divine fluid (and food) through the ages of Egyptian history would be a major task for a specialist. But it is interesting to note the recurrence of the older phrases enough to acquire a sense of the sort of thing which went into the hellenistic mixing bowl from Egypt. After the abolishing of Ikhnaton's reforms, in which figures of light and the sun were supposedly to cover everything, there was a fresh revival of the old phallic tropes. We return to material in which the king is central. "There is life in seeing thee" is said to Seti I.[156] Rameses II is "the water of a god [which came forth] from him; what thou begettest is that which Ra himself has made"; [157] and so he is the "husband of Egypt." [158] Rameses III is "divine water of Ra, which came forth from his limbs." [159] It seems to me not a matter of chance that in the reaction after Ikhnaton the old phallic god Min received an amazing new prominence. Min,[160] presenting his erect phallus, himself crowned with feathers, holding aloft a whip with three lashes,[161] was one of the oldest deities of Egypt, to whom a great festival and a procession were dedicated at harvest time.[162] He was the begetting god, and at the same time the self-begotten, since he was

155. *BD*, 628 (chap. CLXXXIII, 33 f.).

156. Breasted, *Records*, III, 49; cf. 108, Sec. 265.

157. Ibid., 116.

158. Ibid., 210.

159. Ibid., IV, 26.

160. The most recent study of Min is Henri Gauthier, *Les Fêtes du dieu Min*, Cairo, 1931; with a supplementary volume, *Le Personnel du dieu Min*, Cairo, 1931. This study is useful in many details for our purpose but is concerned primarily with discussing the texts, with reconstructing the actual festival of taking the god out of his temple in processions, and with the personnel of the servitors of the god. The more general significance of Min is considered only incidentally. The festival was, he concludes (pp. 289 f.), one so archaic in form that its ritual was in places unintelligible to the performers.

161. The whip has been shown to be itself a fertility symbol. See A. C. Mace and H. E. Winlock, *The Tomb of Senebtisi at Lisht*, 1916, 94–102 (PME, I). It is very close to the fertility symbol of flagellation at the Lupercalia. On the whip as a thunderbolt see the following note. The child born from the lotus frequently bears a whip, which would seem to mark it as a fertilizing gift of life. See the following note. On the whip considered as a symbol of birth see further B. Bruyère, *Mert Seger à Deir el Médineh*, 1930 (*Mém.* Inst., LVIII), 160; and G. Jéquier, *Les Frises d'objets des sarcophages du Moyen Empire*, 1921 (*Mém.* Inst., XLVII), 189. The persistent association of flogging with sexual stimulation is well set forth in the learned work of the seventeenth-century physician, J. H. Meibomius: *Tractatus de usu flagrorum in re medica et venerea*, published in English transl.: *A Treatise on the Use of Flogging in Medicine and Venery*, Paris, 1898. It was shown to me by Dr. Clements Fry of Yale.

162. See below, p. 166. G. A. Wainwright has interesting material to connect Min and his whip with the thunderbolt. This motif may well have been in the symbolism of Min originally, but clearly Min was much more important as the fertility god. See Wainwright's "Some Aspects of Amūn," *JEA*, XX (1934), 139–153. On p. 139, n. 1, he lists his earlier contributions to the subject. In "Some Celestial Associations of Min," *JEA*, XXI (1935), 152–170, he adds to this and connects the sky and

"the bull of his mother Kamephis." [163] After the fall of Ikhnaton's monotheism, when Amon-Ra resumed the position from which Aton had driven him, Amon-Ra is presented with the characteristics of Min, as indeed he had been since the XIIth Dynasty.[164] He frequently appears in this form on later monuments with the king,[165] apparently to carry on the conception of Ikhnaton and his predecessors that the king draws his life from a stream o divine life. In Ptolemaic times Min-Ra is the self-begotten of earlier tradition, the one who gives seeds to all the other gods and goddesses—that is, he is the ultimate source of divine life.[166] It is apparent that whether streams are of rays or of liquid the point is that the stream is an overflowing of divine life almost exactly as Preisigke has described the stream for Ikhnaton.

Over and again in the middle and later periods Min-Ra, or Ra presented in the traditional form of Min, appears with the king before him.[167] In early times Min is shown with "officials," [168] but in later times he, or Amon-Ra in his form, is more usually associated with the king. That this figure with its phallus is not without meaning, and that the god is actually to be taken as giving out the seminal life stream to those before him, is clearly witnessed by several scenes. In one his phallus is over a field which Tuthmosis III cultivates with a plough, where the god can be conceived only as fertilizing the field.[169] Or the king, as in fig. 161,[170] may be in the act of embracing the god.[171]

---

fertility aspects. P. E. Newberry, "The Shepherd's Crook and the So-called 'Flail' or 'Scourge' of Osiris," *JEA*, XV (1929), 84–94, attempts to make the whip into an instrument for gathering laudanum gum; he should, it seems, have taken older accounts into reckoning. Min was associated in figure and processions with lettuce as a fertility symbol: L. Keimer, "Die Pflanze des Gottes Min," *ZaeS*, LIX (1924), 140–143. This was overlooked by S. Schott in his remark about the lettuce of Min: "Das Löschen von Fackeln in Milch," *ZaeS*, LXXIII (1937), 15 f. Gauthier, *Fêtes*, 85, rejects Newberry's thesis but has little himself to say of the whip, except to explain it, with no reference to this literature, as a weapon for castigation of enemies (p. 130). Perhaps Gauthier was thinking of the passage in the ritual of the Opening of the Mouth where the whip is so described: E. A. W. Budge, *The Book of Opening the Mouth*, 1909, I, 108 f. On pp. 162–172, 288, Gauthier discusses the lettuce most interestingly.

163. Erman, *Relig. Ägypt.*, 35 f.

164. Kurt Sethe, *Amun und die acht Urgötter vom Hermopolis*, 1929, 19–22 (Abhandlungen der Preussischen Akademie der Wissenschaften, Phil. Hist. Klasse, 1929, Pt. iv).

165. The connection of Amon-Ra with Min is mentioned by Erman, *Relig. Ägypt.*, 36, 105, 132. But at the last passage he says that Amon-Ra lost all characteristics of Min after his restoration following the Ikhnaton heresy. This seems obviously to ignore the representations to which I am referring. See also G. A. Wainwright, "The Aniconic Form of Amon in the New Kingdom," *ASAE*, XXVIII (1928), 175 ff.

166. A. Scharff, "Ein Denkstein der römischen Kaiserzeit aus Achmim," *ZaeS*, LXII (1926), 88, 94.

167. For example Lepsius, *Denkmäler*, Abt. III, plates 7*e*, 212, 219*b*, 220*b*; in 221*f* the king embraces the god. The figure will frequently be found in almost every volume of the TTS. See also E. Naville, *The Temple of Deir el Bahari*, 1895, I, plates XX, XXIII; II, plate XXVIII. The Epigraphic Survey, H. H. Nelson, et al., *Reliefs and Inscriptions at Karnak*, I, 1936, plates 8, A, D, F, I; 17, 19, 44 (University of Chicago Oriental Institute, XXV). Erman, *Relig. Ägypt.*, 94, explains the figure I have been calling Min-Ra as a popular identification of Amon-Ra with an older and very mysterious phallic deity, Kem-atef, who was the remote creator of the world, a principle popularly thought to be more ultimate than Amon-Ra.

168. P. A. A. Boeser, *Beschreibung der ägyptischen Sammlung des niederländischen Reichsmuseums der Altertümer in Leiden: Die Denkmäler der Zeit zwischen dem alten und mittleren Reich und des mittleren Reiches*, I, 1909, plates XVIII, 27, and XXXII, 42.

[169–171. Following page.]

At Thebes in the later period this ithyphallic figure is most prominent. Anyone who has visited the temple of Karnak will recall how almost omnipresent the figure is. The same is true of the temple of Luxor, from which Gayet has published a large number of the scenes with translations of the inscriptions.[172] In this publication, whose material belongs to the XVIIIth Dynasty, the meaning of the figure becomes quite clear. For example, Gayet shows a scene where the king embraces the ithyphallic Amon-Ra, the same type of scene as in fig. 159. Here one inscription tells that what is represented is "the stable one who makes existence . . . he gives life like the sun eternally." [173] In a similar scene Amon-Ra says to the king who stands before him: "You renew the multitude by making festivals. I grant you permanent renewals by making you alive . . . I give you force and vigor near me." Before the king is the legend: "The Horus-Ra, the powerful bull who erects himself as the giver of life . . . born from his side and lover of himself." [174]

This "Horus-Ra" seems to be the phallus itself, for in another scene of the king with the same deity there are nine invocations of the king to the god, or rather, says Gayet, to the god's phallus:

1. O that which . . . doubly!
2. O that which . . . doubly!
3. O that which erects itself doubly!
4. O that which is doubly great!
5. O that which is doubly powerful!
6. O that which is doubly possessor!
7. O that which is doubly expert!
8. O that which is doubly vigorous!
9. O that which . . . doubly!

Below this register, continues Gayet, are nine vertical lines "repeating nine times that the act which induces the erection of the god is 'performed by the king,' " apparently in the ritual represented.[175]

In still another similar scene the king is performing a ritual in which he gives life to

---

169. Champollion-le-Jeune, II, plate cxcv. Cf. "Er wirkt mit seinem Phallos, um die beiden Länder mit Speisen zu überfluten, die er schafft": H. Junker, "Ein Doppelhymnus aus Kom Ombo," *ZaeS*, LXVII (1931), 55. A very interesting discussion of Min as the fertilizer of the soil is in Gauthier, *Fêtes*, 225, 231–238.

170. From A. Gayet, *Le Temple de Louxor*, I, 1894, plate viii, 46, and p. 43; plate liii, 102, and p. 85 (*Mém.* Miss., XV). See also E. Naville, *The Temple of Deir el Bahari*, I, plate xviii.

171. See also *Rameses III's Temple* [1936], plate 63 (University of Chicago Oriental Institute, XXV).

172. Gayet, loc. cit.

173. Ibid., 43.

174. Ibid., plate x, 59; cf. p. 45. See also plate liii, 100; cf. p. 86.

175. Ibid., plate xiii; cf. p. 48. The ithyphallic Amon-Ra also appears frequently in the Temple at Edfou: Le Marquis de Rochemonteix, *Le Temple d'Edfou*, I, 1897 (*Mém.* Miss., X), plates xxxi*b*, xxxii*a*, xl*b*, xliii*a*. Also at Wadi Hammamat: J. Couyat and P. Montet, *Les Inscriptions hiéroglyphiques et hiératiques de Ouâdi Hammâmât*, 1912 (*Mém.* Inst., XXXIV), plates vii*b*, viii, x, xii, xv, xvi, xviii, xxi, xxxiv.

the four points of the compass as four bulls, while Amon-Ra assures the king, "I have given you countless years of life each day, like Ra." [176]

In a different presentation of the same conception Amon-Khem appears as an ithyphallic image borne by slaves on a platform. Before him the king holds the censer, "the means of the divine renewing which precedes a rebirth," as Gayet explains. "The phallic erection of the god is produced at the same time when the flame rises from the censer." In return Amon-Khem gives the king life.[177] The phallic nature of the sun-stream in the sense of a stream of fire is here reproduced in the notion of the seminal power of fire. So important was this conception that it was even perpetuated for the Roman emperors.[178]

The phallic image or deity, then, is quite explicitly the representation of the divine source of life.[179] Of course this is not "life" merely in the ordinary sense. The ankh symbol which the solar disk gives the king is provided not just to keep him from dying but to give him life in a higher and more mystical sense, both here and hereafter, than is available to other men. The king, whether by the ankh symbol or by the phallus, is given divine or true life, and his royal gift to his subjects is to pass on that life to them.[180] This representation of the king continued down into Ptolemaic times,[181] and, as we shall see,[182] the same image of the god, one in which an erection could be induced by pulling a string, was borne in popular processions. The meaning of this rite would naturally be that the people are now also looking for divine life, along the familiar lines by which royal prerogatives were popularized in later Egypt.

E. PHALLIC GODS OF THE THEBAN TOMBS

SUCH AN IDEA of the cosmic source of life, a conception which has appeared already in the ancient Pyramid Texts, seems to me vividly represented in several types of scenes.

176. Gayet, plate XXXVI; cf. p. 73. See a similar scene from Elephantine: C. Lenormant, *Musée des antiquités égyptiennes*, 1841, plate III, 4: identical with *DE, Antiquités;* Planches, I, plate 37.

177. Gayet, plate XLIX; cf. p. 80. A similar procession is shown in Champollion, *Monuments de l'Egypte et de la Nubie*, III, plate CCXI.

178. See below, VI, 83 f.

179. On Min the giver of life see the inscriptions quoted by Gauthier, pp. 129, 132, 206, 262, 276. In some of these he also gives force and victory: see also pp. 175, 252. Edgerton wrote to me: "In general I have the impression that *all* gods and goddesses pictured and labeled on Pharonic monuments are *commonly* said to give life, as well as force, victory, and all other good and perfect gifts. I fear the singling out of particular deities, such as Min, in this connection, may prove misleading." Edgerton is certainly correct that what I am writing here is misleading if one takes it as a description of Egyptian religion in general. Let me remind the reader again that I am tracing out only those concepts of Egyptian religion which the Greeks later syncretized with Dionysus, especially the idea of divine fluid.

180. For example in the Tell el-Amarna tablets (S. A. B. Mercer, *The Tell el-Amarna Tablets*, 1939) the king is called the "breath of my life" by his subjects, Tablets 141, 143, 144, 297; the king's breath is said to give eternal life, Tablet 149; he is besought to give life, Tablets 74, 198; and he sends life to one of his subjects, "To thee one sends life," Tablet 31*a*. Ernst Percy, *Untersuchungen über den Ursprung der johanneischen Theologie*, 1939, 313, asserts that the ankh is only earthly life in Egyptian ideology. The material here discussed seems to show that he is wrong.

[181–182. Following page.]

First is a most important type found four times in the Theban tombs. Because its first appearance chronologically is most poorly reported to us, I shall consider two of the others before it. One example appeared in the tombs of Rameses VI and is thus to be dated in the middle of the twelfth century.[183] Figure 163 [184] shows the design as photographed for Piankoff. The setting of the scene on the wall as a whole can be seen in fig. 164.[185] A large central figure stands with his body and head in the heavens represented by the sun (depicted twice according to Egyptian convention) [186] and the stars, three on one side, six on the other. The figure has long feminine hair, but a heavy beard as well as an erect phallus. From its body run a series of dotted lines to the heavenly bodies and to a series of little figures, six on a side ranged up a peculiar V-shaped ramp. They hold out their hands to receive little red balls which are apparently what come to them from the central figure along the dotted lines. The three upper figures at the left have their lines connected at right angles with a line which goes up not from the central figure but from the sun behind him. The idea seems a dissemination of light-life which could come from the central figure or from the sun which was his visible appearance. One of the dotted lines, however, leads from the end of the phallus to touch a figure standing at the bottom of the right tier of little figures. This person I shall call the "aspirant." He raises his hands eagerly as though to ascend the tier like a ladder, and himself catches a red ball of light. Beside the line to this figure, likewise connected by a line with the phallus, is the traditional seated figure of the divine child with its finger to its mouth,[187] along with the hieroglyph for fire. The design seems to tell us that the stream is one of fire and of life in the sense of birth at the same time, and that it is this which goes not only to the universe but in a special way to the "aspirant."

At either side of this central group extends the long body of a snake which in another of the instances joins under the feet of the standing figure and clearly is understood to do so here, since the snake's head is on the left end and the tail on the right. Beneath the snake, on either side, a small black figure kneels, or rises from the earth, in adoration, and behind her stand three bearded mummies. To the inscriptions we shall return.

The same design is found also in the tomb of Rameses IX, a few years later.[188] Here our information about the design is much less adequate. Two scholars made sketches of

---

181. W. M. Flinders Petrie, *Tanis*, I, 1885, plate xv (EXF, II). J. W. Crowfoot, *The Island of Meroe*, I, 1911 (ASE, XIX), plate xxiii.

182. See below, VI, 71.

183. In W. M. Flinders Petrie, *A History of Egypt*, III: *From the XIXth to the XXXth Dynasties*, 1905, 172; the dates of Rameses VI are given as 1161–1156 B.C.

184. From A. Piankoff, transl., *The Tomb of Ramesses VI*, ed. N. Rambova, 1954, plates 115 f. (Egyptian Religious Texts and Representations, 1; Bollingen Series XL).

185. From ibid., plate 113. Cf. *Life*, XXIV, iii (Jan. 19, 1948), 82.

186. E. Grébaut, "Des deux yeux du disque solaire," *RT*, I (1870), 72–87, 112–131.

187. For this figure see above, II, 269–272.

188. I call him Rameses IX according to general usage, though Petrie called him Rameses X, and I follow Petrie (above, n. 183), 178–184, in dating him 1153–1134 B.C. Petrie notes that the tomb contains the texts of the Litany of the Sun; chapters 123, 125, 126, 130 of the Book of the Dead; and Parts 1–3 of the Book of Am Tuat. It contains the earliest instance of the Ages of Man, but as five Ages, not the later conventional seven.

it, figs. 165 [189] and 166,[190] but they show the design only after much of it had been destroyed. Three photographs published by Piankoff show what is now left of the scene, and of these I publish one, fig. 167.[191] The original can be reconstructed only by putting these reproductions together along with a sketch made by one of the members of Napoleon's expedition to Egypt.[192] Obviously the design centered in the same great ithyphallic figure, its head with a sun and six stars above it on either side. The central figure stood on a snake, for the snake again curves at either side over three standing figures, and probably a small kneeling one, if we may so interpret the black spot at the left of section two of Lefébure's drawing, fig. 165, and in all probability the snake was joined at the bottom. The central figure, like that in *A*, had both feminine hair and the phallus, but this time we see in Piankoff's photograph a feminine breast line, and the old Napoleonic sketch shows the long feminine dress. The figure was then certainly hermaphroditic and was probably so intended in the tomb of Rameses VI. On the V-shaped ramp at either side are again six little figures with hands outstretched to receive red balls which dotted lines connect directly or indirectly with the central figure. The early Napoleonic drawing shows what is now lost, the "aspirant" standing at the base of the tier on the right, the line to whom begins at the central figure's abdomen but seems tangential also to the phallus, though the destruction of the phallus makes this not certain in the photograph.

The third appearance of this design is in another Theban tomb, that of Princess Tausert, of the close of the thirteenth century B.C.,[193] so that it is the earliest one known. It has been twice published, but the early sketch has no value.[194]

The other copy of the design from Tausert's tomb is reproduced in fig. 168.[195] Lefébure in publishing it made no comment on the scene. It brings out a few details lacking in the first two. We now see that we were correct in supposing that the snake was joined under the feet of the central figure and that this figure was standing upon it. Again a worshiping figure is before three mummiform figures under the snake at either side of the central group. Six figures along the ramps on either side receive the dotted lines, though the ball

189. From E. Lefébure, *Les Hypogées royaux de Thèbes*, 1889, plate 17 (*Mém.* Miss., III, i); the texts are here given without translation, plate 19.

190. From F. Guilmant, *Le Tombeau de Ramsès IX*, 1907, plate XCII (*Mém.* Inst., XV).

191. From Piankoff, *Disque solaire*, plate XXXVI. See also his plates XXXVII f.

192. *DE*, Planches, II, plate 84, fig. 6. In the same work, Descriptions, I, 412, the editor, Costaz, notes that the engraver left out the hieroglyph which means "fire." He also says that the central figure is represented discharging a flow of seminal fluid, from a portion of which the little figure under the phallus is being born. The "aspirant" seems to him also begotten by the phallus, and to represent a brother of the other figure, an older brother since he is larger. He guesses that the central figure is then a great ancestor and that the whole is a way to represent a genealogy, even distinguishing the males from the females. He admitted that the stars perplexed him, suggesting that they had astrological meaning as the gods or stars presiding over the destiny of the family. His interpretation is an excellent example of the danger of a fanciful approach to symbols.

193. See, beside the works listed below, Petrie, *History of Egypt*, III, 127–129, where further bibliography of the tomb is given.

194. *DE*, Planches, II, plate 92, fig. 11. In commenting on this, the editor connects it with *A* but admits that it throws considerable doubt on his theory that *A* represents a genealogical tree: *DE*, *Descriptions*, I, 412 f.

195. From Lefébure, plate 67; cf. p. 133.

which typified what they got is here omitted. Again there are two suns in the heavens, and a group of stars. Seven stars are on one side and six on the other: probably the number in itself had no importance, though six has appeared frequently. The central figure is once more presumably hermaphroditic, since feminine hair goes with beard and phallus. It turns this time to the left, and so the little "aspirant" stands at the bottom of the left tier rather than the right. The seated figure with finger to his mouth is again beneath the phallus. The dotted lines in the drawing seem to me to have been carelessly indicated by either the ancient artist or the modern copyist, but as before we have the sense of radiation from the central figure to all within the "V."

Of much less importance is the fourth sketch of the scene, which appears on the cartonnage, or wrapping, of the mummy of Hor, prophet of Ammon-Ra—king of the gods—and son of the governor of Thebes, fig. 171.[196] It was found in the Ramesseum and therefore is of approximately the same date as the others. Here so many details are omitted that it is clear the painting must have been very carelessly done. But the basic idea is retained.

The design itself seems from the four instances to have been an established one in Egyptian iconography of this period. To reconstruct it we must combine the evidence of all the presentations. It properly consisted of a great ithyphallic figure whose feet were on the snake of the lower world, the head among the sun and stars. The figure, then, seems to force us to consider it a cosmic god of some sort or name, essentially the god who dominates the upper world. From it flows a radiation, what the editors called an "émission de la liqueur séminale." Presumably painted in red like such lines elsewhere, [197] with the sun the same color, along with the ideogram for fire, the liqueur must be a radiation of fire or light. This would seem to be an identification of the divine Light-Stream with the Life-Stream, for birth is from light or fire.[198] It is known that ancient Egyptians described Min as one who "permeates the world in the torrential fire of his phallus," [199] exactly the phenomenon which is here graphically presented, though there is no reason for calling this figure Min. The radiation goes out in streams to the heavenly bodies, and also to twelve little figures each of whom opens her hands to receive it in the form of a little red sun-ball. These figures are divided into two tiers with six in each, one above the other. At the bottom of one of the tiers is a little human figure, the "aspirant" who stretches up his hands as though to ascend the tier like a ladder. He too receives in a dotted line the radiation from the great source, properly from the phallus. Directly from the divine phallus and just under it proceeds a conventional figure for a baby or the divine child,[200] which is appar-

196. From J. E. Quibell, *The Ramesseum*, 1898, plate xxviii; cf. p. 20 (Egyptian Research Account, II).

197. See below, fig. 173.

198. See E. A. W. Budge, *The Egyptian Heaven and Hell*, 1905, I, *The Book Åm-Tuat*, 32 (Books on Egypt and Chaldea, XX), where a drawing shows an ankh, , for the erect phallus of two gods.

199. See above, p. 166.

200. E. A. W. Budge, *An Egyptian Hieroglyphic Dictionary*, 1920, I, p. xcic, no. 72. Cf. A. H. Gardiner, *Egyptian Grammar*, 1927, 436, no. 17. Clement of Alexandria calls it *geneseōs sumbolon*, *Stromata*, v, vii, 41; cf. A. Deiber, *Clément d'Alexandrie et l'Egypte*, 1904, 40 (*Mém.* Inst., X). See above, II, 269–272, where the figure is discussed as meaning the divine baby, or divine birth, in the form of the self-nourished.

ently being born from the phallus and is itself, by the ideograph beneath it, identified as "fire." This figure seems especially to characterize the flow of life and birth to the "aspirant." At each side of this group, under the snake and so in the lower world, are four figures, three male mummies and an adorant, apparently again a human being, with hands lifted to the central group or figure.

Before we can come to any conclusion about the meaning of this scene, however, it is clear that we must know what the inscriptions upon the three representations have to say. Unfortunately they are highly cryptic and do not explain the characters represented as fully as could be wished. For example, Piankoff [201] reports the inscription on the design as it was drawn in the tomb of Rameses VI as follows. The ithyphallic god has no name here but is certainly the one named in the tomb of Rameses IX: "The One who hides the Hours." The child under the phallus is "The Gory One." The gods who are under the snake at the right are named Iaut-her, Kheper-her, and Ua-her. One reads three times with minor variations: "This god is thus: the serpent, the Enveloper, is over him." The fourth god, the adorant, Mem-ta, is identified: "This god is thus: he praises those among whom he is." The inscriptions with the figures on the left are incomplete, but identify them in practically the same terms. The caption for the whole seems to be at the end:

> (Those) who do not see the rays of Ra. They guard in darkness, they breathe when they hear his words. When he passes by, their souls go in his following.

That is, we conclude that the ithyphallic god in the center is Ra himself.

The inscriptions with the scene in the tomb of Rameses IX are much more elaborate. The gods under the snake are characterized:

> These gods who do not see the light of Ra, they keep watch in the shadows, they breathe when they hear his voice and whose soul goes in its course. They bring it about that the Osiris, the king Rameses IX, can enter the inaccessible roads in the West, that the deep obscurity should be illuminated for him, so that he sees Him-who-hides-the-hours.[202]

The inscription with the figures opposite begins like the foregoing, but continues:

> They bring it about that the king Rameses IX enters and leaves in the West, that his soul should not be rejected, that his forms shine with Shetai, the guide, he who is in his hours.

The great central god, we are confident, is Ra, and the "aspirant," the human form about to climb or go through the twelve stations within the "V" is the dead man himself. Piankoff calls him a god, but I am confident it is the deified Rameses IX, or VI, or whatever dead person the design was put with.

With the design in the tomb of Rameses IX we have for the first time inscriptions to

201. *The Tomb of Ramesses VI*, 339 f.

202. The translations of the inscriptions in the tomb of Rameses IX are those of Piankoff, *Disque solaire*, 65 f. Edgerton read this name "The One Hidden in respect to Time." Neither title is meaningful to me except possibly as meaning the "eternal" one, in whom time disappears. But this is a pure guess.

identify the figures inside the "V." Only the top four of the six figures on each side are left. Each of these is marked: "She who presides at his discharging in the Pen-Shetai." This is a sexual allusion, for while the first figure is then specially characterized as "among the bodies of Him-who-hides-the-hours," the second is "who gives birth to his mysterious bodies"; the third, "when his seed descends in *snfy* which receives it"; the fourth, "who gives birth to the mysteries which become children." The suggestion, that is, is that they are definitely playing the sexual role in intercourse and bearing, and this is what the streams of light to them probably indicate. The four figures remaining in the "V" at the left are similarly marked as those who preside over the discharging in Pen-Shetai, but they are in addition only those who guide, illuminate hidden things, and give praise. The little baby who falls from the great phallus and who is marked with the sign of fire is labeled "This god is thus: he procreates the flame . . . *snfy*, he receives [it]. Then this god enters . . . he gives the flame in the place of the damned."

The two tiers of six figures along each side of the "V," we now notice, are not mummies, like the gods of the lower world, as they have been taken to be, but are clearly marked as having their hands free to move. The first impression of these would naturally be that they are the guardians of the twelve gates of Am Tuat, a notion even more obvious when we realize that Parts 1, 2, and 3 of the Book of Am Tuat are written on the walls of the Tomb of Rameses IX. But the twelve doors and personages of Am Tuat belong in the lower world, while the figures in our design seem definitely, with the sun and stars, to belong to the upper world. They are probably the twelve hours of the day, corresponding to the twelve hours of the night, which appear in the Book of Day and Night, twice written in the tomb of Rameses VI and published by Piankoff.[203] In this book the king follows the sun in its daily course. Born in the morning from the vulva of Nut, the sky goddess, the sun (and the king with it) goes along the belly of Nut until at night she swallows them. They must then return through the body of the goddess, a twelve-hour journey, so that she can bear them again in the morning.

On the whole, then, the cryptic inscriptions bear out the impression of the design itself.[204] The world into which the deceased is going is a world which teems with begetting and the creation of light. The central figure is not a god of the lower world but rises from it into the sky and is essentially Ra, the god who dominates the upper world. But the figure is also "He-who-hides-the-hours," and Piankoff [205] has shown that this figure symbolizes the fact that "at a given moment in the night the cosmic machine ceases to function. To

203. A. Piankoff, *Le Livre du Jour et de la Nuit*, Cairo, 1942 (Institut Français d'Archéologie Orientale, Bibliothèque d'Etude, XIII). In English in his *The Tomb of Ramesses VI*, 389 ff.

204. Edgerton tells me that the inscription with the design as it appears in the tomb of Tausert is still more abbreviated. With the figures at the sides of the "V" are such phrases as "Secret in respect of heart," or "Hidden(?) of heart," while over above them are written the familiar phrases, "The Osiris, the Lord of the two Lands, King, True of Voice, given life like Ra for ever and ever," and "Lord of Diadems, Lord of making offerings, Queen Tausert is in the cemetery at the side of his (*sic*) Lords." Where Edgerton sees the large central figure in the tomb of Rameses IX labeled "The One who is Hidden with Respect of Time," in the tomb of Tausert there is only a single character beside him, one which itself means "The Hidden One."

205. In *JEA*, XXXV (1949), 115 f.

set this machine going again and to make the sun god advance on the rim of time, it is necessary to invoke certain forces in the other world, and by appropriate formulas to make the hours go out from the abyss of the nothing." The scenes we have been studying seem to indicate that this daily starting of the celestial machine is a matter of divine birth, of the sending out of life-light in a stream to the constituent parts of the universe.[206] The aspirant identifies himself with this cosmic begetting to come into celestial life himself, and so to "shine with Ra." [207] Imaginative mythology with its names and personalities seems to have given way to a more direct representation through symbols of these deeper hopes, fears, and projections out of which mythologies come.

In these scenes the king is depicted as rising into the cosmic light by a rebirth in which he is identical with the Divine Child. With them we must associate a group of scenes from another wall of the tomb of Rameses IX. For here the same story seems told in a variety of ways.

In the upper register of fig. 172 [208] are a series of figures which have not been identified for me, but in the middle register at the left a scarab rides in a boat across the heavens "upon the coils of the serpent 'O-neḥa," [209] holding in his claws the solar disk. He rides between "Horus eyes," but the scarab through all this panel is of such importance that we must stop with it for a moment.

The scarab was the symbol of Khepera, and from the XIIth Dynasty it was normally represented as carrying the sun disk in its claws. "The idea of the word *Kheper* is 'being,' existence, creation, or becoming; and the god Khepera is the self-existent creator-god." [210] We have an explanation of the nature of the scarab only from the Roman period, but there is good reason to think this explanation very old. Porphyry expands what is to be found in Plutarch [211] and Aelian [212] when he says that the Egyptians, unlike people ignorant of divine things, honored the beetle as the "animate image of Helios. . . . For every scarab is male, and as the sun does in the universe, he ejects his semen in mud and

206. Min himself was "lord of the sky": E. Naville and H. R. Hall, *The XIth Dynasty Temple at Deir el-Bahari*, 1913, III, 4 (EXF, XXXII). But whatever that may have meant in early times, when it is applied to Amon-Ra, the sun god, in later times, the phrase must mean not sky god but literally the lord of the sky: E. Naville, *The Temple of Deir el Bahari*, 1906, V, 7a. Here as often it appears that Amon-Ra is like Min, "the bull of his mother"—that is, the one who by his rays fertilizes the earth. See also above, pp. 155 f.

207. We are reminded of Porphyry's statement that the Egyptians "revered fire and water most of all the elements, since these are the chief causes of our salvation" (*aitiōtata tēs sōtērias hēmōn*): *De abstinentia*, IV, 9 (Hopfner, *Fontes*, 467). I am incompetent to connect these scenes properly with the text of the Book of Kererets, which is found almost complete on the walls of this tomb. The book is largely a series of charms for the safety of the soul in the other world. See A. Piankoff, "Le Livre des Quererts," *Bulletin de l'Institut Français d'Archéologie Orientale du Caire*, XLI (1942), 1–11; XLII (1944), 1–62; XLIII (1945), 1–50; and his *The Tomb of Ramesses VI*, 45 ff.

208. From Guilmant, *Le Tombeau du Ramsès IX*, plate LXIII*b* (*Mém.* Inst., XV).

209. Dr. Ludlow Bull wrote Dr. Etienne Drioton of Paris for me, and Dr. Drioton most kindly sent this translation and those which follow from this panel.

210. W. M. Flinders Petrie, *Scarabs and Cylinders with Names*, 1917, 2.

211. *On Isis*, 10 (355A); 74 (381A).

212. *De natura animalium*, x, 15.

makes it into a ball and gives it an impetus in the opposite direction with his hind feet."[213] That is, the scarab was a solar symbol because its ejection of semen into the ball figured the flow of engendering life from the sun to the universe, and the power of the sun to beget itself each night for new rising each morning. So it is not surprising that in a marginal vignette on a papyrus of the Book of the Dead the scarab is an ithyphallic deity in the "self begotten" pose of masturbation, with the familiar head, feathers, and whip of Min, fig. 169.[214] As here represented, the scarab seems not the sun itself but the ultimate deity of the Pyramid Texts, Atum, who created himself by masturbation and then in the same way (or by spitting) created the primal pair Shu and Tefnet.[215]

The sun, then, fig. 172, goes across the sky toward a row of females, and these are identified, as Drioton translates the text:

> Those who are thus figured are the mysterious-of-face, the guardians of Ra. He passes a moment in their city of sand where are concealed the mysteries of him whose flesh is hidden.[216]

What these figures or their "cities of sand" are I have no notion, but we learn that the scarab is here called Ra, like the sun god in the heavens.

It is the symbols of the lower register that are extremely important for us. At the left is a row of four females again, each standing upon a snake. With them is an inscription which Drioton reads as follows (with comments in square brackets added by me):

> Those who are thus figured are in the abyss. This god [which I take to be the scarab above and in this register] converses with them. They create from him numerous forms and he makes them a gift of their forms [that is, they form themselves?]. This god unites himself to his disk in this crypt where his birth takes place [that is, he begets himself from himself]. Then when this god has passed before these goddesses they stop, and a profound darkness hides them.

213. *De abstinentia*, IV, 9 (Hopfner, *Fontes*, 468). The meaning of the last phrase, *tois opisthiois antanapherei posin*, would be dubious but for the statement of Plutarch, in connection with the scarabs, that the sun "seems to turn the heavens in the direction opposite its own course, which is from west to east": *On Isis*, 74 (381A). The scarab is even more fully discussed by Horapollo Niliacus, *Hieroglyphics*, I, x (ed. A. T. Cory, 1840, 19–22; Hopfner, *Fontes*, 579). It is interesting that the notion reappears in *The Secret of the Golden Flower*, transl. from the Chinese by Richard Wilhelm and thence into English by C. F. Baynes, 1931, where on p. 31 the unknown Chinese author says: "The scarabaeus rolls his ball and in the ball there develops life as the effect of the undivided effort of his spiritual concentration. If now an embryo can grow in manure, and shed its skin, why should not the dwelling place of our Heavenly Heart also be able to create a body if we concentrate the spirit upon it?" This is an example of the power inherent in the union of Yin and Yang, Light and Dark, Male and Female, in the ultimate Tao.

214. From *BD*, ed. Davis, plate LXXIX.

215. See above, p. 152. In the Book of the Dead at this passage a prayer is made for the repose of the soul. "Thou madest me my skin. Thou knowest what I mean, thou knowest it very well. . . . See that I may absorb thee. See that I may rest in the Tuat," etc. This is again the desire for life after death in terms of identification with deity, who is presumably here represented as the scarab in the form of the Self-Caused.

216. They can be seen more clearly on Guilmant's plate LXXX, where it appears that the little mounds are full of dots, apparently "sand."

There is definitely a meaning in the distinction between these registers, then. In the upper one the sun boat goes across the sky, giving illumination. Then in the lower register we are in the "abyss." The same god passes through this, and first meets females, who are recreated, or recreate themselves, as he passes, and who then are left in darkness until he returns.

The scarab also recreates himself, and this he seems to be doing in the extraordinary four figures to the right, which I have reproduced in fig. 170 [217] from the old Napoleonic drawings and in fig. 173 from a later drawing.[218] Since the late eighteenth century some censorious hand has scratched off the phalli. The group originally consisted of four black silhouetted figures each with long woman's hair but also with a phallus. The figures bend backward from the hips to make, with the hair, almost a complete arch. The hair and phallus seem clearly to indicate a hermaphrodite, though Piankoff and I, as we studied the original together in the tomb, could not believe that a feminine breastline was indicated. Above each of the black figures is a red sun disk, while a red stream, a dotted line, goes out from the phallus to produce new birth, the Divine Child again. There is also a red line which goes from the claw of a scarab to the mouth of the figure in the old drawings. In the drawings reproduced from Guilmant and Lefébure the line from only one of the figures is connected with the scarab: the others go straight down to the edge of the picture. But in the same volume, our figure 173, where Guilmant shows the wall as a whole, he indicates that with three of the figures the lines did connect the mouth with the scarab. I strongly suspect that the intention of the design is to show the line as coming up from the scarab to the woman's mouth in every case, since all agree in showing it that way in at least one instance. This would seem to me to mean that the hermaphroditic figure is receiving at the mouth a stream of red (fire or light) from the scarab and is giving off a similar stream to produce a birth from the phallus.[219] The whole may well be identified, as far as the design goes, with the solar disk above it.

With this interpretation, which the design itself seems to indicate, the inscriptions with these strange figures agree. Drioton said that the little inscriptions, numbered 18, 20, 48, and 49 on fig. 173 beside the ithyphallic figures, were enigmatic variations on the word meaning "fire." Nos. 19, 21, and 50 were apparently enigmatic distortions of names which neither he nor Bull could identify. Drioton warned that only an expert could even guess at the identity of these names, and Edgerton was likewise at a loss.

We now have something more definite to go on, however. The scarab is the ultimate source, itself the hypercosmic and unperceived deity, from whom flows out a stream of fire or light which fertilizes a lesser hermaphrodite through the labia of the mouth and so enables the lesser figure itself to produce a full birth from its phallus.

This interpretation is strengthened by the rest of this register, fig. 174,[220] which shows

217. From *DE*, Planches, II, 86, 1.

218. From Guilmant, plates LXXX f. Our figure is made by combining details from these.

219. C. Lenormant, *Musée des antiquités égyptiennes*, 1841, 21, gives the following interpretation without benefit of the inscriptions: "Le sujet . . . représente, sous forme symbolique, l'ordre de la création des astres émanés du scarabée, emblême du monde."

220. From Guilmant, plate LXXX.

variants of the same motif. For at the right of these ithyphallic figures stands a second row. The one at the left of the first in line shows again a god from whose phallus the new divine baby is being born: this time the god holds a snake to his lips, and a scarab is beside his head. At his right is a double-formed god, which suggests in a new way the double nature represented in the other figures. Then at the extreme right is a great sun disk in which stands (i.e. with which is identified) a figure with female breasts. The central part is destroyed, because, I suspect, it was ithyphallic. It seems to me to be the same god as the one which we have just found represented in four places, including this one. Scarabs, one with a smaller sun disk, emerge from this larger disk. That is, they too are being born.

All of this register, especially from the four bent-back figures on, seems to illustrate the sentence of the inscription "This god unites himself to his disk in this crypt where his birth takes place." What is being illustrated in these and the first four hermaphrodites is the daily birth of the new sun from the old sun, for this is the symbol, indefinitely ramified and varied in representation, most beloved by Egyptians for their hope of immortality. Indeed when we look at fig. 175 [221] which stands immediately beside these registers, we see the new birth of the old god, accompanied by the scarab and disk, as well as by the snake, with the inscription which Drioton translates:

> This god, so figured, whose arms are raised and whose feet are in the abyss, the birth of this great god takes place in the crypt where this god is. He speaks to Osiris and Osiris speaks to him. This god is in Dêt [generally written *Dewat,* Underworld] in the deep shadows, Nehep being his guardian. He is illuminated during [or, says Drioton, through, by means of] the birth of Ra.

It is the immortality of Rameses that is in question throughout. He is reborn in the depths, as Osiris "speaks to him," or as Ra, too, is born. And like them he is essentially reborn as his phallus becomes again erect, and he, not quite lost in the darkness, begets himself. The row of "prisoners" below indicate the fate he has escaped, the fate of eternal confinement to the darkness. To be born again and to be "illumined" are, as usual, quite synonymous terms. Likewise, the figures are varied because the idea is essentially mystical. Rameses can hope for immortality as he is born from the divine phallus, or from the scarab, or as, by becoming united with Osiris or Ra, he himself achieves the divine and self-begetting erection. All are figures not essentially of sex but of immortality, the achieving of divine life.

For in all this, we may stop again to remind the reader, sex is used symbolically, not because the Egyptians were frustrated in sex and so presented a Freudian picture but because they were so frustrated and terrified at death. The row of prisoners at the bottom of this register show in a really hideous way the fate every Egyptian hoped to escape, the horror of eternal consciousness within one's grave, eternal frustration indeed. The phallic symbols, the light symbols, which in these designs are being so vividly blended, as well as water symbols, drinking symbols, nursing symbols, and the rest are all basically symbols

221. From ibid., plate LXXVII; cf. for its position fig. 172, above.

of the "life urge," in terms of the divine fluid. They are wish projections, if we may use another Freudian term, by which the Egyptians, for long only the king but ultimately all initiates, could feel their passion for immortality gratified.

F. HERMAPHRODITISM

ANOTHER PIECE of evidence from the tomb of Rameses IX which must be considered here is the Litany of the Sun, which expresses directly many of the ideas we have found in the two scenes from the tomb already discussed. The Litany is too long to give here entire.[222] In it Ra is addressed by many terms which indicate the same underlying conception: Ra is the Scarab born as his own son; [223] he is Tonen who begets his own members, who fashions what is within himself; [224] he is the unique one who forms his own body; [225] he is the image of the bodies of Isis and Nephthys,[226] of Nun [227] and of Nut; [228] he has created the water which emerges from his inner parts; [229] he emits rays and creates bodies, and what he emits from himself is himself; [230] he is the great lion who created the gods.[231] After seventy-five such apostrophes the ritual continues with an elaborate address to the king who is at once Osiris and Ra, to the point where "What Ra begets, it is he [the royal Osiris] who begets it." [232] Repeatedly it is stated: "The royal Osiris is Ra, and vice versa"; [233] "The life of [the royal] Osiris is the life of Ra, and vice versa." [234] This remarkable document, the basic meaning of which Naville has expounded in terms of pantheism,[235] seems to me to express the very heart of the religion of intelligent Egypt as it centered round the king in the second millennium B.C. It is this same religion which was later popularized when all initiates through the ritual strove during life and, as they hoped, even after death to identify themselves with Osiris and hence with Ra, in order to obtain divine immortality.

These prayers have thrown us again into hermaphroditism, since the god is described as having both male and female form. The hermaphrodite is a frequent figure in Egyptian art, where it is usually represented as a human being or god with female breasts and a

222. Edouard Naville, *La Litanie du soleil: Inscriptions recueillies dans les tombeaux des rois à Thèbes*, 1875.

223. Ibid., 2, p. 20. See p. 22, n.

224. Ibid., 3, p. 22. Tonen, Naville explains, is the phallus of Osiris. Cf. 66, p. 66, with Naville's notes. On p. 95 the king as Ra is glorified with the statement: "His phallus is Tonen."

225. Ibid., 6, p. 27. On p. 96 the king as Ra-Osiris is glorified: "he makes the royal Orisis to be born, he produces his own birth."

226. Ibid., 17, 18, p. 37.

227. Ibid., 20, p. 39.

228. Ibid., 16, p. 36. Naville has an interesting note on how Nut is the universal mother, the Female Principle in the cosmos, who corresponds to the *anō sophia* of later Gnosticism.

229. Ibid., 21, p. 40. As such he is the image of Remi, the weeper, and Naville has interesting material to show the Egyptian association of life-giving power with tears. We may in this be confronted with the basic value of the *mater dolorosa*. See also John Lewis, "The Mother Worship in Egypt," *Journal of the Manchester Egyptian and Oriental Society*, XI (1924), 52.

230. Naville, *La Litanie*, 50, 51, p. 58.

231. Ibid., 56, p. 61.

232. Ibid., p. 103.

233. For example ibid., p. 79.

234. Ibid., p. 84.

235. Ibid., pp. 122–130.

man's beard. Such a representation is particularly common for the "two Niles," a figure which will be discussed shortly.[236]

A very interesting representation is a drawing from a papyrus of the British Museum which Piankoff publishes but does not date.[237] It is presumably late. At the right is the familiar representation of Nut, the sky goddess, under whom is usually an earth god, here represented with a serpent's head, and he is called "The one who has created that which is in the mysterious Dewat," and "The great god who is at the head of Men-nefer (Memphis), the seat of peace, T;nn, the Lord of Eternity," as Piankoff translates the inscriptions. Piankoff calls this Nut the day sky. Behind it is a similar figure which Piankoff calls the night sky, since its position indicates that it is the sky, and the stars on its body that it is night. It has a beard and an exaggerated phallus and testicles to indicate its masculinity, but that it takes the position of the figure traditionally considered to be feminine and retains feminine hair certainly suggests that it is hermaphroditic, even though the feminine breasts are lacking. Written beside it is: "Adoration, words spoken: The-risen-one-in-health, the first of the Westerners, who has created the sky, who has created the earth, who has created the Dewat, the great god." Under it is the male god in, so far as I know, a unique position—that is, he is fertilizing himself in the mouth, is the "self-engendered," as Piankoff calls it.[238] He is Geb, and his inscription reads "Geb the father of the gods, the great god who has created the earth and all the circuit of Ra."

Piankoff concludes: "The phallic god covered with stars . . . is evidently the celestial Osiris . . . the Lord of the Dewat of the Pyramid period." [239] I rather incline to see in both figures the fullness of bisexuality. Instead of the male earth and female sky, here we have both sexes in each, or the bisexuality of the Ultimate. It may be the "self-engendered" which is depicted, but I rather think that Piankoff's second parallel is basically more correct, a reference to the notion that the hermaphroditic Ultimate pro-

236. See J. E. Gautier and G. Jéquier, *Fouilles de Licht*, 1902, 33–35, and plate XII (*Mém.* Inst., VI); and below, p. —. Another representation of hermaphroditic origin of life for man is possibly intended in a peculiar design which has appeared to my knowledge, only twice: here the solar disk is extended to give out a stream of life and power toward a table or altar of offerings. This masculine symbol is extended by a pair of arms which are connected with a headless torso consisting only of female breasts. The editor calls this Nut with the descending sun, since the arms and breast come from the western mountains. But the two together may well have carried hermaphroditic significance. See for these B. Bruyère, *Rapport sur les Fouilles de Deir el Médineh (1924–1925)*, 1926, 84 f.; and ibid. *(1926)*, 1927, 26 (G. Foucart, Fouilles de l'Institut Français d'Archéologie Orientale du Caire, III, iii, and IV, iii).

237. See A. Piankoff, "The Funerary Papyrus of the Shieldbearer Amon-M-Saf," *Egyptian Religion*, III (1935), 155, fig. 2. It is Papyrus Brit. Mus. 10018, and this picture was published also by Lanzone, *Dizionario*, plate CLIX. Piankoff's whole discussion is extremely valuable for showing the loss of individuality at later times in the Egyptian gods. They had become local representations of a great pantheistic power, which, although not thought out with the precision of some Greek minds, was keenly felt and believed in.

238. Piankoff refers to the only parallel I know, one which is very obscurely presented by G. Daressy, *Cercueils des cachettes royales*, 1909, plate LII, the left side, bottom register, third design from the left (Catalogue général des antiquités égyptiennes du Musée du Caire). At the bottom of p. 156 Daressy describes the design without mentioning the phallus, but it is clearly visible under a glass.

239. He goes on (p. 155) to expand this with references.

duces all *other* things by copulating with himself, and thus gives birth first to the primal pair Shu and Tefnet.[240] The two conceptions, actually, are one. It is the self-caused or self-engendered from whom other things can come. Hence the accompanying inscription properly calls the figure who fertilizes himself the father of the gods and creator of earth and sky.

So when to Ra the properties of the Ultimate are ascribed, he is the "self-produced." Ra is "self-produced . . . a perfect god, making his body, giving birth to it. He has not come out of a womb, he has come out of cycles." Hence: "Thou art youthful water and old water. They repose in the merits of thee. Thou givest life to the earth by thy stream. Thou art heaven, thou art earth, thou art fire, thou art water, thou art air in the midst of them." [241] "I am the mighty one, who createth his own light. . . . Pure are thine effluxes, which flow from thee." [242] "Hail to thee, Horus of the Two Horizons, who art Chepera Self-originating." [243] "I am the great god, self-produced." [244] "O Ra, thou who art . . . the divine man-child, the heir of eternity, self-begotten and self-born"—that is, by activities both male and female.[245]

> I [Ra or Nu] am the great god who gave birth to himself. . . .[246]
>
> I know the god who dwelleth therein.
> Who then is this?
> It is Osiris; or (as others say), Rā is his name, (or) It is the phallus of Rā wherewith he was united to himself.[247]

Still more clearly the notion emerges in a Hymn to Amon: [248]

> Fashioning himself, there is none who knows his shapes. . . . Forming his images, creating himself. . . . Joining his seed with his body, to create his egg within his secret self.[249]
>
> He had no mother for whom his name was made. He had no father who begot him and who said, "it is I"(?). Shaping his own egg: Force(?) mysterious of births, creating his

240. R. O. Faulkner, "The Bremner-Rhind Papyrus, III," *JEA*, XXIII (1937), 172 (27, 1). Faulkner's translation makes no connection between the divine masturbation and the spitting out of the gods, but Budge's earlier translation in *Archaeologia*, LII (1890), 441 f., represents that the god fertilized his own mouth with the seed after the masturbation, and then produced Shu and Tefnet, the one by evacuation, the other by spitting, so that the one god became three. This makes more sense—if the sense is not Budge's own paraphrase. I can have no judgment in such a case.

241. Translation of S. Birch, "Inscription of Darius at the Temple of El-Khargeh," *TSBA*, V (1877), 296, 301; verses 5, 6, 44 f.

242. *BD*, ed. Renouf and Naville, 206, chap. CXIX; and 296, chap. CXLVII. On p. 207, n. 1, Renouf says that the end of chap. CXLIX reads: "Let me be joined, let me be united with the sap which proceedeth from Osiris." Cf. Naville at p. 307.

243. Ibid., 23, chap. XV. On p. 29 he has an interesting note (5) in which the Egyptian word of the passage is made equivalent to *autogenēs*.

244. Ibid., 35, chap. XVII.

245. *BD*, 10.

246. Ibid., 93, chap. XVII, 9. In his edition of *BD*, 78, line 9, Davis translates "He is the one who fornicates in himself." Edgerton wrote me that the line should be translated: "I am the great god who comes into existence by himself."

247. Ibid., 94 f., chap. XVII, 23–25. The idea of the double-sex manifestation of divinity is brought out on a hypocephalus disk published by P. J.

beauties. Divine god, coming into existence by himself: all gods were created after he began to be.[250]

Faciens vulvam, creans phallum. Primus injecit semen in vaccas(?). Coivit cum eo, quo potius est, siquando non erat vulva. Rising as Re in Nun, giving birth to all that is and is not. Father of fathers, mother of mothers. The bull of these four cows.[251]

Long ago Grébaut [252] discussed some of these texts and concluded that in the case of a god who impregnated his mother with himself, the mother could be only the feminine aspect of the one god, who is really father, mother, and son simultaneously. Grébaut does not call this god hermaphrodite, but it is clear that if the feminine aspect is an aspect of the male god, the conception could be represented pictorially only as hermaphrodite.

When these passages are put together, it becomes apparent that though the Egyptians might represent goddesses as distinct from gods, actually in the highest statement the feminine and masculine elements blend into one supreme god who is supreme precisely because in him gods and goddesses at last are one, and so the psychological urge for completeness is satisfied in the ultimate *causa sui*.

Less common than the hermaphroditic representation to show the "self-caused" is the ithyphallic Min body with the Horus child head [253] and, if the whip is a fertility symbol, the child born holding the whip. For here the begetter and the begotten are fused into a single entity.

So Plutarch says: "They often call Isis by the name of Athena, saying such a phrase as 'I came from myself,' which means that she is a product of her own initiative (*autokinētos phora*)." [254]

The ithyphallic and hermaphroditic figures, then, were for the Egyptians by no means merely an indecent glorification of sexual pleasure. They were symbols of the coming of the life of the god to man and nature, and great was their emotional power.

G. BES AND MONOTHEISM

ONE OF THE most interesting variants in this symbolism appears in a peculiar elaboration of the Bes figure.[255] Bes, who like Min is obviously at all times a phallic deity, was

---

de Horrack, *PSBA*, VI (1884), 126–129. Here at one side the soul of the deceased presents himself to Hathor, the cow, to request rebirth. On the other an ithyphallic snake, with the "eye," represents the male principle. In the center a seated deity, Amon with the whip, is beside a female deity with the lotus, "another symbol of renewed birth." The whole disk, as explained by Horrack, is extremely interesting.

248. A. H. Gardiner, "Hymns to Amon from a Leiden Papyrus," *ZaeS*, XLII (1905), 12–42.

249. Chap. 40, in ibid., p. 25.

250. Chap. 100, in ibid., p. 33.

251. Chap. 400, in ibid., p. 37. The delicate Latin is Gardiner's. Ptah is also hailed as the one who begat himself: W. Wolf, "Der Berliner Ptah-Hymnus," *ZaeS*, LXIV (1929), 18 and 26.

252. "Des deux yeux du disque solaire," *RT*, I (1870), esp. 127 f.

253. Lanzone, *Dizionario*, plate CCCXXXII, 2.

254. *On Isis*, 62 (367A) (Hopfner, *Fontes*, 72). To translate this "self-impelled motion," with F. C. Babbitt in the Loeb ed., as the words would ordinarily mean, is to lose contact with the first part of the sentence and with Egyptian thought.

255. A very interesting collection of Bes types

sometimes identified with the sun, as were almost all Egyptian gods. It is significant that in one hermaphroditic representation [256] the "two eyes," here probably those of the sun, are shown between his legs on either side of his familiar little apron.[257] One most interesting object [258] shows Bes, an ithyphallic figure covered with eyes, with two pairs of arms, two pairs of solar wings and a bird's tail. Its back is represented as that of a bird, whose head is blended into the Bes face. The face is the usual Bes type, but on either side of it are four small heads, which Gressmann lists as, right, a lion, ram, crocodile, jackal; left, a ram, baboon, crocodile, and an unidentified animal. The god stands on a pedestal, around the border of which is the symbol of eternity, a snake curled in a circle with its tail in its mouth. Two others, generally like this but with interesting variants, are published by Lanzone.[259] They are not ithyphallic. One has a similar arrangement of animals at the side of the head, the other not. These two figures are definitely identified with the sun, in the one case by the solar wings and the feathers-and-disk headdress, in the other by a pair of solar eyes on either side of the figure.[260] In the latter, symbolism is immeasurably complex, and all is surrounded by a border made of the ideograph for fire, twelve times repeated, on either side of the arc.

Still another figure of similar type, this time with a lion's head for phallus, is published by Erman.[261] From these types it appears that in all of them Bes is shown to be simply the organizing idea around which all the attributes of deity cluster. Similar combinations of divine attributes, dubiously Bes at all, may have an ithyphallic scarab as the center for a riot of symbolic associations, as in fig. 169. In combinations of this sort Bes may disappear and an ithyphallic hermaphrodite take its place.[262] In spite of a few cases where the ithyphallicism is not indicated, the general meaning of these symbolic combinations is unavoidable. It is that of Deity reduced by combination to abstraction. He contained within himself all the qualities Egyptians associated with divinity, such as power, life, destruction, light, eternity, and the rest, but his most important attribute was the life-giving power represented especially by the erect phallus, though it might be symbolized by the ankh or the fire sign, or in many other ways. By such fusing of divine attributes did

---

was made by Alice Grenfell, "The Iconography of Bes, and of Phoenician Bes-Hand Scarabs," *PSBA*, XXIV (1902), 21–40. See also Lanzone, *Dizionario*, plates LXXIII–LXXXI.

256. B. Bruyère, *Fouilles de Deir el Médineh (1933–1934)*, 1937, 112, fig. 48; cf. fig. 49 for evaluation of the mystic symbolism (Fouilles de l'Institut Francais . . . du Caire, XIV).

257. Grenfell, p. 33, mentions other Bes figures "with female breasts; with teats (sphinx form)."

258. Published by Gressmann, *AOTB*, II, plate CCXXIII, no. 567; cf. p. 162; and by Lanzone, *Dizionario*, plate LXXX, 3, 4; cf. pp. 212–215. See Grenfell, 24, fig. II.

259. Op. cit., plate LXXX, 1 f., and plate LXXXI; cf. pp. 211–212, 215–221.

260. The eyes may be those of the moon.

261. *Relig. Ägypt.*, 310. See also *BD*, ed. Renouf and Naville, 40 (chap. XVII); "The Lion with dazzling mouth and with head bent forwards is the Phallus of Osiris [otherwise of Ra]." See also H. Grapow, "Spruch 17 des Totenbuches," *Urkunden des aegyptischen Altertums (Deutsch)*, V, 38 f. On the frequent connection of Bes with the lion see F. W. von Bissing, "Eine hellenistische Bronzefigur des Gottes Bes," *MDAI, Ath.*, L (1925), 123–132. He shows a very interesting ithyphallic Bes on plate V, 1.

262. Lanzone, *Dizionario*, plates CXXXVI; CXXXVII, 5; CXXXVIII, 1. In plate CXXXVII, 4, the figure is female, with no hermaphroditic indication.

the ancient world ordinarily come to understand monotheism.[263] Hence it is not surprising that, as Osiris was equated with Dionysus by the Greeks, Bes, obviously with the same identification, was very popular in Roman Egypt.[264]

This symbolic approach to the abstraction of monotheism seems to me one of the most important lessons in our study of symbols. People committed to a verbal medium for thinking feel that so long as there are a variety of names and figures for gods we must still be in polytheism. But when the symbols are all crowded upon a single figure, it is clear that those thinking in symbols are thinking in what verbalists would call monotheistic terms. The clustering of symbols upon the single figure is the symbolist's way of expressing the abstraction.

The importance of phallic imagery is made certain by the large number of purely phallic grotesques which constantly turn up in the graves. Some are definitely of the Min form,[265] one is a stone "phallus a half meter long finished like an obelisk on a pedestal." [266] Or there may be images in which the phallus has again become a lion's head on figures otherwise abundantly marked as solar.[267] This is extremely interesting, for the lion's solar head [268] is the favorite fountain spout of antiquity, and here, at least, seems definitely to be made the source of the solar divine fluid.[269] The Egyptian Museum at Cairo has a large

263. The similarity of these figures to the vision of Ezekiel (I, 5–14) is obvious and striking. It may be interesting to recall a statement by Renouf, in a note to his and Naville's translation of *BD*, 122: "In reading this and almost every other chapter of the *Book of the Dead*, it is absolutely necessary to bear in mind that different divine names do not necessarily imply different personalities. A name expresses but *one* attribute of a person or thing, and one person having several attributes may have several names." Conversely, as in Stoic allegory, the names of different gods, and here their symbols, are applied to a single personality to represent monotheism. Renouf might well have quoted his own translation of *BD*, XVII, p. 35: "His [Ra's] names together compose the cycle of the gods."

264. [A.-C.-P. Caylus], *Recueil d'antiquités*, 1759, III, 16, and plate IV, 1; A. H. Sayce, "Some Greek Graffiti from Abydos," *PSBA*, X (1888), 383–386; A. Grenfell, "Note on Scarab 384," *PSBA*, XXIII (1901), 139–141. Dionysus seems himself to have been a beer god, if Jane Harrison's exposition of the epithet Bromios is accurate: *Prolegomena*, 414–417; see also 420.

265. See, for example, G. Daressy, *Statues de Divinités*, I, 1906, plates VI, XXVII (Catalogue général des antiquités égyptiennes du Musée du Caire).

266. B. Bruyère, *Rapport sur les fouilles de Deir el Médineh (1926)*, 1927, 39. Cf. idem, *Mert Seger à Deir el Médineh*, 1930, 161, n. 1 (*Mém.* Inst., LVIII).

267. Daressy, plate XXXVII, pp. 178 f. Horus is represented as an ithyphallic hawk, the phallus ending in a lion's head, in Mariette, *Dendérah*, II, 1870, plate 76. Cf. A. Deiber, *Clément d'Alexandrie et l'Egypte*, 1904, 42, fig. 11 (*Mém.* Inst., X). See above, p. 176.

268. To be discussed in Vol. VII.

269. In describing the figures on a tomb, B. Bruyère, *Mert Seger à Deir el Médinah*, 117, says: "A lion's or a feline's skin covers the body of the priest *Sam*, who performs the rites of resurrection of the dead; a lion's muzzle ornaments the belt of the kings and the priests. Sekhmet, Maut, Tefnut, Mehent are goddesses with lions' heads because they are media of rebirth." We shall return to the lion's head as spout in a later volume but record here that the lion spout is primordially Egyptian. See William Stevenson Smith, *A History of Egyptian Sculpture and Painting in the Old Kingdom*, 1946, 55, where two instances are given from the Fifth Dynasty. See also the lion spout from Lisht in the Metropolitan Museum of New York. Shesemu, the god of the oil press and wine, early changed into a lion; and Shesemu may be the lion who spouts: ibid., 210, n., and Mercer, *Pyramid Texts*, II, 187.

collection of these phallic grave fetishes from the Saïtic period, from which I show a representative selection, fig. 176.[270] These fetishes represent sometimes the phallus alone, sometimes a human figure with an enormous phallus, sometimes a scene of copulation with such a phallus. Put into graves, these could hardly be indecent jests and can only represent a craving and hope for eternal life which the phallus expressed.[271]

With them I must associate the idea in libation texts published by Blackman.[272] Here the dead man is offered, as Osiris, the moisture which "came from thee." Blackman thinks this refers to the body moisture which has been taken from the mummy, so that the new life is possible only when new moisture, par excellence that of Osiris himself, is restored. But there is not a hint in the several texts quoted that it is the body moisture, while the fluid which issues from Osiris seems by now clearly to be the Nile from his phallus, the flow of seminal fluid which gives life. This could be typified by elaborate and expressive paintings of libations, or by putting a cheap model of the phallus itself into the grave.[273]

The stress which Philo lays upon the mystic ascent as typified in the copulations of the Patriarchs shows the notion lifted slightly beyond these direct presentations, and the Christian discussion of the projection of the Logos, the extreme emphasis upon the manner of its incarnation, are perhaps one step further in sublimation. But the mystic quest for union, for identification with the divine, for rebirth in divine life through water, "born of water and the Spirit," in John's words (or perhaps we should translate, "Born of water, i.e. the Spirit"), all are so close to the ideas here set forth without subterfuge or euphemism that two important points seem clear. First, the later euphemisms really have their roots, at first consciously, later unconsciously, in this symbolism; and secondly, the earlier direct expression itself contained at least potentially the lofty idealism which in later formulation would usually be regarded as something much "higher" than the original expression.

Of course phallic images were not the only ones to express mystic aspiration. We have frequently met phrases in which life and breath are put to the nostrils, for example, but

270. Published by permission of the Museum. Cf. A. Moll, *Handbuch der Sexualwissenschaften*, 1912, 573–575. Moll, p. 576, says of these that they are of about 600 B.C., hence in the Saïtic period. He consulted an eminent Egyptologist, he says, who assured him that there was nothing like these in earlier Egyptian periods, and hence that these must come from Greek influence. How Greek influence could have reached down at such a time to make this impression upon the life of the lower classes, who must have used these objects, the "eminent Egyptologist" did not explain. Strange as they are in form, I must see them only as a formal departure from the general Egyptian attitude toward phallicism and its promise of immortality, which is here emerging.

271. Phallic amulets, common in the ancient world, were used with two basic purposes, the warding off of the evil eye and the increase of fertility. See Budge, *Amulets and Superstitions*, 15, 20, 144, 296, 308, 322, 490. Flinders Petrie, *Amulets*, 11, no. 16 (and plate 1) shows several of these from Roman Egypt and remarks: "There is no trace of any such amulet in use by Egyptians." He apparently means ancient Egyptians.

272. A. M. Blackman, "The Significance of Incense and Libations in Funerary and Temple Ritual," *ZaeS*, L (1912), 69–75.

273. Is not the "Water-Spirit," which was the "power" of God coming down from heaven to man, only another variant of this conception? The material is presented, without any such suggestion, by W. Spiegelberg, "Die aegyptische Gottheit der 'Gotteskraft'," *ZaeS*, LVII (1922), 145–148.

274. See F. Daumas, "Sur deux chants liturgiques des mammisis de Dendara," *Revue d'égyptologie*, VIII (1951), 31–46.

this can become a figure of impregnating the goddess for the divine birth, a figure used in liturgy to which some ritualistic act may well have corresponded.[274] A great number of other figures of speech or symbols were used for the mystical ascent by the Egyptians. What concerns us here is to establish the meaning of the symbols of phallus and fluid.

H. MILK

ANOTHER COMMON figure is the one we have met in Mesopotamia, that of getting divinity through being nursed by a goddess. We have already encountered this in several connections [275] but should say a word more about it.

A scene of nursing, usually nursing by Hathor the cow goddess, is one of the commonest symbols in Egyptian art. In fig. 177 [276] a scene is shown which Gayet describes:

> Under the bed of the queen is a row of buckles, *s'hen*. On the bed the "royal mother" Maut m ua, giver of life, is kneeling, her head adorned with the vulture of Maut and the sign of consolidation. Behind her a woman sustains her and makes a magical gesture toward the nape of her neck; the latter has a vase on her head which contains the fertilizing liquid or the blood of the bull Bitaou-Osiris.[277] Before the queen two figures of Hathor-sat, their heads adorned with the disk and the palms of light, nurse the royal child, Horus, Ma neb Ra and his double, whose cartouche is crowned with the disk and palms of light.
>
> Finally, under the bed where the queen gives birth to the child, the royal infant and his "double" are again nursed by the celestial cow. "Speak four times . . . as king of the South and North, giving life, expanding the heart, on the seat of Horus; you guide the living, you govern the double earth as Mâ khérou, like the sun in eternity, and the ages in the dwelling [illegible].[278] She gives all life, all might, all power like Ra, eternally."
>
> The reference is certainly to the dwelling of Hathor. Hathor, being the goddess of the horizon of the setting sun and of the horizon of the rising sun, watches over the king who is born at the rising and over his double who remains in Amenti at the setting. It is again an allusion to the double movement of the vital solar flame which appears at dawn, disappears at the horizon, rising and setting alternately.
>
> In the column placed at the center of this little tablet: "She gives all life, all stability, and all power near her." [279]

Of the nine nurses [280] at the right who have the sign of Neit on their heads, Gayet, in the

275. See above, p. 116.

276. From A. Gayet, *Le Temple de Louxor*, I, 1894, plate LXVI (*Mém.* Miss., XV). The same scene was published more beautifully but less accurately by Champollion-le-Jeune, *Monuments de l'Egypte et de la Nubie*, IV, plate CCCXLI.

277. This is a *nmst* vessel, which contained Nile water, but in presenting the vessel to a king the prophet described it: "I bring to thee that which has issued from Nun, that which first issued from Atum in its name of *nmst*." The succeeding texts make it clear that it is the seminal fluid of the sun god which is in the vessel. See A. M. Blackman, "Sacramental Ideas and Usages in Ancient Egypt," *RT*, XXXIX (1921), 68–78.

278. Is this the "beautiful dwelling of fire," *tcheser?*

279. Gayet, 104 f.

280. These are nurses no less because the child is not actually at the breast. The two positions are interchangeable in Egyptian ideographs for "nurse." See Budge, *An Egyptian Hieroglyphic Dictionary*, I, p. CIII, no. 18 f.

absence of an inscription, has no explanation to offer. Neit is a goddess also identified with the heavenly cow as mother of the sun,[281] but it is conspicuous—what Gayet does not notice—that Neit by the masculine beard is here shown to be a hermaphrodite. The "buckles" to which Gayet calls attention are ordinarily the symbol of Isis, probably of the uterus of Isis.[282] The couch, the usual lion couch of a mummy or of heavenly childbirth, is the love couch which is a psychopomp to carry the soul to the other world, or to indicate the course of the sun.[283] That is, the scene really is an elaborate one for the birth of the sun (Horus) from his mother (Hathor, Mut, Isis, or Neit) and from the still more ultimate source indicated by the jar of seminal fluid which is on the head of the attendant of the heavenly mother. The mystic idea of mediation of heavenly life by the cosmic hermaphrodite, or of the ultimate as hermaphrodite, is represented. And the whole is a sign that the Queen of heaven gives out life and power like Ra. The same hermaphroditism appears in a hymn to Aton, who is ordinarily masculine, where it is said that the earth is nursed (at the breast) by the rays of Aton.[284]

In this sense, I am convinced, we should read the whole mass of nursing scenes from Egypt.[285] The spirit of the scenes is expressed in the passage already quoted from the Pyramid Texts, where the deceased is addressed:

> Ho, whence, pray, art thou come, my son, O king?
> He is come to these his two mothers, the two vultures,
> They of the long hair and hanging breasts,
> who are on the hill of *śḥśḥ*.
> They draw their breasts over the mouth of N.,
> but they do not wean him forever.[286]

In the New Kingdom this process is absorbed into the solar monotheism of Egypt by the devotee's saying to the masculine god of the sun, "Thy rays suckle every field." [287] That is, the figure or symbol of nursing is simply another convention for exemplifying the notion of the heavenly birth and sustentation, which is at the same time the mystic objective of all nature and of human religious experience. Again it is not for an outsider to appraise these scenes in detail.[288] But aside from the conventional scene of Hathor-Isis nursing

281. Erman, *Relig. Ägypt.*, 33.

282. Op. cit., 42. It is not a buckle but a uterus according to Budge, *Dictionary*, I, p. cxxxv, nos. 33 f. Budge discusses this in his *Osiris and the Egyptian Resurrection*, 1911, I, 276.

283. B. Bruyère, *Mert Seger à Deir el Médineh*, I, 1929, 117 (*Mém.* Inst., LVIII); Bruyère and C. Kuentz, *Tombes thébaines*, 1926, 130 f. (*Mém.* Inst., LIV).

284. Quoted by J. H. Breasted, *Dawn of Conscience*, 285.

285. G. Barton, "Milk," *HERE*, VIII, 637, has entirely inadequate evidence for his conclusion to the contrary.

286. Mercer, *Pyramid Texts*, I, 191, lines 1118*a*–1119*b*. Cf. Breasted, *Dawn of Conscience*, 81, 91; A. Erman, *The Literature of the Ancient Egyptians* [1927], 9. See above, p. 153.

287. Erman, 291.

288. A considerable number of these scenes will be found together in E. Chassinat, *Le Mammisi d'Edfou*, I, 1910, plates XIII–XV, XVII, XIX–XXI, XXV, XXX–XXXIII, XXXV–XXXVIII, XLIII f., XLIX, LII (*Mém.*, Inst., XVI). An interesting description of Horus as nursed by Isis and begotten in the embrace of Osiris from Ptolemaic times is in an inscription published by G. Daressy in *ASAE*, XVII (1917), 109. One variant is a bird (probably the Horus

Horus, either as a babe in her lap or as a larger youth standing beside her,[289] it is interesting to note that the hermaphrodite motif is shown in connection with the idea of nursing. The Nile, a masculine deity, appears with a man's beard and woman's breast, fig. 178;[290] he kneels on the ground pouring out water from a frog in his hand and pouring milk from his breast. The frog was itself in Egypt a symbol of fecundity and fertility, new life; as such it appears on one "bronze object in the British Museum at the end of a phallus"[291] and survives even into Christian times on lamps as a symbol of resurrection.[292] In a Ptolemaic scene from Denderah, fig. 179,[293] the Hathor cow is on the sun boat suckling a mystic in the usual way, but the cow is shown certainly to be also a bull. The background of lotus marks the whole as a scene of life giving. From the beginning of the first millennium before Christ comes fig. 181,[294] which represents the apotheosis of a king in the next world as he assumes the role of Horus and drinks from the breast of the goddess. The inscription reads in part: "Mayest thou be nourished with her life. May thy limbs be made firm, which have been fashioned by the great goddess, Semset of the house of provisions."

The symbol of nursing spread from Egypt to join with the Syrian symbol in the north. Miss Goff has directed me to two interesting seals. Fig. 180[295] shows a Phoenician

hawk, but the drawing is not clear) nursing the goddess' breast. Lanzone, *Dizionario*, plate CCCX, 2. See also G. Bénédite, *Le Temple de Philae*, 1893, plates II, XXIII, XXXVIII, and LX (*Mém.* Miss., XIII). Ordinarily the goddess in the sycamore tree pours out from the seminal vase to give new life to the deceased beneath the tree, but in at least one instance the king in a royal tomb at Thebes sucks at a great breast which hangs down from the tree: Arpag Mekhitarian, *Egyptian Painting*, transl. Stuart Gilbert, 1954, 38; cf. 78 (The Great Centuries of Painting, ed. Albert Skira).

289. The significance of both seems to me the same. The chronological age of one who is a "babe in Christ," for example, has nothing to do with the relationship implied.

290. From Lanzone, *Dizionario*, plate CLXXXXVIII, 3. He says on p. 524, n. 31, that he has this from Rosellini. See also a similar one, Bénédite, plate XXXVIII. Another such Nile, without the beard, has the same double flow of milk from the breast and water from a frog in the hand, and hence probably is also hermaphroditic: see Bénédite, plate XXXVI. The Nile is there nourishing a *ka*. Cf. G. Daressy, "Bas-Reliefs d'Athribis," *ASAE*, XVII (1917), 189. The hermaphroditic Niles are most clearly shown in Lanzone, *Dizionario*, CLXXXXVIII, 1 f., and CLXXXXIX, 2. In ibid., 3, the Nile lacks the beard but holds two jars of flowing liquid, which continue the hermaphroditic symbolism. Erman, *Relig. Ägypt.*, 16 f., points out the hermaphroditic character of the Niles, but in n. 1 to p. 17 (on p. 441), he despairs of explaining it. See above, pp. 176 f.

291. Budge, *Amulets and Superstititions*, 143 f.

292. Interesting material is to be found in Budge, *Osiris and the Egyptian Resurrection*, I, 279–281; Lanzone, *Dizionario*, 852–854. In these the frog is discussed as the goddess Heqet. See below, p. 193, and fig. 184. Lanzone publishes a Christian lamp with "I am the resurrection" written around the frog, and with a cross on its back. This is the meaning of the frogs I saw on lamps in the Pontifical Biblical Museum in Jerusalem, Israel. But whether these were Jewish or Christian lamps there was no way to tell. Three presumably Christian lamps with frogs are published in Oscar Wulff, *Altchristliche und mitelalterliche byzantinische und italienische Bildwerke*, I, nos. 1313–1315; see bibliography in Text volume at no. 1313 (Königliche Museen zu Berlin: Beschreibung der Bildwerke der christlichen Epochen). In F. X. Kraus, "Frosch," *Real-encyklopädie der christlichen Alterthümer*, 1882, I, 544 f., it appears that the frog could be the masculine phallus or the sign of a goddess, but in the latter case I strongly suspect hermaphroditic implications, as with the "Niles."

293. From *DE*, Planches, IV, plate 26, 9.

294. From W. M. Flinders Petrie, *The Palace of Apries* (*Memphis II*), 1909, plate XVII; see p. 21 (BSAE, XVII).

295. From C. de Vogüé in *RA*, Ser. II, Vol. XVII (1868), plate XIV, 20; cf. p. 438; see also M. A. Levy, *Siegel und Gemmen*, 1869, 30 f.

seal, in which a priest with Assyrian dress but Egyptian head covering sacrifices a horned female goat who, even as she is slaughtered, suckles four tiny human beings. Her "life" is thereby being doubly released. On the other seal an animal suckles her young between a tree on the one side and an ankh on the other—that is, the suckling is again emphasized with other symbols of the source of life.[296]

Even the conception of the *causa sui* who begets himself on his own mother is expressed in terms of nursing. We saw above [297] how the deceased as Osiris was addressed: "Adjusted(?) for this is thy breast of thy mother, thy breast of thy true self."

I. THE NEW LIFE

ON ANOTHER symbol which has often appeared for the fluid we must say a word in summary. Light has appeared even more commonly than the phallus in Egyptian remains and "illumination" is as universal a figure in religion as is erotic language. One design again brings the two together and, after the manner of religious symbolic pictures, much else also, fig. 183.[298] Here is the sun with its illumination combined with the Egyptian representation of baptism, a double pouring. The person is "sitting on a jar," but the pose suggests the conventional one of new birth or the divine child (although the finger is not at the mouth), and the two ankhs below show that this baptism is one in which the water is giving life, causing the birth, and that at the same time the baptism is what the early Christians called *phōtismos*, illumination.[299] It is significant that in a rite which makes the deceased into a sun god the water of his baptism is a flow of ankhs and *was* scepters,[300] which mean, according to Piankoff, wealth or prosperity. The two together might indicate "the full life." Similar scenes, where the water is shown as a series of ankhs, are familiar, and with one such the accompanying formula reads: "I have purified thee with life and good fortune, so that thou art rejuvenated like (thy) father Ra." [301]

296. C. Clermont-Ganneau, in *Journal Asiatique*, Ser. VIII, Vol. I (1883), 140; no. 16 on a plate bound in II, at p. 304. Below is a winged disk between two uraei, says Clermont-Ganneau with a question mark. He publishes it in a collection of "Seals Syrian, Phoenician, Aramaeam, etc.," without further identification. The name is Astoretᵉoz, which he translates "He of whom Astarte is the power" or "the salvation."

297. See above, p. 144, n. 15.

298. From G. Jéquier, *Les Frises d'objets des sarcophages du Moyen Empire*, 1921, 313 (*Mém.* Inst., XLVII). See also Norman de G. Davies, *Five Theban Tombs*, 1913, 24, and plate XXI (ASE, XXI).

299. Cf. *BD*, ed. Renouf and Naville, 339: "He drinks the running water of the stream, he shines like a star in the sky." This, it is said, will happen to the one observing the instructions of the Book.

300. Cf. A. M. Blackman, "Sacramental Ideas and Usages in Ancient Egypt," *PSBA*, XL (1918), 57–66, 86–91. The idea that divine nature and existence are represented by peace is one of the constants of our symbolism. See above, II, 124–133.

301. Lepsius, *Denkmäler*, III, 124*d;* cf. Blackman, 87, and plate v at p. 90. Parrot's essay on the "cool water" as refreshing from the pain of thirst in hell seems, as we go on, increasingly unsatisfactory (above, p. 147). "O Osiris, Erster der Westlichen: dargebracht wird dir dieses dein kühles Wasser, das in diesem Lande ist, das alle lebenden Dinge erzeugt." The water, the quotation goes on, is the source of Osiris' life, and yet the water is his water; from H. Junker, "Die Stundenwachen in den Osirismysterien, nach den Inschriften von Dendera, Edfu und Philae," *Denkschrift der K. Akad. der Wissenschaften in Wien*, Phil. Hist. Klasse, LIV (1910), 79 f.; also in G. Roeder, *Urkunden zur Religion des alten Ägypten*, 1923, 40.

With this went the longing for purification which is likewise a mystic constant. Indeed, these baptism scenes have usually been taken for purification scenes by Egyptologists, certainly the truth if not the whole truth.[302] Much of the ritual is concerned with purification. Naville paraphrases a papyrus fragment of the Book of the Dead:

> At each pylon there is a dialogue between the deceased and doorkeeper, who asks whether the deceased has been purified, in what water, with what oil he has been anointed, which garment he wears, which stick he holds in his hand.[303]

The ritualistic ceremony of purifying is almost universal, and very generally the happy exclamation "I am pure" accompanies it.[304] "Every son maketh the purification for his father," says a line on a libation vase of the Saïtic period, the long inscription of which is chiefly concerned with the life-giving power of the divine water of Nut, the water of the Nile, the milk of Isis, and the like.[305] Purity, power, life, and ability to give life, are blended in the gift of Ptah Tatunen to Rameses II and III:

> I look at thee, and my heart is rejoiced; I embrace thee in my golden arms; I wrap thee in life everlasting and pure; I endow thee with strength and happiness; I make enter into thee joy, ecstasy, peace, pleasure, and delectations. I grant it to thee that thy heart shall become young again like mine; I have elected thee, I have chosen thee, I have put within thee a perfect heart and excellent words; there is absolutely nothing, from ancient times to the present, which thou dost not know; thou makest the inhabitants of the earth alive by thy wisdom.[306]

This is a small part of the divine gifts to the king cited in the inscription. Each individual needed purification to face the dread judgment of Osiris or Thoth and their assistants. The ritual of The Book of the Dead is largely concerned with phrases which will guarantee this purification:

> And I, entering and ascertaining who cometh forth through that gate of the Inviolate one, I purify myself at that great stream where my ills are made to cease, and that which is wrong in me is pardoned and the spots which were on my body upon earth are effaced.[307]

Such a rite continued to seem important down into Ptolemaic times. In the excavation of West Hermoupolis (Touna el-Gebel) a house, perhaps to be dated just before the

302. The article by A. M. Blackman, "Purification (Egyptian)," *HERE*, X, 476–482, is excellent. See also his "Some Notes on the Ancient Egyptian Practice of Washing the Dead," and "The House of the Morning," *JEA*, V (1918), 117–124, 148–165.

303. In Renouf's and Naville's translation, p. 295.

304. See A. Wiedemann, "Bronze Circles and Purification Vessels in Egyptian Temples," *PSBA*, XXIII (1901), 263–274.

305. P. Pierret, "Libation Vase of Osor-Ur preserved in the Museum of the Louvre (No. 908)," *PSBA*, 1880, 57–60.

306. E. Naville, "Le Décret de Phtah Totunen en faveur de Ramsès II et de Ramsès III," *TSBA*, VII (1882), 122, line 7. I have translated his French version into English.

307. *BD*, ed. Renouf and Naville, 155 (chap. LXXXVI); cf. 165 (chap. XCVII), 175 (chap. CV). Cf. A. M. Blackman, "Sacramental Ideas and Usages in Ancient Egypt," *PSBA*, XL (1918), 57–66.

Roman conquest, was discovered with an elaborately painted funerary room, one scene in which is shown in fig. 186.[308] Here the deceased (who wears sometimes Greek costume, sometimes Egyptian) is in Greek clothing getting the divine flow of fluid from Thoth and Horus, while her ka or ba, a black silhouette, watches. Above the woman is the falcon; largely destroyed, which may have been thought of as Horus again as in another scene in the same room,[309] but which in any case seems to be the sun. The deceased actually continues to receive the fluid of the sun god.

It is extremely hard to say how much connection all this craving for purity had to do with practical ethics. Blackman has shown abundantly that purification was essentially a process of rebirth in the vital fluid of Osiris,[310] although he can establish little connection between ethical practice and religious aspiration for purity. In spite of his excellent material,[311] in which are gathered the statements of Egyptian ethical idealism, the sanction of hell, and the rest, Egyptian monuments as a whole give the overwhelming impression that ceremonial purification and rebirth are in themselves adequate to take care of man's purity and to conduct him safely through his posthumous ordeals. "I have come out of the womb; I have been an infant like my father; there are no perverse actions of mine in the various events of my lot." [312] A small but highly important body of gnomic literature has remained,[313] but the absence of connection between it and the symbolism in the graves and temples is conspicuous. It is worldly wisdom, moral advice of a fine, sometimes lofty, character but advice, singularly, given without reference to divine will, or to divine sanction here or in the coming judgment. The powerful section of the advice of an early Pharaoh to his son is in another vein,[314] as well as the devout attitude taken by Amen-em-Apt. In the latter, a fear of the coming judgment in various forms, including the lake of fire, is vivid,[315] for the gods are close watchers of man's conduct.[316] Hence moral conduct has divine sanction, and man not only must watch his conduct but must carefully observe the divine rites,[317] and still more he must pray to God for strength and the necessities of life,[318] commit himself personally to God's care,[319] even to "seating oneself on the two arms of the

308. From Sami Gabra, *Rapport sur les fouilles d'Hermoupolis Ouest* (Touna el-Gebel), Cairo, 1941, plate XIII, 2; cf. pp. 44 f.

309. Ibid., plate XVI, 2; cf. p. 48.

310. In his studies quoted in notes 299 and 302; see also *RT*, XXXIX (1921), 44–78.

311. "Righteousness (Egyptian)," *HERE*, X, 793–800.

312. *BD*, ed. Renouf and Naville, 347 (chap. CLXX).

313. A collection of some of this material was made by Budge, *The Teaching of Ȧmen-em Ȧpt, Son of Kanekht*, 1924. See also Gressmann, *AOTB*, I, 33–46. A recent discussion of the subject, where references to much material are to be found, is Hermann Moderau, "Die Moral der alten Ägypter nach Kapitel 125 des Totenbuches," *Archiv für Orientforschung*, XII (1937/9), 258–268. He shows how a few people seem to have had a real conception of divine justice when Osiris came to take the place of Ra, or the Ra-king, as the guardian of justice. But this seems to have had little effect upon religion in general. "Trotz des strengen Totengerichts kein Gebet um Gnade in den negativen Konfessionen" (p. 268).

314. A. H. Gardiner, "New Literary Works from Ancient Egypt," *JEA*, I (1914), 27, 13.

315. Budge, *The Teaching of Ȧmen-em Ȧpt*, vss. 96–101; 150, vss. 131–133; 157, vs. 229.

316. Ibid., 162, vs. 292; 163 f., vss. 321–328; 166, vss. 358–362.

317. Ibid., 151, vss. 144–147.

318. Ibid., 154, vss. 185–188.

319. Ibid., 159, vs. 253.

God." [320] For "the love of God is more precious (and) estimable than the reverence of the nobleman"; [321] God is the builder, whoever may mix the mud and straw; [322] man's mind is the very nose of God.[323]

Interesting as this text is, it is difficult to use it for any generalization about Egyptian religion, for its religious ethic is unique in Egypt, and it is apparently the product of foreign influence.[324]

Nor do I feel any moral reality in the "Negative Confessions" listed in the Book of the Dead, by which at each of the forty-two gates the soul professes that it is innocent of the sin against which the watcher of that gate is guarding.[325] The list itself is again a splendid code of morality. But there is no indication that the man who glibly made the confessions was ever guided by them in his personal conduct with his slaves or fellows. As Budge points out, the deceased prays: "Blot out my evil deeds, and put away my culpable deeds committed upon earth, and destroy anything of evil that clings to me, and let there be nothing in me to alienate you from me. Let me pass through the Åmmeḥet, and enter Restau, and pass through the secret gates of Åmentt." The prayer is answered, the correct words are pronounced; and the very avengers of divine Truth say to him, "Come, for we have blotted out thy evil deeds, and put away thy sin and thy culpable deeds committed upon earth, and we have destroyed every evil thing that clung to thee upon earth. Enter therefore into Restau, and pass through the secret pylons of Åmentt."

That is, in spite of the great emphasis upon the final judgment, it is hard to find a trace of ethical sensitivity or deep moral conscience, at least conscience with a religious compulsion, in the Egyptian religious literature or drawings. Egyptian religion was not "ethical religion" of the sort taught by the prophets of Israel. Ethical conduct was of course

320. Ibid., 173, vs. 457.

321. Ibid., 177, vss. 525–526.

322. Ibid., 174 f., vss. 482–489.

323. Ibid., 174, vss. 473 f.

324. The dissertation of R. O. Kevin, *The Wisdom of Amen-em-Apt and Its Possible Dependence upon the Hebrew Book of Proverbs*, 1931, reprinted from *The Journal of the Society of Oriental Research*, XIV (1931), 115–157, gives the bibliography of this disputed text. Breasted, *The Dawn of Conscience*, 1933, makes much of the document in the development of his thesis that religion in the sense of religious ethics was first conceived in Egypt. See especially pp. 321 ff. That this element was present in Egypt is clear, but that it took the central place in Egyptian religion to which Breasted assigned it seems to me still undemonstrated. As for the Egypt which the Greeks came to know, Breasted admits that the ethical aspects were in the last thousand years replaced by the "magical," which is saying in his own terms what I go on to say above in mine. And the "magical," that is, the efficacy of rite and ritual, seems to me a much more important element throughout Egyptian religion than Breasted implies. The same point of view was anounced almost simultaneously by A. Moret at the Congress of Orientalists at Rome in 1935, but not printed until later: "Le Doctrine de Maât," *Revue d' Egyptologie*, IV (1940), 1–14.

325. See for example *BD*, ed. Renouf and Naville, 214–216, chap. cxxv; see also pp. 216–220; Budge (above, n. 313), 30–45; Gressmann, *AOTB*, I, 9–12. A. H. Gardiner, "Ethics and Morality (Egyptian)," *HERE*, V, 479, says of these impressions: "Their aim, so far from being an ethical one, was essentially, though perhaps not quite consciously, anti-ethical. Accepting the prevalent belief that happiness in the hereafter is conditioned by a previous life of innocence upon earth, they proceeded to elaborate an incantation such as might hoodwink the Divine Judge and enable the dead man to evade the natural consequences of his sins." It is such a state of affairs that made G. F. Moore remark that morality and religion were never combined but to the hurt of both.

important. The gods were righteous and loved righteousness,[326] and social injustice was deplored,[327] but the efficacy of the ritual was complete.[328] To be sure, one had to be careful to have a tomb, proper embalming and burial, and proper tendance of one's remains by one's children.[329] But the ethical agonies of the penitential psalms, of Christian liturgy (or the mourner's bench), and of some Babylonian literature are entirely removed by the placid efficacy of the ritual.[330]

There are, however, other values in religion than those commonly regarded as social and ethical. I must remind the reader again of Jung's remark that the purpose of organized religion is to anticipate the questions of the soul with answers which satisfy its possible cravings, so that the soul does not have to go out, alone into the Alone, to face reality. There is no religion in history which seems to me so completely to have done this for its devotees as the Egyptian. And it was probably the very perfection of its symbolism which made it so attractive to men of the hellenistic and Roman world, who saw their own questions and longings anticipated in it, and answered. Yet the efficacy of this symbolism suffered when transplanted. For where it was challenged by rival myths and symbols, it could not act so potently as during the successive millennia in Egypt when the outside world touched only the periphery of society, and the child grew up in harmonic resolutions before the discords of life had begun to jangle within him.[331] Of course the tragedies of oppression, hunger, social injustice, and personal relations must have been as common in ancient Egypt as at any time since. Yet none of these, so far as we know, made men question the ultimate truth of their religion. Social problems never seem to have become cosmic for Egyptians, at least to an extent which affected the form in which religion presented itself to the people. Thirty years ago when I was studying kingship [332] as it appeared in the ancient world, I was puzzled by the fact that while the oriental kings, Babylonian and Persian and to some extent those of Israel, were representatives of God or the gods insofar

326. Gardiner, 479 f. See also Breasted, *Dawn of Conscience*, 191 f., 221, 249, 259. But on Breasted's material see above, note 324.

327. See the "Meditations and Complaints" in A. Erman, *The Literature of the Ancient Egyptians* [1927], 85–131.

328. Even to providing prosperity and peace in this life: Erman, 140, no. 3. On the efficacy of the rites see also G. Jéquier, *Les Frises d'objets des sarcophages du Moyen Empire*, 1921, 314 (*Mém.* Inst., XLVII).

329. Budge, op. cit. (above, n. 313), 239, quotes a fine passage from "The Teaching of Ani" on this matter. A single confession of sin is quoted from one of the Theban Tombs by Breasted, *Dawn of Conscience*, 317: "*Punish me not for my many sins.* I am one ignorant of his own body, I am a man without understanding." But here again the unique difference of the instance only emphasizes the opposite spirit of Egyptian religion as a whole.

330. A possible exception is the poem quoted in Erman, 89:

Lo, my name is abhorred, Lo, more than the odor of carrion
On days in summer, when the sky is hot, etc.

331. This does not mean that there is no trace of skepticism in Egyptian remains. Drinking Songs 2 and 3 from the New Kingdom, quoted by Erman, 251–254 (see his comments) are of the universal *carpe diem* type. But I insist again that the religion of Egypt soared untroubled above such frivolity. A more serious exception is the brief penitential hymn to Ra quoted by Erman, 307. See also pp. 308, 311.

332. See my "The Political Philosophy of Hellenistic Kingship," *Yale Classical Studies*, I (1928), 53–102; "Kingship in Early Israel," *JBL*, XLVIII (1929), 169–205.

as they presented themselves to men as the incarnation of the law and justice of God, this legal and ethical aspect of the divine king did not appear in Egypt at all. The reason now seems to me to be that the gods of Egypt were essentially metaphysical rather than legal and ethical and that man came into relation with them by rising into a new nature rather than by trying to reproduce divine righteousness and justice on earth. Christians came later to try to combine these two approaches to religion, as did hellenized Jews before them. Individual Orientals must have added mystical aspiration to their legalism, just as individual Egyptians seem occasionally to have added legalism and divine righteousness to their metaphysical mysticism. All I am saying here is that the religion of Egypt seems as strangely to lack the ethical and legal approach as in general did Jews of the Old Testament the mystical. The motive of the love of God appears in the Egyptian writings, but it is triumphant announcement on a cosmic scale:

> All people were happy, cheerful of mind, and with glad hearts; all men cried out for joy, and all people adored his (Osiris') goodness: "How deeply we love him! His goodness traverseth the hearts, and great in all is the love of him." [333]

And the tone occasionally becomes vividly erotic:

> Love of Thee [Amon, the god of Thebes, the ithyphallic Min-Amon-Re] is diffused throughout the Two Lands, and thy rays shine in the eyes. (It is) the well-being(?) of mankind when thou arisest; the beasts wax languid when thou shinest.
>
> Thou art beloved in the southern sky, and art pleasant in the northern sky. Thy beauty captivateth the hearts, and the love of thee maketh languid the arms. Thy fair form maketh feeble the hands; the heart forgetteth when one looketh upon thee.

The longing is not in vain:

> The gods make obeisance unto thy majesty, and extol the might of their creator. They rejoice when he that begat them draweth nigh, and they say unto thee: "Welcome, in peace!" [334]

Here is the ecstasy of gratification, no uncertainty of ethical failure. The Egyptian people had their inconceivable duration and essential changelessness not merely because of their geographical isolation but also because they had a religion which solved the problems of their souls. The devotee not only worshiped the gods: he was to be identified with them through the rites.[335] Such is the power of effective religious symbolism. The

333. Erman, 144: from a hymn to Osiris on a tombstone of the XVIIIth Dynasty, now in Paris.

334. Erman, 286. These hymns, pp. 282–288, are worth careful study throughout.

335. The identification of the deceased with Osiris is proverbial in Egyptian religion. But we have seen that he was to be fully deified by taking on all the various types of divine manifestation. A. M. Blackman, "The Rite of Opening the Mouth in Ancient Egypt and Babylonia," *JEA*, X (1924), 47–59.

true mystic was not only "justified before the great god": he was "begotten of the worthy," [336] while the only dread was that the divine seeds might not be implanted within him.[337] Indeed the effect made by describing the terrors of the "damned" in Egypt was like that of a sermon on hell in orthodox Christian circles. It was a gruesome pleasure, but nevertheless intense, to visualize the terrors from which the saved would *escape*.[338] And the dead man with the right passwords in Egypt had no need for self-searching: he would surely escape, not by his own merits, but by those of the formulae. I cannot see in this how Egyptian religion could have been an active ethical force in daily life. Its function was quite different, the allaying of the fears and uncertainties of life and death. As the prophet Amos was well aware, religion always tends to become ethically weaker as its ceremonies of purification and absolution become more automatically effective.

J. OSIRIS

TWO POINTS must be stressed as we leave this ancient Egyptian material for a time to go into the Greek world and then to see what happened in the hellenistic mixing bowl to all that we have considered. First, the Greeks still had Ammon, with whom Alexander and the Ptolemies could be identified, while Thoth and Anubis, Min and Bes continued to have functions. But the functions of all gods were by that time ancillary to Osiris, or to the trinity of Osiris, Isis, and Horus. Ra and Atum and the other great solar or suprasolar gods had been almost entirely swallowed up. This is a phenomenon already noticeably begun in the transition from the Pyramid Texts to the Book of the Dead. Osiris simply took into himself all the values we have been encountering in the names of the other great gods. But we have seen those values so fluently transferable from one god to another even in ancient Egypt that it is no surprise to find them finally settling in Osiris. For example, the symbolism in early times for the begetting of Osiris by Ra was used likewise for the begetting of Horus by Osiris, or for the primitive pairs begotten by Atum. And in temples and tombs of later periods where the concern is more definitely for Osiris than for Ra this same symbolism continues. Again it is the symbol, in this case the divine begetting, which persists through god after god and myth after myth—persists with unchanged value. The important thing is the begetting, usually in a special way, some miraculous, wonderful way. God the begetter and God the begotten were the basic constants in all the myths and names. So Min was associated with Osiris [339] and with Horus.[340] The ithyphallic figure of

336. A. H. Gardiner, "The Tomb of Amenemhet, High-Priest of Amon," *ZaeS*, XLVII (1910), 91.

337. "Ihr Abscheu ist, wenn der Arm des Gottes auf sie fällt, und der Gottesschatten [a name for the ithyphallic Min: see author's note] sie geschlechtlich missbraucht. Nicht tritt sein Samen in (sie) ein." H. Kees, "Ein alter Götterhymnus als Begleittext zur Opfertafel," *ZaeS*, LVII (1922), 110.

338. Hermann Kees, *Aegypten*, 1933, 321 (Kulturgeschichte des alten Orients, I), ascribes the lack of horror in representations of the underworld by Egyptians to their lack of imagination. I suspect that it was Kees who lacked imagination.

339. On the relation of Min and the ithyphallic Amon-Ra to Osiris see G. Parthey, *Plutarch über Jsis und Osiris*, 1850, 178.

340. The ithyphallic Min figure was also used for Horus. See A. Piankoff, "Le Naos D29 du Musée du Louvre," *Revue d'Egyptologie*, I (1933), 168 and 177.

Osiris was often represented within a snake, as in fig. 182,[341] indicating that he lies thus in the lower world. Carried on from earlier patterns, in drawings at Denderah, Osiris frequently lies ithyphallic on the lion couch. He may be simply ithyphallic,[342] or Isis in the form of a hawk may be drawing impregnating seed from his phallus.[343] In this way the scene is universally interpreted: but I cannot resist pointing out that the gesture of masturbation of Osiris in fig. 184 [344] cannot be without significance in view of the Egyptian emphasis upon creation by masturbation which we have already encountered. Here Isis as a hawk receives the seed of the dead Osiris who still can masturbate. The frog, whether as masculine or feminine potency, is at his feet, and Hathor at his head. The notion of begetting by masturbation was evidently important at Denderah, since another scene shows three deities in the same act.[345] It is clear in all these that Isis' role in the begetting was quite subordinated to the primeval notion of the procession from the Self-caused and Self-sufficient. The accompanying texts throw little light on the meaning of these pictures. But by this time one may be allowed to presume that in the figure of Osiris in later cults the old religious values were continued. No special meaning of the phallic imagery when applied to Osiris can be reconstructed. His general connection with fertility is familiar, and certainly the longing to be identified with Osiris meant to the devout a personal longing for life. There is a prayer to Osiris, "Thou mummy with the long phallus," [346] and the conception is again powerfully expressed in the statement already quoted: "I am Osiris, the lord of the heads that live . . . with a phallus which goeth to the remotest limits [where] men and women [live].[347] Breasted says of the pictures of Osiris as an ithyphallic mummy that they "show him even in death as still possessed of generative power." [348] And it is a fair guess that Osiris' erection may itself be a symbol of the resurrection, as Bruyère explains the erection of Seb.[349]

Osiris as the fertility god or source of life might be pictured as a mummy, from whose body vegetation comes, fig. 185,[350] but the more common form was the burial of an Osiris image stuffed with grain or with grain and dirt,[351] and these images were usually ithy-

341. From H. Frankfort, *The Cenotaph of Seti I at Abydos, 1933*, II, plate XXXI. A figure wrapped in a snake was an ideograph in Egyptian for eternity: see Budge, *An Egyptian Hieroglyphic Dictionary*, I, p. XCVIII, no. 29.

342. Flinders Petrie, *Denderah, 1898*, 1900, II, plate XXV*a* (first at left in fourth row).

343. See *DE*, Planches, IV, 27, no. 9: cf. for a discussion of these scenes and their earlier parallels A. Wiedemann, "Notes et remarques," *RT*, XX, N.S., IV (1898), 134–136. See also G. Daressy, "Les Temples d'Abydos," *RT*, XXI (1899), 4; Mariette, *Dendérah*, IV, plates 68–70, 88–90; Erman, *Relig. Ägypt.*, 70, and cf. F. Guilmant, *Le Tombeau de Ramsès IX*, 1907, plates XC f. (*Mém.* Inst., XV). See below, pp. 195 f.

344. From Budge, *Osiris and the Egyptian Resurrection*, I, 280.

345. See *DE*, Planches, IV, plate 27, no. 10. And see above, p. 177.

346. Quoted by Erman in *ZaeS*, XXXVIII (1900), 31.

347. *BD*, 234 (chap. LXIX).

348. *Dawn of Conscience*, 98; cf. 101. On p. 99 Breasted says: "The Nile was but the source and visible symbol of that fertility of which Osiris was the personification."

349. B. Bruyère, *Mert Seger à Deir el Médineh*, 1930, 200 (*Mém.*, Inst., LVIII).

350. From Erman, *Relig. Ägypt.*, 40, fig. 29.

351. M. A. Murray, *The Osireion at Abydos*, 1904, 27 (Egyptian Research Account, IX).

phallic.[352] That is, there seems much more reason for the Greeks to associate phallic worship with Osiris than was at first supposed by Egyptologists.[353] To the Greek emphasis upon the phallus of Osiris in the Nile (which would seem to connect the fertilizing power of the Nile with this imagery) we shall return.

Hence the rising sun is hailed as Horus, "who travels over the heavens, thou child who came out of the phallus, thou fire-child, with radiating brilliance, who drives away darkness and shadow." [354] Erman says he does not know what the phallus here means, but the statement suggests that the visible Sun God who rises is a birth from a more ultimate principle, whose essential characteristic is its power of light-generation. An interesting illustration of the mingling of conceptions of Osiris and Ra is the Book of the Traversing of Eternity, as presented on the stele of an Osirian priest. This priest not only is in the presence of Osiris, but is definitely united with Ra in the eternal solar cycle they represent.[355]

For our purpose, accordingly, the problem of the relation of Osiris and Ra, Nile and Sun, may be ignored. What is important is to see that in the Egypt the Greeks came to know that solar imagery was associated with the water-stream and both were treated as variants of the single divine stream of light, life, and fertilization on which the hope of man depended. In spite of the utter difference in approach and type of figure used, it seems likely that this stream was for Egyptians what "Grace" was for later Christians, and the two seem as closely similar in their psychological value for the devotee as they are different in their symbolic presentation. The Gnostics, as we shall see, made the same identification.[356] Budge has assured us that we may be certain that the phallus of Osiris "played a very prominent part in the beliefs of the Egyptians concerning resurrection." [357] Indeed, the confusion of mythological persons and functions becomes clear only as we see that mythology was, for the Egyptians, of but secondary importance. Of consistently primary importance was the basic desire, so deep as to be often subconscious, to represent visibly that the ultimate, by whatever name, is the source of existence and life for the universe and is available, by ritualistic or mystical appropriation, to the individual in this world and the next. Of this ultimate source the phallus was a recurrent, because vividly expressive, symbol.

This leads us to the second matter that should be considered before we leave ancient Egypt, the problem of how much all this was purely funerary and eschatological, and how far it went into the everyday life of the people. Even in the funerary material we have frequently met phrases which show that the power of the god, even his phallus, was available to give life not only to the deceased but to all people and districts of Egypt. And in

352. J. G. Wilkinson, *A Second Series of the Manners and Customs of the Ancient Egyptians*, 1841, II, 300, n. I saw many of these in the Egyptian Museum in Cairo.

353. See Murray, 27–29.

354. Published by Erman, *ZaeS*, XXXVIII (1900), 21; cf. 25.

355. W. Wreszinski, "Das Buch vom Durchwandeln der Ewigkeit nach einer Stele im Vatikan," *ZaeS*, XLV (1908), 111–122.

356. See below, VI, 92–106.

357. Budge, *Osiris and the Egyptian Resurrection*, II, 96, with references in n. 2. Cf., for Osiris in Pompeii, ibid., 295.

the hymn to Osiris quoted above [358] we have an address to the gods which seems much more appropriate for the living than for the dead, a thoroughly mystic prayer. For mysticism is anticipated eschatology, life eternal achieved here and now.

It is extremely difficult to say how far this went into common life. But certainly the Egyptian life was full of festivals and rituals for the living, and if in these mystic aspiration was largely expressed in liturgy and symbol, there is every reason to suppose that the worship addressed to such gods as we have met would be largely designed to get fertility and security, life in the fullest sense, for the living as it was for the dead.

Blackman [359] has correctly identified the meaning of the "cool water" of Egyptian embalming and funerary rites. At the annual re-enactment of the embalming of Osiris, he recalls, such water was poured out to the god hourly through the night, a libation which represented not only washing but revivification. The latter conception is made especially clear in the formula for the second hour:

> O Osiris Khentamenthes, take to thee this thy cool water which is in this land, which begets all living things, all things which this land gives. It is the begetter of all living things, yea, all things issue from it. Thou partakest thereof, thou livest thereon, thou art healthy thereby. Thou breathest the air that is in it (the water). It hath begotten thee, and thou comest forth living on all things thou desirest.[360]

The formula of the third hour represents Osiris as reborn from the water of the second hour, when he is now Ra and solar. Indeed Blackman (p. 75 f.) properly connects this ritual with formulae in which the water of libation and purification is definitely made the seminal fluid of both Osiris and Atum, the fluid in which the king, later any initiate after the popularization of rites, was reborn as the son of the god.[361]

This sort of mysticism, and what it meant to the devotee, is amazingly set before us in the magnificent Songs of Isis and Nephtys recently published.[362] Here is a long ritualistic poem recited by two virgins ceremoniously attired and with the names Isis and Nephtys inscribed on their arms. The recitation took place at the festival of the Two Kites in the temple of Osiris and in his presence:

358. See above, p. 191.

359. A. M. Blackman, "Sacramental Ideas and Usages in Ancient Egypt," *RT*, XXXIX (1921), 67. For further documentation see John Lewis, "The Mother Worship in Egypt," *Journal of the Manchester Egyptian and Oriental Society*, XI (1924), 51 f.

360. Op. cit., 75.

361. Chnum, the creator god, is discussed as twofold by Erman (*Relig. Ägypt.*, 44), one in the form of creator and the other as the god (or gods), "Masters of the cool water." In view of the seminal meaning of this phrase, I do not see that the two are not both the same god, Chnum, who begets all creation. The libation in funerary rites is repeatedly described: "This libation is for thee, O Osiris . . . it cometh forth from thy son, it cometh forth from Horus"; see Budge, *The Liturgy of Funerary Offerings*, 1909, 51 f., 87, 96 f.

362. R. O. Faulkner, "The Bremner-Rhind Papyrus-I: A. The Songs of Isis and Nephthys," *JEA*, XXII (1936), 121–140. References are made by column and verse as there given. This was published earlier by Budge in *Archaeologia*, LII (1890), 398–414; 457–491.

O fair Stripling, come to thine house;
For a very long time we have not seen thee.[363]
Come thou: O young Child, in peace,
O our Lord, that we may see thee;
Consort thou with us after the manner of a male.[364]
O thou who art fair of countenance, lord of love,
O Bull who impregnates cows,
Come, O Sistrum-player, gleaming of countenance,
O thou who art uniquely youthful, beauteous to behold,
Lord among women,
Male of cows,
O Child, master of beauty,
O that we might see thee in thy former shape.[365]

Such, at much greater length, was the song addressed to Osiris. But it was certainly more than an address to the god. The mystic drama must have represented vividly to the devotee the craving of the Female Principle for impregnation. And as the mystic identified himself or herself with the actresses, the two virgins depilated for the sacred marriage, his or hers was the vicarious experience of divine impregnation from the divine fluid. On a higher level the more advanced mystic, who had achieved identification with Osiris, might have the still more exalted experience of cosmic begetting. For at the top of this ascent the mystic became himself the Light of the World whose light was life.

The Egyptian, Mesopotamian, and Syrian material we have been considering has all been studied for its possible contribution to an understanding of the divine fluid in Greco-Roman syncretism. The material is so full for the religion of ancient Egypt that it seemed extremely important to see from it just what it was which Greeks later identified so enthusiastically with their own religious objectives. For the phallic symbols of Egypt [366] were the symbols which, we shall see, from the first made the Greeks confident that Osiris

363. Ibid., I, 10 f.

364. Ibid., II, 7–9.

365. Ibid., III, 5–12.

366. I am under no illusion that I have done more than open the subject of phallicism in Egyptian religion. Many other symbols seem to me to have phallic meaning. For example one recalls the omnipresent lotus, which gives life; which is held to the face, especially by women, when it gives them life, just as do the ankh-hands from the sun. It is from the lotus that the seated figure of infancy frequently springs; cf. *DE*, Planches, I, plate 95, nos. 1, 3; E. Chassinat, *Le Mammisi d'Edfou*, I, 1910, plate XLV (*Mém.* Inst., XVI); G. Maspero, *The Dawn of Civilization*, 1894, 136. The last seems to me decisive: the figure of birth can emerge from the lotus as it does from the erect phallus. Erman, *Relig. Ägypt.*, 62, connects this figure with one of the many myths of creation. One myth has the young sun god emerge from an egg, another from a lotus growing out of the *Urwasser*, and by another the Horus child is on the back of a cow swimming in the *Urwasser*. All are birth stories, figuring the origin of the "Self-Begotten." The lotus is used on scarabs to represent the "fluid of life"; W. M. F. P[etrie], "The Grenfell Collection of Scarabs," *Ancient Egypt*, 1916, 26. But if the lotus is sometimes phallic, is it always so? We must leave the subject of phallicism in Egyptian religion in general to Egyptologists. To Serapion our design represented the rising sun: Plutarch, *De Pyth. Orac.*, 12 (400A); cf. *On Isis*, 11 (355B).

was but the Egyptian name for Dionysus. Clearly the phallic meaning is something which the Greek wine god carried with him and which, with virtually no Greek texts on the meaning of that symbol in Greek religion, we have found much illuminated in Egyptian usage. In the following volume we shall trace the symbolism of the divine fluid through the Greco-Roman world and examine its relevancy to the Jewish remains.

[*The contents of Volume V is indexed at the end of Volume VI.*]

LIST OF ILLUSTRATIONS

ILLUSTRATIONS

Discussion of the objects or designs listed below will be found in the text as indicated by the page numbers in parentheses. Acknowledgments for the figures individually likewise appear there. Names of museums, collections, etc. accompanying the captions give the present location of the item designated.

FIGURE

FIGURE

ILLUSTRATIONS

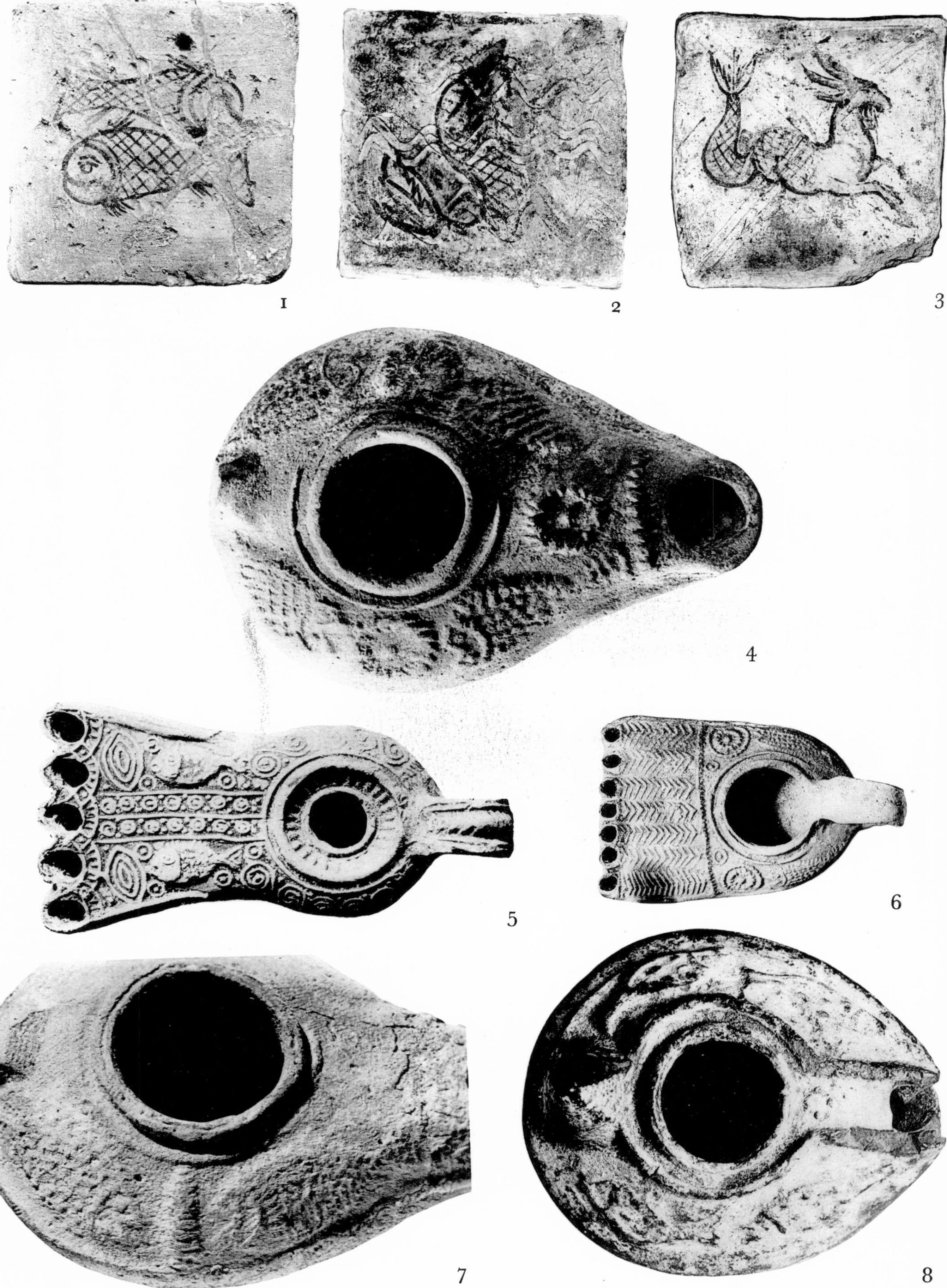

I
2
3
4
5
6
7
8

9

10

11

12

13

14

15

16

17

18

19

20

21

22

23

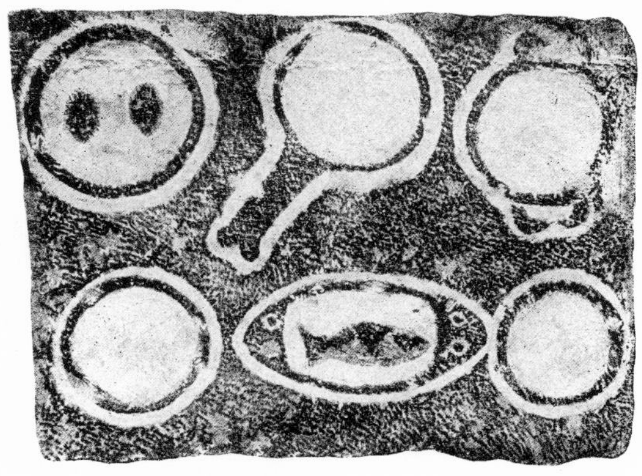
24

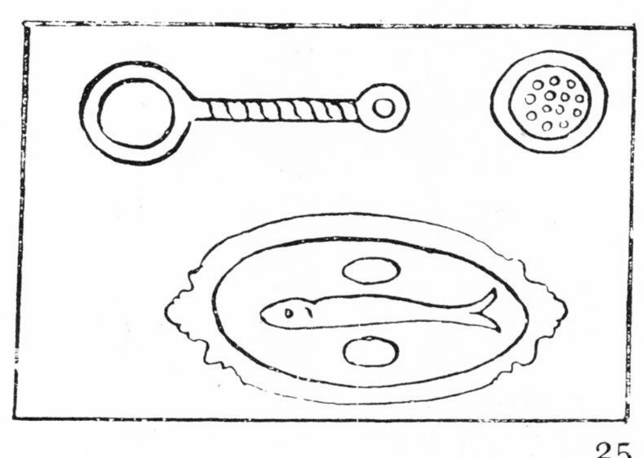
25

26

27

28

30

29

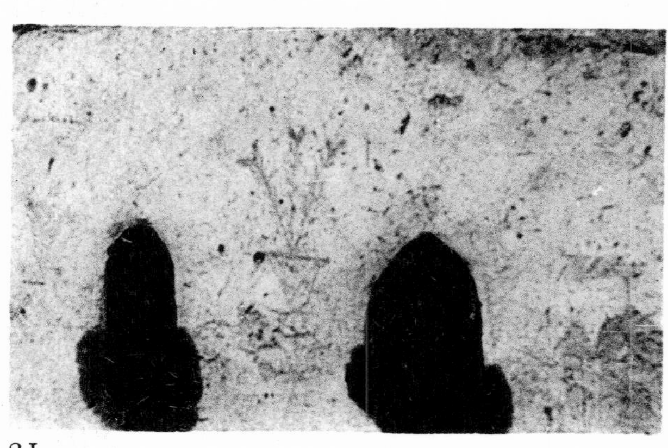
31

32

33

34

35

36

37

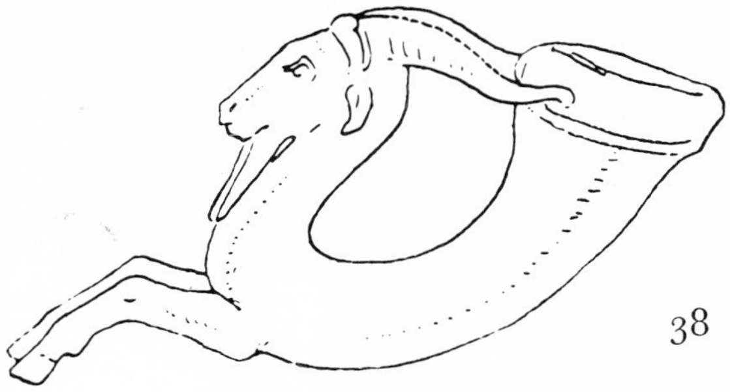

38

39

40

41

42

43

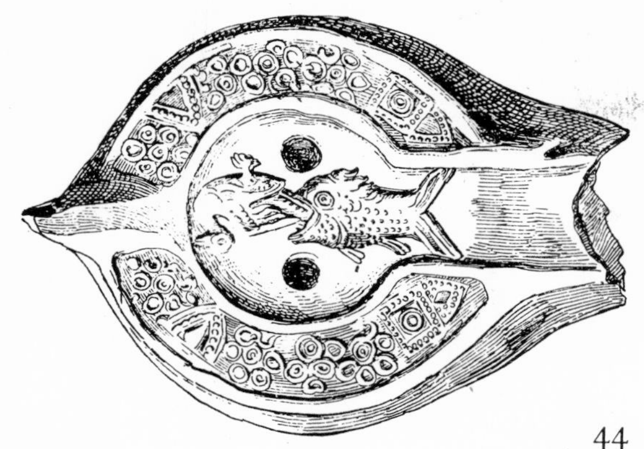

44

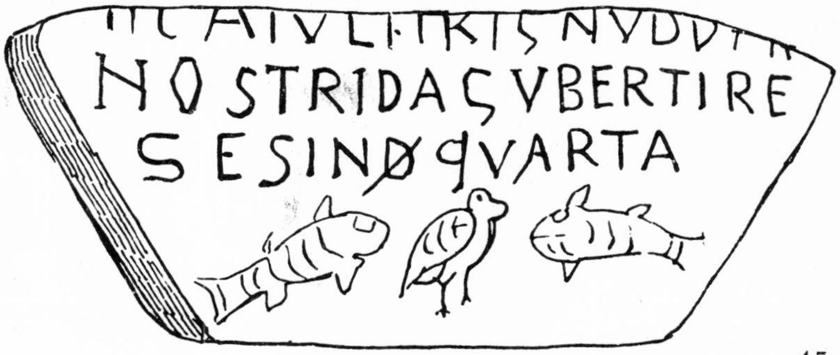

NO STRIDAS VBERTIRE
SESINØ QVARTA

45

46

47

48

49

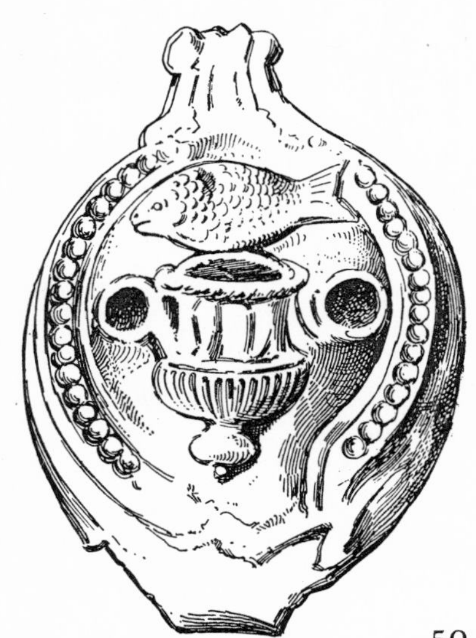

50

51

52

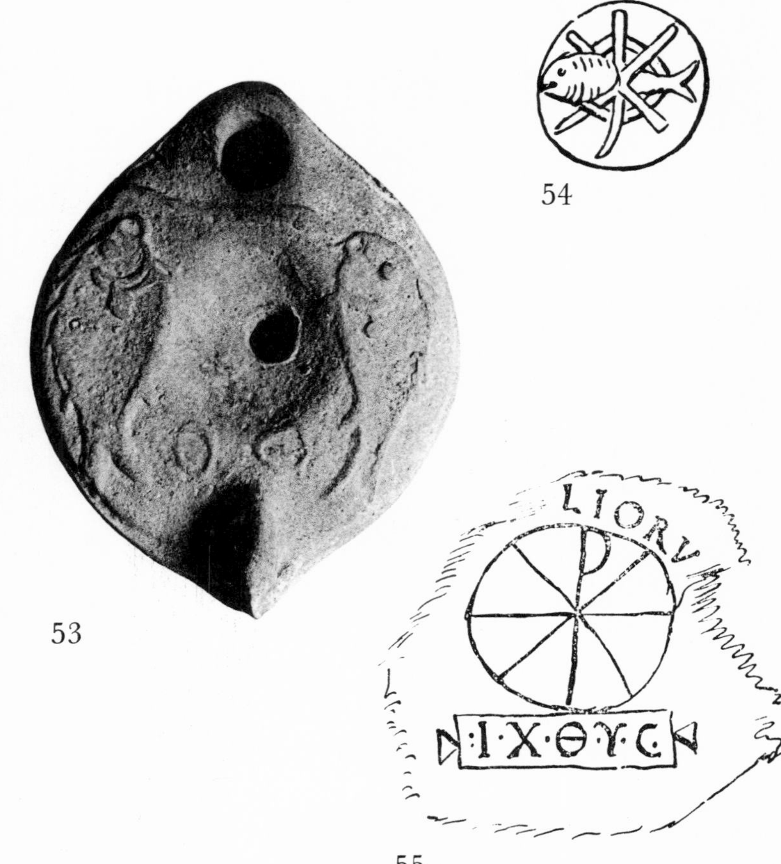

53

54

55

SYNTROPHI ON

56

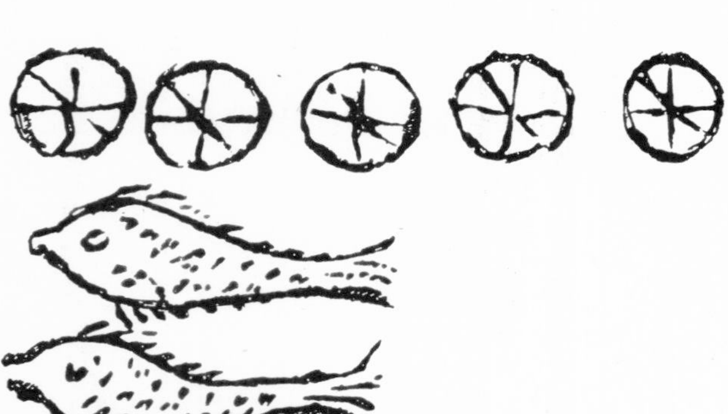

57

58

59

60

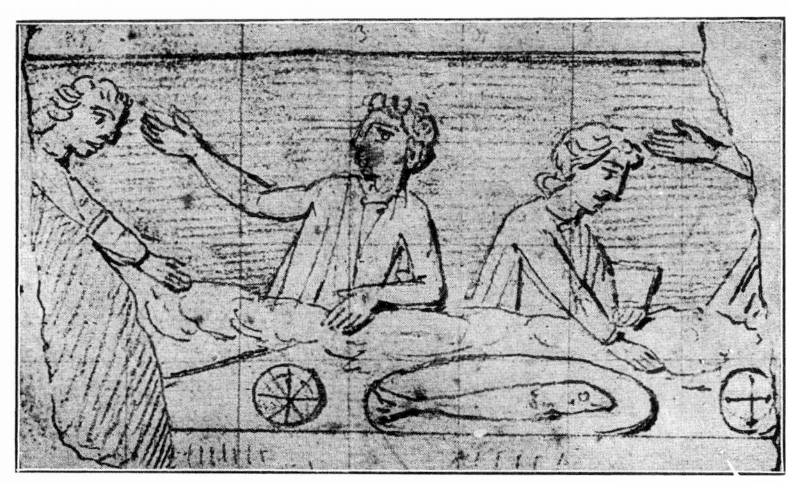

61

62

63

64

65

66

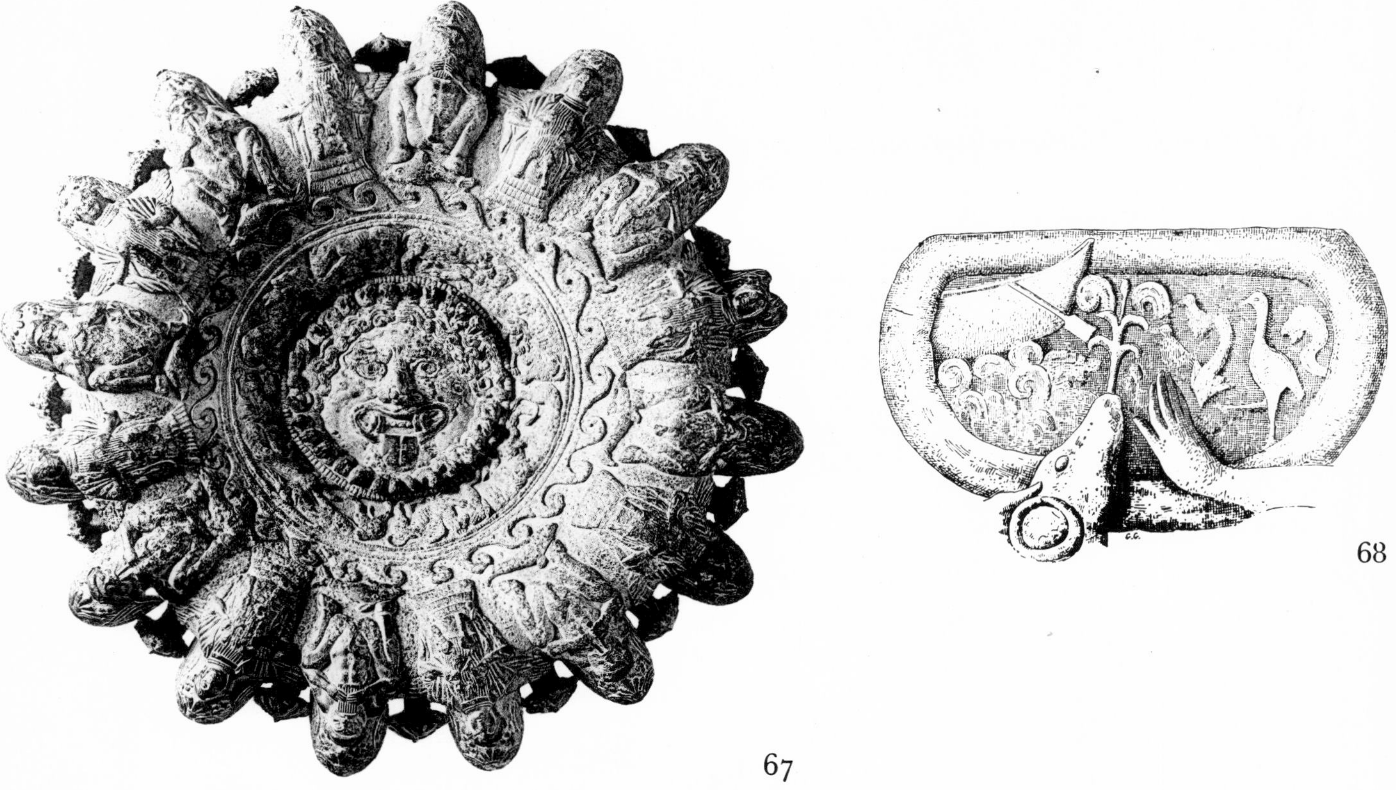

67

68

69

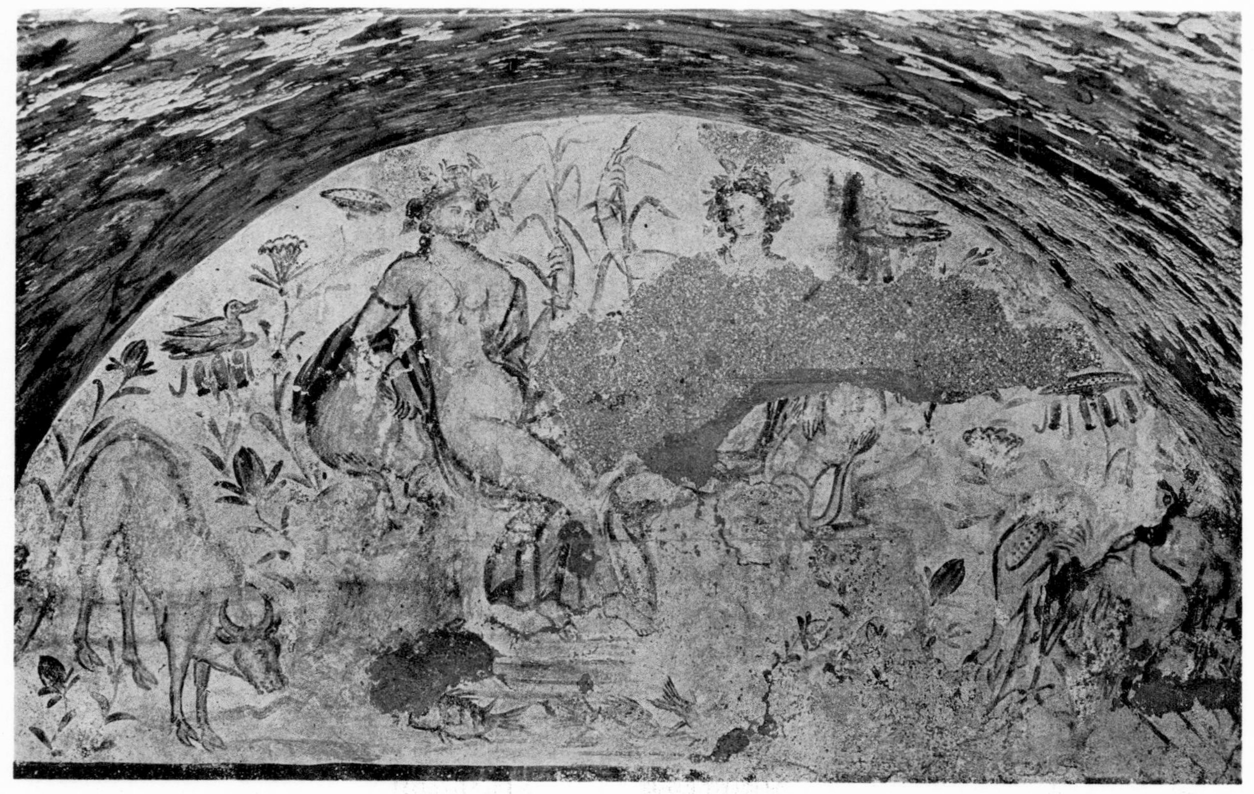

70

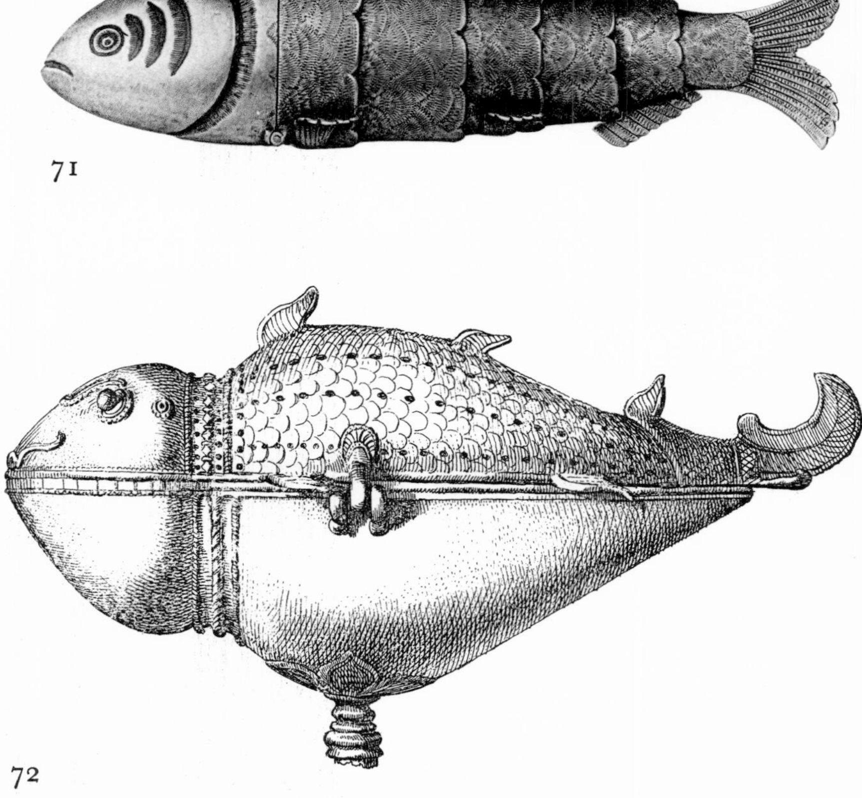

71

72

73

74

75

76

77

78

80

79

81

82

83

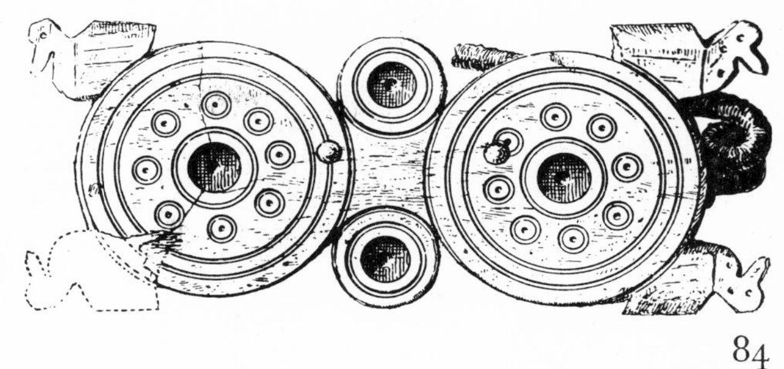

84

85

86

87

88

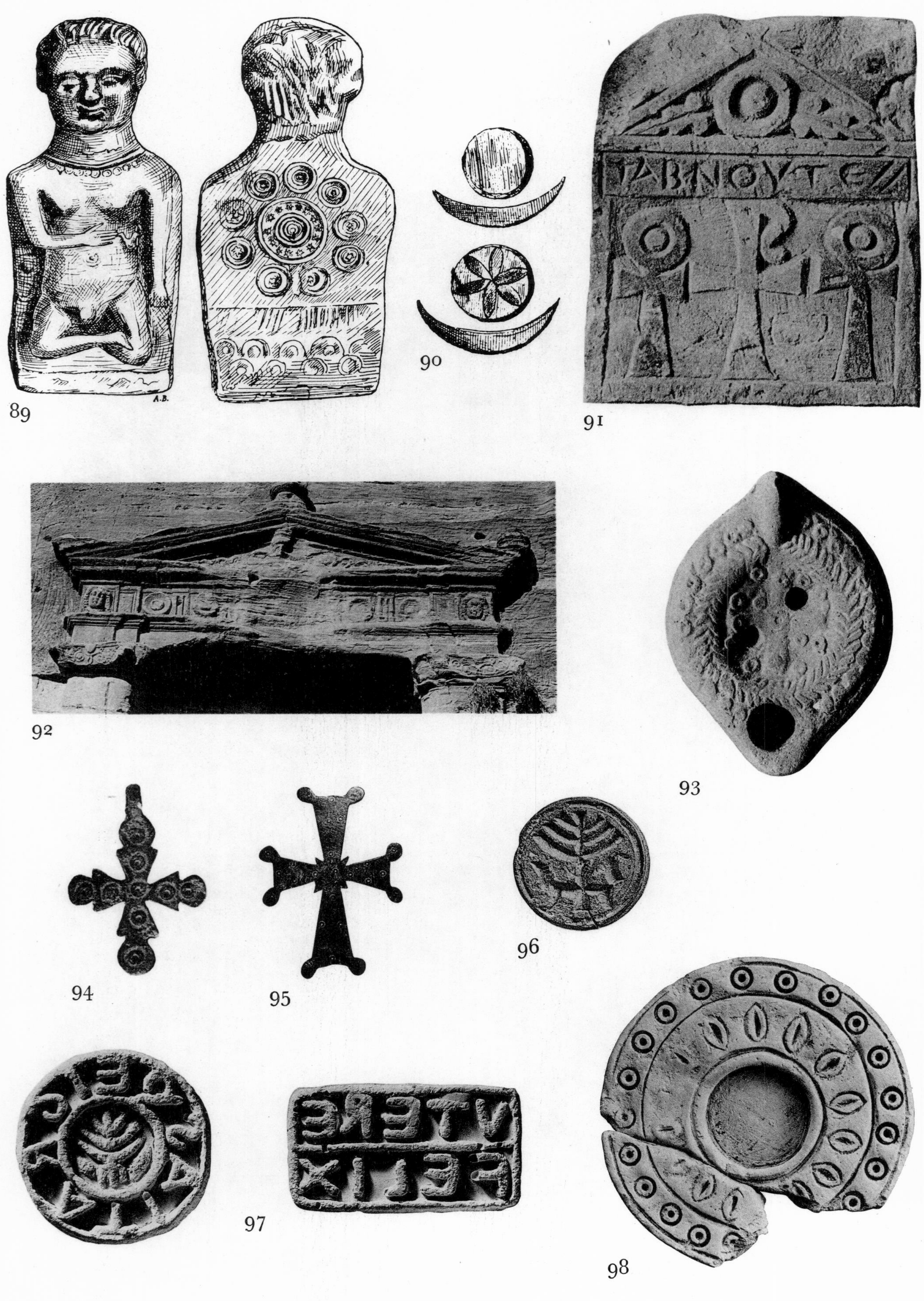

89 90 91 92 93 94 95 96 97 98

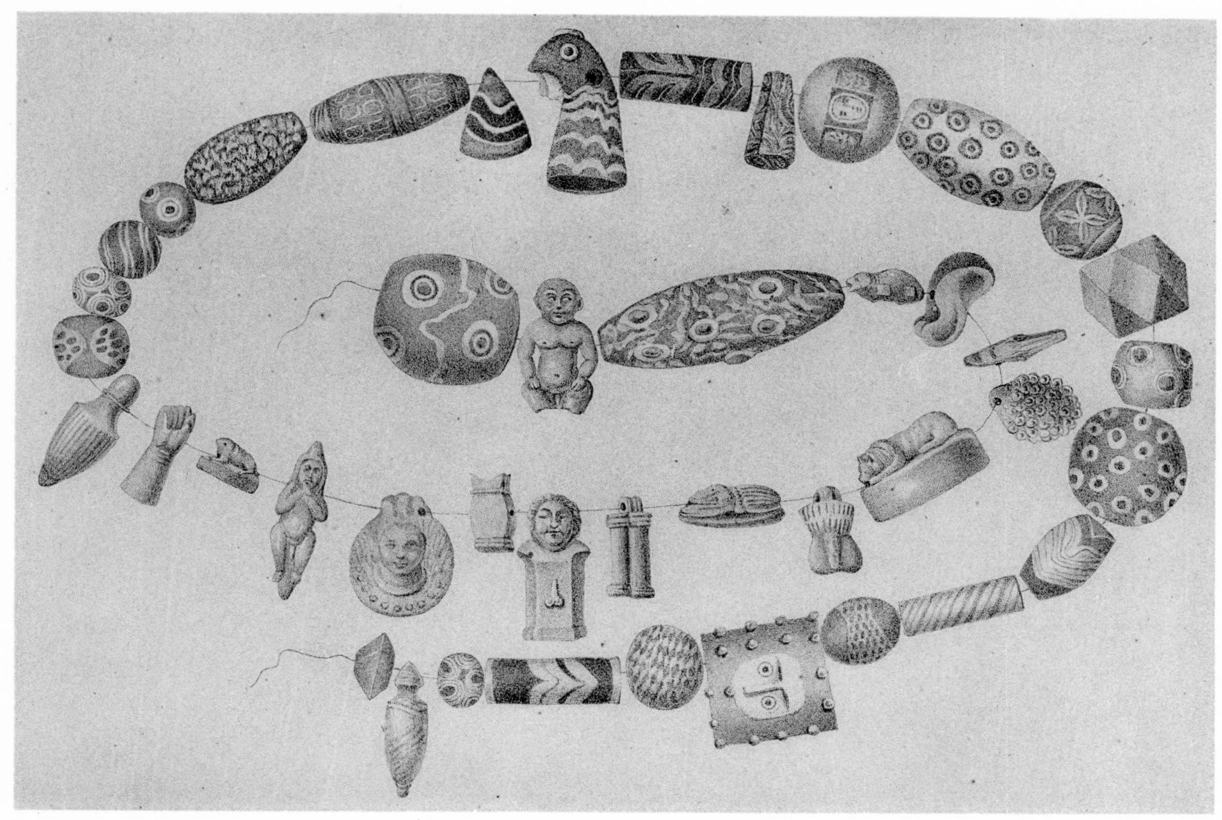

99

100

101

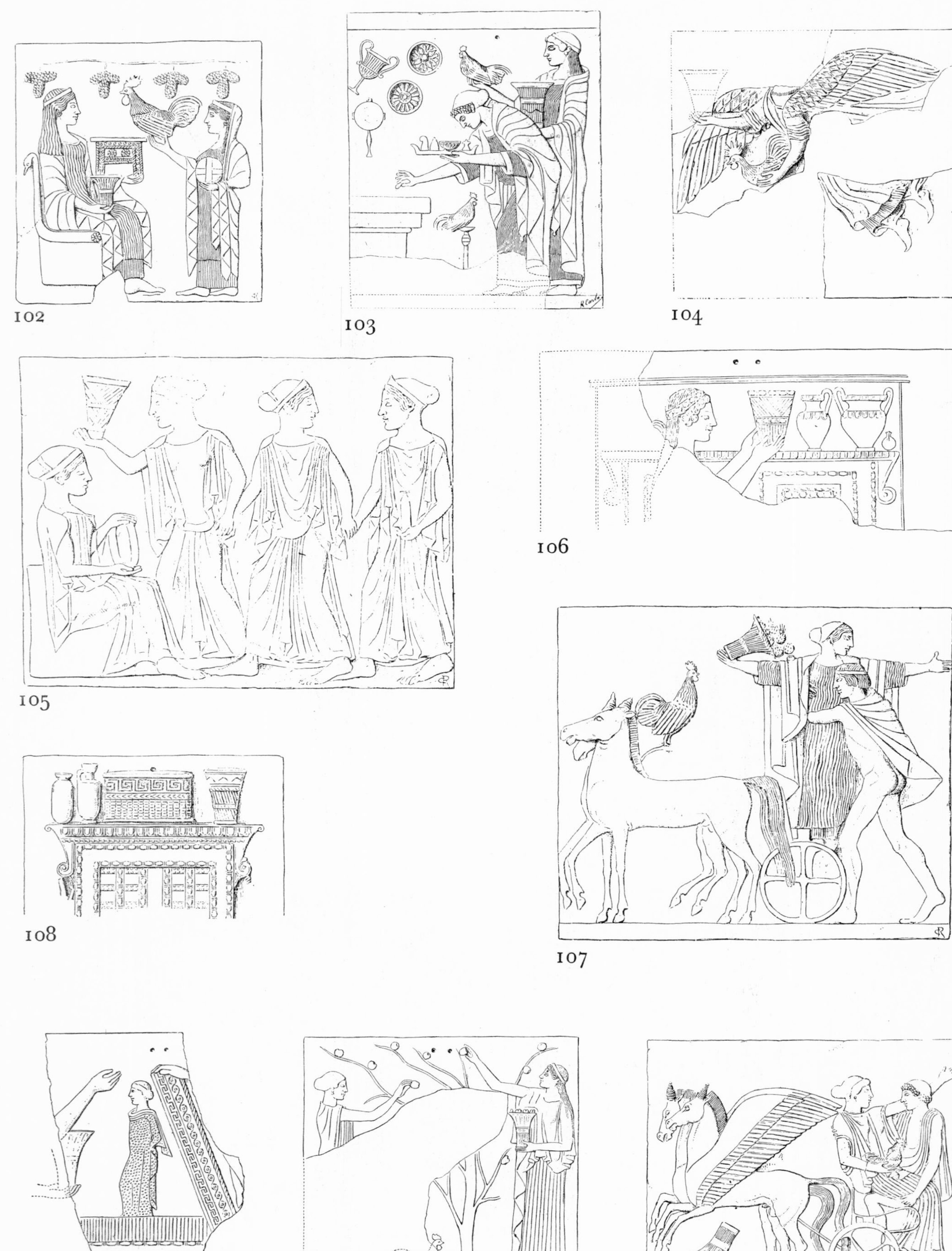

102 103 104

105 106

108 107

109 110 111

112

113

114

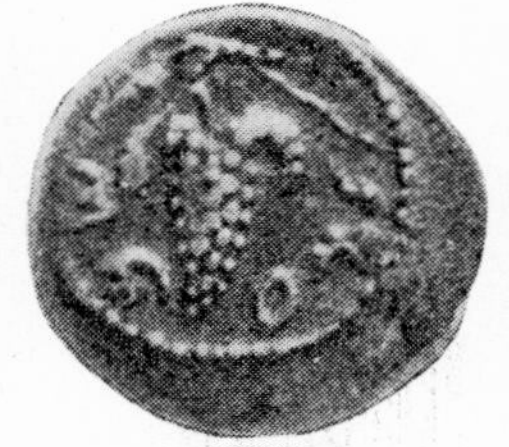

115

116

117

118

120

121

122

123

124

125

126

127

128

129

130

131

132

133

134

135

136

137

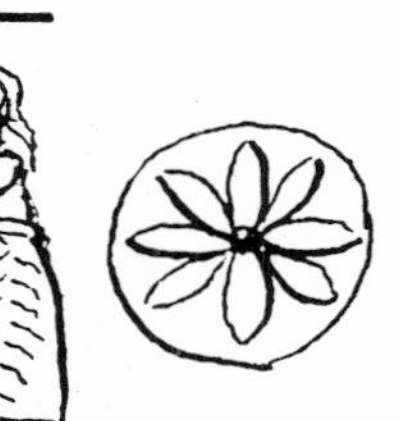

138

139

140

141

142

143

144

145

146

147

149

150

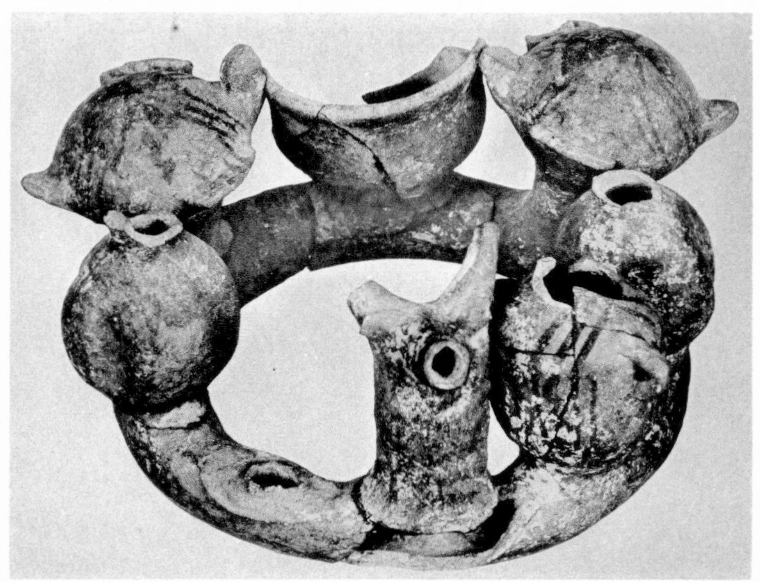

151

152

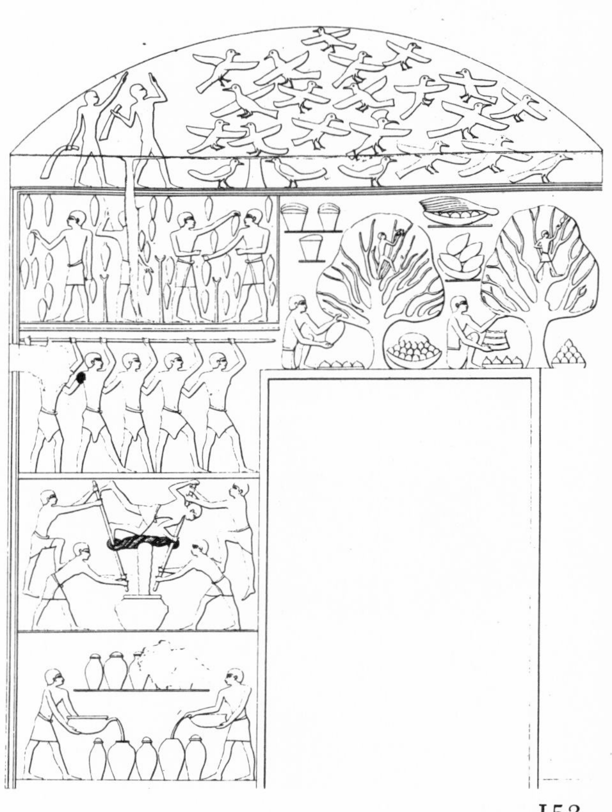

153

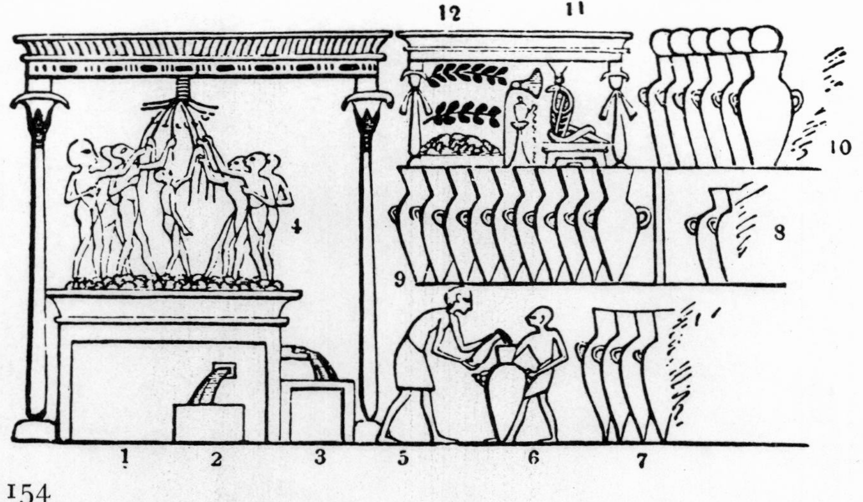

154

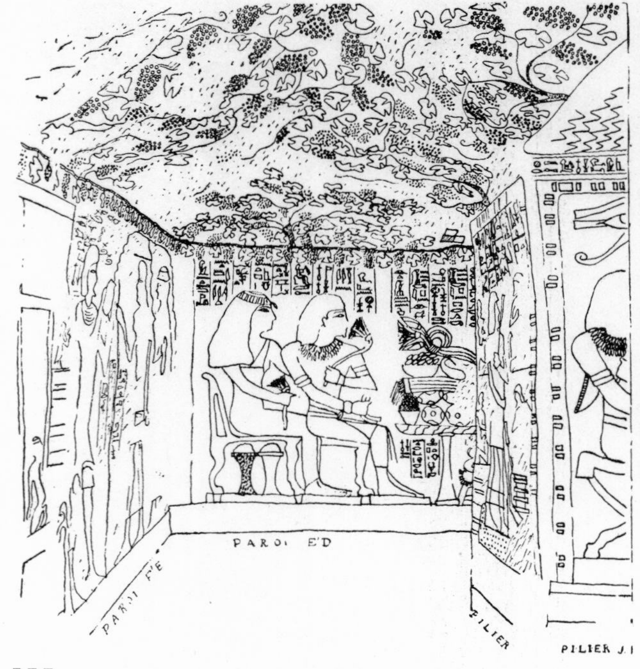

155

156

157

158

159

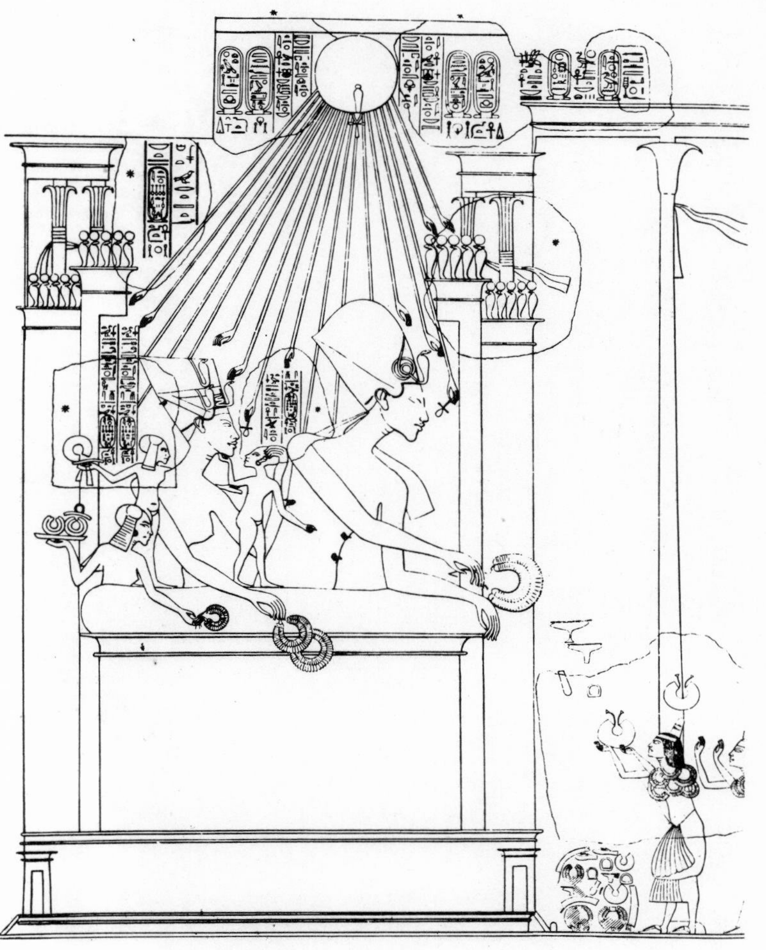
160

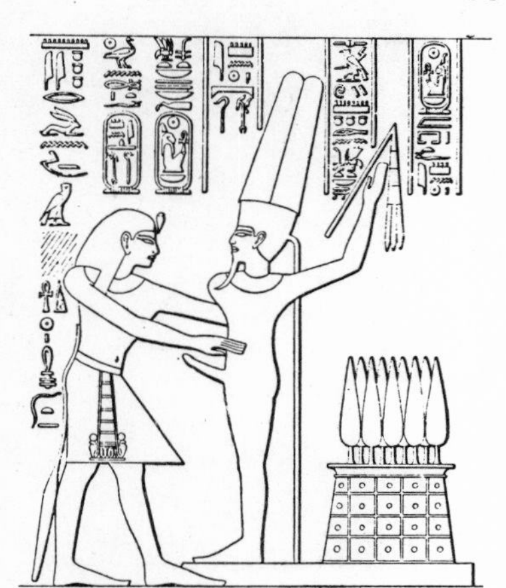
161

162

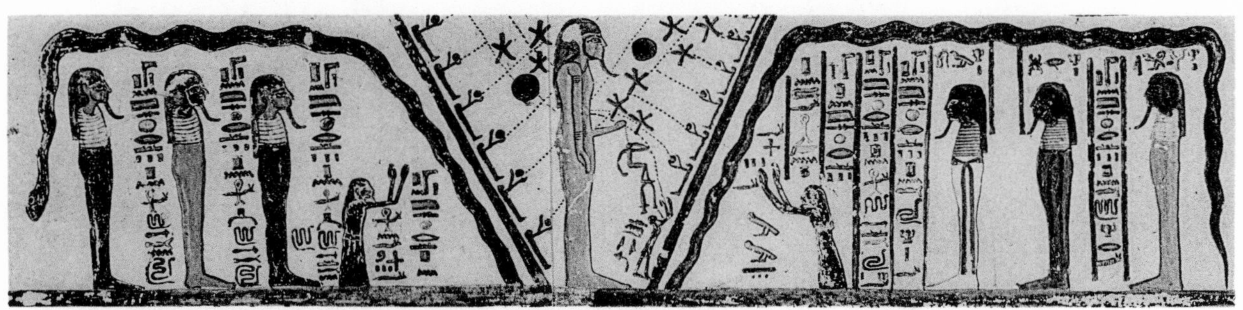
163

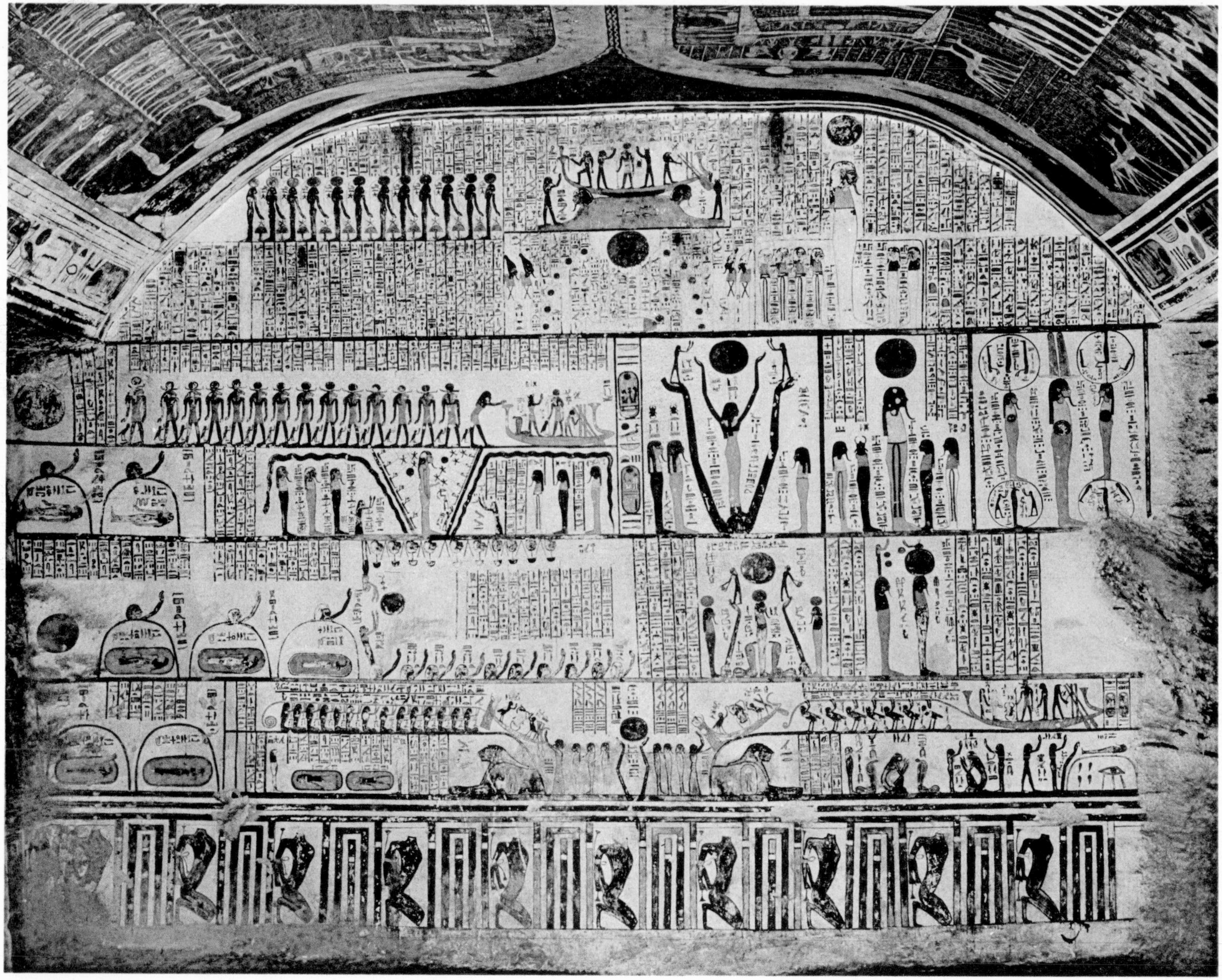

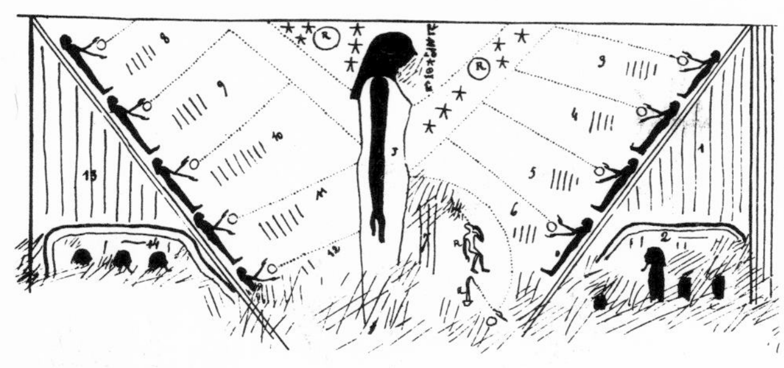

165

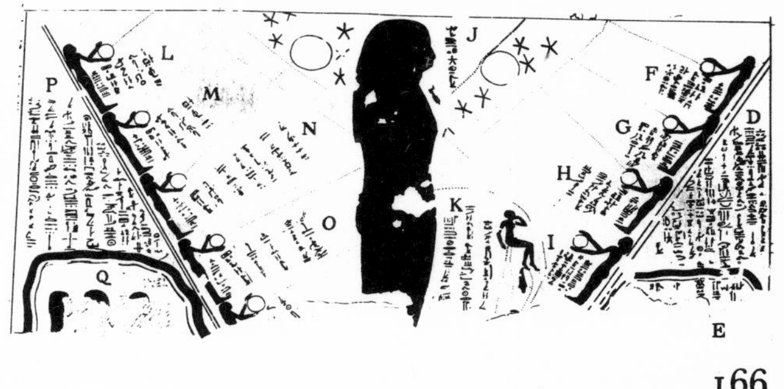

166

167

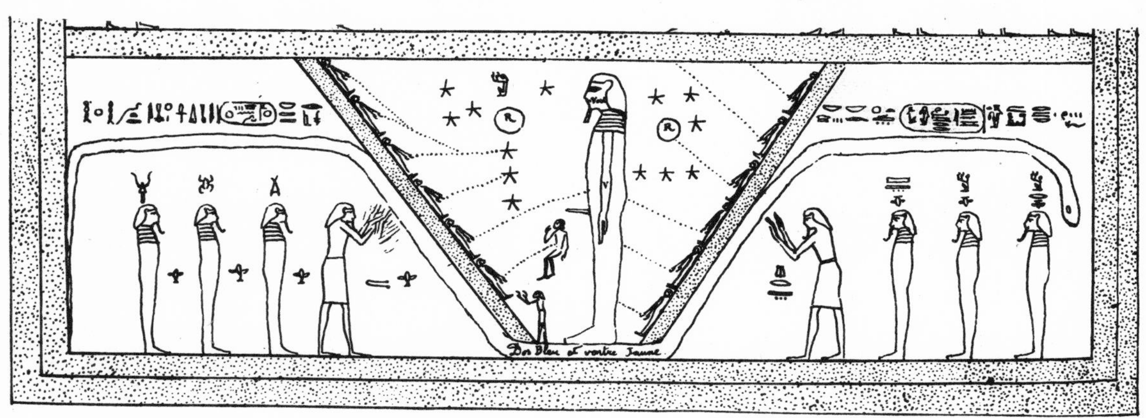

168

169

170

171

172

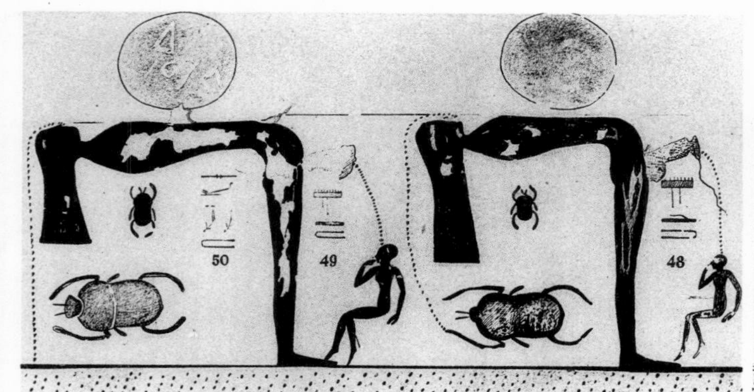

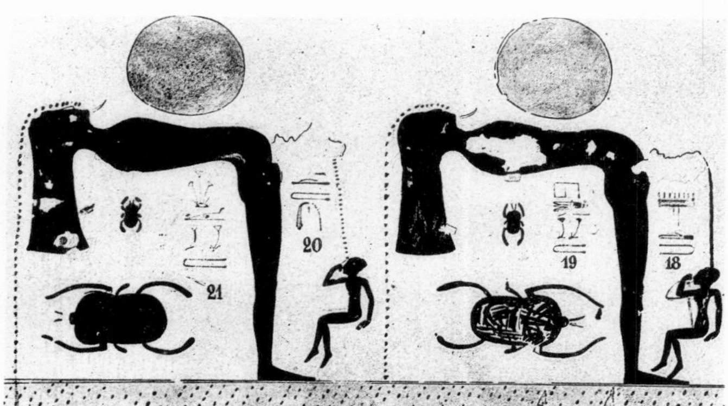

173

174

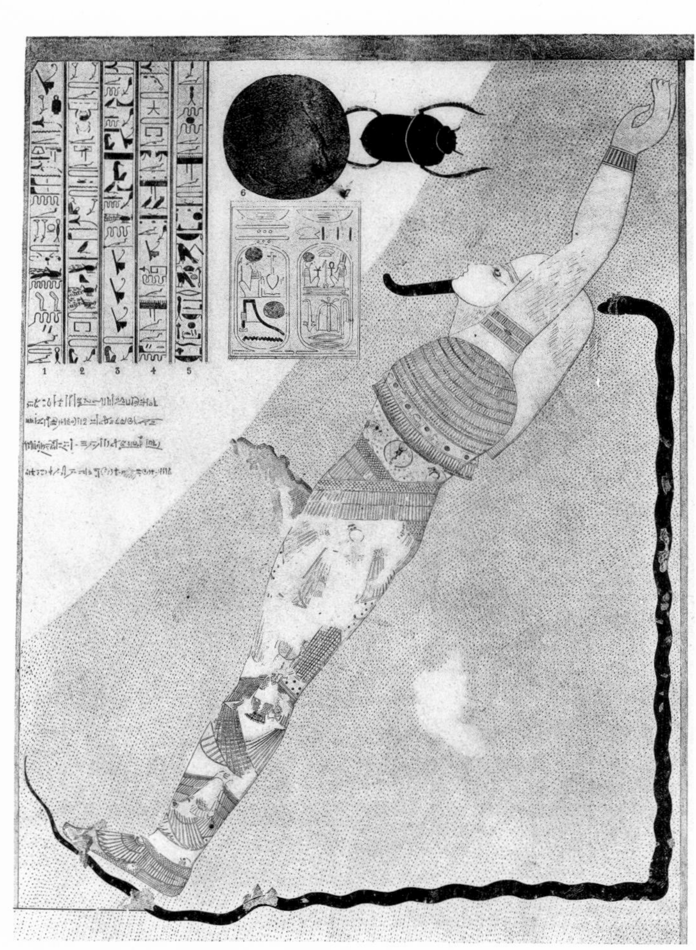

175

176

177

178

179

180

181

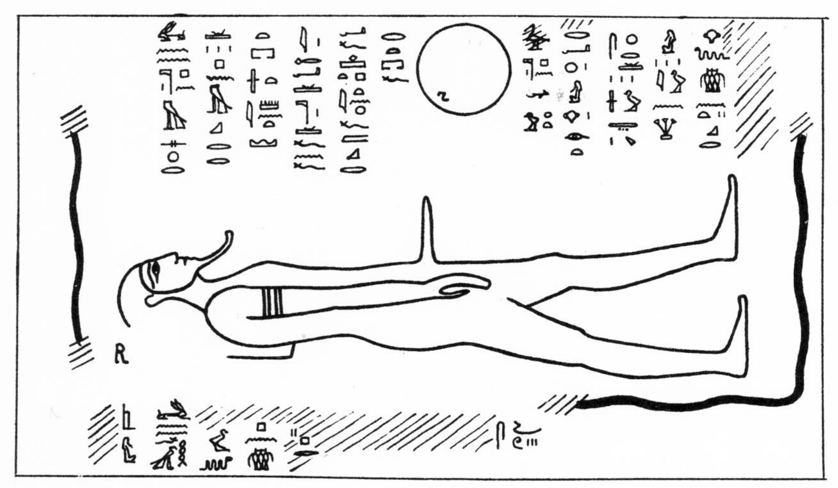

182

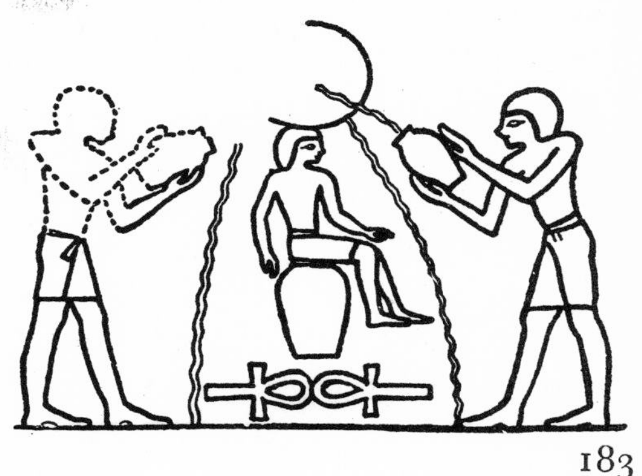

183

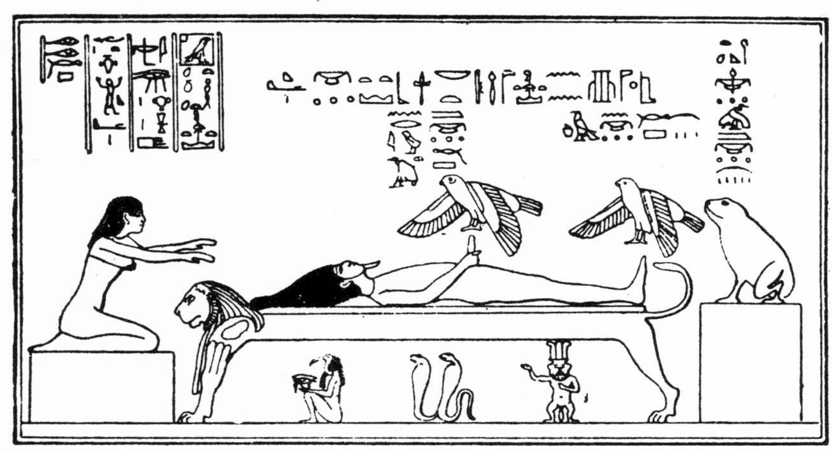

184

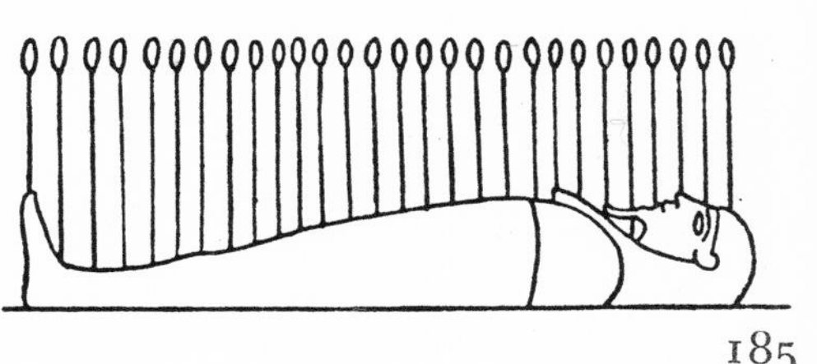

185

186